St Antony's Series

Series Editors

Halbert Jones
St Antony's College
University of Oxford
Oxford, United Kingdom

Matthew Walton
St Anthony College
University of Oxford
Oxford, United Kingdom

The St Antony's Series publishes studies of international affairs of contemporary interest to the scholarly community and a general yet informed readership. Contributors share a connection with St Antony's College, a world-renowned centre at the University of Oxford for research and teaching on global and regional issues. The series covers all parts of the world through both single-author monographs and edited volumes, and its titles come from a range of disciplines, including political science, history, and sociology. Over more than thirty years, this partnership between St Antony's College and Palgrave Macmillan has produced about 200 publications.

More information about this series at
http://www.springer.com/series/15036

Pedro Fortes • Larissa Boratti • Andrés Palacios Lleras • Tom Gerald Daly
Editors

Law and Policy in Latin America

Transforming Courts, Institutions, and Rights

palgrave
macmillan

Editors
Pedro Fortes
FGV Law School
Rio de Janeiro, Brazil

Andrés Palacios Lleras
Estudios Palacios Lleras SAS
Bogota, Colombia

Larissa Boratti
Ilarraz Advogados
Porto Alegre/RS, Brazil

Tom Gerald Daly
Edinburgh Centre for
Constitutional Law
University of Edinburgh
Edinburgh, United Kingdom

St Antony's Series
ISBN 978-1-137-56693-5   ISBN 978-1-137-56694-2   (eBook)
DOI 10.1057/978-1-137-56694-2

Library of Congress Control Number: 2016958187

Cover illustration: Marcin Leszczuk / Alamy Stock Photo

Printed on acid-free paper

This Palgrave Macmillan imprint is published by Springer Nature
The registered company is Macmillan Publishers Ltd.
The registered company address is: The Campus, 4 Crinan Street, London, N1 9XW, United Kingdom

PREFACE

No field of academic study addresses a broader variety of human activity, and no field involves a broader range of human catastrophes and human triumphs, than the study of law. Yet no academic field suffers so much from parochialism. Even in the twenty-first century, the laws of one jurisdiction still differ from those of another; the techniques of one area of law differ from those of another; the study of substantive law can easily be divorced from the challenges of dispute resolution and enforcement; the study of any area of the law can be abstracted from the study of its economic and social and political context. And since the past seems to us to be another country, we are prone to the parochialism of people who forget their history.

All the resulting barriers between disciplines are barriers to understanding. I congratulate the editors of this volume, and the authors, for the many ways in which they have promoted understanding of the challenges for law and public policy in Latin America, by knocking down barriers. They have done so by putting the study of law together with the study of policy, economics and politics. They have done so through comparative study of the laws of Latin American jurisdictions, and study of the relations between the Inter-American Human Rights System and the law and politics of particular countries. They have done so by connecting the study of law and policy with the study of history. They have done so by putting questions of the substance of the law in the context of the challenges of process and enforcement, and by focusing on the role of institutions. The topics covered are of importance to every region in the world today: legal integration; the role of law in economic and social development; the challenges of developing effective international techniques for the protection of human rights (and the challenges of the interaction of such techniques with domestic rights regimes); financial regulation; constitutional transformation; and emerging technologies and their implications for copyright and patent regimes and competition law. Each of these areas, of course, has particular resonance and importance in Latin America, but I think it is fair to say that Europe, North America, Africa, Asia and Australasia all have lessons to learn from the work in this volume, and from the authors' approach to law and policy in Latin America.

The conference in Oxford organised by the editors was a first for us in focusing on the law and policy of Latin America. And the event was itself an exercise in knocking down barriers. The diversity of disciplinary speci-alities of the speakers and of the participants was very striking, as was the diversity of countries represented (including England, Scotland, Germany, Switzerland, Ireland, Nigeria, Canada, the USA, Argentina, Brazil, Chile and Colombia). It is also noteworthy that the organisers managed to bring together the Latin American Centre, St Antony's College, the Centre for Socio-Legal Studies and the Faculty of Law in Oxford in an unprece-dented collaboration. And I am particularly glad that the event brought together UCL and the University of Oxford.

The Oxford conference was a step towards deeper engagement at our university with the law in Latin America, and this volume is a lesson to us: if we are to engage intelligently in the study of problems of law and policy in Latin America, we cannot be satisfied with barriers.

Timothy Endicott
Oxford, UK
September 2015

ACKNOWLEDGEMENTS

We are especially grateful to St. Antony's College, University of Oxford, for hosting the II Graduate Conference on Latin American Law and Policy on 7 March 2014 and for encouraging us to organise this volume as part of the St. Antony's Series with Palgrave Macmillan. We owe special thanks to the series editors, Leigh Payne, Paul Betts and Halbert Jones, for their invaluable support and assistance with all editorial matters over the past two years.

We are also thankful to Palgrave Macmillan and everyone involved in the book's production, particularly Imogen Gordon Clark, Sara Crowley-Vigneau and Jemima Warren. An anonymous reviewer gave us enthusiastic feedback at a decisive moment and we would like to express our gratitude regarding her praise for the project at such an early stage of the editorial process.

This volume is the direct result of two successful conferences on Latin American law and policy, which were organised in two successive years at University College London (UCL) and at the University of Oxford. Both events attracted large audiences and we must thank numerous institutions and individuals for their generous collaboration with us in supporting them.

At Oxford we benefited from the sponsorship of the Faculty of Law, the Centre for Socio-Legal Studies and the Latin American Centre, and we owe special thanks to the heads of these departments – Dean Timothy Endicott, Dr Marina Kurkchiyan-Banks and Prof. Leigh Payne – for their leadership, vision and extremely generous support. At UCL, the conference held at Bentham House was supported entirely by the Faculty of Law and we must thank the Dean of UCL Laws – Prof. Dame Hazel Genn – for her generosity, encouragement and sponsorship.

We also benefited from the presence and participation of faculty members from the University of Oxford and UCL. We are especially grateful to Dean Timothy Endicott, Dr Fernanda Pirie, Prof. Timothy Power, Vice-Dean Cheryl Thomas, Prof. William Twining, Prof. Denis Galligan, Dr Bettina Lange, Prof. Eduardo Posada-Carbó, Dr Virginia Mantouvalou and Dr Florian Wagner von Papp for their opening, chairing and discussing the conference papers with us.

Furthermore, we would like to thank the staff from UCL and the University of Oxford for their invaluable assistance, especially Kirsten Yost and Katie Hayward of the Centre for Socio-Legal Studies, Elvira Ryan at the Latin American Centre, and Jackie Hall and Michelle Robb from the Oxford Faculty of Law.

Additionally, we are especially grateful to the University of St. Gallen, the Max Planck Institute of Hamburg, the University of Toronto and Queen Mary University of London for the presence and participation of Prof. Dr Dr Peter Sester, Tilman Quarch, Associate Dean Mariana Prado and Prof. Gabriel Gari with us as chairs and discussants of conference papers.

Moreover, FGV Law School (Rio de Janeiro), Universidad de Los Andes (Bogotá) and Universidad Torcuato di Tella (Buenos Aires) deserve a special mention for sending Dean Joaquim Falcão, Dean Helena Alviar, and Prof. Roberto Gargarella as keynote speakers for the Oxford conference. We were honoured by their participation and we are also extremely pleased with their valuable contributions to this book.

Likewise, we would like to thank everyone involved with the conferences and all authors who contributed to this book for accepting our invitations. As junior scholars who are still just starting our international academic careers, we have considered it a unique privilege to have the opportunity to gather senior and junior scholars from various countries, multiples perspectives and different stages to discuss law and policy in Latin America at UCL, the University of Oxford and now as part of the St. Antony's Series. We would like to thank everyone who was involved in these projects with us.

Pedro would also like to thank, in particular, his wife Christiane and his daughter Floriana for their patience, love and understanding about this and other projects during his academic period in Oxford. Without this essential family support, none of the projects developed during this time would have been possible and any eventual success has to be shared with them both. Pedro is also grateful to all the inspirational friends and colleagues he had the opportunity to meet and learn from at Oxford, Stanford, Harvard, PUC/Rio, UFRJ, FGV, Bennett and the Ministério Público do Rio de Janeiro.

Larissa is particularly grateful to the UCL Laws research community, a truly inspiring and motivating academic environment from which she has benefited greatly. She acknowledges CAPES Foundation, the Ministry of Education in Brazil, for the financial support to pursue a PhD in the UK. She is also thankful to her family for their encouragement to her in embarking on this academic journey overseas – the most special gratitude to Marcelo Ilarraz. Last but not least, Larissa would like to thank her fellow editors for the extraordinary team effort in bringing such a challenging project together.

Andrés is very thankful to Pedro and Larissa for joining him in the organisation of the conferences at UCL and the University of Oxford. He also extends his gratitude to his peers at UCL and to the members of the faculty who have been involved in this effort. Furthermore, this project would not have been possible without the support of his wife Tatiana Rodriguez, and the help of all his good friends in London and Oxford. Finally, he would like to extend his very warm appreciation to Pedro, Tom and Larissa for their hard work in making this book a reality. *Muchas gracias!*

Tom would like to thank his slee (cool) niece Mia, the research community at Edinburgh Law School, and all those who have helped to enhance his knowledge of Latin America (and Brazil in particular), especially Prof. Oscar Vilhena Vieira, Prof. Conrado Hübner Mendes and Prof. Roberto Gargarella. Particular thanks go also to the Supreme Court of Brazil, the Brazilian Society of Public Law, and FGV Law School (São Paulo), who were excellent and informative hosts during a research visit in summer 2013. Finally, to all his Latin American friends, who now include his co-editors, many thanks for welcoming an Irishman into the Latin American fold. *O meu muito obrigado a todos/muchas gracias a todos!*

Pedro Fortes, Larissa Verri Boratti, Andrés Palacios Lleras,
and Tom Gerald Daly
Oxford, London, and Edinburgh, March 2016.

CONTENTS

Part I   Courts, Constitutionalism and the
          Inter-American System   1

1   Brazilian 'Supremocracy' and the Inter-American Court
     of Human Rights: Unpicking an Unclear Relationship   3
     Tom Gerald Daly
     1   *From Dictatorship to 'Supremocracy' in 30 Years*   5
     2   *State Policy and the Inter-American Court*   7
          Brazil and the Inter-American System before Acceptance
              of the Inter-American Court's Jurisdiction   7
          Brazil and the Inter-American Court   8
          General Signs of Greater Openness to International
              Human Rights Norms   10
          A Qualified Openness   10
     3   *The Supreme Federal Court and the Inter-American Court*   11
          The Recent Nature of the Relationship   11
          The Constitutional Status Accorded to Inter-American
              Norms and Jurisprudence   11
          Rare References to Inter-American Court Jurisprudence   12
          Divergence from Settled Inter-American Court Case Law   13
     4   *Conclusion: Key Questions Raised by this Inter-Court*
          Relationship   15
     Notes   16

2   Transnational Legal Process and Fundamental Rights in
    Latin America: How Does the Inter-American Human
    Rights System Reshape Domestic Constitutional Rights?   21
    Marcelo Torelly
    1   The Movement of International Law Towards Judicialisation   22
    2   Latin American Cases of Transnational Legal Process   24
         Transnational Legal Process at the Inter-American
             Commission   24
         Transnational Legal Process in the Inter-American Court   26
    3   Does Constitutional Architecture Matter?   29
    4   Transversal Human Rights Governance and New
         Constitutional Actors   32
    5   Conclusions   34
    Notes   34

3   Complying (Partially) with the Compulsory Judgments
    of the Inter-American Court of Human Rights   39
    Damián González-Salzberg
    1   The Method Used for Measuring Compliance   40
    2   Measuring Compliance with 330 Measures   42
         Paying Compensation   42
         Acknowledging Human Rights Violations   47
         Prosecuting Human Rights Violators   47
         Adapting Domestic Legislation   48
    3   Possible Paths for Improving Compliance   48
    4   Conclusion   50
    Notes   51

4   Media Representations of the Inter-American System
    of Human Rights   57
    Diego Gil, Rolando Garcia, and Lawrence M. Friedman
    1   Background   59
         Brief Description of the Inter-American System   59
         Media Coverage as a Proxy for Legal Culture   61
    2   Method   62
    3   Findings and Discussion   63
    4   Conclusion   69
    Notes   71

**Part II   Institutional Development: Policy Implementation
and Change   75**

**5   The Evolving Relationship Between Law and Development:
Proposing New Tools   77**
Helena Alviar
1   *The Purely Instrumentalist Approach: Law in the Margins*   79
2   *Instrumentalist Law-Centred Approach*   83
      The 1960s Wave   83
      The 1990s Wave   84
3   *The Elements of the Dynamic Approach*   86
4   *Final Thoughts*   89
Notes   89

**6   Transnational Legal Indicators: The Missing Link in
a New Era of Law and Development   95**
David Restrepo Amariles
1   *Transnational Legal Indicators and the Law and
      Development Moments*   96
      *The First Moment of Law and Development: USAID
            and SLADE*   97
      The Second Moment: The World Bank and the CPIA   98
2   *Law and Performance Measures: A New Era in Law
      and Development Policy*   99
      *A New Development Rhetoric: Governance and the
            Rule of Law*   100
      The Third Moment: World Governance Indicators   101
3   *Evidence-Based Policy: The Way Ahead?*   102
      Legal Indicators and Legal Reform in Business Law   103
      *Evidence-Based Reform and the Mathematical Turn
            in Development Policy*   104
      Evidence-Based Law and Development Policies   104
      Indicators and the Mathematical Proceduralisation of Law 106
4   *Concluding Remarks*   108
Notes   108

7 Institutional Bypasses in Brazil: Overcoming
Ex-Ante Resistance to Institutional Reforms 113
Mariana Mota Prado
1 *What Is an Institutional Bypass?* 114
2 *Institutional Bypasses in Brazil* 115
3 *Overcoming Ex-Ante Resistance to Reforms* 116
Self-Interested Resistance 117
Overcoming Cognitive Resistance 119
4 *Conclusion* 123
Notes 125

Part III Institutional Challenges: Integrating Markets and
Regulation 129

8 Convergence, Coordination and Collusion in Securities
Regulation: The Latin American Integrated Market 131
Jose Miguel Mendoza
1 *Convergence, Coordination and Collusion* 133
Regulatory Convergence 134
Regional Coordination of Enforcement Policies 136
Collusive Delegation and the Political Economy
Benefits of MILA 138
2 *Conclusion* 142
Notes 142

9 Using Judicial Actions to Address Corporate
Human Rights Abuses: Colombia, 2000–2014 149
Laura Bernal-Bermudez
1 *Global Regulatory Framework* 150
2 *Factors Influencing Judicial Outcomes* 152
Political Opportunities 152
Global Pressure 152
Profile of the Firm 153
The Role of Civil Society 153
Type of Abuse 153
3 *Colombia's Conflict and Political Economy* 154

4 Preliminary Findings   156
5 Conclusions   162
Notes   163

10 Multiple Strategies of Financial Regulation Adopted
    in the Colombian Securities Market: The Case of
    Over-the-Counter Derivatives   167
    Ligia Catherine Arias Barrera
    1 Brief Description of the Colombian OTCDM   168
    2 Strategies of Regulation Adopted in the Colombian
       Securities Market   169
       Risk-Based Regulation: The Colombian Approach   169
       Risk-Based Regulation in the Institutional Context   171
    3 What Hinders the Growth of OTCDMs in Colombia?   175
    4 Final Remarks   177
    Notes   178

11 A Counterhistory of Anti-Trust in Latin America   185
    Andrés Palacios Lleras
    1 The Development of Anti-Trust Law in Latin America:
       The Dominant Narrative   186
    2 Continuity and Discontinuity in Latin
       American Anti-Trust   189
       The Enduring Allure of Legal Reform   189
       Discontinuity in Economic Doctrines   193
    3 Conclusions   196
    Notes   197

Part IV Constitutional Engine Room: Between Individual
         Autonomy and Collective Self-Government   203

12 Latin American Constitutionalism, 1810–2010:
    The Problem of the 'Engine Room' of the Constitution   205
    Roberto Gargarella
    1 1810–1850: Constitutionalism in the Independence Years   206
    2 1850–1917: The Founding Period of Latin American
       Constitutionalism   208

3   1917–1950: The Advent of Social Constitutionalism   209
4   1950–2010: Constitutionalism and Human Rights   211
5   The 'Engine Room' of the Constitution   213
6   Conclusion   215
Notes   216

13   **Addressing Poverty through a Transformative
     Approach to Anti-Discrimination Law in Latin America**   221
     Alberto Coddou McManus
     1   *A Transformative Approach to Anti-Discrimination Law:
         Socioeconomic Lens*   222
         Purposes and Boundaries   222
         A Transformative Approach to ADL in Latin America 224
         Socioeconomic Lens   227
     2   *ADL and Poverty in Argentina*   229
     3   *Conclusion*   233
     Notes   234

14   **Gender Quotas, Legislative Resistance and
     Non-Legislative Reform**   239
     Malu A. C. Gatto
     1   *Gender Quota Adoption and Strengthening*   241
     2   *Measuring Gender Quota Strength*   242
     3   *Results*   244
     4   *Conclusion*   251
     Notes   253

15   **Human Rights and Remains: A Policy Proposal to
     Prevent Human Rights Violations in Brazil**   257
     Pedro Fortes
     1   *Allegations of Torture in Contemporary Brazil*   258
     2   *Structural Elements within the Criminal Justice System* 262
     3   *A Policy Proposal to Prevent Human Rights Violations
         in Brazil*   265
     4   *Final Remarks*   267
     Notes   270

Part V *Mundus Novus:* **Emerging Technologies and Rights** 273

16 *Mundus Novus:* **The Construction of a Free Flow
of Information from the Navigators of Yesterday
to the Internauts of Today** 275
Joaquim Falcão
1 *The Road of Autograph Letters in the Fifteenth Century* 277
2 Mundus Novus *and the Misattribution of Authorship* 279
3 *The Free Flow of Cooperative Information* 282
4 *On the Current Legal Obstacles to the Free Flow
of Information* 284
5 *The Multiple Nature of Ambition* 287
Notes 289

17 **Digital Culture, Copyright and the Orphan Works Issue:
A View from Brazil** 293
Paula Westenberger
1 *Digitisation, Orphan Works and Cultural Institutions:
From Human Rights to International Copyright Law* 295
2 *Existing Solutions for the Orphan Works
Issue Internationally* 297
3 *Brazil's Copyright System and Constitutional Rights* 298
4 *Projects of Reform of Brazil's Copyright Law* 300
Preservation 300
Accessibility 301
Specific Provisions for Orphan Works 302
Problems Not Addressed by the Projects of Reform 302
5 *Conclusion* 303
Notes 303

18 **The Incorporation of a Right to Health Perspective into
Brazil's Patent Law Reform Process** 311
Emmanuel Kolawole Oke
1 *The Tension between Patent Rights and the
Right to Health* 312
The Right to Health and Access to Medicines 312

The Tension Between Patent Rights and the Right to Health in Brazil   313

2 *The Relationship Between Patent Rights and the Right to Health*   315

3 *Brazil's Patent Law Reform Process and the Right to Health*   316

Eliminating Patents on New Uses or New Forms of Known Drugs   318

Raising the Standard for Determining an Inventive Step   319

Clear Rejection of Data Exclusivity   319

Clarifying ANVISA's Role in the Examination of Patent Applications for Pharmaceutical Products and Processes   321

4 *Conclusion*   323

Notes   323

19 Constitutional Environmental Protection in Brazil: A Rights-Based Approach   327

Julia Mattei and Larissa Verri Boratti

1 *From Inside: The Fundamental Rights Approach to Environmental Protection in Brazil*   329

Scope and Structure   330

Implementation   333

2 *Looking Backwards: Environmental Protection in the Context of Latin American Constitutionalism*   335

3 *Looking Elsewhere: Other Approaches to Environmental Protection*   337

4 *Conclusion*   338

Notes   339

Index   347

Notes on Contributors

Helena Alviar is Dean and Full Professor of Law at Universidad de los Andes, Bogotá.

David Restrepo Amariles is Assistant Professor of Law at HEC Paris and a Researcher at the Perelman Centre of Legal Philosophy (Université Libre de Bruxelles), Brussels.

Ligia Catherine Arias Barrera is Lecturer at Externado de Colombia University and Assistant Lecturer at the University of Warwick.

Laura Bernal-Bermudez is a doctoral candidate in sociology at the University of Oxford and a Colombian lawyer.

Larissa Verri Boratti is a doctoral candidate in law at University College London and a Brazilian lawyer.

Tom Gerald Daly is Associate Director of the Edinburgh Centre for Constitutional Law and a consultant on the rule of law, human rights and democracy-building.

Joaquim Falcão is Dean and Professor of Law at FGV Law School, Rio de Janeiro.

Pedro Fortes is Professor of Law at FGV Law School, Rio de Janeiro, and a public prosecutor at the Attorney General's Office of Rio de Janeiro.

Lawrence M. Friedman is the Marion Rice Kirkwood Professor of Law at Stanford Law School, California.

Rolando Garcia is a doctoral candidate at Stanford Law School.

Roberto Gargarella is Professor of Law at Torcuato di Tella, Buenos Aires, an Associated Researcher at CONICET, Buenos Aires, and at CMI, Bergen, and an Argentinean lawyer and sociologist.

Malu A.C. Gatto is a doctoral candidate in politics at the University of Oxford.

Diego Gil is Lecturer in Law and Teaching Fellow at Stanford Law School.

Damian Gonzalez-Salzberg is Lecturer in Law at University of Sheffield.

Julia Mattei is Lecturer in Environment and Planning Law at Nürtingen-Geislingen University, a doctoral candidate in law at the University of Cologne and a Brazilian lawyer.

Alberto Coddou McManus is Professor of Law at Diego Portales University, Santiago.

Jose Miguel Mendoza is Head of Enforcement for the Colombian Superintendence of Companies and Associate Professor of Corporate Law at Universidad de Los Andes, Bogotá.

Emmanuel Kolawole Oke is a doctoral candidate in Law at University College Cork.

Andrés Palacios Lleras is doctoral candidate in Law at University College London and a Colombian lawyer.

Mariana Mota Prado is Associate Dean for the Graduate Program and Associate Professor at the Faculty of Law at the University of Toronto.

Marcelo Torelly is a Postdoctoral fellow at University of Brasilia School of Law, Project coordinator at IOM-Brazil, and the former Director of the Transitional Justice Program at the Brazilian Federal Government and the United Nations Development Programme.

Paula Westenberger is Postgraduate Teaching Associate and a doctoral candidate at Queen Mary University London and a Brazilian lawyer.

ABBREVIATIONS

ACHR	American Convention on Human Rights
ADL	Anti-Discrimination Law
ANVISA	Agencia Nacional de Vigilancia Sanitaria (National Health Surveillance Agency)
AR	anti-trust regime
AUC	Autodefensas Unidas de Colombia (United Self-Defence Forces of Colombia)
BOPE	Batalhão de Operações Policiais Especiais (Police Special Operations Battalion)
BOVESPA	Bolsa de Valores, Mercadorias & Futuros de São Paulo (Brazilian Securities, Commodities and Futures Exchange)
BR	Banco de la Republica (Central Bank, Columbia)
CAA	corporate abuse allegation
CCP	central counterparty
CEJIL	Center for Justice and International Law
CEPAL	Comisíon Económica para América Latia y el Caribe (Economic Commission for Latin America and the Caribbean (ECLAC))
CERLALC	El Centro Regional para el Fomento del Libro en América Latina y el Caribe (Regional Centre for Book Development in Latin America and the Caribbean)
CESCR	Committee on Economic, Social and Cultural Rights
CESR	Committee of European Securities Regulators
CHRD	Corporations and Human Rights Database
CPIA	Country Policy and Institutional Assessment
CSJN	Corte Suprema de Justicia de la Nación (Supreme Court of Argentina)
CSR	corporate social responsibility

DRT	debt recovery tribunal
ECLAC	Economic Commission for Latin America and the Caribbean
ECOSOC	Economic and Social Council
EU	European Union
FAC	Financial and Accounting Circular
FARC	Fuerzas Armadas Revolucionarias de Colombia (Revolutionary Armed Forces of Colombia)
FDI	Foreign direct investment
FSC	Financial Superintendence of Colombia
GDP	gross domestic product
GFC	Global Financial Crisis
HR	human rights
IACtHR	Inter-American Court of Human Rights
ICESCR	International Covenant on Economic, Social and Cultural Rights
IGQS	Index of Gender Quota Strength
ILO	International Labour Organization
IMF	International Monetary Fund
INADI	Instituto Nacional contra la Discriminación, la Xenofobia y el Racismo (National Institute Against Discrimination, Xenophobia and Racism)
INPI	Instituto nacional da propriedade industrial (National Institute of Industrial Property)
IOSCO	International Organization of Securities Commissions
ISI	Import Substitution Industrialisation
MHCP	Ministerio de Hacienda y Crédito Público (Ministry of Finance, Columbia)
MILA	Mercado Integrado Latinoamericano (Latin American Integrated Market)
MIS	Marco Integrado de Supervision (Integrated Supervision Framework)
MOU	memorandum of understanding
NGO	non-governmental organization
OAS	Organization of American States
OECD	Organisation for Economic Co-operation and Development
OTC	over-the-counter
OTCDM	over-the-counter derivatives market
SCJN	Suprema Corte de Justicia de la Nación (Supreme Court of Mexico)
SENASP	National Secretariat of Public Security (Secretaria Nacional de Segurança Pública)
SFC	Superintendencia Financiera de Colombia (Financial Superintendency of Colombia)

SLADE	Studies in Law and Development
SUS	Sistema Único de Saúde (Unified Health System)
TLP	Transnational Legal Process
TRIPS	Trade Related Aspects of Intellectual Property
UCL	University College London
UN	United Nations
UNCITRAL	United Nations Commission on International Trade Law
UNCTAD	United Nations Conference on Trade and Development
UNDP	United Nations Development Programme
UNESCO	United Nations Educational, Scientific and Cultural Organization
UNGPs	UN Guiding Principles on Business and Human Rights
UPP	Unidades de Polícia Pacificadora (police pacification units)
USAID	United States Agency for International Development
WGIs	World Governance Indicators
WIPO	World Intellectual Property Organization
WTO	World Trade Organization

List of Figures

Fig. 4.1   Types of article concerning the Inter-American System   65

Fig. 4.2   Level of domestic and international media coverage   66

Fig. 4.3   Articles specifically concerning the Inter-American System   67

Fig. 4.4   References to institutions of the Inter-American System   68

Fig. 4.5   References to case law of the Inter-American Court   70

Fig. 9.1   Distribution of observations per sector of the economy   157

Fig. 9.2   Distribution of types of abuse by year of violation   158

Fig. 9.3   Use of judicial actions by type of abuse   160

Fig. 14.1   Values of the IGQS and its individual components, as distributed in Latin America   245

Fig. 14.2   Strength of original gender quota policy designs in Latin America, as measured by the IGQS   246

LIST OF TABLES

Table 3.1	The 330 measures ordered by the Inter-American Court	43
Table 3.2	Degree of compliance	47
Table 4.1	Total number of articles for each newspaper	63
Table 8.1	Aggregate data for MILA stock exchanges	134
Table 9.1	Types of abuse: frequency and percentage	157
Table 9.2	Remedy and accountability outcomes	161
Table 14.1	Strength of policy revisions in Latin America as measured by changes in the IGQS and its individual component scales	248

INTRODUCTION

The present study developed from two conferences on Latin American law and policy organised by the editors in 2013 and 2014 at University College London (UCL) and the University of Oxford, respectively, aimed at discussing the diverse and far-reaching legal reforms taking place across Latin America as a region, providing a forum for sustained discussion about the particularities and specific challenges shaping the law in the region, and bringing together the growing international band of scholars who are addressing the regional context in English-language scholarship.

In recent decades, Latin American states have embarked on ambitious legal reforms, from the adoption of new constitutions to the elaboration of new legislative frameworks dealing with copyright law, environmental protection and anti-trust. These transformations have brought changes in government structures and individuals' perceptions of their relationship with state power. Fundamental rights are now as important as the notion of efficiency. Central banks and regulatory agencies have become key institutions in the state's finances. *Technopols* have displaced the traditional bureaucracy in state administration. However, old problems remain: entrenched income inequality, corruption and environmental pollution continue to be pervasive. Yet, as these reforms have focused on law and legal institutions, the role of law continues to be highly important in reshaping social relations in Latin America.

This book draws together scholars from Argentina, Brazil, Colombia, Chile, Ireland, Mexico, Nigeria and the USA to analyse intersections between law and policy across the region, focusing especially on transforming courts, institutions and rights. As there is a growing interest in recent Latin American transformations, our purpose is to offer for a broad audience studies on legal innovations and political transformations in this region. In this context, this volume is interdisciplinary and explores various perspectives from different fields of social sciences on how these legal reforms occurred and their impact on transforming not only courts, institutions and rights, but also politicojuridical integration, socioeconomic development, and access to knowledge, medicines, and a healthy environment.

Therefore, our book contrasts with other works on Latin American legal and political issues: these are usually limited to the domains of 'black letter' law or specialised social sciences, whereas this collection comprises sociolegal studies of law in context. In addition, all chapters focus on concrete regional problems, providing detailed case studies and proposals to address rights enforcement, underdevelopment, and inequality in Latin America. The theme of courts, institutions and rights cuts across all studies, as rights enforcement depends on functioning courts and institutions – a relationship seen throughout the volume. The studies here also offer a transnational perspective, as authors seek to establish a dialogue on Latin American law and policy based not only on their local knowledge but also on their international expertise. Therefore the reader will find a collection of texts that analyse the most important sociolegal transformations in Latin America and their impact on courts, institutions and rights.

The chapters comprising this study are organised under five headings. Given the centrality of courts in transformative legal and political arrangements, Part I investigates how the Inter-American Court of Human Rights has transformed local courts, Latin American constitutionalism and rights enforcement across the region. Tom Gerald Daly (Chap. 1) provides an overview of the difficult and underexplored relationship between the Supreme Federal Court and the Inter-American Court, set against the overall state relationship with the Inter-American Court. By highlighting a number of questions posed by the Supreme Court's stance, the contribution goes to the heart of our understanding of the transnational system centred on the Inter-American Court, concerning the precise requirements of 'conventionality control'; the limits of 'dialogue' as a metaphor for interlevel court interaction; the extent to which the Inter-American Court's jurisprudential approach can accommodate opposing domestic positions; and the possible need for greater deference towards domestic courts in general.

Focusing on institutional dialogue among courts for human rights protection, Marcelo Torelly (Chap. 2) analyses how domestic constitutional regimes from Latin America interact with the Inter-American Human Rights System. He argues that structural transformations in international law together with the decline of statehood leads to broader legal interaction at the transnational level, allowing new players (such as non-governmental organisations and victims) to act as constitutional actors, articulating political claims in the linguistic register of rights. This process spurs the reshaping of constitutional law, allowing civil society organisations to bypass institutional obstacles for human rights enforcement in the domestic arena, and also leading to a new set of legitimacy problems concerning law-making. Comparing case law from Argentina, Brazil, Chile and Mexico, this chapter reveals an enormous variation in the way states interact with the Inter-American Human Rights System, but also a general trend to consider its precedents, if not as a binding normative source, at least as a reflective interpretative tool. Torelly concludes that constitutional engagement is an interesting answer to the growing need for legal integration in the region.

Damián González-Salzberg (Chap. 3) also discusses the transformations caused by the Inter-American Court of Human Rights, focusing on human rights enforcement by nation-states. He offers a comprehensive empirical study of the level of compliance with judgments of the Court. This study uses an empirical method to survey compliance with the totality of judgments issued until mid-2011 and monitored by the Court by the end of June 2013, covering five types of measure of reparations ordered in those judgments. In brief, it analyses a total of 330 measures of reparations ordered within 112 judgments, making it one of the most comprehensive empirical studies published on the topic. In addition to presenting the empirical results, this chapter proposes different paths to improving the level of compliance with the Court's judgments.

Diego Gil, Rolando García and Lawrence M. Friedman (Chap. 4) contribute to this debate by exploring representations of the Inter-American Court in the media through a detailed empirical study of media coverage in several countries. The results are, in a way, discouraging, indicating that newspapers in Latin America generally pay little attention to the Court's work; surely a factor which helps to produce the general obscurity in which the Court labours. The authors suggest that the feeble media coverage reflects the Court's status, and no doubt also reinforces it: not all countries have subjected themselves to the jurisdiction of the Court; others feel free to ignore its judgments; individuals cannot petition it directly; and it remains, in addition, a part-time institution.

Part II focuses on institutional development and different strategies for policy implementation and change. In her study of the evolving relationship between law and development, Helena Alviar (Chap. 5) compares and contrasts three different methods: the purely instrumentalist; the instrumentalist law-centred; and the legally centred. These three perspectives share a view of the relationship between law and economic development as direct: once your economic development goals are clear or the benefits of legal transformation are evident, these ideas can easily be translated into legal texts. However, Alviar argues that the true relationship between law and economic development remains elusive and that there is a range of interactions taking place that haven't been adequately analysed. For this reason, she proposes unpacking this relationship with a set of tools that foreground the theoretical dialogue taking place between economists and lawyers, as a step towards acquiring a more complex understanding of the exchange that is taking place. A detailed unpacking of the set of ideas that underlie the role of law and legal reform in society is necessary and it means understanding not only what the idea of law is in the background of both economists and policy-makers, who will inevitably take different views of the power of the judiciary, the executive branch or the legislature, but also fundamental definitions of liberty and equality. According to Alviar, development depends on a deep understanding of the dynamics of courts, institutions and rights enjoyment.

In his study of transnational legal indicators and institutional change in Latin America, David Restrepo Amariles (Chap. 6) adopts an original approach by analysing indicators in the context of governance through development, which characterises most contemporary development policy. He argues that transnational legal indicators reflect new dynamics of legal reform and development policy based on the premises of new public management, regulatory competition and the emergence of a global market of rules. Indicators promote the idea not only that there is only one model of development, but also that there is only one model of law in development. They define the rule of law as a *proxy* of legal systems and expand its rhetoric to include business law and regulation, and promote a mathematical proceduralisation of legal concepts that strips legal phenomena away from their context and intrinsic complexity. The chapter concludes that transnational legal indicators are useful and necessary tools to understanding and assessing the transformation of legal institutions across the world as they provide reforms with new comparative and empirical knowledge. It also sets out a series of recommendations to improve existing legal metrics and encourage the creation of new ones with regional focus.

In her study of institutional bypasses in Brazil, Mariana Mota Prado (Chap. 7) investigates the conditions under which an institutional bypass is likely to help policymakers overcome initial resistance to reforms. She analyses two municipal case studies from Brazil: a bureaucratic reform in the 1990s (Poupatempo); and a police reform in the 2000s (Unidade de Polícia Pacificadora). Her case studies reveal that these bypasses may be a helpful strategy for policy implementation and institutional change, and may also foster rights protection and enforcement.

Part III discusses contemporary institutional challenges of Latin American law and policy, focusing particularly on market integration and regulation. In his contribution on securities regulation, Jose Miguel Mendoza (Chap. 8) explains how stock exchange integration under the Latin American Integrated Market (MILA) may help overcome some of the political economy challenges to capital market development. The onset of MILA has reopened a longstanding debate concerning the operation of capital markets in Latin America and has set the stage for a serious assessment of the region's experience with the regulation of listed firms, and, perhaps more importantly, for any course corrections that are deemed necessary. However, policy-makers in Latin America are still struggling to come up with a well-defined framework for the regulation of capital markets, with some consensus still to be reached as to the top policy priorities that must be pursued. The discussions presented here are meant to inform the efforts of policy-makers in understanding different approaches to the regulation of listed firms in the developing countries of Latin America. Although MILA and the developing Pacific Alliance have created space for serious institutional change, the dearth of independent research in the field of Latin American capital markets could undermine ongoing efforts to introduce effective reform.

Next, Laura Bernal-Bermudez (Chap. 9) addresses a different institutional problem by analysing redress mechanisms and the prosecution of corporate human rights abuses. She evaluates the reliance of current regulatory measures on judicial actions to prosecute corporations by analysing explanatory factors of corporate accountability and/or remedies for victims: the political environment where a trial takes place; institutions in charge of the prosecution/trial; the corporation that committed the abuse; the type of abuse committed; and the role of civil society in the trial. Using

Colombia as a case study, she indicates instances where accountability and remedy are possible, despite high obstacles for access to justice, and presents some patterns and conclusions regarding the use of judicial actions. The chapter uses a large data sample from the Corporations and Human Rights Database (CHRD), which is the first Large-N database on corporate human rights abuses in existence, to study corporate involvement in human rights abuses with a broader scope and a more representative sample for analysis.

Ligia Catherine Arias Barrera (Chap. 10) investigates institutional strategies in the Colombian derivatives market. She describes how the lack of interconnectedness among the multiple regulatory strategies adopted in the Colombian over-the-counter derivatives market (OTCDM) affects regulation and supervision, and, as a consequence, market growth. Colombia has implemented predominantly a risk-based approach to the regulation of the securities market; initially with a separated regulation and supervision approach to the banking and securities system, and afterwards reaffirmed by specific legislation. However, the case of Colombia responds more to a mixture of regulatory approaches, including risk-based regulation and regulatory capture. The evolution of securities market regulation shows a prevailing move towards International Organization of Securities Commissions and Organisation for Economic Co-operation and Development principles, some risk-based regulation principles and ultimately a strong emphasis on investor protection. Inconsistencies in the approach to the regulation of the securities market have arguably triggered failures in the regulation and supervision of the OTCDM, adversely impacting the use of derivatives in commodities trading. The chapter contributes to the scarce Colombian OTC derivatives literature by proposing some recommendations for the better regulation and supervision of the market.

This part ends with Andrés Palacio-Lleras's analyses of historical transformations in Latin American competition law. He takes an original approach to competition law in Latin America by suggesting that historical analysis should not take sides in debates about free markets, yet acknowledging that legal rules determine the degree of market freedom. Understanding the evolution of its institutions requires an investigation of the transplantation of foreign rules and doctrines into Latin American contexts. Likewise, research should focus on channels of diffusion of these rules and doctrines, the individuals and institutions involved in their transplantation, and their interactions as litigants, government advisors and international experts. Overall, the chapter provides some interesting ideas about how to understand the history of competition law in Latin America and points to new paths of research that have not yet been explored.

Part IV discusses constitutional transformations in Latin America and how they have affected individual autonomy and collective self-government. Roberto Gargarella (Chap. 12) provides a brief descriptive history of Latin American constitutionalism (1810–2010) and offers some tools for critically examining the region's constitutional development. In its descriptive part the chapter organises the history of Latin American constitutionalism around four periods: (1) the independence years (1810–1850); (2) the 'founding period' of Latin American constitutionalism (1850–1917); (3) the coming of social constitutionalism (1917–1950); and (4) the latest wave of constitutional reforms (1950–2010). In his critical analysis, Gargarella mainly argues that the implementation of social and economic constitutional rights is impeded by the absence of necessary, correlative reforms in the organisation of power of those same constitutions. In spite of its brevity, the chapter is quite exceptional in its scope and ambitions: it aims to cover 200 years of the region's constitutional history, and to speak in comparative terms for the entire region.

Next, Alberto Coddou McManus (Chap. 13) focuses on equality and anti-discrimination law in the region. He addresses the possibilities and limits of the anti-discrimination project for Latin America. Anti-discrimination law guiding principles – anti-classification, anti-subordination and the intervention principle – offer answers to two traditional critiques from both the left and the right. He proposes an institutional articulation of an anti-discrimination project centred on Gargarella's *egalitarian-dialogic constitutionalism*. McManus offers the basis to craft an anti-discrimination project that takes advantage of the distinctiveness of the understanding of equality and its relation with both social rights and anti-discrimination law in Latin America.

Malu A. C. Gatto (Chap. 14) also discusses inequality in her contribution by analysing gender quotas, legislative resistance and non-legislative reforms. As a type of affirmative action policy for women, gender quotas have the potential to direct the candidate-recruitment process (previously solely managed according to party discretion) and limit the space for male candidates – the vast majority of political incumbents and party leaders. Gatto uses a newly developed database of all cases of gender quota adoptions (and revisions) in Latin America to derive an indicator to measure the strength of gender quotas comparatively, and to consecutively map the designs of quotas in Latin America. In addition, she examines the role of executive decrees and judicial decisions for the strengthening of gender quota policies. Her analysis is crucial for mapping the strength of policies in the region and how they are being adopted and revised. Beyond elucidating the importance of specific parts of quota legislations, quota adoption and revision also tell another story: gender quotas may be the result of various processes of negotiation and decision-making that involve more than one branch of government; women's rights depend on courts and other institutional actors.

Pedro Fortes (Chap. 15) sets out his empirical research, investigating human rights violations committed by police in contemporary Brazil. His study reveals a pattern of complaints of torture and other forms of police abuse made by criminal defendants, without any proper investigation by judges, prosecutors or public defenders owing to the structural features of the Brazilian criminal justice system. These structural factors, he suggests, include an asymmetry of information caused by long delays between killings and their official communication to judicial authorities, or by imprisonment and judicial testimony in which torture was finally alleged; an inadequate regime of incentives for judicial cooperation, such as an absence of plea bargaining and sanctions for perjury, which induce criminal defendants to lie and which lead to most testimonies being discredited in the courtroom; and the lack of an investigative structure at the attorney general's office, which discourages initiatives to investigate allegations of police violence made by criminal defendants. The chapter concludes with a policy proposal addressing each structural factor to prevent human rights violations in Brazil.

Part V focuses on emerging technologies and rights, addressing how courts and institutional actors should guarantee access to knowledge, medicine and a healthy environment. Joaquim Falcão (Chap. 16) takes a historical parallel as a vantage point from which to address the issue of copyright: the flow of information in the fifteenth century, the age of maritime exploration and discovery by the great navigators. Using a concrete case as an example—the *Mundus Novus* letter attributed to Amerigo Vespucci, which made him famous and which justified naming the continent discovered by Columbus not Columbia but America—the argument shows how a lack of restriction on the reproduction, citation and use of the content by other authors had a decisive impact on the life of this historical individual, and on the Americas. Based on this example, Falcão demonstrates that the same principle should apply today: that there are no reasons to limit and excessively regulate copyright, trademarks and patents in the cybernetic age, and that complete freedom in this area has positive consequences. This is an innovative chapter inasmuch as it departs from the standard academic practice in comparative law and legal history by taking history and sociology as its starting point, tracing a parallel with the present to regulate the future. Comparison with a well-known concrete example strengthens the case against the regulation of copyright, attempting to use facts rather than mere legal argumentation to persuade the reader that the free flow of information in public creation is necessary for incremental innovation and knowledge accumulation, and combating the severe constraints imposed by legal obstacles.

Paula Westenberger (Chap. 17) discusses the issue of digitisation and orphan works in cultural institutions from the Brazilian perspective. The originality of this study is the in-depth analysis of the current copyright legislation and of the proposals for legal reform in the area still pending submission to the Brazilian Congress. The analysis is contextualised by reference to the relevant human rights and Brazilian constitutional provisions and is contrasted with solutions adopted in other jurisdictions. Legislative solutions proposed in this chapter aim to strike a balance between the interests of authors in protecting their rights and those of society at large in promoting access to culture. The relevance of analysing the Brazilian perspective is based on the fact that Brazil is currently considered a potentially influential world leader in terms of internet rights as a result of the recent implementation of the 'Internet bill of rights'.

In his contribution Emmanuel Kolawole Oke (Chap. 18) argues that incorporating a right to health perspective into the design, implementation and interpretation of a country's patent law entails recognising patent rights as instrumental rights that should serve fundamental social needs by facilitating both pharmaceutical innovation and access to medicine. Therefore the incorporation of a right to health perspective into the Brazilian patent law reform process, which was launched in October 2013, is a step in the right direction. The chapter examines the proposed reforms to the Brazilian patent law and highlights how these proposals will enhance enjoyment of the right to health. This perspective does not necessarily mean that patent rights should be unprotected but that they cannot prevent access to essential medicine. These proposed reforms may make the acquisition of frivolous patents for essential drugs more difficult and facilitate the early entry of cheaper, generic drugs into the market on the expiration of the patent term of protected drugs. If eventually enacted, these measures will assist the Brazilian Government in fulfilling its right to health obligations. Oke concludes that other developing countries can follow the Brazilian model by incorporating a right to health perspective in their national patent laws.

Finally, Julia Mattei and Larissa Verri Boratti (Chap. 19) discuss Brazilian constitutional environmental law by exploring alternative models for normative concepts on environmental protection. They offer an instrumental perspective and develop a contextualised, grounded analysis of one specific approach to the constitutionalisation of environmental rights by grappling with the implications of the Brazilian constitutional formulation of a right to the environment, and by contrasting it with other normative models and provisions. First, their study gives an overview of the fundamental right to a healthy environment established in the 1988 Brazilian Federal Constitution, in terms of its scope and the extent of its interpretation and implementation. In such a context, legal-political progress resulted from allowing litigation on public interest grounds and creating forms of direct judicial protection of such a right, namely enhanced quality of domestic legislation and a strong judicial protection. Then it refers to Latin American experiences and to European Union (EU) law, addresses the rise of a Latin American constitutionalism with the purpose of giving context to the Brazilian constitutional reforms, grounded on claims for social justice, and discusses the recognition of a fundamental right to a clean and healthy environment in EU law as an example of a model that addresses the environmental duty of governments without necessarily creating environmental rights. Once again, courts, institutions, and rights are intertwined in their law and policy analysis.

The editors are grateful to the Faculty of Law at UCL and to the Latin American Centre, the Centre for Socio-Legal Studies, and the Faculty of Law at the University of Oxford for the use of their facilities and for the generous funding of these two conferences. The chapters comprising this volume are versions of some of the papers presented at these events, and the editors would like to thank all of the participants for their presentations and lively contributions, which have led to this timely collection.

Pedro Fortes, Larissa Verri Boratti, Andrés Palacios Lleras,
and Tom Gerald Daly
Oxford, London, and Edinburgh, March 2016.

PART I

Courts, Constitutionalism and the Inter-American System

CHAPTER 1

Brazilian 'Supremocracy' and the Inter-American Court of Human Rights: Unpicking an Unclear Relationship

Tom Gerald Daly

The post-war era has witnessed two distinct trends concerning courts: the proliferation and growing power of domestic constitutional and supreme courts;[1] and the rise of regional human rights courts.[2] This has led to two results: a 'judicialisation' of politics, whereby courts now govern areas of policy and politics previously considered outside their domain; and a blurring of the lines between constitutional law and international law as domestic courts apply the decisions of regional human rights courts, and as the latter have characterised themselves as 'constitutional' courts on a wider, regional, scale.[3] The tendency in Europe and South America, the two regions with the most developed human rights courts, is to present a picture of a shared 'transnational' judicial space, with the courts at the

The author wishes to thank the National University of Ireland (NUI) for providing the Travelling Studentship in International Law to support this research. Thanks are also owed to Prof. Conrado Hübner Mendes, Prof. Oscar Vilhena Vieira, FGV Direito São Paulo, the Brazilian Society of Public Law, the Supreme Federal Court of Brazil, and the Global Justice Academy at the University of Edinburgh for their assistance with this research.

T.G. Daly (✉)
University of Edinburgh, Edinburgh, UK

domestic and regional levels working together as part of a common judicial project to constrain arbitrary state action and uphold human rights.[4]

In South America in particular, the regional shift to electoral democracy from the late 1970s ushered in a 'double' judicialisation of politics. At one level, apex domestic courts have—at different paces—thrown off their timidity in the face of the other branches of government and assumed increasingly prominent positions in the democratic order. At a second level, the Inter-American Court[5] of Human Rights (hereinafter Inter-American Court) has through its forceful case law managed at times to exert an effect on domestic constitutional orders not only rivaling, but even surpassing, the impact of the European Court of Human Rights across the member states of the Council of Europe. In recent decades a strong perception has arisen of a 'harmonic resonance'[6] between domestic apex courts and the Inter-American Court. This 'structural coupling', as Marcello Torelly has observed, has blurred the boundaries between the domestic and international orders, fostering a 'transconstitutionalization of fundamental rights problems' and the evolution of a transnational community of courts.[7]

It is important to emphasise that, with all South American governments displaying some resistance to the Inter-American Court's rulings, and with constitutions in the region differing in their openness to international human rights law, it is largely the domestic courts' openness to Inter-American case law which has led to its increasing centrality in domestic constitutional orders. In the last two decades in particular, most apex courts in South America have incorporated Inter-American case law as a parameter for constitutional interpretation: many (though certainly not all) courts have gone so far as to include Inter-American norms in a formal 'constitutional block' comprising constitutional law and international human rights norms. In this environment, courts such as the Supreme Court of Venezuela—which was a vocal critic of the Inter-American Court before Venezuela left its jurisdiction in 2012[8]—appear anomalous: a 'captured' court merely echoing executive opposition to Inter-American oversight.

Much more difficult to characterise is the underexplored relationship between the Supreme Federal Court of Brazil (hereinafter Supreme Federal Court) and the Inter-American Court. In stark contrast to many of the neighbouring democratisation processes, Brazilian democratisation has largely witnessed a 'single' or 'unipolar' judicialisation of politics. While the power, centrality and assertiveness of the Supreme Federal Court has increased dramatically, there has been very limited penetration of Inter-American case law in the domestic constitutional order owing to the Supreme Federal Court's somewhat 'closed' stance towards the Inter-American Court's jurisprudence, even despite growing openness towards the latter at the overall state level.

As such, the Brazilian context appears to invert the more familiar regional scenario whereby the domestic apex court tends to be more open to Inter-American norms than the other governmental branches. This contribution, by providing a brief overview of the relationship between the Supreme Federal Court and the Inter-American Court, and the void it represents at the heart of the regional judicial community in Latin America, seeks to highlight a number of key questions, which are crucial to our understanding of the transnational system centred on the Inter-American Court. Section 1 provides a brief account of the Supreme Federal Court's rise in the domestic order after 1988. Section 2 charts the increasing (albeit non-linear) openness in state policy towards the Inter-American Human Rights (hereinafter Inter-American System) from dicta-torship to the present. Section 3 focuses on the relationship between the Supreme Federal Court and the Inter-American Court. Section 4 con-cludes by returning to these key questions.

1   FROM DICTATORSHIP TO 'SUPREMOCRACY' IN 30 YEARS

The rise of the Supreme Federal Court has been well charted in the past two decades and need not be rehearsed at length here.[9] Established under Brazil's first republican Constitution of 1891, and having enjoyed some 'political prominence' and periods of fertile jurisprudence, during the First Republic (1891–1930), the Supreme Federal Court displayed resistance during the early years of the military dictatorship (1964–1985)[10] before being brought to heel by the military regime. However, unlike many of its counterparts in neighbouring states, it was never fully subordinated,[11] retained at least some of its integrity and public support into the democratic transition, and did not suffer a purge on the return to democratic rule.[12]

Although the Supreme Federal Court had become a peripheral state organ by the mid-1980s, the new democratic Constitution of 1988 pushed it firmly into the limelight. The text amplified its role at the centre of the constitutional order as 'guardian of the Constitution'[13] by narrowing its previously broad jurisdiction to almost exclusively constitutional mat-ters.[14] It also significantly enhanced the Court's review powers through the introduction of two new abstract review mechanisms, to operate alongside the existing diffuse review system, which permits limited constitutional review by ordinary courts in concrete cases. These reforms have led to the Court operating akin to a classic 'European-style' constitutional court in many ways, although it remains at the apex of, rather than separate from, the ordinary judiciary.

The enormous and ambitious 1988 Constitution, with its 'open texture, programmatic norms and indeterminate provisions',[15] set the scene for the judicialisation of Brazilian politics. In the context of political, economic and legal flux following the adoption of the Constitution, and with a pressing need for clarification of the outsized and rights-heavy constitutional text and the constitutional boundaries between the branches of government, political and civil society actors were strongly incentivised to bring actions before the Supreme Federal Court. Today, virtually every controversy of social and political significance comes before the Court, with abstract review being the backbone of its key jurisprudence.

However, this is not due to an 'activist' approach of the Supreme Federal Court comparable to, say, the Constitutional Court of Colombia since 1992. Indeed, until 2000, the Supreme Federal Court adopted a rather restrained posture in its case law, only occasionally taking bold positions against the executive, and evincing timidity in the use of its generous powers (e.g. the power to address legislative omission).[16] Kapiszewski attributes its general restraint to its institutional security and stability: with a long history, no judicial purges since well before democratisation; full and real guarantees of tenure and judicial independence; autonomy regarding budgetary matters; procedural continuity through the change of regime; a sense of the institution as separate from individual judges; and a professional ethos of collegiality.[17] Others suggest that the legacy of its suppression under military rule simply left the Court ill-equipped to fulfil its much more expansive role under the new Constitution.[18]

The Supreme Federal Court's more assertive turn in recent years—especially as regards its fundamental rights jurisprudence—has been facilitated by successive enhancements of its review powers since the 1990s, through constitutional reform in 1993, two laws in 1999 and further constitutional reform in 2004.[19] These reforms progressively added more competences to the Court: including two new mechanisms for abstract review to expand its oversight role; permitting it to hold public hearings where clarification is required concerning complex matters and to modulate the effect of findings of unconstitutionality; and introducing a system of precedent and amplifying the binding nature of its decisions, which has diminished the significance of diffuse constitutional control by lower courts. Moreover, unlike other courts in the region, the Supreme Federal Court has not suffered threats or attacks from the other branches of government in reaction to assertive decisions,[20] although this is certainly not to say that it is immune to criticism.

In recent years, Brazilian scholars such as Oscar Vilhena Vieira have begun warning of the perils of 'supremocracy', with the Supreme Federal Court enjoying supremacy vis-à-vis not only other courts but also as against other state powers.[21] While perhaps somewhat hyperbolic, the phrase nevertheless captures the current totemic status of the Court in Brazil's constitutional order and, crucially, its pre-eminence in the judicial architecture of the state; a constitutional court in a polity where far greater expanses of law and policy have been 'constitutionalised' than is the norm.

2   State Policy and the Inter-American Court

While the Supreme Federal Court's star has risen ever higher during the past 25 years, the Inter-American Court has tended to remain at the periphery of Brazilian political and legal consciousness.

Despite being one of the first states in South America to begin the transition to electoral democracy in the 1970s, placing great emphasis on fundamental rights protection in its post-transition Constitution, and signing the American Convention on Human Rights (ACHR) in the early months of the return to civilian rule in 1985,[22] Brazil has appeared reluctant to engage with the Inter-American System. It was the second last of the current contracting parties to ratify the ACHR (in 1992) and the third last to accept the jurisdiction of the Inter-American Court (in 1998). However, state policy appears to have become increasingly open to the Court's oversight since 1998.

Brazil and the Inter-American System before Acceptance of the Inter-American Court's Jurisdiction

During military rule, state policy was generally hostile to international human rights oversight. Brazil adhered to very few international human rights treaties[23] and the state was not a signatory to either of the principal Inter-American rights instruments, the American Declaration of the Rights and Duties of Man and the ACHR. While, as an implied consequence of Organization of American States (OAS) membership[24] the state was subject to the individual application procedure before the Inter-American Commission on Human Rights (hereinafter the Inter-American Commission; which permits the Commission to examine individual claims of rights violations), requests for information from the Commission were routinely ignored in a climate of human rights abuses directly perpetrated by the state. Even where the state was found to be responsible for human rights violations, it refused to implement the Commission's recommendations.[25]

In the early years of democratic rule, despite a shift from state-led human rights violations to violations by private actors, the signing of a number of human rights treaties, including the ACHR,[26] and some minimal engagement with the Inter-American System, the state still had a tendency to ignore the Inter-American Commission or to be extremely late in responding to it.[27] Between 1985 and 2000 there was little further engagement, with the Commission issuing only one merits decision, in 1998.[28] Since 2000, the number of cases against Brazil before the Commission has risen gradually,[29] but Cavallaro's observation in 2002 that 'use of the system against Brazil continues to be relatively limited' appears broadly true over ten years on.[30]

It has been observed that the state's engagement with cases before the Inter-American Commission, and implementation of the Commission's decisions, tends to require intensive lobbying by national civil society actors, including the media.[31] A good example is the *Maria da Penha* case,[32] in which the Commission had in 2001 recommended prompt and effective compensation for a victim of serious domestic abuse and the adoption of measures at state level to address domestic violence. For more than two years the federal government failed to act but, after considerable pressure from women's movements and the Special Secretariat of Public Policy for Women, it finally enacted a law on domestic violence against women, which came into effect in 2006.[33]

Brazil and the Inter-American Court

Brazil's relationship with the Inter-American Court is little over a decade old but it was dramatic from the outset. The Court's first decision against Brazil in 2002[34] arose in the context of an effort to protect prisoners at the Urso Branco ('polar bear') penitentiary in Rondônia state, north-west Brazil. Following a prison massacre and evidence of an unacceptably high death rate and violence,[35] the Inter-American

Commission sought provisional measures from the Court. In an 'unprecedented and sweeping decision',[36] the Inter-American Court granted the measures, ordering Brazil to adopt all necessary means to protect the life and personal safety of all prisoners, to investigate the facts surrounding the massacre in order to identify and prosecute those responsible, and to report on its progress in this regard to the Court within 15 days, and thereafter every two months. However, the year the decision was issued this did not have immediate effect due to the federal nature of the Brazilian state: in short, the authorities in Rondônia refused to bow to the Court's judgment.[37]

To date, the Inter-American Court has handed down no more than five full merits judgments in cases against Brazil, between 2006 and 2010. These concern a mixture of matters related to very widespread human rights deficiencies, and authoritarian practices which bled into the democratic era, such as mistreatment of the mentally ill, police 'death squads', police wiretapping and violent evictions of landless workers, and the validity of the 1979 Amnesty Law.[38] In all of these cases bar one,[39] the Court has found Brazil responsible for violations of the ACHR—a remarkable strike rate by any standards.

Spatial constraints preclude a detailed analysis of these cases. It suffices to state that, while generally complying with orders for pecuniary or symbolic compensation, the state's compliance with orders to investigate, prosecute and punish crimes is impeded by a serious lack of familiarity with the Inter-American System among key state actors charged with compliance, such as the judiciary and the police force.[40]

Nonetheless, the state, in response to the most recent judgment in the *Guerrilha do Araguaia* case, while refusing to fully implement the decision by ordering investigations and prosecutions concerning the disappearances, or to repeal the 1979 Amnesty Law, which precludes the prosecution of various crimes perpetrated during military rule, took three significant steps in response to the decision: (1) enacting a law to give effect to the constitutional right to information by establishing a full framework for access to such information and protection of privacy; (2) ratifying the International Convention for the Protection of All Persons from Forced Disappearance in 2010; and, (3) perhaps most important, establishing in November 2011 Commissão Nacional de Verdade (National Truth Commission), which in December 2014 produced a report on human rights abuses committed from 1946 to 1988.[41] This, it should be noted, was achieved in the teeth of strong military opposition.[42]

General Signs of Greater Openness to International Human Rights Norms

Allied to these specific implementation measures, a more general development in the past decade tends to suggest state policy towards greater openness to the Inter-American System. A constitutional amendment of 2004 (No. 45/2004) amended Article 5 of the Constitution (concerning fundamental rights) to provide that international human rights treaties and conventions approved by Congress under the procedure required for constitutional amendments (i.e. by a supermajority of three-fifths of the votes, in two rounds of voting) 'shall be equivalent to constitutional amendments', as well as enshrining Brazil's accession to the International Criminal Court in the constitutional text and providing recourse to federal courts in cases of serious human rights violations. The first amendment in particular appeared to lay the foundations for an 'internationalisation' of the constitutional order, in a similar manner to constitutional law in various other Latin American states (e.g. Argentina and Colombia).

A Qualified Openness

It is important not to overstate the state's openness towards the Inter-American Court. The federal nature of the Brazilian state continues to be identified as one of the obstacles to the implementation of Inter-American decisions, and, as Cavallaro has noted, the federal government's stance towards the system is 'far from monolithic'.[43] Moreover, despite significant progress in the last 16 years, and Brazil's 'increasingly intense'[44] participation in the Inter-American System, domestic 'conventionality control' by public officials and judicial actors, under which they themselves ensure that state action is compatible with the ACHR, remains absent.[45]

Bernardes notes that the state remains 'resistant to the scrutiny of its public policies by international bodies',[46] citing the Inter-American Commission decision of 2011 ordering provisional measures to suspend the construction of a hydroelectric plant at Belo Monte, which was met with a fierce response from the Brazilian Government, including suspension of the transfer of financial contributions to the Commission and recalling Brazil's ambassador to the OAS.

That said, and although it is clearly not entirely linear, the general trajectory of State policy for the past decade in particular has been toward greater openness to the Inter-American System, and the Inter-American Court more specifically.

3   THE SUPREME FEDERAL COURT AND THE INTER-AMERICAN COURT

The stance of the Supreme Federal Court towards the authority of the Inter-American Court is more difficult to characterise. As we will see, one of the greatest stumbling blocks towards greater understanding of the Supreme Federal Court's position is that it has never been expressly articulated. However, a number of signs provide a slightly clearer understanding of the Court's position.

The Recent Nature of the Relationship

It is worth emphasising that for the first decade of the Supreme Federal Court's post-1988 operation, Brazil was not subject to the jurisdiction of the Inter-American Court (although it had ratified the ACHR) and, as seen above, the latter did not deliver its first decision in a case against Brazil until 2002.

Thus, unlike many of its counterparts in the region, in states which accepted the Inter-American Court's jurisdiction much earlier,[47] the Supreme Federal Court initially carved out its role in the new democratic dispensation without any formal link to the Inter-American Court, and without any requirement to enter into any form of 'dialogue' with it. This, to some extent, helps to explain the very limited penetration of Inter-American jurisprudence in the Supreme Federal Court's case law, but it does not explain the latter court's continuing stance towards the Inter-American Court since the turn of the century.

The Constitutional Status Accorded to Inter-American Norms and Jurisprudence

As indicated in the introduction to this chapter, Inter-American instruments and Inter-American Court jurisprudence are accorded constitutional status in the legal orders of various South American states: in some cases, this flows from the constitutional text (e.g. Argentina); in others (e.g. Colombia and Peru), it has been achieved by the apex court through the doctrine of the 'constitutional block'. The Supreme Court of Argentina has gone as far as to assert, since 1995, that even Inter-American Court case law concerning other states might be seen as binding, seen to full effect in the Supreme Court's *Simon* decision of 2005, invalidating Argentina's amnesty laws in compliance with longstanding

Inter-American jurisprudence in the area.[48] As such, Inter-American Court case law is widely used across the region as a parameter for interpretation of the Constitution.

By contrast, the Supreme Federal Court has never precisely articulated the status accorded to the jurisprudence of the Inter-American Court, although it has acknowledged that, through presidential decree 4.463 of 2002, the authority of the latter's final decisions concerning Brazil has been fully recognised by the state.[49]

As regards the instruments of the Inter-American System, the Supreme Federal Court traditionally accorded international treaties a subconstitutional status equivalent to ordinary law, allowing international norms to be revoked or amended by subsequent legislation under the 'later in time' (*lex posterior*) rule.[50] This changed in 2008, with a Supreme Federal Court decision addressing a direct clash between provisions of the Constitution and the ACHR concerning imprisonment for civil debt.[51] The Court recognised that simply following the 'later in time' rule would be problematic, allowing international treaties to be superseded by domestic legislation.

However, as regards constitutional amendment No. 45/2004, the Supreme Federal Court made a clear distinction between international treaties adopted before and *after* the amendment came into force. The latter would, as the amendment requires, attain constitutional status. However, the former—including the ACHR, ratified in 1992—would be accorded an intermediate status of 'supra-legality'; subconstitutional, and therefore not subject to the 'later in time' rule, but nevertheless subject to compliance with the Constitution.[52]

The decision has been decried as a missed opportunity to finally accord constitutional status to Inter-American norms and to strengthen the dialogic relationship between the Supreme Federal Court and the Inter-American Court, long urged by various Brazilian scholars, and sought by a minority of justices in the decision itself.[53] Yet, while the 'supra-legality' doctrine precludes any formal use of Inter-American jurisprudence as a parameter for interpreting the Constitution, it has been suggested that in practical terms it appears to open the door to this approach: in the instant case concerning civil debt, for example, the constitutional provision at odds with the ACHR was divested of any legal effect.[54]

Rare References to Inter-American Court Jurisprudence

Beyond the formal status accorded to the ACHR in the Supreme Federal Court's doctrine, or any formal status accorded to the Inter-American

Court's case law, a useful indicator is the extent to which reference is made to this case law in the former's jurisprudence. As Torelly notes, even the Constitutional Court of Chile, which resists any formal 'constitutional block' doctrine, nevertheless 'reflexively' uses Inter-American jurisprudence to reinterpret domestic law.[55]

By contrast, while Moreira Maués rightly points out that the *textual provisions* of the ACHR have been influential in the Supreme Federal Court's interpretation of constitutional provisions concerning due process guarantees and the freedom of expression[56]—even before the 'supra-legality' decision discussed above—references to the *case law* of the Inter-American Court are extremely rare in the former's decisions. Gustavo Ferreira Santos, for example, notes a study revealing that, of 138 sample decisions of the Supreme Federal Court, not one made reference to the Inter-American Court's case law, while no fewer than 80 references are made to decisions of the Supreme Court of the United States, and 58 citations of decisions of the Federal Constitutional Court of Germany.[57]

The Supreme Federal Court displays no aversion to citing external jurisprudence and continues to expand its range of citations, including case law of the European Court of Human Rights.[58] However, reliance on Inter-American Court decisions—as seen, for example, in the Supreme Federal Court's decision of 2009 finding a domestic diploma requirement for journalists to violate the Constitution[59]—are rare and isolated examples, and they do not appear to reflect any systematic shift in the Supreme Federal Court's approach to the Inter-American Court's case law. As a consequence, and in stark contrast to much of Latin America, Brazilian constitutional case law can be considered almost entirely distinct from the latter's case law.

Divergence from Settled Inter-American Court Case Law

The Supreme Federal Court's stance towards the Inter-American Court, specifically, comes into question most sharply in its 2010 judgment on Brazil's 1979 Amnesty Law.[60] At the time when the case came before the Court, settled Inter-American Court jurisprudence indicated that the law violated several provisions of the ACHR and must be divested of legal effect. Indeed, various other apex courts in the region (including those of Argentina, Chile, Colombia and Peru) had already followed the Inter-American jurisprudence by invalidating domestic amnesty laws or restricting their application in line with ACHR's requirements.

However, the Supreme Federal Court, in a decision of 29 April 2010, rejected the challenge: the rapporteur-judge, Justice Eros Grau, argued that the Court was not in a position to review the political negotiation and agreement on which the amnesty was based, and a considerable majority of 7–2 voted with him. As Mezarobba notes, 'The decision was harshly criticized by human rights organizations both inside and outside Brazil.'[61] The decision is striking for two reasons.

First, it was an unexpectedly timid decision from a court which had appeared to have moved towards a more assertive fundamental rights jurisprudence since 2000, and which had in recent years struck down a number of laws from the authoritarian era (including the press law discussed in Section 3.3), and against the regional backdrop where many courts had moved towards a common approach in line with the Inter-American Court's case law.

Second, and most importantly for the present purposes, despite the undeniable salience of existing Inter-American jurisprudence, all seven majority opinions characterised the matter as a domestic legal issue, going to some lengths to avoid treating it as solely a rights issue, and ignoring the case law of the Inter-American Court. While fleetingly recognising that the authority of that Court's final judgments was fully recognised by the state in 2002, Justice Grau refused to strike down the law as unconstitutional, stressing the 'bilateral' character of the amnesty;[62] the dangers of focusing on human dignity at the cost of other values;[63] the Court's clear historical case law (from the 1900s, 1950s and 1980s), which consistently upheld a broad interpretation of successive amnesty laws;[64] and the amnesty law's formal status as a 'legal measure' (*lei-medida*), addressing a particular historical issue rather than a law of general application.

Indeed, only one judge, Justice Lewandowski, cited the relevant Inter-American case law to argue that the application of the amnesty should be decided on a case-by-case basis using criteria elaborated in the Supreme Federal Court's historical amnesty jurisprudence.[65]

Mere months later, the Inter-American Court handed down its own decision in a separate action taken against the 1979 Amnesty Law, holding that certain provisions of the law, in precluding the investigation and punishment of severe human rights violations, are incompatible with the ACHR and have no legal basis.[66] At paragraph 177 it expressly noted that the state authorities, including the Supreme Federal Court, had failed to carry out any 'conventionality control' to assess the 1979 Amnesty Law against Brazil's obligations as a party to the ACHR, as required under its 2006 decision in *Almonacid Arellano v Chile*.[67] Sooner or later, it seems, the Supreme Federal Court will have to provide a response as challenges to the law continue to be taken.[68]

4 CONCLUSION: KEY QUESTIONS RAISED BY THIS INTER-COURT RELATIONSHIP

At present it is difficult not only to characterise the Supreme Federal Court's position towards the Inter-American Court but also to identify the reasons for its failure to engage with the latter. Does it constitute opposition to the international court's regional hegemony; an aversion to the Inter-American Court's lack of deference towards domestic courts; scepticism about the international court's pedigree (democratic, professional or otherwise); a resistance to interference by *any* international adjudicative body; a mere preference for citing 'Western' courts; a slow adjustment by a court unaccustomed to sharing normative supremacy; or merely yet another example of Brazilian exceptionalism compared with its regional neighbours?

Regrettably, in the absence of any explicit articulation by the Supreme Federal Court of its relationship with the Inter-American Court, its position concerning the binding nature of the Inter-American Court's decisions, or its view of possibly problematic aspects of that Court's jurisprudence, one is left to mere conjecture. In the 1979 Amnesty Law decision, for instance, the Supreme Federal Court never states that it believes the Inter-American Court's position on amnesty laws is *wrong* or that it is not bound by the latter's line of authority concerning amnesty laws. It simply avoids the question entirely.

This silence may be compared to the European context, where at least a minority of courts are wont to occasionally express open difference with the European Court of Human Rights: witness, for instance, the *Horncastle* decision of the Supreme Court of the United Kingdom in 2009, where Lord Phillips took great pains to explain why the Court refused to follow a decision of the European Court of Human Rights, and the latter's subsequent modification of its position to accommodate the Supreme Court's decision.[69] In the Brazilian context, in place of 'dialogue'—admittedly a highly overused metaphor—we are left with parallel monologues from each court, which never quite intersect.

The lack of articulation also leaves it entirely unclear whether, and in what way, the Supreme Federal Court may change its position towards the Inter-American Court in future. What can be said is that the Supreme Federal Court's position raises a range of fundamental and difficult questions at the heart of the evolving regional transnational community of domestic apex courts and the Inter-American Court, which certainly warrant further exploration: the precise requirements of 'conventionality control'; the limits of 'dialogue' as a metaphor for interlevel court interaction; the extent to which the Inter-American Court's jurisprudential approach can accommodate opposing domestic positions; and the possible need for greater deference towards domestic courts in general.

This, it may be said, is a research agenda that will benefit the constitutional conversation not only in Latin America but also in Europe and Africa, as well as in other regions in which the creation of regional human rights courts is being contemplated or advocated. In short, and as underscored by many of the other contributions to this collection, the Latin American conversation has an increasingly global resonance.

NOTES

1. Constitutional courts and supreme courts with the power to review the compatibility of state actions and laws with the Constitution are now found in over 100 countries worldwide. See e.g. C Neal Tate and Torbjörn Vallinder, *The Global Expansion of Judicial Power* (New York University Press 1995).

2. Regional human rights courts were established in Europe in 1959, in the Americas in 1978 and in Africa in 2004.

3. See e.g. Alec Stone Sweet, 'On the Constitutionalisation of the Convention: The European Court of Human Rights as a Constitutional Court' (2009) Faculty Scholarship Series Paper 71; and Manuel Eduardo Góngora Mera, *Inter-American Judicial Constitutionalism: On the Constitutional Rank of Human Rights Treaties in Latin America through National and Inter-American Adjudication* (Inter-American Institute of Human Rights 2011).

4. Ibid.

5. The Inter-American system for the protection of human rights, which is a creation of the Organization of American States (OAS), includes the Inter-American Court of Human Rights and the non-judicial Inter-American Commission on Human Rights, as well as various special rapporteurs focused on discrete topics (e.g. freedom of expression, rights of the child).

6. Diego Rodríguez-Pinzón, 'The Inter-American human rights system and transitional processes' in Antoine Buyse and Michael Hamilton (eds), *Transitional Jurisprudence and the ECHR: Justice, Politics and Rights* (Cambridge University Press 2011).

7. Marco Torelly, 'Transnational Legal Process and Constitutional Engagement in Latin America: How do Domestic Constitutional Regimes deal with International Human Rights Law?' SLS II Graduate Conference on Latin American Law and Policy, Oxford 7 March 2014, 39.

8. See Alexandra Huneeus, 'Courts Resisting Courts: Lessons from the Inter-American Court's Struggle to Enforce Human Rights' (2011) 44 Cornell International Law Journal 493, 500.

9. See e.g. Oscar Vilhena Vieira, 'Supremocracia' (2009) 8 Revista Direito GV 441; Loiane Prado Verbicaro, 'Um Estudo Sobre as Condições Facilitadoras da Judicialização da Política no Brasil' (2008) 4 Revista Direito GV São Paulo 389; and Oscar Vilhena Vieira, 'Descriptive Overview of the Brazilian Constitution and Supreme Court' in Oscar Vilhena Vieira, Frans Viljoen and Upendra Baxi (eds), *Transformative Constitutionalism: Comparing the Apex Courts of Brazil, India and South Africa* (Pretoria University Law Press 2013).

10. See Keith Rosenn, 'Separation of Powers in Brazil' (2009) 7 Duquesne Law Review 839, 845.

11. See e.g. Mark J Osiel, 'Dialogue with Dictators: Judicial Resistance in Argentina and Brazil' (1995) 20 Law and Social Inquiry 481, 527–532.

12. Diana Kapiszewski, 'How Courts Work: Institutions, Culture and the Brazilian *Supremo Tribunal Federal*' in Javier Couso, Alexandra Huneeus and Rachel Sieder (eds), *Cultures of Legality: Judicialization and Political Activism in Latin America* (Cambridge University Press 2010) 56.

13. Article 102 Federal Constitution of 1988.

14. Other superior courts were established to deal with non-constitutional (e.g. military and labour) matters.

15. Prado Verbicaro (n 8) 390.

16. Kapiszewski (n 11) 72–73.

17. Ibid. 61 et seq.

18. J Zaiden Benvindo, *On the Limits of Constitutional Adjudication: Deconstructing Balancing and Judicial Activism* (Springer 2010) 92 et seq.

19. Constitutional Amendment No.45/2004.

20. See e.g. Gretchen Helmke and Jeffrey K Staton, 'The Puzzling Judicial Politics of Latin America: A Theory of Litigation, Judicial Decisions, and Interbranch Conflict' in Gretchen Helmke and Julio

Rios-Figueroa (eds), *Courts in Latin America* (Cambridge University Press 2011).

21. Vilhena Vieira, 'Supremocracia' (n 8).
22. Tullo Vigevani and Gabriel Cepaluni, *Brazilian Foreign Policy in Changing Times: The Quest for Autonomy from Sarney to Lula* (Lexington Books 2009) 16–17.
23. Ratification of the International Convention against Racial Discrimination was a rare exception.
24. See James L Cavallaro, 'Toward Fair Play: A Decade of Transformation and Resistance in International Human Rights Advocacy in Brazil' (2002) 3 Chicago Journal of International Law 481, 482.
25. Cecília MacDowell Santos, 'Transnational Legal Activism and the State: Reflections on Cases Against Brazil in the Inter-American Commission on Human Rights' (2007) 7 SUR—International Journal on Human Rights 29, 39–40.
26. The state signed the ACHR, the two International Covenants (International Covenant on Civil and Political Rights and International Covenant on Economic, Social and Cultural Rights (ICESCR)) and the UN Convention against Torture in the mid-1980s but did not ratify most treaties until the 1990s.
27. MacDowell Santos (n 24) 39–40; and Cavallaro (n 23) 485–486.
28. Only one significant case, concerning the human rights of the indigenous Yanomami community, came before the Inter-American Commission during this time—in 1985.
29. Until May 1994, only two of the hundreds of cases pending before the Inter-American Commission concerned Brazil, and fewer than 30 by 1998. By 2010, Brazil ranked fifth in the number of cases pending before the Commission: Cavallaro (n 23) 483–484; and Marcia Nina Bernardes, 'Inter-American Human Rights System as a Transnational Public Sphere: Legal and Political Aspects of the Implementation of International Decisions' (2011) 15 SUR —International Journal on Human Rights 131, 137.
30. Cavallaro (n 23) 485.
31. Ibid. 488.
32. *Maria da Penha Maia Fernandes* IACommHR Case 12.051 Report 54/01 (16 April 2001).
33. See MacDowell Santos (n 24) 44–47.
34. Order of the Inter-American Court of Human Rights (18 June 2002).

35. Cavallaro (n 23) 489.
36. Ibid.
37. Cavallaro (n 23) 489.
38. *Ximenes Lopes* IACtHR Series C 149 (4 July 2006); *Nogueira de Carvalho* IACtHR Series C 161 (28 November 2006); *Escher* IACtHR Series C 200 (6 July 2009) (see also the Inter-American Court's interpretation of the judgment: IACtHR Series C 208 (20 November 2009)); *Garibaldi* IACtHR Series C 203 (23 September 2009); and *Gomes Lund ('Guerrilha do Araguaia')* IACtHR Series C 219 (24 November 2010).
39. *Nogueira de Carvalho* ibid.
40. Bernardes (n 28) 139–140.
41. *Relatório da Comissão Nacional da Verdade* 10 December 2014. http://www.cnv.gov.br/.
42. See, for example, Gary Duffy, 'Brazil Truth Commission Arouses Military Opposition' *BBC News* (11 January 2010). http://news.bbc.co.uk/1/hi/8451109.stm.
43. Cavallaro (n 23) 487.
44. Bernardes (n 28) 133.
45. Ibid. 144–146.
46. Ibid. 136–137, 150 n 6.
47. Argentina, Chile, Colombia and Uruguay had all accepted the Inter-American Court's jurisdiction by 1990.
48. Damian A Gonzalez-Salzburg, 'The Implementation of Decisions from the Inter-American Court of Human Rights in Argentina: An Analysis of the Jurisprudential Swings of the Supreme Court' (2010) 15 SUR—International Journal on Human Rights 113, 121.
49. See e.g. Justice Grau's vote in the Amnesty Law decision of 29 April 2010, addressed below.
50. See Antonio Moreira Maués, 'Supra-Legality of International Human Rights Treaties and Constitutional Interpretation' (2013) 18 SUR—International Journal on Human Rights 205, 206–207.
51. RE 349703 (3 December 2008).
52. Ibid. 29.
53. Gustavo Ferreira Santos, 'Treaties X Human Rights Treaties. A Critical Analysis of the Dual Stance on Treaties in the Brazilian Legal System' (2013) 15 European Journal of Law Reform 20, 27, 33.
54. Moreira Maués (n 49) 209.

55. See e.g. Góngora Mera (n 3) 139; and Torelly (n 6) 31.
56. Moreira Maués (n 49) 209–211.
57. Ferreira Santos (n 52) 26–27.
58. See Tom Gerald Daly, 'The Differential Openness of Brazil's Supreme Federal Court to External Jurisprudence', IACL World Congress, Oslo 16–20 June 2014. http://www.jus.uio.no/english/research/news-and-events/events/conferences/2014/wccl-cmdc/wccl/papers/ws5/w5-daly.pdf.
59. In RE 511.961 (17 June 2009) the rapporteur-judge, Justice Gilmar Mendes, cited extensively from a Consultative Opinion of the Inter-American Court of 1985: Advisory Opinion OC-5/85 IACtHR Series A 5 (13 November 1985). See also the more recent judgment in RE 591054 (17 December 2014).
60. ADPF 153 (29 April 2010).
61. Ibid. 18.
62. Ibid. 28.
63. Ibid. 25.
64. Ibid. 28–30.
65. Ibid. 130.
66. *Gomes Lund ('Guerrilha do Araguaia')* (n 37).
67. *Almonacid Arellano* et al. *v Chile* IACtHR Series C 154 (26 September 2006).
68. One of the latest challenges arose in the context of the prosecution of a government official for the kidnapping of members of the Araguaia guerrilla movement in the 1970s. See 'Brazil Prosecutes Retired Colonel over Disappearances in Challenge to Amnesty Law' *The Pan American Post* (14 March 2012). http://panamericanpost.blogspot.com/2012/03/brazil-prosecutes-retired-colonel-over.html.
69. See *R v Horncastle* [2009] UKSC 14 (SC); and *Al-Khawaja and Tahery v The United Kingdom* (2012) 54 EHRR 23. For more on the European context, see Nico Krisch, *Beyond Constitutionalism: The Pluralist Structure of Postnational Law* (Oxford University Press 2010) ch 4.

CHAPTER 2

Transnational Legal Process and Fundamental Rights in Latin America: How Does the Inter-American Human Rights System Reshape Domestic Constitutional Rights?

Marcelo Torelly

How does Transnational Legal Process (TLP), based on international human rights law, affect domestic constitutional law? This chapter aims to address this question by analysing how domestic constitutional regimes in Latin America interact with the Inter-American System. It argues that structural transformations in international Law together with broader legal interaction have allowed new players to behave as constitutional

The author would like to thank Carlos Gaio, David Kennedy, Diego Garcia Sayan, Federico Andreu Guzman, James Cavallaro, Karinna Fernández Neira, Kathryn Sikkink, Koen Lemmens, Leigh Payne, Leonardo Filippini, Naomi Roht-Arriaza, Marcelo Neves, Pablo Saavedra Alesandri, Par Engstrom, Pedro Salazar, Roberto Gargarella, Sergio Garcia Ramirez, Vicki Jackson and William Twining for helpful information, interviews, advice and comments on drafts of this chapter. The usual caveats apply.

M. Torelly (✉)
University of Brasilia, Brasilia, Brazil

P. Fortes et al. (eds.), *Law and Policy in Latin America*,
DOI 10.1057/978-1-137-56694-2_2

actors articulating political claims in the language of fundamental rights by means of the Inter-American System. This process inaugurates possibilities of reshaping constitutional law, allowing civil-society actors to bypass institutional obstacles to human rights enforcement in the domestic arena. The parallel development of the Inter-American System as an independent regime with a plurality of domestic answers to its normative growth leads to a unique path of development, adding an interesting set of models of transversal human rights governance to the broader field of 'global governance'.

1　THE MOVEMENT OF INTERNATIONAL LAW TOWARDS JUDICIALISATION

International law in the twentieth century was marked by an important structural shift in three stages.[1] In the first half of the century, for international lawyers and diplomats working on codifying norms, and identifying and systematising sources of law, legal positivism was the foremost theoretical reference. Characteristic problems concern whether international law was actually law, and how to reconcile theories of the will of the state with binding norms derived from customary practices.[2] States were engaged in building international organisations able to allow decision-making processes based on plenary deliberation, by consensus if possible. The League of Nations represents well this project of international law as a 'cosmopolitan dream'.[3]

After the failures of this first assembly moment, efforts were put into building executive institutions. From the 1950s to the 1980s, with the establishment of the United Nations (UN) and the growth of its independent agencies, specialised regimes in charge of policy management started to appear as 'independent' or 'self contained'.[4] They exercised an executive rather than a legislative style of governance, characterised by a 'combination of technocratic strength and political weakness'.[5] The idea of 'balance of power' took the place of 'consensus building', legal concerns moved from codification to administration, and positivism lost ground to realism and functionalism.[6] The growth of specialised regimes led to an unprecedented legal pluralism, which some defined as a 'fragmentation of International Law'.[7] The Inter-American System was born in this context, first with a monitoring body and later with the addition of a judicial court.

A third moment, from the 1980s on, is characterised by a systematic attempt to exclude politics from international law, as if its current configuration expressed the result of broader international agreement throughout the 'international community'. Since the end of the Cold War, international judicial bodies, assumed to be less politicised than other international organisations, have been affirmed as the best bodies to manage conflicts. This belief reinforces the widespread consolidation of independent judicial bodies designed to promote conflict resolution inside specialised regimes. The Inter-American Court, established in 1979, has become increasingly important regarding human rights governance in Latin America, especially since the 1990s.

The prevalence of neoliberal values in this historical quarter has meant a promotion of the idea of individual resolution of conflicts, reinforcing the role of courts as bodies able to manage conflicts in a 'technical' rather than a 'political' way. Global norms have become a trend, and transnational bodies have broken the previous monopoly of domestic institutions to interpret and enumerate rights.[8]

The actors have also changed: not only are states and international organisations considered relevant players, but also corporations, non-governmental organisations (NGOs) and even individuals are now able to intervene, sometimes even being considered as subjects with an international legal personality.[9] International NGOs have become key players, denouncing abuses and promoting an agenda for rights.[10,11]

International law has amplified its scope, establishing a 'liberal focus not on state-to-state interactions ... but on an analytically prior set of relationships among states and domestic and transnational civil society'.[12] In this context, the idea of TLP gains terrain. According to Koh, 'Transnational legal process describes the theory and practice of how public and private actors ... interact in a variety of public and private, domestic and international *fora* to make, interpret, enforce, and ultimately, internalize rules of transnational law.'[13]

While interacting, all players are producing and enforcing legal regulation. If at first scholars were arguing whether norms made without explicit state agreement could be called 'real' law, currently legal pluralism prevails and new players and 'law-makers' are widely operating everywhere, in an outstanding structural change. The role of courts has also grown dramatically. Regional human rights courts openly address contentious domestic issues, sometimes even performing a role of supranational judicial review. In the domestic dynamic, there are three possible reactions concerning international law and international decisions: convergence, engagement and resistance.[14]

When domestic judges and policy-makers assume a posture of *convergence*, they tend to understand 'domestic constitutions as a site for the implementation of international norms' and themselves 'as participants in a decentralized but normatively progressive process of transnational norm convergence'.[15] This model leads to a hierarchy between domestic and international law in a pattern of interaction that better performs the traditional expectations of compliance.

Conversely, domestic judges and policy-makers may assume a posture of indifference to international law, stating the supremacy of national sovereignty. This *resistance* model tends to ignore or underestimate both the existence of an overlapping jurisdiction (transversal governance) and the possibility of learning from another legal regime.

Finally, one may *engage* with the international. In the engagement model there is no assumption of an a priori precedent but there is openness to 'the idea that the concept of domestic constitutional law itself must now be understood in relation to transnational norms …'.[16] Engagement may lead to harmonisation or dissonance. The difference in relation to the previous models is that here, international law is neither hierarchically superior nor prima facie disregarded but is considered as a whole.

While domestic constitutions traditionally define individual and social guarantees as 'constitutional rights', international law calls the very same kind of rights 'human rights'. So, both constitutional and human rights law deal with *fundamental rights.*[17] In this sense, TLP may impact domestic constitutional law, inserting new actors and norms into the decision-making process concerning fundamental rights interpretation and enumeration. Opening up international law to new actors, TLP allows forms of transnational legal activism 'viewed as an attempt not simply to remedy individual abuses, but also to re-politicize law and re-legalize HR politics by invoking and bringing international courts and quasi-judicial systems of HR to act upon the national and local juridical-political arenas'.[18]

2 LATIN AMERICAN CASES OF TRANSNATIONAL LEGAL PROCESS

Transnational Legal Process at the Inter-American Commission

Two exemplary cases illustrate well how TLP can lead to constitutional engagement at the Inter-American Commission: Argentina's *DNA Compulsory Extraction* case and Brazil's *Maria da Penha* case.

There was an illegal policy during military rule in Argentina (1976–1983) of secretly giving up the children of killed political opponents for adoption, attributing them with false identities. With democratisation, NGOs started to search for those children, with significant success. In two cases, however, the supposed kidnapped children declined to cooperate with the legal procedures. In the *Vázquez Ferrá* case[19] they appealed a decision that imposed DNA extraction, arguing before the Supreme Court of Argentina[20] that compulsory extraction constituted an 'inadmissible intrusion of the State into one's intimacy; it damages one's constitutional guarantees of physical integrity ... affects one's dignity' ... and it violates the procedural constitutional guarantee that allows one not to testify when this may produce evidence against one's family nucleus'.[21]

The Supreme Court of Argentina accepted this argument and overruled the compulsory extraction. The same legal construction was mobilised during the *Prieto* case.[22] Here the Supreme Court argued that there was a conflict between Prieto's right to self-determination and his assumed grandparents' right to truth, ruling against the compulsory extraction.[23]

On 31 March 2003, the defeated grandmothers of *Vázquez Ferrá* filed a petition at the Inter-American Commission arguing that due to the Supreme Court of Argentina's ruling the Argentinean state had violated sections 5 (humane treatment), 8 (fair trial), 17 (rights of the family) and 25 (judicial protection) of the ACHR. On 11 September 2009 a friendly settlement was reached, stating that Argentina should change its domestic legislation in order to ensure that the country 'effectively investigates and adjudicates the abduction of children during the military dictatorship'.[24]

On 27 November Argentina's National Congress approved Law 26,549, changing article 218 of the Penal Procedural Code, allowing judges to order compulsory DNA extraction whenever needed in criminal cases, even without the DNA owner's consent. In practical terms, human rights TLP has been successfully used to *reshape the scope of constitutional rights* to self-determination, physical integrity, human dignity and constitutional procedural guarantees, as well as to reinforce the right to truth.

The second example took place in Brazil in 1983. Ms Maria da Penha was shot by her husband in a domestic struggle and became paraplegic. After several other aggressions and another attempt on her life, she denounced him. For 15 years the authorities failed to fairly prosecute the case. On 20 August 1998, the victim filed a petition against Brazil at the Inter-American Commission.

On 4 April 2001 the Commission published its report. It concluded that the state had violated the right to a fair trial and judicial protection, and that the measures adopted to reduce tolerance of domestic violence and improve its prosecution 'have not yet had a significant impact ... in particular as a result of ineffective police and judicial action'.[25] In its recommendations, it urged Brazil to quickly complete the criminal procedures against the aggressor, to investigate the irregularities in the previous procedures, to compensate the victim, and to continue and expand legal reforms aiming to end domestic violence.

On 7 August 2006, Law 11,340 was enacted, establishing new criminal procedures and creating a system of specialised courts to address violence against women. Owing to social mobilisation, the bill became known as the 'Law Maria da Penha'. Here, the Inter-American Commission was used as *political leverage* in the domestic struggle for public policies and the recognition of rights.

In both examples, the victims were not alone in the Inter-American System. The Argentinean case was proposed by the Association of Grandmothers of the Plaza de Mayo; the Brazilian one by the Center for Justice and International Law (CEJIL) and the Latin American and Caribbean Committee for the Defence of Women's Rights. Both cases combined *individual litigation* with *strategic goals.*

What do these cases tell us about TLP at the Inter-American Commission? One clear conclusion is that TLP is used as a broader *strategy of mobilisation for legal change.* Beyond the individual case, mobilisation aims to rebuild legal institutions and public policy. The Inter-American System is used to produce a 'boomerang effect'[26] where domestic demands are issued internationally in order to be resent to the domestic level with higher pressure for implementation. Combining domestic and international mobilisation, specific civil society actors are able to reshape fundamental rights by non-traditional means.

Transnational Legal Process in the Inter-American Court

When the Inter-American Commission is unable to unravel a case, it sends it for litigation in the Inter-American Court. Domestic amnesty cases from Argentina, Brazil and Chile illustrate well how international litigation may impact fundamental rights.

In Argentina, the military self-amnesty was annulled during the Alfonsín administration (1983–1989), but new impunity laws were put in force by the democratic parliament in 1986 (Ley de Punto Final) and 1987 (Ley de Obediencia Debida). The Supreme Court of Argentina ruled both laws to be constitutional.[27] The next president in office, Carlos Menem, issued ten presidential decrees granting pardons to members of the repressive apparatus who were then being prosecuted, as well as to leaders of the junta (military rulers) who had previously been convicted.[28] The Supreme Court also upheld these decrees.[29] Law 25,779 from 2003 finally revoked these impunity measures.

In 2005 the Supreme Court of Argentina reinforced Law 25,779 and declared the impunity laws and decrees to be unconstitutional, changing its original precedent from 1987. Two key issues influenced this change. First, a constitutional reform in 1994 gave some human rights treaties constitutional rank.[30] Second, the Inter-American precedent from *Velazquez Rodriguez v. Honduras*, explicitly quoted by the Supreme Court,[31] helped to develop the idea that under the ACHR states have a duty to investigate and prosecute human rights violations.[32]

This cornerstone decision allowed two kinds of use of international law to be distinguished: *normative* and *reflective*. International law may be used as a set of *normative rules*, but also as an *interpretative tool* to better understand domestic legal provisions. Argentina was not convicted in *Velázquez Rodrigues* (a ruling that only binds Honduras) but has used the decision to reinterpret its own constitutional provisions. In this case, the reflective process leads to normative convergence.

In Chile and Brazil, amnesties were enacted in 1978 and 1979, respectively, and these are still valid. The Chilean amnesty was challenged in the Supreme Court of Chile just after transition, and upheld in August 1990.[33] In Brazil, the Supreme Federal Court upheld the amnesty law in April 2010, 25 years after the transition.[34] In 2006 the Inter-American Court ruled against the Chilean amnesty in *Almonacid Arellano*,[35] and in 2010 against Brazil in *Julia Gomes Lund*.[36] The main difference is that Chilean courts were able to circumvent the amnesty even before the Inter-American ruling, while in Brazil, prosecutions remained blocked.

How did prosecutions use international law in Chile?[37] The original successful attempts focused on circumventing the law in cases not covered by the amnesty.[38] In 1993 the District Court of Lautaro for the first time withdrew the amnesty law, arguing that the kidnapping of a child who is never recovered constitutes a permanent crime. This is fundamentally a factual argument but the judge added, 'with no prejudice to the validity of elementary principles of political law, recognized by civilization in international documents such as the Universal Declaration of HR ..., and the American Convention on HR'.[39] This decision was one in a series where local courts engaged in international law in a reflective way.[40]

The most significant legal change happened in 1998, when the Supreme Court of Chile's Criminal Chamber provided a new interpretation of the scope of the amnesty law. In *Pedro Poblete Cordoba*[41] the Court derived two important legal criteria from international law. First, it declared that in order to receive amnesty a criminal must be identified and the crime elucidated, in order to avoid a 'blanket amnesty.' Second, it stated that as Chile had declared a 'State of War' during military rule, the Geneva Convention applied. In the following year, the Supreme Court of Chile also reinforced the ruling, stating that the amnesty law should not apply to kidnapping and illegal detention when those crimes are characterised as continuous over time.[42]

When the Inter-American Court ruled in *Almonacid Arellano*, in September 2006, international law was already being applied as a subsidiary source in prosecutions for human rights violations (*reflective engagement*). So what difference did the Inter-American ruling make? Did Chilean courts accept the international decision as a *normative* kind of judicial review?

On the one hand, less than three months after the Inter-American decision, the Supreme Court of Chile, for the first time, declared crimes against humanity to be not subject to statutes of limitation (in a case concerning summary executions, *Hugo Vásquez Martínez and Mario Superby Jeldres*[43]). In grounding the ruling, it explicitly used the ACHR as a reflective element, and quoted paragraphs 96 and 99 from *Almonacid*. The same arguments would be reinforced in the *Manuel Tomás Rojas Fuentes*[44] and *José Matías Ñanco*[45] homicide case rulings, and in the ruling on the *Ricardo Troncoso Muñoz and others*[46] kidnapping. On the other hand, Chile has rejected *Almonacid* as a normatively binding judicial review ruling: it never complied with the command to nullify the amnesty law. These are examples of when the Chilean court has *engaged*. As the amnesty law is still in force, full compliance has not been achieved; the international decision has helped to reshape victims' fundamental rights, however.

Brazil has followed the opposite path when dealing with accountability. While in Argentina and Chile, the courts were widely used to advance transitional justice, in Brazil, most efforts concentrated on the administrative level, especially in reparations.[47] In the first two decades after military rule, almost no cases have been presented to the courts.

Brazilian amnesty law has faced only two substantive challenges in courts. In 1995, victims' relatives from the Araguaia Guerilla, Human Rights Watch and CEJIL filed a petition at the Inter-American Commission, which led to the November 2010 Inter-American Court *Gomes Lund* ruling. In 2008 the Brazilian Bar Association filed a suit in the Supreme Federal Court arguing that amnesty for torture and gross human rights violations should be considered unconstitutional. The Supreme Federal Court ruled the case in April 2010,[48] six months earlier than the Inter-American Court. By seven votes to two, the judges upheld the amnesty.[49] Over the years, both strategies—to circumvent or overturn amnesty—have failed in Brazil. In this scenario, did the Inter-American Court ruling change anything?

The Supreme Federal Court did not pronounce on amnesty after *Gomes Lund*, but the Federal Prosecutors Office changed its interpretation of the amnesty law due to the international ruling. In response to the Inter-American Court, the Criminal Chamber of the Prosecutor's Office created a working group on transitional justice and organised a workshop in order to strategise how better to comply. The results are available in *Documento 02/2011*, which can be considered as an institutional turning point.[50] In the document, the institution draws up an engagement strategy that reproduces elements of the Chilean model: advancing prosecutions using international law to restrain rather than nullify the domestic amnesty. Since then, nine lawsuits have been filed and prosecutors are analysing 195 other cases.[51] None of those lawsuits has reached a final verdict so it would be premature to say whether the Brazilian courts will converge, engage or keep resisting international law. Nevertheless, it is worth noting that even without compliance the ruling has produced substantive effects.

3   Does Constitutional Architecture Matter?

Eight Latin American constitutions give human rights some sort of constitutional rank: Argentina (1994),[52] Bolivia (2009),[53] Brazil (2004),[54] Colombia (1991),[55] Ecuador (2008),[56] Mexico (2011),[57] Peru (1979)[58] and Venezuela (1999).[59] How does this openness to international law effectively impact constitutional law?

Where constitutions stimulate the interaction between domestic and international law, non-traditional constitutional change is more likely to happen, both in the *normative* and the *reflective* sense. However, constitutional architecture alone does not lead to broader human rights TLP impact. Examples of three 'open architecture' countries illustrate this assumption: Brazil exemplifies lower interaction and resistance. In contrast, Argentina exemplifies convergence with international precedence.

Mexico raises the interesting question of an emerging multilevel heterarchical system.

The 2004 Brazilian constitutional reform granted constitutional rank to human rights treaties ratified under a special procedure. Later, the Supreme Federal Court set a precedent stating that human rights treaties approved before the reform are ranked between ordinary and constitutional norms.[60] This applies both to the Inter-American Court and the International Criminal Court treaties, so judges can always refer to constitutional arguments to prevent international law application. Regardless of a state's international obligations and the constitutional provisions for openness, in hard cases such as those mentioned above relating to amnesty law, judges tend to ignore international human rights law. This resistance is probably better explained by cultural rather than normative reasons.

The Argentine Constitution states that 'the American Convention on HR ... has constitutional rank'.[61] This creates an institutional architecture that favours convergence. In different situations, the Supreme Court of Argentina has faced the challenge of dealing with conflicts arising from Inter-American cases that contradict domestic decisions. Despite some isolated episodes,[62] the Supreme Court has systematically complied. Two examples can help a better understanding of how Argentina conforms to a convergence model.

In *Bulacio*,[63] a case concerning a death inflicted by the security forces in the 1990s, the Inter-American Court ruled that Argentina must investigate and prosecute those involved in a crime whose original prosecution was barred due to ordinary statutes of limitation. The Supreme Court of Argentina emphasised in its ruling that due process had been strictly followed by the lower courts, and that under domestic law there was no legal reason to reopen the case. Nevertheless, it recognised that 'the mentioned ruling is mandatory to the Argentinean state, therefore this Court ... must subordinate its rulings to those of the aforementioned International Court'.[64] The Supreme Court therefore reopened the case, creating a normative legal exception to the criminal's constitutional guarantees in order to allow convergence.

Carranza Latrubesse is an even more explicit example.[65] A judge was purged from his functions in the 1980s. Domestic courts answered his claim by stating that the administrative purge was non-justiciable. He filed a petition at the Inter-American Commission, which asserted that by precluding a decision on the petitioner claim 'the Argentine State violated his rights to a fair trial and to judicial protection provided for in Articles 8 and 25 ... of the American Convention',[66] using its legal prerogatives to recommend that Argentina adequately compensate Mr Carranza.

After several legal detours, the case reached the Supreme Court of Argentina, where it sparked a debate on the duty to comply, not with Inter-American Court *rulings* but with Inter-American Commission *recommendations*. The Supreme Court understood that without a friendly settlement, the Inter-American System procedures allow only one final decision: an Inter-American Court ruling or an Inter-American Commission recommendation.[67] As a final decision binds the state regardless of its source, the Supreme Court understood that 'it must reject the National State grievance and recognize the mandatory nature of recommendations from section 51.2 from the American Convention issued in the Inter-American Commission report 30/97'.[68] This was the first ruling of this kind in Latin America and set an extremely relevant precedent concerning the nature of the legal obligation of states under the jurisdiction of the Commission, usually understood as a *political* rather than a *judicial* body.

Mexico's 2011 constitutional reform points towards a hybrid model. The country has added a clause stating that 'the HR norms are interpreted in accordance with this constitution *and* the HR treaties',[69] adding that 'all public authorities ... have the obligation to promote, respect, protect, and fulfil HR'.[70] This second provision has a special significance. Mexican justice, like that of Brazil and Argentina, constitutes a federal system where local courts share a *diffused* power of judicial review, besides the *concentrated* power of the country's Supreme Court of Justice of the Nation. This opens up avenues towards the possibility of *domestic conventional review* in both concentrated and diffused ways. Mexican scholars have argued that multiple kinds of constitutional-like precedents will co-exist in the Mexican legal system:

> The first is the traditional vertical way, derived from decision from SCJN[71] ... But after the reform another vertical way has been activated that comes from the Inter-American HR Court and generates binding precedents for all judges, and, potentially, a multidimensional way that implicates all the judges of the country will be activated.[72]

In evaluating the legal rank of *Radilla-Pacheco*,[73] the Supreme Court stated that all the resolutions of the Inter-American Court against Mexico are binding (including the interpretative criteria applied[74]) and that it lacks powers to reanalyse, review or change Inter-American rulings.[75] This is quite similar to Argentina, but the pending issue is how courts will behave in cases of constitutional collisions. Will they maintain international precedence, as Argentina did in *Bulacio*, or will the double-vertical model find its limits when this sort of collision happens?

4   TRANSVERSAL HUMAN RIGHTS GOVERNANCE AND NEW CONSTITUTIONAL ACTORS

One of the most remarkable effects of human rights TLP is the reshaping of the framework used to understand and explain constitutional law. As shown, TLP includes new actors in the constitution-making process, such as the Inter-American Commission, the Inter-American Court and, even more important, individuals and NGOs.

Traditional ways to understand international norm compliance used to fit well into previous frameworks where sovereign national states were the main actors. However, this approach misses much of what really happens in a pluralistic legal system, where regimes constantly interact mediated by different public and private players. An approach focusing on interactions and reciprocal influence better captures strategic movements that lead to norm change at the constitutional level. Taking an example as *Compulsory DNA Extraction*, it is easy to realise how non-traditional actors effectively mobilise to change the scope of constitutional rights.

The traditional framework for thinking about constitutions includes the idea that 'the people' get together to establish a political system and a set of guarantees. To change this agreement a special procedure is required. The courts must implement the rule of law and interpret the constitution. All the rights and guarantees are derived from this process. In the *Compulsory DNA Extraction* case the Supreme Court of Argentina interpreted the constitution and ruled on a set of individual guarantees. After that, an NGO went to an international body and reached an agreement that led to a new constitutional arrangement of rights. Also, in *Bulacio* the Constitution was momentarily set aside.

Many other cases have this very same structure: well-organised civil society groups go to an international body using international law to claim that the domestic understanding on the existence or extension of certain rights restricts or fails to protect a human right. Governments are called to enforce decisions and recommendations. Precedents influence or bind courts. The final scope of the fundamental right is set transversally in the interactions among these players. 'The people', constitutional assemblies and sometimes even the legislative branch are partially displaced in this process of constitutional transformation.

This use of strategic litigation is coherent with current developments of international law, focused on dispute resolution by 'technical' means in legal bodies rather than consensus-building in political organisations. TLP leads to the abovementioned 'boomerang effect', with political pretensions at the domestic level being submitted to international bodies and resent to the domestic regimes. Legal scholars define this process as a 're-entry',[76] with international politics affecting domestic law, allowing legal change. This does not imply that human rights TLP is substituting the traditional domestic processes of law-making and constitutional change. Those processes stay alive and relevant. The fact to be noticed is that human rights TLP appears as *a new way to reshape fundamental rights*, changing traditional boundaries. It does not substitute but rather displaces traditional constitutional procedures.

The Inter-American System translates political claims into the language of fundamental rights, granting those claims a special legal status domestically. By doing so it creates fundamental rights norms 'ad hoc when a current conflict assumes constitutional dimensions and requires constitutional decisions'.[77] For example, Chilean society reached no new consensus regarding the amnesty, but the courts translated a political claim for justice into law ad hoc.

The work of the Inter-American System also leverages and legitimises domestic struggles for human rights, which means that even when full compliance is not achieved, an impact may be made by other means. The Inter-American System has been used not only to influence laws' interpretation or to set new normative grounds in courts, but also to impact legislative deliberation and public policy-making.

A closer look at how courts use precedents from the Inter-American System and the rise of conventional review as a domestic legal tool allows the identification of a trend of non-hierarchical institutional ways of domestic-international interaction, as seen in the Mexican example. This means domestic institutions are responding to Inter-American standards and incorporating international law as a whole. As human rights and constitutional rights are both kinds of fundamental rights, growing interaction means that TLP will gradually gain terrain in human rights transversal governance, influencing and reshaping constitutional law. Domestic regimes seem to be equipping themselves for the task.

5   CONCLUSIONS

The set of cases analysed present huge variation regarding how states interact with the Inter-American System, but also a general trend to consider its decisions, if not as a binding normative source then at least as a reflective interpretative tool. In responding to claims from civil society, the Inter-American System contributes to redefining the scope of fundamental rights. It translates political claims into the language of international human rights law, allowing courts to decouple international law into fundamental rights provisions that make sense in domestic constitutional terms.

Strategic litigation examples demonstrate how NGOs have taken advantage of changes in the transnational governance structure to use individual litigation to achieve collective goals, leveraging processes of struggle for rights. The Inter-American System allows these organisations to function as constitutional players that are able to make use of both the legal outcomes of litigation to boost constitutional change in the courts, and the political outcomes to mobilise society around a specific political agenda. In other words, HR TLP may repoliticise international law and generate broader domestic incidence and pressure for policy-making.

As TLP challenges traditional constitutional theory, the fact that domestic regimes are equipping themselves with institutional tools to interact without losing their own constitutional identity is probably the most relevant trend one can observe in the set of cases here presented. Rising transversal human rights governance is a challenge that constitutional theory will have to face in the coming years. Latin America seems to be on the threshold of this process.

NOTES

1. David Kennedy, 'One, Two, Three, Many Legal Orders: Legal Pluralism and the Cosmopolitan Dream' (2007) 31 NYU Review of Law and Social Change 641.
2. Joseph G Starke, 'Monism and Dualism in the Theory of International Law' (1936) 17 British Year Book of International Law 66.
3. Kennedy (n 1) 641.
4. Bruno Simma and Dirk Pulkowski, 'Of Planets and the Universe: Self-contained Regimes in International Law' (2006) 17(03) European Journal of International Law 483, 491.
5. David Kennedy, 'The International Style in Postwar Law and Policy' (1994) Utah Law Review 7.

6. Hans Morgenthau is an earlier proponent of this way of understanding international law. See Hans J Morgenthau, 'Positivism, Functionalism, and International Law' (1940) 34(2) American Journal of International Law 260.

7. International Law Commission, *Fragmentation of International Law: Difficulties Arising from the Diversification and Expansion of International Law* (Report of the Study Group of the International Law Commission, finalised by Martii Koskenniemi 2006).

8. In a similar sense, see Martti Koskenniemi, 'The Future of Statehood' (1991) 32(02) Harvard International Law Journal 397, 410.

9. Christian Walter, 'Subjects of International Law' (2007) 57 Max Planck Encyclopedia of Public International Law 634.

10. See Margaret F. Keck and Kathryn Sikkink, *Activist beyond Borders* (Cornell University Press 1998).

11. Jackie Smith, Ron Pagnucco, George Lopez, 'Globalizing HR: The Work of Transnational HR NGOs in the 1990s' (1998) 20(2) Human Rights Quarterly 379.

12. Anne-Marie Slaughter, 'International Law and International Relations Theory: A Dual Agenda' (1993) 87(2) American Journal of International Law 205, 207.

13. Harold H Koh, 'Transnational Legal Process' (1996) 75 Nebraska Law Review 181, 183–184.

14. Vicki C Jackson, *Constitutional Engagement in a Transnational Era* (Oxford University Press 2010).

15. Ibid. 08–09.

16. Ibid. 09.

17. Gerald L Neuman, 'Human Rights and Constitutional Rights: Harmony and Dissonance' (2003) Stanford Law Review 1863.

18. Cecília M Santos, 'Transnational Legal Activism and the State: Reflections on Cases against Brazil in the Inter-American Commission on HR' (2007) 4(7) Sur International Journal on Human Rights 30.

19. V. XXXVI 30 September 2003, CSJN (Argentina).

20. Corte Suprema de Justicia de la Nación (CSJN).

21. *Vázquez Ferrá* (n 19) 05 (my translation).

22. V. XXXVIII 11 August 2009, CSJN (Argentina).

23. For a case review, see Marcelo Ferrante, 'Proof of Identity in Criminal Prosecutions for Abduction of Children and Identity Substitution' in CELS (ed), *Making Justice* (Siglo XXI) 143–161.

24. Report 160/10 Inter-American Commission on Human Rights (IACommHR) item 2.1.

25. Report 54/01 IACommHR item 60.3.
26. Keck and Sikkink (n 10).
27. Jaime Malamud-Goti, 'Punishing HR Abuses in Fledgling Democracies: The Case of Argentina' in Naomi Roht-Arriza (ed), *Impunity and HR in International Law and Practice* (Oxford University Press 1995) 160.
28. Graciela Daleo, 'El Movimiento Popular y la Lucha Contra la Impunidad en la Argentina' (2007) 5 Revista HMiC: Història Moderna i Contemporània 221, 224.
29. The Supreme Court of Argentina analyses the legitimacy of the decrees only if the president has the prerogative to pardon not only convicted criminals but also those still facing prosecution. See Aquino 14 October 2002, CSJN (Argentina).
30. Reforma Constitucional de 1994 22 August 1994 (Argentina).
31. See the vote of Judge Enrique Santiago Petracchi.
32. Christine AE Bakker, 'A Full Stop to Amnesty in Argentina The Simón Case' (2005) 3(5) Journal of International Criminal Justice 1106, 1112.
33. Cath Collins, 'Human Rights Trials in Chile during and after the "Pinochet Years" ' (2010) 4(1) International Journal of Transitional Justice 67, 74.
34. Paulo Abrão and Marcelo Torelly, 'Resistance to Change: Brazil's Persistent Amnesty and its Alternatives for Truth and Justice' in Francesca Lessa and Leigh Payne (eds), *Amnesty in the Age of Human Rights Accountability* (Oxford University Press 2012) 151.
35. *Almonacid Arellano et al. v Chile* IACtHR Series C 154 (26 September 2006).
36. *Gomes Lund ('Guerrilha do Araguaia') v Brazil* IACtHR Series C 219 (24 November 2010).
37. See Pamela Pereira, 'The Path to Prosecutions: a Look at the Chilean Case' in *Transitional Justice – Handbook for Latin America* (International Center for Transitional Justice 2011) 271.
38. Collins (n 33) 74.
39. Ruling by Lautaro's Judge Christian Alfaro Muirhead, Causa Rol 37.860, 5th consideration (my translation).
40. Karinna F Neira, 'Breve Análisis de la jurisprudencia Chilena, en Relación a las Graves Violaciones a los Derechos Humanos Cometidos Durante la Dictadura Militar' (2010) 8(1) Estudios Constitucionales 467, 471.

41. Rol n° 469–98 09 September 1998, CS Chile (Segunda Sala Criminal).
42. Rol n° 248–98 07 January 1999, CS Chile (Segunda Sala Criminal). See also Karinna F Neira, *La prescripción gradual, aplicada a los delitos de lesa humanidad* (MSc Dissertation, University of Chile 2010) 76–82.
43. Rol n° 559–04 13 December 2006, CS Chile (Segunda Sala Criminal).
44. Rol n° 3125–04 13 January 2007, CS Chile (Segunda Sala Criminal).
45. Rol n° 2666–04 18 January 2007, CS Chile (Segunda Sala Criminal).
46. Rol n° 3452–06 10 May 2007, CS Chile (Segunda Sala Criminal).
47. Paulo Abrão and Marcelo Torelly, 'The Reparations Program as the Lynchpin of Transitional Justice in Brazil' in *Transitional Justice – Handbook for Latin America* (International Center for Transitional Justice 2011) 443.
48. Ação de Descumprimento de Preceito Fundamental n° 153/2008 STF Brazil (Supreme Federal Court).
49. For a broad overview of the ruling, see Marcelo Torelly, *Justiça Transicional e Estado Constitucional de Direito: Perspectiva Teórico-comparativa e Análise do Caso Brasileiro* (Fórum 2012) 299.
50. MPF Brazil, 2ª Câmara, 'Documento n° 02/2011' (2012) 7 Revista Anistia Política e Justiça de Transição 358.
51. MPF Brazil, Segunda Câmara de Coordenação e Revisão, *Atividades de Persecução Penal desenvolvidas pelo Ministério Público Federal (2011–2013)* (Grupo de Trabalho Justiça de Transição 2014) 248.
52. Reforma Constitucional de 1994 (Argentina), Article 75(22).
53. Constitución Política del Estado (Bolivia 2009), Article 256.
54. Constituição da República Federativa do Brasil, Article 5(3) (new text from Constitutional Amend 45).
55. Constitucion Política de la Republica de Colombia, Article 93.
56. Constitución de la República (Ecuador), Article 11.
57. Constitución Política de los Estados Unidos Mexicanos, Article 1 (new text from 2011 Constitutional Reform).
58. Constitución Política del Peru, Disposiciones Finales y Transitórias, Fourth Transitorial Disposition.
59. Constitución de la República Bolivariana de Venezuela, Articles 19 and 23.
60. Flávia Piovesan, 'Hierarquia dos Tratados Internacionais de Proteção dos Direitos Humanos: Jurisprudência do STF' (2008) 6 Revista do Instituto de Hermenêutica Jurídica 105.
61. Reforma Constitucional de 1994 (n 54).

62. For a critical assessment of non-compliance, see Damián A Gonzalez-Salzberg, 'The Implementation of Decisions from the Inter-American Court of Human Rights in Argentina: An Analysis of the Jurisprudential Swings of the Supreme Court' (2011) 15 Sur International Journal on Human Rights 113.

63. *Bulacio v Argentina* IACtHR Series C 100 (18 September 2003).

64. Miguel Angel Espósito E.224.XXXIX 23 December 2004, CSJN (Argentina, my translation) item 07.

65. Gustavo Carranza Latrubesse C.568.XLIV C.594.XLIV 06 August 2013. CSJN (Argentina).

66. Report 30/97 IACommHR item 83.

67. Ibid. item 8.

68. Ibid. item 18 (my translation).

69. Constitución Política de los Estados Unidos Mexicanos (n 59).

70. Ibid. (my translation).

71. Suprema Corte de Justicia de la Nación (Supreme Court of Mexico).

72. Pedro Salazar et al., *La reforma constitucional sobre Derechos Humanos – Un Guia Conceptual* (Ciudad de Mexico: Senado de la Nacion 2014) 160 (my translation).

73. *Radilla Pacheco v Mexico* IACtHR Series C 209 (23 November 2009).

74. *Resolución dictada por el Tribunal Pleno en el expediente varios 912/2010* 14 July 2019, SCJN (Mexico), section 19.

75. Ibid. section 17.

76. Marcelo Neves, *Transconstitutionalism* (Hart 2013) 32, 41, 75.

77. Gunther Teubner, *Constitutional Fragments: Societal Constitutionalism and Globalization* (Oxford University Press 2012) 52.

CHAPTER 3

Complying (Partially) with the Compulsory Judgments of the Inter-American Court of Human Rights

Damián González-Salzberg

The Inter-American Court is a judicial body whose main purpose is to judge and decide cases concerning the violation of human rights protected by the ACHR. The Court's rulings in the exercise of this adjudicatory role are binding upon the states parties that are respondents to the case in question. States that have ratified the ACHR and accepted the jurisdiction of the Court have undertaken the obligation to comply with its judgments pursuant to Article 68(1) of the ACHR. However, the overall level of compliance with judgments is far from perfect. The 2013 Annual Report of the Inter-American Court shows that, by the end of that year, 148 of the 166 judgments issued by the Court were at the stage of monitoring of compliance.[1] The fact that, by the end of 2013, only 18 judgments had been fully complied with means that the overall level of compliance with

An earlier version of this work was published as 'Do States Comply with the Compulsory Judgments of the Inter-American Court of Human Rights? An Empirical Study of the Compliance with 330 Measures of Reparation' (2013) 13 Revista do Instituto Brasileiro de Direitos Humanos 93.

D. González-Salzberg (✉)
University of Sheffield, Sheffield, UK

© Palgrave Macmillan, a division of Macmillan Publishers Limited 2017
P. Fortes et al. (eds.), *Law and Policy in Latin America*,
DOI 10.1057/978-1-137-56694-2_3

the Court's judgments was extremely low at just over 10 %.[2] Regardless of what this low degree of compliance might suggest, the states are certainly not indifferent to the Court's rulings, as I have argued in a previous article,[3] and as the Court itself started highlighting from its 2010 Annual Report.[4] In most cases the states have taken actions to comply with the measures of reparation imposed by the Court, even if they have not fully complied with them all.

The increasing attention given to the level of compliance with the Inter-American Court's judgments attests to its relevance as an object of analysis. In 2010, two original studies on compliance with the decisions of the organs of the Inter-American System were published.[5] While my previous article focused exclusively on the rulings of the Court, the work of the Association for Civil Rights covered selected judgments, together with certain decisions of the Inter-American Commission. A comparative analysis of the case law of both the Inter-American Court and the European Court of Human Rights was published in 2011,[6] and an increasing number of articles have focused on compliance with the Inter-American Court's rulings by specific states.[7]

Notwithstanding the attention given to this topic, this chapter offers a much needed up-to-date empirical study of the level of compliance with the Inter-American Court's judgments. I analyse a total of 330 measures of reparation, ordered in 112 judgments issued by the Court. The study will show the level of states' compliance with the measures of reparation imposed by the Court in order to propose the lessons that can be learned from this experience. Section 1 explains the method followed so as to measure the degree of compliance with the Court's judgments. Section 2 presents the results of the empirical study conducted. In Section 3 I discuss possible ways to improve the level of compliance by the states. In Section 4, conclusions will be drawn.

1   The Method Used for Measuring Compliance

The method used for the classification of the measures of reparation ordered by the Inter-American Court and for measuring their degree of compliance is an amended version of that developed in my previous work.[8] While the Court has a broad competence concerning the ability to order reparations,[9] the focus of the analysis is on five types of reparation traditionally ordered by the Court. These measures are the payment of pecuniary compensation; the publication of certain parts of the judgment;

the performance of an official and public act of acknowledgment of state responsibility; the investigation of violations of human rights in order to prosecute and punish those responsible for such violations; and the amendment of domestic legislation to bring it into conformity with the provisions of the ACHR.[10]

Within the Inter-American System, the Inter-American Court has assumed the task of monitoring compliance with its own judgments.[11] Therefore I have obtained data concerning whether or not the measures of reparation have been complied with from the orders on monitoring compliance with the judgments issued by the Court.[12] The determination of the degree of compliance with each measure is assessed as complied with (C), not complied with (N) or partially complied with (P). The criteria used to establish when a measure has been partially complied with are described below. Regarding the payment of compensation, this measure is considered as partially complied with when at least one of the payments ordered as compensation has been made by the state. As to the publication of the judgment, this measure is considered to have been partly complied with when at least one of the publications has been completed. Concerning the public act of acknowledgment of international responsibility, owing to the nature of the measure, which requires the performance of one particular public act, this is the only measure in which partial compliance cannot take place. In relation to the investigation of the facts, and the judgment and prosecution of those individually responsible, this measure is considered to be partially complied with when, after the ruling of the Court, at least one person has been subject to disciplinary measures. Finally, the duty to amend domestic legislation is labelled as partially fulfilled in those cases in which more than one piece of internal legislation should have been passed and one of them has already been enacted.

I want to make a clarification regarding the decision to measure partial compliance in this study. The main reason is that the Inter-American Court considers certain measures as being partially fulfilled when it monitors compliance.[13] However, I do not fully agree with the Court measuring partial compliance. The compulsory nature of the judgments may well suggest that they should be considered by the Court as not complied with until the measure is completely fulfilled. Moreover, if the Court decides to continue measuring partial compliance, the criteria for deciding when a specific order should be seen as partially fulfilled, instead of plainly unfulfilled, should be made explicit.

The analysis that follows covers all judgments on reparations issued by the Inter-American Court before mid-2011 that have been monitored by the Court up to mid-2013, making a total of 114 judgments. This number comprises every judgment issued by the Court from the *Velásquez-Rodríguez* case in 1989 to the *Vera Vera* case in 2011, excluding the five cases in which the Court has not ruled against the state,[14] and the 13 cases in which the Court has not issued an order monitoring compliance with the judgment before mid-2013.[15] Furthermore, the two cases against Trinidad and Tobago are shown in Table 3.1[16] but they are not included in the subsequent statistical analysis, given that the state abandoned the Inter-American System and did not report to the Court on its compliance with the judgments. Consequently, the analysis concerns 112 judgments. The total number of measures under examination is 330 and the results of the empirical study are shown in Tables 3.1 and 3.2, which show the level of compliance with the judgments issued by the Court in just over two decades.

2   MEASURING COMPLIANCE WITH 330 MEASURES

This section presents the results of the empirical study in Tables 3.1 and 3.2, and in different subsections it discusses the compliance with each type of measure. Table 3.1 shows the 330 measures of reparation ordered by the Inter-American Court in 112 judgments and the degree of compliance with them.[17] It indicates the state against which the Court ordered each measure and in which cases the measures were ordered. It shows the degree of compliance with each measure, indicating whether it has been complied with (C), partially complied with (P) or not complied with (N). It also highlights in bold the 16 cases that have been fully complied with by the states, which means that all measures ordered by the Court have been complied with and not only the five types of reparation under analysis.[18] Table 3.2 shows the number of cases in which each of the measures has been ordered, and it also presents, in percentages, the level of full compliance, partial compliance and non-compliance with each measure.

Paying Compensation

The payment of compensation for both pecuniary and non-pecuniary damages is the oldest measure of reparation ordered by the Inter-American Court, and it has been constant in its case law since the *Velásquez-Rodríguez*

Table 3.1 The 330 measures ordered by the Inter-American Court

		Pecuniary compensation	Publicity of judgment	Public apology	Prosecution	Amendment of legislation
Peru	Neira-Alegría	C				
	Loayza-Tamayo	C			N	C
	Castillo-Páez	C			C	
	Castillo-Petruzzi					C
	Cesti-Hurtado	P			P	
	Durand and Ugarte	C	P	C	N	
	Cantoral-Benavides	C	C	C	N	
	Constitutional Court	P			N	
	Ivcher-Bronstein	C			P	
	Barrios Altos	P	C	C	P	P
	'Five Pensioners'	C			N	
	Gómez-Paquiyauri	C	C	C	N	
	De La Cruz-Flores	C	C			
	Lori Berenson	–	C	–	–	C
	Huilca Tecse	C	C	C	N	
	Gómez Palomino	P	C		N	N
	García-Asto	P	P			
	Baldeón-García	N	C	N	N	
	Aguado-Alfaro	N				
	Castro-Castro Prison	N	N	N	N	
	La Cantuta	P	P	C	P	
	Cantoral-Huamaní	P	N	N	N	
	Acevedo Buendía	P	C			
	Abrill-Alosilla	C	C	–	–	–

(continued)

Table 3.1   (continued)

		Pecuniary compensation	Publicity of judgment	Public apology	Prosecution	Amendment of legislation
Guatemala	Blake	C			P	
	'White Van'	P			N	
	'Street Children'	C			N	C
	Bámaca-Velásquez	C	C	C	N	P
	Myrna Mack-Chang	C	C	C	P	
	Maritza Urrutia	C			N	
	Plan de Sánchez	P	C	C	N	
	Molina-Theissen	C	C	C	N	N
	Carpio-Nicolle	C	C	N	N	
	Fermín Ramírez					N
	Raxcacó-Reyes		C			N
	Tiu-Tojín		C		N	
	'Las Dos Erres'	P	C	C	P	N
	Chitay Nech	C	P	N	N	
Colombia	Caballero-Delgado	C			N	
	Las Palmeras	C	C		P	
	19 Tradesmen	P		C	N	
	Gutiérrez-Soler	C	C		N	
	Mapiripán	P	C		P	
	Pueblo Bello	P	C	C	N	
	Ituango	C	C	N	P	
	La Rochela	P	C		P	
	Escué-Zapata	P	P	C	P	
	Valle-Jaramillo	C	C	N	P	
	Cepeda-Vargas	C	C	C	N	
Ecuador	Suárez-Rosero	P			N	
	Benavides-Cevallos	C			N	
	Tibi	C	C	C	N	
	Acosta-Calderón	**C**	**C**	–	–	–
	Zambrano-Vélez	P	C	C	N	C
	Chaparro-Álvarez	P	P			P
	Albán Cornejo	C	C			
	Salvador-Chiriboga	P	P			
	Vera Vera	C	P			

Table 3.1 (continued)

		Pecuniary compensation	Publicity of judgment	Public apology	Prosecution	Amendment of legislation
Argentina	Garrido and Baigorria	C			N	
	Cantos					
	Bulacio	C	C		P	P
	Bueno-Alves	P	C		N	
	Kimel	C	C	C	–	C
	Bayarri	C	C		N	
Paraguay	**Canese**	C	C	–	–	–
	Juvenile Reeduc. Instit.	P	C	N		
	Yakye Axa	P	N	C		N
	Sawhoyamaxa	P	P			N
	Goiburú	P	C	N	P	N
	Vargas-Areco	C	C	C	N	C
Honduras	**Velásquez-Rodríguez**	C	–	–	–	–
	Godínez-Cruz	C	–	–	–	–
	Juan H. Sánchez	P	C	C	N	
	López-Álvarez	C	C		N	
	Servellón-García	C	C	C	P	
	Kawas-Fernández	C	C	C	N	
Venezuela	El Amparo	C			N	
	The Caracazo	C	C		N	
	Blanco Romero	N	N		P	N
	Montero-Aranguren	N	N	N	N	N
	Apitz-Barbera	N	N			N
Panama	Baena	P				
	Heliodoro-Portugal	C	C	C	N	P
	Tristán-Donoso	C	C	–	–	–
	Vélez Loor	C	C		N	
Suriname	**Aloeboetoe**	C	–	–	–	–
	Gangaram Panday	C	–	–	–	–
	Moiwana	C		C	N	N
	Saramaka People	P	C			N

(continued)

Table 3.1   (continued)

		Pecuniary compensation	Publicity of judgment	Public apology	Prosecution	Amendment of legislation
Chile	*The Last Temptation*	–	–	–	–	C
	Palamara-Iribarne	C	C			P
	Claude Reyes	–	C	–	–	C
	Almonacid-Arellano		C		N	N
Mexico	*Castañeda-Gutman*		C			N
	'Cotton Field'	C	C	C	N	
	Radilla-Pacheco	C	C	C	N	N
Nicaragua	*Genie-Lacayo*	C	–	–	–	–
	Mayagna	C	–	–	–	C
	Yatama	P	P			N
Bolivia	*Trujillo-Oroza*	C	C		N	C
	Ticona-Estrada	C	C		P	
	Ibsen-Cárdenas	C	C		P	
Brazil	*Ximenes-Lopes*	C	C		P	
	Escher	C	C	–	C	–
	Garibaldi	C	C		N	
Trinidad	*Hilaire*	?				?
	Caesar	?				?
El Salvador	*Serrano-Cruz*	C	C	C	N	
	García-Prieto	C	C		N	
Barbados	*Boyce*					N
	Dacosta-Cadogan					N
Dominican Republic	*Yean and Bosico*	C	C	N		N
Costa Rica	*Herrera-Ulloa*	C	–	–	–	C
Uruguay	*Gelman*	C	C	C	N	P

and *Godínez-Cruz* cases.[19] From the judgment on reparations in the *El Amparo* case in 1996, the Court has adopted a measure aimed at protecting the payment in favour of the victims by placing an obligation on the state to pay interest in the case of arrears.[20] This makes pecuniary measures the only ones that include an automatic penalty mechanism in cases of non-compliance. As shown in Table 3.1, only 12 of the 112 judgments on reparations have not established the payment of compensation as a measure of reparation, making this type of reparation the one most frequently

Table 3.2 Degree of compliance

	Total	Complied with	Partially complied with	Not complied with
Pecuniary compensation	100	65 % (65)	29 % (29)	6 % (6)
Publicity of judgment	79	80 % (63)	13 % (10)	7 % (6)
Public apology	40	73 % (29)	0	27 % (11)
Prosecution	72	3 % (2)	28 % (20)	69 % (50)
Amendment of legislation	39	31 % (12)	18 % (7)	51 % (20)

ordered (89 % of the cases). Table 3.2 shows the level of compliance with this measure, which has a relatively high degree of full compliance (65 %) and a very low degree of non-compliance (6 %).

Acknowledging Human Rights Violations

The obligation to publish certain parts of the judgment against the state, and the duty to conduct a public act of acknowledgment of state responsibility, have been adopted since the judgments on reparations in the cases of *Cantoral-Benavides* and *Durand and Ugarte*.[21] The measure of publishing certain sections of the judgments usually consists of the publication of the facts of the case and the operative paragraphs in both the *State Official Gazette* and another newspaper with national circulation.[22] As shown in Table 3.2, the order to publicise the ruling against the state has become a very frequent measure of reparation. It has been ordered in 79 cases out of the 112 under analysis (just over 70 % of the cases). This measure appears to enjoy a high level of compliance because its degree of full compliance is 80 %. Concerning the public acknowledgment of state responsibility, this measure traditionally consists of a public act performed by some of the highest authorities of the state in the presence of the victims and their next of kin.[23] As shown in Table 3.1, this type of measure has been ordered by the Inter-American Court in 40 out of the 112 judgments under analysis (35 % of the cases). The level of full compliance with this measure, which by its own nature does not admit partial compliance, is relatively high at 73 %.

Prosecuting Human Rights Violators

One of the most characteristic measures of reparation decided by the Inter-American Court is the obligation for the domestic authorities to conduct investigations into the facts that constituted human rights violations in order to prosecute those individually responsible for the violations and to impose due legal sanctions on them. The obligation to prosecute and punish was ordered for the first time in the judgment on reparations in the case of *El Amparo*.[24] Since then it has become common for the Court to order this type of measure, having been imposed on states in 72 out of the 112 judgments under analysis (64 % of the cases). Nevertheless, this type of reparation is the one with the lowest level of compliance with a full compliance rate of only 3 %. As can be seen in Table 3.1, only in two cases has the Court considered full compliance to have been achieved with this measure. However, only in the *Castillo-Páez* case did the prosecution and conviction take place.[25] The second fulfilled order refers to the *Escher* case, in which the Court accepted the application of statutory limitations because the case did not concern a grave violation of human rights but instead a violation of the right to privacy.[26]

Adapting Domestic Legislation

The obligation to amend domestic legislation was imposed by the Inter-American Court for the first time in the judgment on reparations in the *Loayza-Tamayo* case, in which it ordered the state to adapt two pieces of criminal legislation to render them compatible with the ACHR.[27] Since that ruling, the Court has ordered this measure in 39 out of the 112 judgments examined (35 % of the cases). As shown in Table 3.2, the overall level of compliance with this measure is relatively low, having a full compliance rate of only 31 %. The level of partial compliance with this measure is also low (18 %), showing the cases in which more than one measure was ordered—either the adoption or the suppression of a piece of domestic legislation and where at least one measure has already been adopted, but not all of them.

3   POSSIBLE PATHS FOR IMPROVING COMPLIANCE

As I mentioned at the beginning, the overall level of compliance with the Inter-American Court's rulings is just above 10 %. This study presented some relatively optimistic data, showing that certain measures of reparation have a high level of compliance, but it also demonstrated that the level of compliance with other measures can be as low as 3 %. Therefore it remains imperative to continue searching for possible ways to improve the level of compliance with the Court's rulings. There are specific measures that can be adopted by different actors of the Inter-American System in order to improve the level of compliance. In particular, I will focus on civil society, the states and the Court.

Concerning civil society, as highlighted in previous articles, I continue to believe that the pressure from within states remains fundamental for improving the degree of compliance.[28] Many governments of the Americas tend to proclaim their commitment to the protection of human rights. Nonetheless, these public pronouncements are not always followed by the states' compliance with their international obligations. A conscientious civil society that can see beyond empty rhetoric and that recognises the important role played by the Inter-American System towards the protection of human rights can be essential for putting pressure on the states to comply with their international obligations. Indeed, governments would be forced to take every possible step to comply with the Inter-American Court's orders if the political support of the public depended on the actual steps adopted towards complying with human rights obligations.

Regarding specific measures that the states can adopt, the level of compliance with the Court's judgments would improve if the states were to create a political organ with the ability to supervise their conduct concerning compliance. I strongly support the idea developed by the former president of the Court Cançado Trindade to create a body composed of representatives of the states that have ratified the ACHR and have accepted the jurisdiction of the Inter-American Court.[29] In fact, I believe it would be essential to restrict participation in this organ to those states subject to the Court's jurisdiction since states that have committed to the regional protection of human rights by accepting the jurisdiction of the court should not be subject to the authority of those states that have not assumed this essential obligation.

Nevertheless, I recognise that the political interest of the states in creating an organ with the power to supervise their conduct concerning compliance with the Inter-American Court's judgments is doubtful. A clear sign of the states' lack of interest in reinforcing the Inter-American System can be inferred from their collective behaviour in recent years when faced with Venezuela's denunciation of the ACHR and its consequential abandonment of the system.[30] It was worrisome that the governments of the system displayed an almost complete lack of public concern regarding Venezuela's decision to deprive the people within its jurisdiction of the protection of the Inter-American Court. This questionable decision of the Government of Venezuela has been criticised by human rights bodies, such as the Office of the High Commissioner for Human Rights and the Inter-American Commission, and by various NGOs.[31] However, regardless of their proclaimed concern about the protection of human rights, the governments of the region have mostly been silent on the issue.[32]

As for the been Court, a mechanism that could be further developed is the applicability of Article 65 of the ACHR. This provision establishes the Inter-American Court's obligation to periodically inform the General Assembly of the OAS (the parent organisation of the Inter-American System) about the cases in which a state has not complied with its judgments, a duty which the Court performs by indicating the judgments pending compliance in its Annual Report. Nonetheless, the provision also grants the Court the authority to make specific recommendations, and the Court has taken advantage of this power in specific cases, highlighting the lack of compliance with certain judgments and requesting the General Assembly to urge the state to fully comply with such rulings.[33]

Two judges of the Inter-American Court have expressed conflicting views regarding the circumstances that justify the full applicability of Article 65. On the one hand, former President García-Sayán has argued that this faculty shall be exercised by the Court only when the state has expressly indicated that it will not comply with the measures ordered.[34] On the other hand, Judge Vio Grossi has adopted a more flexible view of the circumstances in which the Court should resort to informing the General Assembly regarding non-compliance, asking for political measures to be adopted.[35] This debate regarding the applicability of Article 65 is certainly welcome and deserves due attention from everyone interested in the topic of compliance with the Court's judgments. I consider that the best possible outcome from this debate would be for the Court to agree on specific criteria that would allow resorting to Article 65. Nevertheless, these criteria cannot be as extreme as depending on an express refusal of the state to comply with the Court's judgments, as argued by Judge García-Sayán. If reasonable criteria were to be developed by the Court,[36] the applicability of Article 65 could prove to be an effective mechanism to improve the level of future compliance with the Court's judgments.[37]

4   Conclusion

There is widespread concern about the level of compliance with the judgments of the Inter-American Court, as can be inferred from the increasing level of attention given to the topic by various scholars. The comprehensive empirical analysis conducted within this chapter presents relatively optimistic data. While the overall level of full compliance with the Court's judgments almost reached an impressive 90 % of non-compliance by the end of 2013, the chapter showed that compliance with specific measures is much greater. In particular, compliance with the orders concerning the payment of compensation, as well as the orders regarding the public acknowledgement of state responsibility, is relatively good. However, the optimistic data are limited to those measures because the ones ordering criminal prosecution and the amendment of domestic legislation have a much lower level of compliance. These results show the need to seriously consider possible strategies to improve the level of compliance with the Court's judgments.

The chapter presents some possible paths to be adopted by different actors of the Inter-American System, which deserve further consideration. On the one hand, the idea of the creation of a political organ, as described above, might currently sound unrealistic. The level of political commitment of the states to reinforcing the Inter-American System can be questioned given the lack of objections publicly raised about Venezuela's decision to abandon the system. On the other hand, I continue to believe in the importance of civil society in achieving a higher level of compliance with the Inter-American Court's judgments. The commitment of civil society and the ways in which this can be channelled into pressurising the states to comply with the Court's rulings is a topic that merits further academic research, and it is an issue that should be thought about by social and political actors. Lastly, the suggestion that the Court should develop further the use of Article 65 is certainly a realistic possibility. It only depends on the will of the current judges to discuss and agree on the criteria that should be followed in deciding the submission of a particular case to the consideration of the General Assembly. This could improve the level of compliance with the Court's judgments and it could become a legacy that the current composition of the Court leaves to its successor.

NOTES

1. Inter-American Court of Human Rights, 'Annual Report 2013'.
2. The 18 cases fully complied with are *Velásquez-Rodríguez* IACtHR Series C 4 (29 July 1988); *Godínez-Cruz* IACtHR Series C 5 (20 January 1989); *Aloeboetoe* et al. IACtHR Series C 11 (4 December 1991); *Gangaram-Panday* IACtHR Series C 16 (21 January 1994); *Genie Lacayo* IACtHR Series C 30 (29 January 1997); *'The Last*

Temptation of Christ' IACtHR Series C 73 (5 February 2001); *Mayagna (Sumo) Awas Tingni Community* IACtHR Series C 79 (31 August 2001); *Herrera-Ulloa* IACtHR Series C 107 (2 July 2004); *Ricardo Canese* IACtHR Series C 111 (31 August 2004); *Lori Berenson-Mejía* IACtHR Series C 119 (25 November 2004); *Acosta-Calderón* IACtHR Series C 129 (24 June 2005); *Claude-Reyes* et al. IACtHR Series C 151 (19 September 2006); *Kimel* IACtHR Series C 177 (2 May 2008); *Castañeda-Gutman* IACtHR Series C 184 (6 August 2008); *Tristán-Donoso* IACtHR Series C 193 (27 January 2009); *Escher* et al. IACtHR Series C 200 (6 July 2009); *Abrill-Alosilla* IACtHR Series C 223 (4 March 2011); *Mejía-Idrovo* IACtHR Series C 228 (5 July 2011).

3. Damián González-Salzberg, 'The Effectiveness of the Inter-American Human Rights System: A Study of the American States' Compliance with the Judgments of the Inter-American Court of Human Rights' (2010) 16 International Law: Revista Colombiana de Derecho Internacional 115.

4. Inter-American Court of Human Rights, 'Annual Report 2010' 12; Inter-American Court of Human Rights, 'Annual Report 2011' 14; Inter-American Court of Human Rights, 'Annual Report 2012' 13; Inter-American Court of Human Rights, 'Annual Report 2013' 71.

5. González-Salzberg, 'Effectiveness' (n 3); Fernando Basch, Leonardo Filippini, Ana Laya Mariano Nino, Felicitas Rossi and Bárbara Schreiber, 'La Efectividad del Sistema Interamericano de Protección de Derechos Humanos: Un Enfoque Cuantitativo sobre su Funcionamiento y sobre el Cumplimiento de sus Decisiones' (2010) 12 Sur – Revista Internacional de Derechos Humanos 9.

6. Darren Hawkins and Wade Jacoby, 'Partial Compliance: A Comparison of the European and Inter-American Courts of Human Rights' (2011) 6 Journal of International Law and International Relations 35.

7. Alexandra Huneeus, 'Rejecting the Inter-American Court: Judicialization, National Courts, and Regional Human Rights' in Javier Couso, Alexandra Huneeus and Rachel Sieder (eds), *Cultures of Legality: Judicialization and Political Activism in Latin America* (Cambridge University Press 2010); Damián González-Salzberg, 'La Implementación de las Sentencias de la Corte Interamericana de Derechos Humanos en Argentina: Un Análisis de los Vaivenes Jurisprudenciales de la Corte Suprema de Justicia de la Nación'

(2011) 15 Sur – Revista Internacional de Derechos Humanos 117; Marcia Nina Bernardes, 'Sistema Interamericano de Direitos Humanos como esfera pública transnacional: aspectos jurídicos e políticos da implementação de decisões internacionais' (2011) 15 Sur – Revista Internacional de Dereitos Humanos 134.

8. González-Salzberg, 'Effectiveness' (n 3).
9. Dinah Shelton, 'Reparations in the Inter-American System' in David Harris and Stephen Livingstone (eds), *The Inter-American System of Human Rights* (Clarendon Press 1998) 151–172, 152–153.
10. I have supressed the category of 'costs and expenses' used in my 2010 analysis. The reason for this is that sometimes the Inter-American Court includes the payment of expenses in the category of compensation, making it difficult to assess the compliance with this measure independently because it can be dependent on compliance with the payment of compensation.
11. *Baena-Ricardo* et al. (Competence) IACtHR (28 November 2003) para 72.
12. The procedure for monitoring compliance has changed over time. The current mechanism is based on written reports, but the Inter-American Court is allowed to convene hearings when it deems it appropriate. Rules of Procedure of the Inter-American Court of Human Rights, approved by the Court during its LXXXV Regular Period of Sessions (2009), Article 69.
13. *Durand and Ugarte* (Monitoring Compliance with Judgment) IACtHR (5 August 2008) op para 3; *La Cantuta* (Monitoring Compliance with Judgment) IACtHR (20 November 2009) op para 2; *Heliodoro Portugal* (Monitoring Compliance with Judgment) IACtHR (19 June 2012) op para 2.
14. The cases *Cayara* and *Alfonso Martín del Campo-Dodd* were dismissed due to the admission of preliminary objections, and the case *Maqueda* was dismissed due to the discontinuance of the action by the Inter-American Commission. The cases *Fairén-Garbi and Solís-Corrales* and *Nogueira de Carvalho* are the only two in which the Inter-American Court has found no violations of the ACHR by mid-2011. *Cayara* IACtHR Series C 14 (3 February 1993); *Alfonso Martín del Campo-Dodd* IACtHR Series C 113 (3 September 2004); *Maqueda* IACtHR Series C 18 (17 January 1995); *Fairén-Garbi and Solís-Corrales* IACtHR Series C 6 (15 March 1989); *Nogueira de Carvalho* et al. IACtHR Series C 161 (28 November 2006).

15. *Acevedo-Jaramillo* et al. IACtHR Series C 144 (7 February 2006); *Yvon Neptune* IACtHR Series C 180 (6 May 2008); *Ríos* et al. IACtHR Series C 194 (28 January 2009); *Perozo* et al. IACtHR Series C 195 (28 January 2009); *Reverón-Trujillo* IACtHR Series C 197 (30 June 2009); *Anzualdo-Castro* IACtHR Series C 202 (22 September 2009); *Barreto-Leiva* IACtHR Series C 206 (17 November 2009); *Usón Ramírez* IACtHR Series C 207 (20 November 2009); *Xákmok Kásek Indigenous Community* IACtHR Series C 214 (24 August 2010); *Fernández-Ortega* et al. IACtHR Series C 215 (30 August 2010); *Rosentdo-Cantú* IACtHR Series C 216 (31 August 2010); *Gomes-Lund* et al. IACtHR Series C 219 (24 November 2010); *Cabrera-García and Montiel-Flores* IACtHR Series C 220 (26 November 2010).

16. *Hilaire, Constantine and Benjamin* et al. IACtHR Series C 94 (21 June 2002); *Caesar* IACtHR Series C 123 (11 March 2005).

17. The only case that does not show any indications regarding compliance is the *Cantos* case, because none of the measures ordered by the Inter-American Court belonged to the types of reparations analysed in this work. *Cantos* IACtHR Series C 97 (28 November 2002).

18. The *Castañeda-Gutman* case does not appear as fully complied with since its compliance was confirmed by the Inter-American Court after mid-2013. *Castañeda-Gutman* (Monitoring Compliance with Judgment) IACtHR (28 August 2013).

19. *Velásquez-Rodríguez* IACtHR Series C 7 (21 July 1989); *Godínez-Cruz* IACtHR Series C 8 (21 July 1989).

20. *El Amparo* IACtHR Series C 28 (14 September 1996) para 49.

21. *Durand and Ugarte* IACtHR Series C 89 (3 December 2001) op para 4; *Cantoral-Benavides* IACtHR Series C 88 (3 December 2001) op para 7.

22. *Molina-Theissen* IACtHR Series C 106 (4 May 2004) op para 4; *Gómez-Paquiyauri Brothers* IACtHR Series C 110 (8 July 2004) op para 11; *Ricardo Canese* IACtHR Series C 111 (31 August 2004) op para 8.

23. *Myrna Mack-Chang* IACtHR Series C 101 (25 November 2003) op para 8; *19 Tradesmen* IACtHR Series C 109 (5 July 2004) op para 8; *Serrano-Cruz Sisters* IACtHR Series C 120 (1 March 2005) op para 8.

24. *El Amparo* IACtHR Series C 28 (14 September 1996) op para 4.

25. *Castillo Páez* (Monitoring Compliance with Judgment) IACtHR (3 April 2009) op para 1.

26. *Escher* et al. (Monitoring Compliance with Judgment) IACtHR (19 June 2012) para 21 and op para 2.
27. *Loayza-Tamayo* IACtHR Series C 42 (27 November 1998) op para 5.
28. González-Salzberg, 'Effectiveness' (n 3) 133; González-Salzberg, 'Implementación' (n7) 118.
29. Antônio Augusto Cançado Trindade, *Informe: Bases para un Proyecto de Protocolo a la Convención Americana sobre Derechos Humanos, para Fortalecer Su Mecanismo de Protección*, Vol II (2nd edn Corte Interamericana de Derechos Humanos 2003) 47–48, 664, 795 and 919–921.
30. Following Trinidad and Tobago in 1998, Venezuela became the second state to denounce the ACHR.
31. High Commissioner for Human Rights, 'UN Warns of Negative Effects of Venezuela's Withdrawal from Rights Convention' (10 September 2013). http://www.un.org/apps/news/story.asp?NewsID=45808&Cr=venezuela&Cr1#.VeV9UZfQMp1; Inter-American Commission of Human Rights, 'IACHR Deeply Concerned over Result of Venezuela's Denunciation of the American Convention' (10 September 2013) Press Release 64/13. http://www.oas.org/en/iachr/media_center/PReleases/2013/064.asp; International Coalition of Human Rights Organizations in the Americas (2013), 'Denunciation of the American Convention on Human Rights by Venezuela Weakens Protection of the Fundamental Rights of its Citizens' (9 September 2013). http://cejil.org/en/comunicados/denunciation-american-convention-human-rights-venezuela-weakens-protection-fundamental-r; Amnesty International, 'Venezuela's Withdrawal from Regional Human Rights Instrument Is a Serious Setback' (6 September 2013). https://www.amnesty.org/en/latest/news/2013/09/venezuela-s-withdrawal-regional-human-rights-instrument-serious-setback/.
32. It is also surprising that the Inter-American Court has not been more vocal in criticising Venezuela's decision. It would certainly be welcome if, in future, it were to adopt a more explicit position if faced with the denunciation of the ACHR.
33. Inter-American Court of Human Rights, 'Annual Report 1999' 42–43; Inter-American Court of Human Rights, 'Annual Report 2003' 42–43; Inter-American Court of Human Rights, 'Annual Report 2012' 62; *Case of Benavides Cevallos* (Monitoring Compliance with Judgment) IACtHR (27 November 2003) op para 3; *Case of*

Hilaire, Constantine and Benjamin et al. (Monitoring Compliance with Judgment) IACtHR (27 November 2003) op para 5; *Case of Apitz Barbera* et al. (Monitoring Compliance with Judgment) IACtHR (23 November 2012) op para 1.

34. *Case of Blanco Romero* et al. (Monitoring Compliance with Judgment) IACtHR, 22 November 2011, concurring opinion of Judge Diego García-Sayán para 8; *Case of Servellón García* et al. (Monitoring Compliance with Judgment) IACtHR, 22 November 2011, concurring opinion of Judge Diego García-Sayán para 8; *Case of the Saramaka People* (Monitoring Compliance with Judgment) IACtHR, 23 November 2011, concurring opinion of Judge Diego García-Sayán para 8.

35. *Case of Blanco Romero* et al. (Monitoring Compliance with Judgment) IACtHR, 22 November 2011, concurring opinion of Judge Eduardo Vio Grossi; *Case of Servellón García* et al. (Monitoring Compliance with Judgment) IACtHR, 22 November 2011, concurring opinion of Judge Eduardo Vio Grossi; *Case of the Saramaka People* (Monitoring Compliance with Judgment) IACtHR, 23 November 2011, concurring opinion of Judge Eduardo Vio Grossi.

36. These criteria need to consider not only the time elapsed since the Inter-American Court's judgment but also the measures adopted by the states to comply with the reparations ordered, and the states' willingness to inform the Court of such measures and their development.

37. On the applicability of Article 65, see Antônio Augusto Cançado Trindade, *El Ejercicio de la Función Judicial Internacional: Memorias de la Corte Interamericana de Derechos Humanos* (3rd edn Corte Interamericana de Derechos Humanos 2013) 38–39.

CHAPTER 4

Media Representations of the Inter-American System of Human Rights

Diego Gil, Rolando Garcia, and Lawrence M. Friedman

The OAS has two institutions that were designed to protect civil liberties in the Americas.[1] These are the Inter-American Commission and the Inter-American Court. The Commission is charged with providing general supervision over human rights in the region; the Court, as its name suggests, decides cases in which some country in the OAS has allegedly committed a violation of human rights. The oversight function of the Commission may involve any country that is part of the OAS; the jurisdiction of the Court, on the other hand, is limited to those member states that have accepted its jurisdiction.[2]

Both the Commission and the Court have a role in deciding cases on the violation of human rights. The Court hears only cases that the Commission brings to its attention; and the Commission also takes part in the litigation. The social and political context in which these institutions operate is a difficult one; many countries subject to the jurisdiction of the Court have had very unstable and undemocratic governments; and some have gone through periods in which governments have perpetrated mass

D. Gil (✉) • R. Garcia • L.M. Friedman
University of Stanford, Stanford, CA, USA

© Palgrave Macmillan, a division of Macmillan Publishers Limited 2017 57
P. Fortes et al. (eds.), *Law and Policy in Latin America*,
DOI 10.1057/978-1-137-56694-2_4

crimes, or directly or indirectly supported mass murder.[3] The jurisprudence of the Court contains rulings that order very concrete and detailed remedies to mitigate human rights violations. The Court has also exercised the authority to monitor closely the implementation of its rulings, and usually requests states to report on compliance.[4] But compliance is in fact an issue. The Court is fairly activist—at the decisional level. It has less success in getting countries to do what it takes to carry out the Court's decisions. The European Court of Human Rights has had more success in this regard.[5] However, it functions in a much more stable democratic context than its Inter-American counterpart.[6]

A recent study by Alexandra Huneeus demonstrates how little impact the Inter-American Court actually has. She finds that rulings that require money compensation are complied with over half of the time; decisions that request legal reforms are implemented around 10 % of the time; and judgments that order the state to investigate and punish those responsible for crimes are never fully complied with.[7] Huneeus also suggests that states are less likely to comply when the implementation of the Court's decision involves many actors,[8] which leads her to conclude that the Court should engage more with the institutions that compose the local justice system.[9] Along similar lines, Cavallaro and Brewer, who also mention lack of compliance as a problem, feel that the Court could be more effective in promoting human rights practices within states if it partnered with local activists and progressive officials in order to improve the implementation of its rulings.[10]

The compliance problem suggests that the Commission and the Court have not really made a mark on the legal culture of Latin American countries; these institutions hover in the shadows, only dimly perceived as relevant. The human rights movement and consciousness of human rights are key elements of modern legal culture.[11] However, the menu of rights varies considerably from place to place; the consciousness of what is a human right, and how it is to be enforced, is both historically and culturally contingent.[12] There is no question that the human rights culture has flourished in the late twentieth century and into the twenty-first. Country after country has adopted new constitutions; and these constitutions typically include bills of rights, and provide for judicial review. Many countries in Latin America have either established a separate court to perform this function or granted powers of judicial review to their supreme courts. Courts are crucial institutions in the human rights culture; they are formally responsible for making these rights a reality. However, whatever the state of legal culture, these rights and institutions mean very little without strong structural and political backing. It hardly matters, for example, what the Cuban Constitution says, or what the Argentine Constitution said during the period of military dictatorship. If local courts are not empowered to enforce human rights, one can hardly expect an international court to play much of a role.

International courts suffer from an additional handicap. The very fact that they are international is problematic. The USA, for example, considers itself a model democracy; most Americans probably think that their country is, in this regard, as close to perfect as one can get. Foreign interference is decidedly unwelcome. The USA has not signed on to the jurisdiction of the Inter-American Court. Other countries in the hemisphere have decided to stay out of the Inter-American System; and still others, as soon as they lose a case, pack their bags and leave.[13] In the light of these facts, it seems likely that the Inter-American System has not managed to take root in the local legal culture to the degree that, say, the European Court of Human Rights has.

Legal culture is elusive and hard to measure.[14] In this chapter we use media coverage as a proxy for legal culture: imperfect, to be sure, but better than nothing. We have looked at the treatment of news about the Inter-American System, through content analysis of a sample of news reports in four elite newspapers in four Latin American countries. Since human rights issues sometimes involve complex topics, we have assumed that elite newspapers are the most likely media to cover it.

The main finding of this work is that media coverage of the Inter-American System is sporadic and inadequate. In general, elite newspapers tend to report on domestic issues related to the Commission or the Court rather than on decisions that affect other countries. In most instances, the Inter-American institutions are not the main subject of their reports and there is very scanty coverage of the case law of the Court.

1   BACKGROUND

Brief Description of the Inter-American System

The Inter-American System is a product of the late twentieth century, the era after the Second World War. The OAS dates from 1948; the Commission came into existence in 1959 as part of the same impulse that gave rise to the American Declaration of the Rights and Duties of

Man, adopted in Bogota in 1948.[15] The powers of the Commission were also shaped gradually, with the adoption of several international human rights instruments. Seven commissioners sit on the Commission. They are supposed to act as individuals; not as representatives of a country. They are elected by the General Assembly of the OAS for a period of four years. They can only be re-elected once. They meet several times a year. The headquarters is located in Washington, DC.[16] The mandate of the Commission is very broad. It includes, among other things, receiving and analysing individual petitions that claim specific violations of human rights in the region. These can eventually reach the Court. The Commission can also carry out onsite visits to evaluate the human rights situation in a country; it can analyse the general condition of human rights in member states and publish reports about the situation; and it can raise public awareness of human rights issues through studies, seminars, reports and so on.[17]

The Commission was particularly active in the years when a number of Latin American countries were under military dictatorship, and it gained a good reputation during that period.[18] It continues to be an active organisation with a heavy workload. In 2013 it held three regular sessions, adopted 113 reports on individual cases of alleged violations of human rights, and held 114 hearings and 36 working meetings.[19] It carried out 6 onsite visits,[20] referred 11 cases to the jurisdiction of the Court,[21] requested two provisional measures to the Court for two specific victims,[22] participated in several hearings before the Court[23] and submitted written observations to reports about country compliance with the Court's orders,[24] among other activities.

The Court was established in 1979, after the ACHR (popularly known as 'Pact of San José'), which had been adopted in 1969, became enforceable in 1978.[25] The Court is an autonomous judicial institution responsible for the interpretation and application of the ACHR.[26] It consists of a panel of seven judges, who are elected by the OAS member states.[27] The Court sits in San José, Costa Rica.[28] The OAS has 35 member states but only 20 of them have formally accepted the compulsory jurisdiction of the Court.[29] The Court has three key functions. Its main function is to decide on disputes that arise when a state which is subject to the Court's jurisdiction is accused of a human rights violation; it can also monitor compliance with its decisions.[30] The Court can only decide cases that are submitted by the Commission, which acts as a filter, screening out those cases that do not deserve the Court's attention.[31] A second function is the power to order provisional measures if individuals or groups find themselves in some sort of extreme situation and need protection; here the Court can intervene without a formal submission of a case.[32] Finally, the Court has the authority to provide advice, through advisory opinions, to OAS member states on issues related to the interpretation of the ACHR.[33]

The Court is not a permanent tribunal; it has regular meetings during the year, at which the judges hear and decide cases. In 2014 it held five regular sessions and two special sessions.[34] During that year, 19 new cases were submitted to the Court,[35] which held 12 public hearings[36] and produced 16 judgments, 13 on contentious cases and 3 on interpretative requests.[37]

Media Coverage as a Proxy for Legal Culture

The media play an important role in modern societies. Much of what people know, or think they know, about the legal system comes from the media. Political figures reach the public through the media. The media are not only a venue through which the public gets information about the legal system; they can also be an important source of information for legal officials and practitioners.[38]

The media influence the legal system by shaping the public agenda, prescribing which topics are important and which are not; and by influencing how people think about salient issues.[39] The media provide 'frames' through which we absorb information and interpret reality, including the reality of the legal order.[40] These frames favour certain understandings of society, typically those held by powerful groups.[41]

Little empirical research has been done on the media coverage of judicial institutions, especially outside the USA. In the USA some studies have explored the ways in which the media frame public understanding of the Supreme Court of the United States and its work.[42] However, news reports about the Supreme Court, aside from coverage of the judicial appointment process, are limited and typically focus on specific decisions. A small percentage of the Supreme Court's decisions are reported, and the coverage emphasises the result of the case and little else.[43] Outside the USA there is the study by Bogoch and Holzman-Gazit, who investigated coverage of the Israeli High Court of Justice in two newspapers, one popular and one elite. Both of the newspapers gave extensive, positive coverage of the High Court. The Israeli newspapers reported not only on the outcome of cases but also news about other stages in the litigation process. In Israel the media helped to reinforce the idea of the High

Court as a powerful institution that guarantees and protects democratic values.[44] We build on this body of literature to analyse the coverage of the Inter-American System.

2   METHOD

The objective of this study is to explore how the Latin American media report the work of the Inter-American System. In particular, we are interested in understanding how deep or complex is the coverage of the system and whether there are important regional variations. As we explained before, media coverage of legal institutions is one window on the legal culture with regard to those institutions. Accordingly, we collected information from articles in four different elite newspapers published in four different Latin-American countries.

The four countries are Argentina, Chile, Mexico and Venezuela. All are important regional actors, all of them are, or were, part of the Inter-American System and all of them have a national press that, we expect, should be capable of covering the system. These countries give us a good deal of geographic diversity. They also have different histories and traditions and, more important perhaps, in all four, local political forces have some kind of confrontation with the system. Moreover, each had available a newspaper that we could access via an online database.

From each of the countries we selected one major newspaper and collected detailed information about the way the newspaper covered the Inter-American System. We reviewed articles published in *La Nación* for Argentina, in *El Mercurio* for Chile, in *Reforma* for Mexico and in *El Nacional* for Venezuela. We selected these publications because they are among the most important national elite newspapers in their countries, widely circulated, widely read and, as important national newspapers, covering the widest variety of topics.

For each of the four, we collected information from three different years: 2009, 2011 and 2013. The objective was to cover a period broad enough to give us a better picture of media coverage of the Inter-American System in the four countries. Taking a single year might have skewed the data if some particularly salient case or event occurred in that particular year.

We used the Lexis online database of world news. For each newspaper and each year we searched for three key terms that are generally used to refer to the Inter-American System.[45] For all of the articles we recorded

Table 4.1 Total number of articles for each newspaper

Articles reviewed				
	2009	2011	2013	Total
El Mercurio	6	11	12	29
El Nacional	65	83	72	220
La Nación	16	19	33	68
Reforma	52	120	64	236

the name of the newspaper and the date when the article was published.[46] Then we coded information from one out of every two articles that mentioned the Inter-American System.

In addition to the newspaper and date of publication, for all of the articles in the database for which we collected detailed information, we gathered data on the following set of variables: title of the article, type of article, whether the issue that the article covered was domestic or international, whether the article referred specifically to the Inter-American System, which of the two main institutions of the system was mentioned in the article (Inter-American Court, Inter-American Commission or both), and whether the article made any reference to the case law of the Court. We were interested in the amount of coverage, the complexity and sophistication of the coverage, and the type of issues related to the Inter-American System that attracted the attention of the Latin American media.

Table 4.1 shows the total number of articles from which we collected detailed information for each newspaper, for the years covered in the study, and the totals. Information was gathered from 553 articles (Table 4.1).[47]

3   Findings and Discussion

The results are, in a way, discouraging. The findings show that, in general, newspapers in Latin America pay little or no attention to the work of the Commission or the Court, except when the issue directly involves the particular country. Additionally, coverage tends to be superficial; it is limited to reporting certain basic facts with little or no analysis. Finally, in not a few cases, the articles showed a certain amount of confusion about the differences between the two institutions that make up the Inter-American System.

First, as Table 4.1 shows, there is great variation in the number of articles about the system published in each of the newspapers.

The differences between, on the one hand, *El Mercurio* (Chile) and, on the other, *Reforma* (Mexico) and *El Nacional* (Venezuela) are remarkable. *El Mercurio* (Chile) published approximately a tenth of the number of articles that *Reforma* (Mexico) and *El Nacional* (Venezuela) published on this topic.[48] *La Nación* (Argentina) published twice as many articles as *El Mercurio* (Chile). Nonetheless, this number is very small when compared with the number of articles published in the Mexican and Venezuelan papers.

There is, of course, no automatic connection between the number of articles published and the complexity of the media coverage. The quality of the coverage is fundamental. Nonetheless, it is worth mentioning that a reader of *El Mercurio* (Chile) who read the entire newspaper every day during the whole three years that this study covered would have read fewer than 60 articles on the Inter-American System. The situation would not have been that different in the case of a reader of *La Nación* (Argentina). For these two newspapers, the system certainly does not loom very large.

Reforma (Mexico) had a clear peak in reporting in 2011. A series of major decisions went against Mexico towards the end of 2009, and this had an important domestic impact over the next two years. For the other three countries the number of articles about the system remained relatively constant throughout the three years.

Unfortunately there is no clear baseline for comparison—no way we can measure the work of the Latin American media against the work of the media in other places and at other times. This is something that could use further exploration. We can say, however, that compared with media coverage of domestic high courts, the number of articles that we identified is very small. We also did a quick search of coverage of the European Court of Human Rights in *El País*, one of Spain's elite newspapers, using key terms similar to the ones used for the Latin American media. We found that the European Court of Human Rights is reported much more prominently in *El País* than coverage of the Inter-American System in the Argentinean and Chilean newspapers. However, the number is close to the total articles identified in the Mexican and Venezuelan newspapers. One caveat, though, is that the European Human Rights System does not have an institution comparable to the Inter-American Commission; all of the coverage in *El País* refers to the European Court of Human Rights.

One indicator of the depth of coverage is the type of article. News reports are, in general, descriptions of facts that in some cases involve some form of brief explanation or contextualisation but usually do not

Type of Article

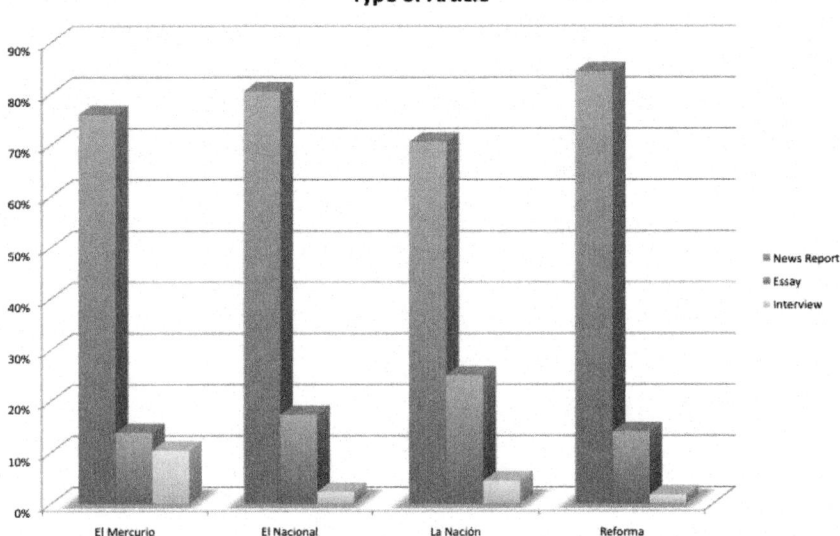

Fig. 4.1 Types of article concerning the Inter-American System

include much in the way of analysis. The point is mainly to inform the readers about events rather than to analyse those events or provide commentary. Editorials and op-ed pieces (we lumped them together under the heading of 'essays'), and also interviews, offer deeper analysis of issues, and typically provide comment or reflection on those issues.

We divided our articles into three categories: news reports, essays and interviews.[49] As Fig. 4.1 shows, news reports form the overwhelming majority of articles—more than 80 % in the case of the Mexican paper. Coverage, as we mentioned, is quite superficial for all the newspapers. News reports are descriptive without much analysis or commentary. Essays and interviews, which could provide more depth, constitute a very small percentage of the articles published. When observed through the Latin American media, the Inter-American System is, in general, a distant and rather obscure entity. Newspapers in the region seem to report only basic facts about the actions of these institutions or conflicts related to them.

The Inter-American System is, of course, a regional system that has an impact on member countries. For the countries in this study, the system has both a domestic and an international component. It is domestic when the actions or decisions of the Inter-American Court or the Inter-American

Domestic or International Issue

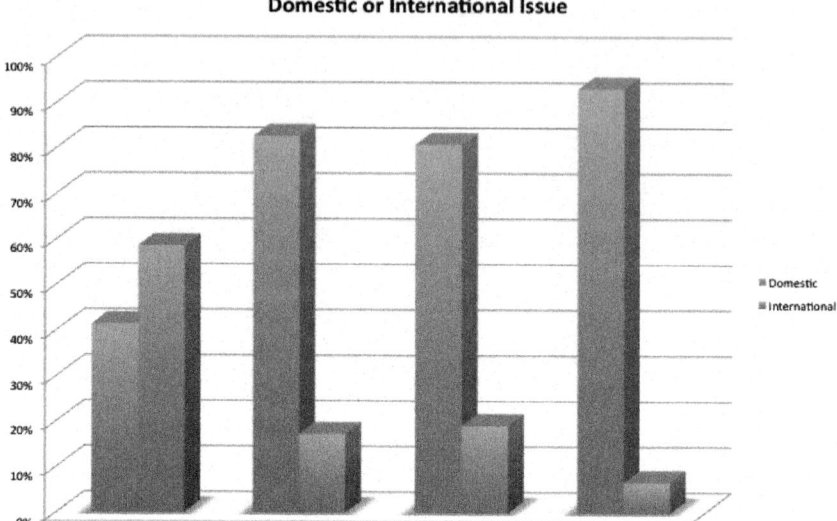

Fig. 4.2   Level of domestic and international media coverage

Commission have a direct effect on the particular country. It is international when the actions or decisions of the system have an impact on a different country. To observe to what extent the media are interested in the international dimension of the system, we classified the articles according to whether they were reporting a domestic or an international issue. Any issue that directly involved the particular country in which the newspaper is published was considered domestic; the rest were considered international.

As Fig. 4.2 shows, media coverage is highly domestic. If the story did not concern the country in which the newspaper was published, it was very unlikely to appear. For example, more than 90 % of the articles in *Reforma* (Mexico) were about a domestic issue. This is remarkable because *Reforma* was the newspaper with the most articles in our database. The Inter-American System is, by nature and purpose, regional; its jurisdiction is supposed to span the whole hemisphere. Yet its regional character is largely ignored by the media. Only *El Mercurio* (Chile) devoted more articles to international issues than domestic issues. The total number of articles in this newspaper, however, was very small, and most international issues that it reported were not related to the jurisprudence of the Court but rather to political conflicts within the system, especially the

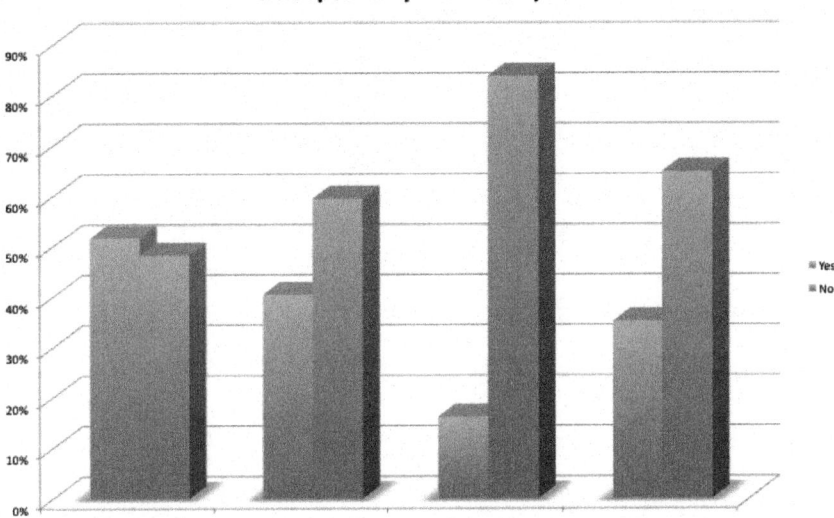

Refers Specifically About the System

Fig. 4.3 Articles specifically concerning the Inter-American System

conflict between some countries in Latin America and the Commission. Therefore, even in the case of Chile, the media coverage does not reflect the regional nature of the Inter-American System.

We also measured whether an article was specifically about the Inter-American System or if the mention of the system was only minor, secondary or incidental. An article covering a new decision of the Court or about the impact of a report of the Commission would be classified as one that was specifically about the system. In contrast, some articles mention the system but do not refer to it in any specific way, or discuss it—for example, a news report that describes a conflict between an individual and the government and simply notes that one party claimed that the dispute could eventually end up in the Court.

As Fig. 4.3 shows, in general the news articles do not refer specifically to the Inter-American System. In *La Nación* (Argentina), fewer than 20 % of the articles specifically addressed the system. Even in the case of *El Mercurio* (Chile), only slightly more than half of the articles referred specifically to the system. Figure 4.3 shows that, in general, the coverage of the system is superficial, and only a very small subset of the articles that mention it actually focus on it.

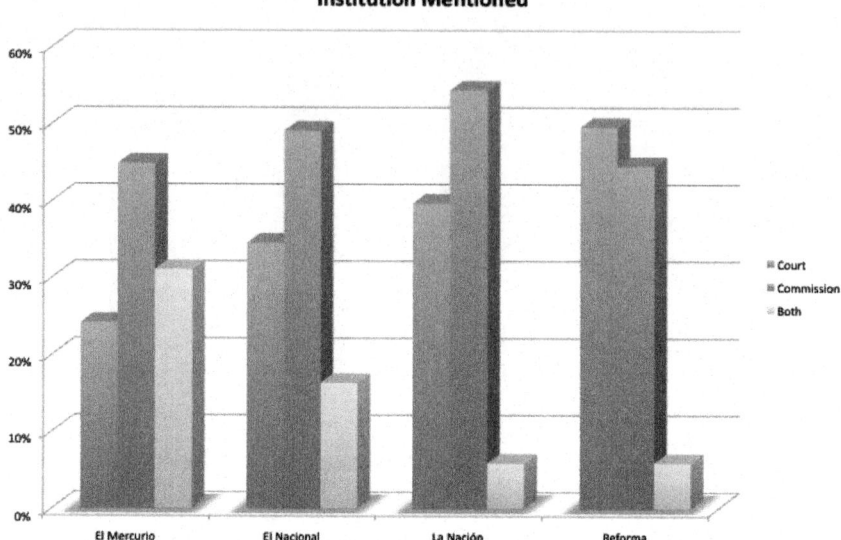

Fig. 4.4 References to institutions of the Inter-American System

For Fig. 4.4 we classified the articles according to whether the article talked about the Court, the Commission or both institutions. Interestingly, we found that in three newspapers the Commission was mentioned in more articles than was the Court. It was only in *Reforma* (Mexico) that the Court was mentioned more than the Commission.

As we mentioned before, the Court is not in permanent, continuous session. Its main function, of course, is to decide cases that are brought before it. The newspapers we studied report on the Court, for the most part, only when a decision directly affects the country in which the newspaper is published. This is not a frequent event. The Commission, however, interacts more often with particular countries, making visits and issuing reports. Thus it attracts more local attention than the Court.

Also as mentioned before, only in *Reforma* (Mexico) was the Court more often the object of attention than the Commission. This was probably because of several decisions in which the Court held that Mexico had violated its international duties. In particular, the *Rosendo Radilla* case, which was decided in 2009, had an impact on the Mexican legal system: it called for significant change in the regulation of military tribunals.[50]

Moreover, the Supreme Court of Mexico changed its interpretation of the basic rules of the Mexican system of judicial review. In other words, the domestic repercussions of the *Rosendo Radilla* decision stimulated a number of articles about the Inter-American Court in the Mexican newspaper.

We also found that coverage of the Inter-American System is not particularly accurate. With some frequency, articles seemed confused about the distinction between the Commission and the Court. An article might mention the one, but the context makes it clear that the article is really about the other. This situation reinforces the perception that the system does not loom very large in the world of Latin American media (Fig. 4.4).[51]

We also looked to see whether or not the newspapers mentioned the role of the Court in building up a body of case law. If an article reported a decision of the Court but failed to mention earlier decisions, we classified this article as one that did not mention the body of case law of the Court.

The overwhelming majority of the articles made no reference to the case law of the Court. This was true for all of the newspapers that we studied. *La Nación* (Argentina) had the highest percentage of articles that made reference to decisions of the Court, but even here the percentage was less than a third of all the articles.

In short, media coverage of the Inter-American System tends to be superficial with little or no analysis. The absence of articles that mention the Court's jurisprudence shows again that there is no real attempt to provide sophisticated analysis or reflection about what the Court and the Commission are doing. With this type of coverage, readers of the newspapers can hardly be expected to develop informed opinions about the work of the Court and of the system in general (Fig. 4.5).

4   Conclusion

The results of our study, reported here, are, as we said, in a way quite discouraging. Newspapers in Latin America pay little or no attention to the work of the Inter-American System except when a case concerns the country in question. Even then, coverage is sparse and sometimes confused.

The failure of media coverage is surely a factor which helps to produce the general obscurity in which the system labours. As we noted, the Inter-American System, compared with (say) the European Court of Justice or the European Court of Human Rights, works in a more challenging environment. The USA and a number of other countries are simply not

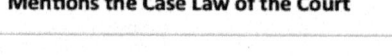

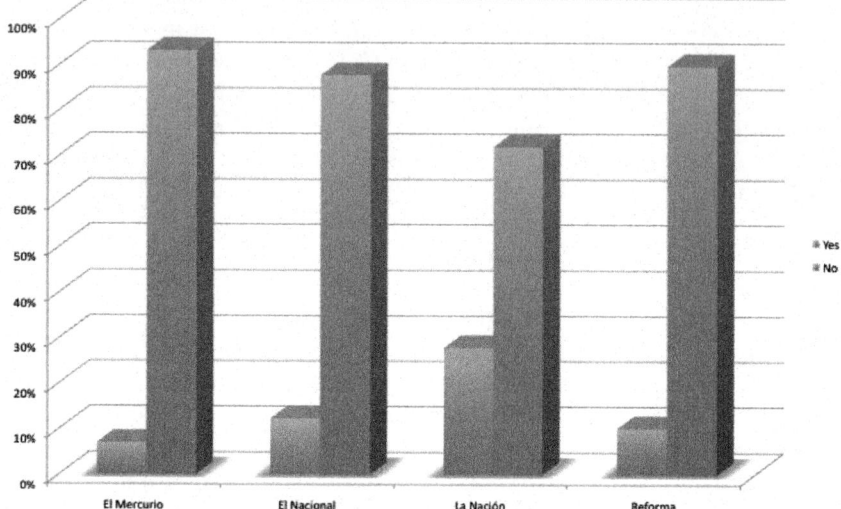

Fig. 4.5   References to case law of the Inter-American Court

subject to the Inter-American Court. Other countries pay attention when its decisions suit them, and then ignore it when these do not. The Inter-American Court is a part-time court. Those countries that fall short of democratic rule can hardly be expected to obey the Court, which, after all, holds to a vision of human rights to which the regime in some countries does not subscribe.

These contextual and structural problems contribute to the weakness of the Court. Feeble media coverage might also play a role. It seems likely that the average Brazilian or Peruvian hardly realises that the Inter-American System exists. The media in Latin America certainly do nothing to make information about the system accessible. Strong traditions and a powerful sense of legitimacy are pillars on which successful regional and international tribunals rest. The Nuremberg trials, after the Second World War, were headline news; they were filmed, debated and discussed. The European Court of Human Rights is a forceful and respected institution. Perhaps some day the Inter-American System will attain this position. But, as of now, it works in the shadows. It would be interesting to know whether other new international tribunals—the International Criminal Court, for example, or the international tribunals for Rwanda,

Cambodia and the former Yugoslavia—suffer from the same obscurity in Latin America, and elsewhere in the world.

Since the media ignore all but the most locally relevant cases, the public in Latin America have no idea of the work of the Inter-American System: the doctrines that it has developed and the ways in which it interprets the hemispheric charter. There is a scholarly literature (fairly formalistic), but if the Inter-American Court and the Inter-American Commission are developing an important body of law on human rights, its doctrines have little hope of penetrating deeply into Latin American legal culture. In this regard, too, the Inter-American System differs from the European regional system.

NOTES

1. The only two regional systems that are comparable to the Inter-American System are the European Human Rights System and the African Human Rights System. See Alexandra Huneeus, 'Courts Resisting Courts: Lessons from the Inter-American Court's Struggle to Enforce Human Rights' (2011) 44(3) Cornell International Law Journal 493, 497.
2. See n 29.
3. Huneeus (n 1) 500.
4. Ibid. 501.
5. See Laurence R Helfer and Anne-Marie Slaughter, 'Toward a Theory of Effective Supranational Adjudication' (1997) 107(2) The Yale Law Journal 273.
6. Ibid.
7. Huneeus (n 1) 507–08.
8. Ibid. 508–11.
9. Ibid. 531–33.
10. James L Cavallaro and Stephanie Erin Brewer, 'Re-evaluating Regional Human Rights Litigation in the Twenty-First Century: The Case of the Inter-American Court' (2008) 102(4) The American Journal of International Law 768, 770.
11. See, generally, Lawrence M Friedman, *The Human Rights Culture: A Study in History and Context* (Quid Pro 2011).
12. Ibid.
13. Famously, in 2013, Venezuela withdrew from the ACHR and it is no longer subject to the jurisdiction of the Inter-American Court. See Freedom House, 'Venezuela's Withdrawal from the American

Convention on Human Rights a Serious Setback'. https://freedomhouse.org/article/venezuelas-withdrawal-american-convention-human-rights-serious-setback.

14. See Lawrence M Friedman, 'Law, Lawyers, and Popular Culture' (1989) 98(8) The Yale Law Journal 1579.

15. For a brief history, see Inter-American Commission on Human Rights, 'What is the IACHR'. www.oas.org/en/iachr/mandate/what.asp

16. Inter-American Commission on Human Rights, Annual Report (2013) 1.

17. Ibid. 2–3.

18. See Huneeus (n 1) 498–99.

19. Inter-American Commission on Human Rights (n 16) 13.

20. Ibid. 16–19.

21. Ibid. 19.

22. Ibid. 25.

23. Ibid. 25–26.

24. Ibid. 26–27.

25. Inter-American Court of Human Rights, Annual Report (2014) 3.

26. Ibid.

27. Ibid.

28. Ibid.

29. Argentina, Barbados, Bolivia, Brazil, Chile, Colombia, Costa Rica, the Dominican Republic, Ecuador, El Salvador, Guatemala, Haiti, Honduras, Mexico, Nicaragua, Panama, Paraguay, Peru, Suriname and Uruguay. Recently, Venezuela withdrew from the jurisdiction of the Inter-American Court. Canada, along with the USA, has never recognised the jurisdiction of the Court. Nor has Cuba, for example. Ibid. 4.

30. Ibid. 5–8.

31. Ibid. 5.

32. Ibid. 9.

33. Ibid.

34. Ibid. 12.

35. Ibid. 15.

36. Ibid. 23.

37. Ibid. 25.

38. See Friedman (n 14).

39. Bryna Bogoch and Yifat Holzman-Gazit, 'Mutual Bonds: Media Frames and the Israeli High Court of Justice' (2008) 33(1) Law & Social Inquiry 53, 55–56.

40. Ibid.
41. Ibid.
42. See, for example, Rorie L Spill and Zoe M Oxley, 'Philosopher Kings or Political Actors: How the Media Portray the Supreme Court' (2003) 87(1) Judicature 22.
43. Ibid.
44. Bogoch and Holzman-Gazit (n 39).
45. The three key terms that we included in our search are *Corte Interamericana*, *Comisión Interamericana* and CIDH. The last one is the abbreviation in Spanish of the Inter-American Court and Commission. We identified all of the articles in which any of these key terms appeared. In the course of analysing the articles, we looked for other potential key terms that might lead us to additional relevant articles. However, we did not find others in addition to the three that we used.
46. There were a few cases where a news article had one of the key terms in the text but the article clearly was not about the Inter-American System. For example, articles that referred to an Inter-American Commission that was not the Inter-American Commission. We excluded those articles from the database. Similarly, whenever the same article appeared twice in the search results, we eliminated the duplicate from the database.
47. Since we captured detailed information from one out of every two published articles that mentioned the Inter-American System, the total number of published articles that mentioned the system during this period is double the number reported in the table.
48. As we mentioned before, Table 4.1 contains the number of articles from which we collected detailed information. The total number of articles published by each newspaper is twice the number reported in the table.
49. The category 'essay' includes editorials from the newspapers as well as regular and invited columnists.
50. *Radilla Pacheco v Mexico* IACtHR Series C 209 (23 November 2009).
51. Certainly the very limited coverage of the Inter-American System makes it difficult for the journalists working for Latin American newspapers to develop the technical knowledge necessary to accurately report on the work of the Inter-American Commission and the Inter-American Court.

PART II

Institutional Development: Policy Implementation and Change

The Evolving Relationship Between Law and Development: Proposing New Tools

Helena Alviar

The relationship between law and social transformation has been a part of theoretical and academic debates for a very long time. Some legal theorists consider law a closed, formal, rational system which works in order to arbitrate the disputes that emerge among individuals, as well as the conflicts between citizens and the power of the state. From this perspective, law is not an agent of social transformation but merely a frame within which human interaction occurs. For other academics, law can and should be used as an engine for economic, social and political change. This instrumental view understands law as an open, flexible system that is, and should be, constantly influenced by external issues such as sociological phenomena, resource distribution goals, and national and historical contexts.

The literature regarding law and development is clearly framed within this second approach. Nevertheless, exactly how this interaction should occur is a topic that has been widely debated since the second half of the twentieth century. The field has been characterised by the search for answers to questions such as: Should law be an instrument for economic development? Is economic development intimately linked to a specific view of law? When does law promote or hinder economic development?

H. Alviar (✉)
University Los Andes, Bogotá, Colombia

© Palgrave Macmillan, a division of Macmillan Publishers Limited 2017   77
P. Fortes et al. (eds.), *Law and Policy in Latin America*,
DOI 10.1057/978-1-137-56694-2_5

These queries are not only important from a purely academic or theoretical perspective but also have been extremely relevant for policy-makers in the Third World.

There have been, broadly speaking, three methods of addressing these issues. The first I shall call the purely instrumentalist one. This approach assumes that economic policies can easily be translated into legal tools and institutions. Since the mid-1950s, this purely instrumental interpretation has been characteristic of many technocrats and policy-makers in the Third World.

Then there is the instrumentalist law-centred approach, which has 1960s and 1990s adaptations. According to the 1960s model, transforming the legal system is a prerequisite to achieving a correct framework that will enhance the conditions in which economic development happens. This transformation of the legal structure should entail the establishment of a classic liberal legal system as well as the strengthening of the technocratic executive branch and centring the importance of public administrative law. This in turn would serve as the basis for development. During the 1990s the centrality of law was exemplified by the Rule of Law project promoted by the World Bank.[1] As was the case in the 1960s, this version of the law-centred approach considers legal transformation as a fundamental first step towards achieving economic development. Nevertheless, it is a critique of what was understood as the excesses of a powerful executive and an administrative public law-centred approach. As a consequence of this critique, during the 1990s, various reforms were introduced that aimed at the consolidation of private law in order to secure market transactions, as well as supporting the judiciary in order to restrain the state and facilitate the free exchange of goods.

For these two last approaches, law is understood as both a frame and an instrument. In the 1960s it was a frame to set in place a classic liberal legal system and an instrument to promote Import Substitution Industrialisation (ISI). In the 1990s it was a frame to secure market transactions and an instrument to promote the free market and export-led growth.

These three perspectives share a view of the relationship between law and economic development as direct: once your economic development goals are clear or the benefits of legal transformation are evident, these ideas can easily be translated into legal texts.

In my opinion, these perspectives underestimate the dynamic ways in which law and ideas about economic development interact. In the dialogue between economic and legal technocrats, there is a range of theoretical interactions happening, which make the translation of objectives much more complex. I take the word 'translation' as an insight provided by David Kennedy in his article 'Law and Development Economics: Toward a New Alliance'. According to him, the use of the word 'translation' foregrounds the difficulties that must be surpassed in order to apply any legal or economic goal.[2]

The objective of this chapter is to provide a different set of tools to interpret what I call the dynamic interaction between policy-makers, economists and lawyers. To do this there are three sections. In the first, I describe in greater detail the instrumentalist approaches mentioned above. In addition, I will set out a series of examples from the Colombian context. The second section provides a description of the dynamic approach I am proposing. It will both outline the difference with instrumental approaches and explain the landscape of the elements that the dynamic approach includes. Finally, I will present some conclusions and propose possible research avenues.

1   THE PURELY INSTRUMENTALIST APPROACH: LAW IN THE MARGINS

As I described in the introduction, many policy-makers in the Third World have understood that economic development goals can easily be translated into legal instruments. In a way, this perspective assumes that the law is a malleable device that can easily contain broader economic development objectives. From this point of view, whatever the definition of development is, ISI or export-led growth should be the guiding principle and the legal system should reflect this. As a consequence, the transformations that are needed are set forth mainly through administrative law, and their interaction with the rest of the legal system (constitutional law, case law etc.) is not taken into account. In addition, it is assumed that because technocrats have a more precise knowledge of economic development goals, the other branches of government should be deferential to their policy design.

In the Colombian context, the golden era of the purely instrumentalist approach was the period from 1960 through to the late 1980s. I am not saying that this view does not exist today among a range of policy-makers; I am arguing that during the late 1960s the understanding that law was an instrument was easily defended, given the relevance that public administrative law had for the development agenda. As a matter of fact, in 1968 there was a fundamental constitutional amendment, which significantly increased the power of the president and his capacity to regulate the economy through administrative law. This constitutional amendment was guided by a very particular definition of economic development, which in general terms interpreted growth as a consequence of industrialisation. In order to industrialise, a country with the characteristics of Colombia had to design a set of protectionist measures that in turn would strengthen local production. In addition, and in order to increase the demand for goods being produced nationally, a degree of resource redistribution was necessary through state subsidy of certain basic goods and by achieving the goal of full employment.

To do this, the president who led this reform, Carlos Lleras Restrepo, as well as his aides, thought that serious changes in state institutions were necessary. This meant restructuring public institutions into a range of public and semipublic enterprises (Sociedades de Economía Mixta, Empresas Industriales y Comerciales del Estado, Establecimientos Públicos) that shared some characteristics with private sector projects but were run by the central government technocrats. He decided to attract individuals from local and international universities with doctoral-level degrees and strong technical knowledge to work on deploying the amendment, regardless of party affiliation.

Indeed, according to academics writing in this period, the administrative reform of 1968 tried to promote a more centralised, apolitical, technocratic institutional setting through the creation of a range of state enterprises and the strengthening of government in order to handle economic matters. In accounts of the debate surrounding the constitutional amendment, members of the Congress of Colombia assumed that this was a project of a technical spirit and as a consequence it did not have ideological implications in political parties' doctrine.[3]

For example, a leading administrative academic, Jaime Vidal Perdomo, said that this meant centralising power and translating economic development goals into governmental regulation:

> Taking into account the difficulties posed by economic management, the speed of the phenomena produced by economic factors, and the greater government experience in this field, this 1968 amendment substantially changes the former scheme and gives way to a new and more flexible legal system providing additional power to the executive branch in order to: organize public credit, accept national debt and decide on its payment, regulate exchange and international trade and modify customs duties, tariffs and any other customs-concerning regulations.[4]

Therefore, and as the above quote suggests, the 1968 amendment led to important changes, such as broadening the capacity of the executive power to intervene in the economy. Some scholars have even compared the Colombian president to a demigod, who had extended his presidential power especially with the constitutional reform of 1968.[5] Indeed, even though the 1886 Constitution[6] explicitly allowed the president to use decree laws during specific periods and on particular subjects that were defined by law,[7] there are various examples of the president pushing the limits of that power by intervening in the economy, especially after the constitutional reform of 1968.[8]

Among these one can observe the president's ability to declare a state of economic emergency, which allowed the executive to intervene selectively in specific areas of the economy to prevent crises or facilitate development plans. During this economic or social crisis, the president could use these emergency measures to raise revenue and adopt short-term economic plans.[9]

The amendment adopted in 1968 also widened the scope of governmental authority by giving the president control over the national budget, revenues and expenditures. It made economic planning constitutionally mandatory.[10] Economic planning, with the implementation of the policies established in the National Planning Department, led to a range of private economic activities.[11] It allowed the executive to intervene in specific areas of the economy in order to facilitate development plans.[12]

In addition, the constitutional amendment included the protection of both free enterprise and private initiative with a strong government intervention in the general direction of the economy. This direction of the economy included production, distribution, use and demand of goods and services through centralised economic planning.[13] It also authorised the government to take part in the economy by controlling wages and salaries in both the public and the private sectors.[14] Finally, it allowed the president to directly intervene in the functioning of the central bank.[15] According to another leading legal academic writing at the time,

> The essence of the 1968 reform lay in the reduction of Congress's power to organize the national budget and to control the planning policies guiding the economic activity of the state. With this reform, the process of overwhelming growth of presidential power reached its crowning point.[16]

There was such concentration of power that even the judicial branch protected it. In a 1972 ruling, the Supreme Court of Colombia argued that a law, which set up a publicly funded corporation to provide credit for agricultural development, violated the exclusive power granted to the president.[17]

In sum, the combination of an increase in presidential power and administrative regulation, economic development policy was seen as a technical matter easily translatable into legal regulation:

> Then, the reform, as we have already mentioned, is not ideological but instrumental and has as its center the composition of the public powers, excepting the jurisdictional one, its functions and the relations among them. The first aspect does not mean that it does not adjust itself to a State conception, since it obeys to the inspiration of modernizing the power instruments to adapt them to the demands of the economic and social development and of going back to the traditional rules of the democratic game, partially and transitorily altered by the 1957 Plebiscite.[18]

There are many contemporary examples of this classic view. From the late 1980s until the late 1990s, Colombian development strategy shifted from promoting industrialisation and full employment to strengthening the competitive mechanisms of the market as the only suitable way to achieve economic growth. ISI policies were gradually abandoned in favour of free trade[19] and strong market institutions:

> the national economy made a transit from an economic model with an emphasis on the development of the domestic market, import substitution industrialization, to a model of opening and internationalization of the economy. The objective of that process was not only to insert the Colombian economy into the world market, but also to increase the efficiency of the economy, through the reduction of the State's 'size' and its regulatory function of the economic process.[20]

The abandonment of ISI and full employment as the primary objectives of development policy was set in place through a range of legal transformations and administrative regulations. Again, the reforms were motivated by the hope that the new development strategy could easily be translated into legal instruments, which would be enough to achieve the new objectives. For example, workers' benefits were eliminated and direct state investment in health and education was diminished. Rural poverty alleviation programmes were greatly weakened. These reforms were accompanied by the privatisation of the institutional arrangement that provided social benefits.[21] Poverty alleviation policies changed their macroeconomic status, and became more focalised and defined by microeconomics. Social policy shifted from instruments related to promoting formal and total employment, aiding the rural population,[22] and measures to respond to violence and poverty simultaneously,[23] to the setting in place of cash transfers originally designed to help out households in times of structural adjustment.[24] All of these reforms were set forth through laws and administrative regulations which had as their overarching goal to transform the structure of the state that was established during the late 1960s. As had happened before, the transformations started out with an idea of economic development (the free market and shrinking of the state) and set it forth through a range of legal and regulatory changes.

2 Instrumentalist Law-Centred Approach

The 1960s Wave

As I stated in the introduction, another way of interpreting the relationship between law and development is what I call the instrumentalist law-centred approach, which has a 1960s version and a 1990s version. According to the 1960s version, the establishment of a classic liberal democratic rule of law was necessary in order to achieve economic development. In other words, a specific type of law and legal transformation, on its own, was a requirement to reach economic development. As a consequence, this specific classic liberal legal model created the conditions for economic development.[25] The set of necessary reforms had nothing to do with economic development goals or definitions. Rather, they were concerned with transforming law into a system where law is universally applied to everyone, citizens influence legal transformation through a democratic process, there is a clear separation of powers, and judges adjudicate according to clearly established rules.

Because legal transformation was so important, legal education reform had an essential role. As a consequence, there was a range of projects set in place in many developing countries aimed at changing the way in which law was thought of and taught. For example, USAID (the US government's development agency) and the Ford Foundation promoted a range of legal education reforms during the 1960s in Asia, Africa and Latin America (mostly in Chile, Brazil and Colombia). The main objective of these transformations was the construction of critical thinking for future lawyers so that they would inspire profound and ambitious social changes in the public and private sectors of their countries.[26]

Previously I have described this transformation in Colombian legal education in the following terms:

> Specifically, the objective was to transform the understanding and interpretation of law from a closed, rigid system to an open, flexible one that is influenced and transformed by social needs, economic objectives and public policy choices. In this sense, and given the depth and complexity of development policies aimed at state led industrialization and redistribution, the transformation of traditional legal education was necessary.[27]

In this law-centred approach, it was very clear that along with the setting up of a classic liberal legal system, future lawyers in charge of policy-making needed to have a different set of tools:

> These proposals were directed toward the institutional organization of law schools, the curriculum, the teaching methods, and the goals of legal education. The reforms were in reaction to the general sense that law schools were failing to provide students with adequate knowledge of their social and cultural context and were not adapting to the contemporary needs of a developing society. It was thought that the reforms would produce a revitalized law school that equipped its graduates with greater reasoning skills, greater capacity for comprehension of their role in problem solving, and an acute sense of the law's relationship to social interests, values and systems.[28]

In conclusion, this period was characterised by both the objective of promoting changes in the legal system which were unrelated directly to economic development goals and the aim of making these changes permanent through the transformation of legal education. The changes that were suggested focused on the establishment of a classic liberal frame in which there is a strict separation of powers, formal equality, and where judges apply the law to both citizens and the government, who follow the rules. To permanently transform the legal framework, a major overhaul of the way law was taught was necessary. This transformation involved shifting from a formalist, text-centred approach to a more open, problem-solving one.

The 1990s Wave

The 1990s were characterised by a return to the idea that legal transformation was desirable on its own. An example of this is the increasing interest and research, led by the World Bank, regarding the relationship between the rule of law and development:

> It is widely believed that well-functioning law and justice institutions and a government bound by the rule of law are important to economic, political and social development. As a result, practitioners in the development field have turned increasing attention to reforms intended to improve law and justice institutions.[29]

In its presentation of the idea that legal reform was a necessary precondition for economic development, the World Bank stated that the 1960s experiment had failed because of the lack of an adequate theoretical underpinning:

> The lack of well developed conceptual and empirical underpinnings is a serious concern, especially in light of past efforts to reform legal institutions-most notably the Law and Development Movement of the 1960s-that are widely believed to have failed due to flawed or insufficient theoretical foundations.[30]

Therefore, even though during the 1960s it was argued that legal reform was necessary on its own, the link between that and economic development was not straightforward. Starting in the 1990s, this link was strongly supported by the insights provided by institutional economics. In very broad terms, this meant that Third World countries would enhance development if a set of institutions worked efficiently. One of these institutions was a functioning judiciary. The World Bank describes this link on its website in the following terms:

> One reason the development community is fostering legal and judicial reform is the belief that, beyond their intrinsic worth, such reforms will help improve economic performance. This belief in the power of legal and judicial reform to spur economic development is supported by a growing body of research showing that economic development is strongly affected by the quality of institutions-including the quality of a nation's legal institutions.[31]

Law was once again in the spotlight. What were understood to be meaningful legal institutions differed slightly from the description of the 1960s. The 1990s version of legal transformation included the strengthening of private law in order to secure transactions and to avoid legal unpredictability, the guarantee of clear property rights, and increasing the importance of judges in order to restrain the state and facilitate market operation:

> Indeed, current research suggests that the capacity of national institutions to protect property rights, reduce transaction costs, and prevent coercion may be decisive in determining whether economic development takes place.[32]

As a consequence, local legal reforms were aimed at this objective. An example in Colombia would be the unending reforms intended to strengthen the judiciary and make it more efficient, as well as to promote access to justice. Some of these reforms took place during the 1990s with significant support from USAID, through the Justice Reform and Modernization Program.[33]

To summarise, the 1990s brought a surge in the understanding of law as being essential to economic development. The similarity with the 1960s approach was that it understood legal reform, on its own, as a necessary condition to reach economic transformation. Nevertheless, the differences were also striking. First, there was a greater interest in providing an economic theoretical background, and this came in the form of institutional economics. Second, and as a consequence of the relevance of institutions, many reforms included the strengthening of the judiciary.

3   THE ELEMENTS OF THE DYNAMIC APPROACH

The relationship between law and economic development continues to be an elusive topic, notwithstanding the different perspectives described above. In my opinion, there is a range of interactions taking place that have not been adequately analysed and for this reason I propose unpacking this relationship with a set of tools that foreground the theoretical dialogue taking place between economists and lawyers.

As a consequence, it is essential to understand the basic assumptions that both lawyers and economists have about law, and how these create biases and distribute resources. David Trubek and Marc Galanter were among the first academics to engage in the study of what these assumptions are and how they work. In the article 'Scholars in Self Estrangement: Some Reflections on the Crisis in Law and Development Studies in the United States', they describe this analytical impulse in the following terms:

In the early years of the law and development movement many scholars and assistance officials shared a tacit set of assumptions about the relationship between law and development. In this section we shall set out the basic presuppositions of this paradigm—which we shall call "liberal legalism"— in the form of a series of propositions about the role of law in society and the relationship between legal systems and development. Only by making the tacit assumptions explicit can we understand and examine the ideas that shaped the early law and development efforts. The task of turning presuppositions into propositions, however, is a difficult one. Although the basic elements we seek are fundamental, they are also hard to uncover. The analyst must strive to make them clear and explicit, without at the same time distorting or caricaturing them.[34]

This interaction between ideas about law and its role in society with economic development goals is constantly evolving. The changes come from shifts in laws, institutions, styles of legal reasoning and their interface with market-oriented ideas of development or state-led industrialisation.

To acquire a more complex understanding of the exchange that is taking place, there is a set of issues that must be fleshed out. First, a detailed unpacking of the set of ideas that underlie the role of law in society is necessary. This means understanding what idea of law is in the background of both economists and policy-makers. Do they believe that law is a neutral frame that regulates market transactions or that it is an instrument to promote social transformation and redistribution? Each one of the answers to these questions will deploy a different view of the power of the judiciary, the executive branch or the Congress of Colombia. In addition, background definitions of liberty and equality are essential to limit the possibilities of any legal reform. Finally, this step in the analysis entails understanding the multiple ways in which legal transformations as well as theories about law have shifted historically, more or less in the style of Section 1.

Second, it is essential to understand the multiple ways in which law structures the market. In the US legal tradition, Robert Hale was one of the first legal theorists to explain to what extent the market is not a natural entity but is determined by legal entitlements that are far from being neutral.[35] Duncan Kennedy brilliantly summarises Hale's contribution in the following terms:

In the 1920s and 1930s, the legal realist institutional economists, and most particularly Robert Hale, worked out an analysis of the role of law in the distribution of income between social classes. That analysis retains its power today. The basic idea is that the rules of property, contract and tort law (along with the criminal law rules that reinforce them in some cases) are 'rules of the game of economic struggle.' As such, they differentially and asymmetrically empower groups bargaining over the fruits of cooperation in production.[36]

This idea is extremely enlightening for thinking about law and development. David Kennedy clearly expands it to topics that are frequently mentioned in the literature regarding the field:

> The turn to law is important. Capital is after all, a legal institution- a set of entitlements to use, risk and profit from resources of various kinds. Law defines what it means to 'own' something and how one can successfully contract to buy or sell. Financial flows are also flows of legal rights. Labor is also a legal institution—a set of legal rights and privileges to bargain, to work under these and not those conditions, to quit, to migrate, to strike, to retire and more. Buying and selling are legal institutions—rooted in what it means to own or sell in a given legal culture, in the background legal arrangements in whose shadow people bargain with one another over price. Markets are built upon a foundation of legal arrangements and stabilized by a regulatory framework. Each of these many institutions and relationships can be defined in different ways-empowering different people and interests. Legal rules and institutions defining what it means to 'contract' for the sale of 'property' might be built to express quite different distributional choices and ideological commitments. One might, for example, give those in possession of land more rights—or one might treat those who would use land productively more favorably.[37]

The third step entails describing, in a detailed form, the interaction between different branches of government when targeting a development policy. This means understanding the different ways in which legislators, judges and members of the executive branch act in order to structure a specific goal. Within this description it is important to foreground the choices that policy-makers, legislators and judges make about the best way to reach a development goal. It is not obvious that a development policy should be naturally pursued through administrative law. It could be designed as the creation of a set of incentives in the private sphere.

The fourth tool is related to unfolding the contradictions and clashes between economic policy goals and constitutional provisions such as social and economic rights. As I described in section 2.2, during the 1990s one of the economic development goals was to reduce the size of the state, weaken its role in the distribution of resources, and understand the market as the most efficient and neutral way to allocate goods in society. Even though this was the development goal, the removal of welfare-style policies faced important local existing constitutional restrictions. As a matter of fact, privatisation and the elimination of subsidies were framed within a constitution that includes a generous bill of social and economic rights. Therefore social and economic rights, including special provisions that demand from the state an obligation to guarantee human dignity, and to provide education, health and access to land property to all the population, provide a backdrop against which any social policy must interact. As a matter of fact, then, the Constitution had a very determinant effect on the content of the norms, the type of regulation established and the role of the judges. In other words, the 1991 Constitution has provided a frame for both executive branch technocrats and legislators, in terms of targeting social policies, aiming to reach universal coverage in health[38] and education,[39] as well as guaranteeing a minimum wage[40] and access to land property, among others.

4   Final Thoughts

The objective of this chapter is to analyse diverse historical approaches to law and development, providing examples from the Colombian context. This analysis is provided in order to start to think about the limitations that these approaches have had in terms of both transforming societies in underdeveloped countries and constructing a theoretical bridge between lawyers and economists.

The chapter provides a few tools that could start to pave the way for this dialogue. In the future, these insights could be used to study topics that have captured the imagination of both economists and lawyers, such as property or social and economic right, from a comparative perspective. This comparative perspective should include countries with diverse political regimes, including leftist progressive regimes and those more to the right in Latin America.

Notes

1. For more on the Rule of Law project, see World Bank, Rule of Law and Development. http://web.worldbank.org/WBSITE/EXTERNAL/ TOPICS/EXTLAWJUSTINST/0,contentMDK:20934363~menuP

K:1989584~pagePK:210058~piPK:210062~theSitePK:1974062,00. html#rule_of_law.

2. David Kennedy, 'Law and Development Economics: Toward a New Alliance' in David Kennedy and Joseph Stiglitz (eds), *Law and Economics with Chinese Characteristics: Institutions for Promoting Development in the 21st Century* (Oxford University Press 2013) 5.

3. Jaime Vidal Perdomo, *History of the 1968 Constitutional Amendment and its Legal Reach, Biblioteca Juridical Contemporánea* (Publicaciones de la Universidad Externado de Colombia 1970) 82.

4. Ibid. 213.

5. Manuel José Cepeda Espinosa, *Estado de Sitio y Emergencia Económica* (Contraloría General de la República 1985).

6. Article 76 of the 1886 Constitution.

7. Article 76(12) of the 1886 Constitution: Endowing, *pro tempore*, the President of the Republic with specific extraordinary powers, when necessity requires or public conveniences so advise.

8. Scott Mainwaring and Matthew Soberg Shugart (eds), *Presidentialism and Democracy in Latin America* (Cambridge University Press 1997).

9. Dennis M Hanratty and Sandra W Meditz (eds), *Colombia: A Country Study* (Library of Congress 1988). http://countrystudies.us/colombia/.

10. Carlos Caballero Argáez, 'La impronta de Carlos Lleras Restrepo en la economía colombiana de los años sesenta del siglo XX' (2009) 33 Revista de Estudios Sociales 91. http://res.uniandes.edu.co/view.php/599/view.php.

11. Ibid.

12. In relation to Congress, the President must 'Timely submit to Congress the plans and programs referred to in the 4th ordinal of Article 76 (National Development Plans) …'. Article 39, Legislative Act 1 of 1968.

13. Free enterprise and private initiative within the limits of the common good are guaranteed, but the general direction of the economy will be in the charge of the state. It will intervene, by mandate of law, in the production, distribution, use and consumption of goods and public and private services, and plan the economy in order to achieve integral development. Article 6, Legislative Act 1 of 1968. Hanratty and Meditz (n 9).

14. 'The State will intervene, according to the rule of law, to give full employment to the human and natural resources within income and wage policies …'. Article 6, Legislative Act 1 of 1968.

15. Article 120(14): 'Exercise, as their own constitutional powers, the necessary intervention in the Issuing Bank and the activities of individuals or companies that directly affect the handling or use and investment of funds from private savings.'
16. Alfredo Vásquez Carrizosa, *El poder presidencial en Colombia* (Ediciones Suramérica 1986) 412.
17. Article 120(14) of the 1886 Constitution. Vásquez Carrizosa, ibid.
18. Vidal Perdomo (n 3) 154.
19. The National Development Plan of 1990 establishes two principles in terms of macroeconomic policies. First, free trade and an open economy are basic for development. In this sense, it points out: 'unlike the recommendations of professors and students of the fifties and sixties ... nowadays, an open economy is identified as a basic strategy for development'. Second, State 'intervention must not replace the market; it must correct its distortions'. See https://www.dnp.gov.co/Plan-Nacional-de-Desarrollo/Paginas/Planes-de-Desarrollo-anteriores.aspx (last visited 31 July 2014).
20. Luis Javier Orjuela, 'El Estado colombiano en los noventa: entre la legitimidad y la eficiencia' (1998) 1 Revista de Estudios Sociales 56. http://res.uniandes.edu.co/view.php/28/view.php.
21. For a detailed description of the privatisation goal, see Helena Alviar, 'The Classroom and the Clinic: The Relationship between Clinical Legal Education, Economic Development and Social Transformation' (2008) 13 UCLA Journal of International Law and Foreign Affairs 197, 210–211.
22. Examples of those measures are the Caja de Crédito Agrario, the Instituto Colombiano de Reforma Agraria and the Fondo de Desarrollo Rural Integrado, designed to alleviate rural poverty by increasing credits and resources for small landowners in order to make them more productive. Nevertheless, Colombian agrarian structure remains highly unequal, and the lack of land continues to be an obstacle to development. See Helena Alviar, 'Social Policy and the New Development State: The Case of Colombia' in David M Trubek, Helena Alviar Garcia, Diogo R Coutinho and Alvaro Santos (eds), *Law and the New Developmental State: The Brazilian Experience in Latin American Context* (Cambridge University Press 2013).
23. The Plan Nacional de Rehabilitación was created in 1982 to allocate social benefits to people, regions and activities affected by poverty and

violence, and marginalised by social and economic progress. See Alviar, 'Social Policy', ibid.

24. Ibid.
25. David Trubek and Marc Galanter describe the content of the liberal legalist model in the following terms: 'The liberal legalist model is a general model that explains the relationship between law and society and specifically explains the how legal systems and development relate. It contains six basic characteristics: (1) Society consists of individuals, intermediates and the State. The State has the power to coerce individuals and works through individuals. Both the State and intermediates are instruments used by individuals whom pursue their own welfare. (2) The State controls individuals through law. It does so, according to rules through which the State itself is coerced. (3) Rules are designed to achieve social purposes or attain social principles, in a conscious way. The rule making process is pluralist and there is no systematic advantage of some population over another. Intermediates are the principal actors in the rule-making process because they aggregate individual interests. (4) Rules are equally enforced for all citizens. (5) The legal order applies, interprets and changes universalistic rules. The central institutions of the legal order are Courts, which have the final saying in defining the social significance of law. The typical decisive mode of legal action is adjudication, which follows authoritative rules and doctrine as its outcome. (6) The behavior of social actors tends to follow the rules. When the population does not comply with the rules, officials will enforce them.' David Trubek and Marc Galanter, 'Scholars in Self-Estrangement: Some Reflections on the Crisis in Law and Development Studies in the United States' (1974) Wisconsin Law Review 1062, 1070–1072.
26. César Rodríguez, 'El regreso de los programas de derecho y desarrollo' (2000) 25 El otro Derecho ILSA 13. http://ilsa.org.co:81/biblioteca/dwnlds/od/elotrdr025/elotrdr025-01.pdf
27. Alviar, 'The Classroom' (n 21) 206.
28. Ibid. 207.
29. World Bank, Rule of Law and Development (n 1).
30. Ibid.
31. Ibid.
32. Ibid.
33. USAID, Assessment of USAID/Colombia's Justice Reform and Modernization Program. http://pdf.usaid.gov/pdf_docs/PDACR349.pdf 3.

34. Trubek and Galanter (n 25) 1070.
35. Robert Hale, 'Coercion and Distribution in a Supposedly Non-Coercive State' (1923) 38(3) Political Science Quarterly 470.
36. Duncan Kennedy, *Sexy Dressing Etc.: Essays on the Power and Politics of Cultural Identity* (Harvard University Press 1993) 83.
37. Kennedy (n 2) 2.
38. In 2008 the Colombian Constitutional Court declared that the right to health should be adjudicated in the same rank as civil and political rights. This ruling is important for three reasons. First, the Colombian Constitutional Court ruled that the right to health is an independent fundamental right. In previous rulings, the right to health had been protected when it was linked to life risks or human dignity. Second, the Court stated that health coverage in Colombia was not as universal as it should be and therefore ordered the government to take the necessary measures to ensure universal coverage and to report every six months to the Constitutional Court the progress obtained in relation to this aim. Third, the tribunal pointed out that even though there is a contributive and a subsidised regime, there is discrimination inside the system among the members of those regimes. Therefore the Court ordered the government to unify both regimes.
39. There are many decisions by the Colombian Constitutional Court about this subject. Among them the most useful ar: T-236 of 2001; T-943 of 2004; C-1109 of 2001; C-673 of 2001; and C-925 of 2000.
40. For example, in 2003, the Colombian Constitutional Court declared unconstitutional an increase of 2 % in the value added tax on products that are considered essential for family subsistence (*canasta familiar*). The Court said that this increase went against the taxation system principles of progressivity and equity, and that it would disproportionately affect the poorest segments of society given that most of their income is spent on the goods included in the *canasta familiar*. Corte Constitucional, Sentencia C-776 de 2003, MP Manuel Jose Cepeda Espinosa. Along the same lines, in 2001, in a highly controversial decision, the Court decided that the salary of low-wage public workers could not be increased by less than the inflation rate. Corte Constitucional, Sentencia C-1064 de 2001, MP Manuel Jose Cepeda and Jaime Cordoba Triviño.

CHAPTER 6

Transnational Legal Indicators: The Missing Link in a New Era of Law and Development

David Restrepo Amariles

At a recent event in New York University, a member of the World Bank's Global Indicators Group presented the updated results of regulatory and legal reform projects associated with the Doing Business indicators.[1] The consolidated figures were impressive. Among others, she reported that since 2003, more than 50 economies have formed 'Reform Committees' around the results of Doing Business indicators, most often at the inter-ministerial level or reporting directly to the president or prime minister. In the same period, governments implemented more than 600 legal and regulatory reforms also informed by Doing Business indicators. For instance, Peru has pursued reforms since 2008, seeking to facilitate the creation and development of new business corporations. The World Bank's Global Indicators Group reports the elimination of four procedures that cut in half the time needed to create a new business. As a consequence, Peru escalated 13 positions in the 'starting a business' rank, moving from 102 in 2008 to 89 in 2015.

The seemingly successful strategy of the World Bank Group to advance business law reforms through Doing Business indicators reflects a wider transformation in the way international organisations design, promote and implement legal and regulatory reforms today. This chapter argues that

D.Restrepo Amariles (✉)
HEC Paris, Jouy-en-Josas, France

© Palgrave Macmillan, a division of Macmillan Publishers Limited 2017   95
P. Fortes et al. (eds.), *Law and Policy in Latin America*,
DOI 10.1057/978-1-137-56694-2_6

legal indicators mark the beginning of a new era of law and development policy characterised by the use of performance measures with governance purposes. In particular, it shows that as law progressively became a substantive field of development policy it also became increasingly shaped and disciplined, alongside other fields of development policy, by measurements and indicators.

The chapter is divided in three sections. First, I trace the origins of indicators in law and development policy following David Trubek and Alvaro Santos' moments of law and development. Second, I bring forth the shift towards governance in development policy in the early 1990s, and the rating of law as a substantive field of development policy subject to performance measures. Third, I discuss two possible implications of the shift towards indicator-based legal reform in law and development policy—namely, (1) the emergence of an evidence-based practice of legal reform; and (2) a mathematisation of its concepts and drivers.

1   TRANSNATIONAL LEGAL INDICATORS AND THE LAW AND DEVELOPMENT MOMENTS

The law and development idea is certainly older, wider and more complex than David Trubek and Alvaro Santos have recently suggested.[2] These authors provide an orthodox account which covers predominantly the post-war period, views the law and development movement from a typically US perspective, and focuses mainly on the geographical region of Latin America. This account overlooks earlier waves of the intellectual project of law and development in modern history, such as those that France, the Netherlands and the UK carried out as colonial powers in Africa, Asia and the Caribbean several centuries ago. Moreover, it fails to account for the different narratives of law and development existing around the world, and especially those which highlight the local views and legacies in the relationship between law and development, and give greater relevance to unofficial law.

Nonetheless, Trubek and Santos' account is probably the most critical and complete analysis of contemporary debates in the USA about law and development. In this section, I trace and characterise the role of indicators and performance measures in two of the three moments in which they divide law and development policy in the post-war period. I show in each of them that development organisations such as USAID and the

World Bank conducted initiatives seeking to quantify the performance of state legal systems, and occasionally to link it with socioeconomic performance.

The First Moment of Law and Development: USAID and SLADE

With the process of decolonisation in the 1960s, law was increasingly seen as a significant tool in the discourse of development agencies. According to Trubek and Santos, development policies from the 1950s until the beginning of the 1980s focused on the role of the state in managing the economy and transforming traditional societies.[3] In this first moment, law was an instrument used to modernise newly independent states, create formal structures for macroeconomic control in developing and independent states, and promote social change.[4]

The USA played a significant role in shaping development policy and financing the production of legal measures. At the end of the Second World War, the World Bank, the main development international organisation today, lacked the resources to conduct research on the impact of reforms. Additionally, it had not yet rated law as a developmental discipline, and thus legal reforms had little weight in its budget.[5] The global development agenda in the 1960s was largely set and financed by the USA through USAID, which was and remains a key instrument of US foreign policy.

Most likely the first large-scale empirical and comparative research in the field of law and development took place in the 1970s. John H Merryman and Lawrence Friedman launched the ambitious Studies in Law and Development (SLADE) research project at Stanford University.[6] After having surveyed the field, they concluded that the main weakness of research in law and development was the lack of a solid empirical base. Merryman and Friedman requested a grant to USAID with the purpose of developing a 'new body of theory and method—a "social science" of law and development—to provide the intellectual framework for effective study, research and decision-making'.[7] The objective was two-fold. First, SLADE aimed to produce quantified and comparable knowledge of legal systems in the form of legal indicators, and second, it intended to explore the relations and correlations between them and social indicators.[8]

To operationalise and disaggregate the concept of law for quantification, it defined it in terms of legal system—that is, in terms of institutions, processes and actors, and not in terms of rules.[9] Merryman and his colleagues wanted to advance the idea that legal systems could be usefully described in quantitative terms through these categories. Their definition was very much in line with the prevailing understanding of law within the development field, but it contrasted sharply with the view of law as a system of rules prevailing in legal scholarship and, most particularly, in comparative law.

SLADE conducted research on the legal systems of Latin America and Mediterranean Europe for three years. It obtained 26 measurements of different variables spanning a period of 25 years (1945–1970). Most of the empirical work relied on fieldwork in each of the countries and on available national and regional statistics. Unfortunately, SLADE ran out of funding before analysing the data, and USAID turned down a request for an additional grant. The data collected remains mostly unprocessed and of little use in academic and policy research.[10] Merryman explained that when SLADE completed the empirical research, USAID had lost interest in law as a component of development while scholars began to find it more productive to look elsewhere.[11]

The Second Moment: The World Bank and the CPIA

Beginning in the 1980s, the second moment of law and development experienced the creation of the World Bank's indicators through the Country Policy and Institutional Assessment (CPIA). These were the first transnational legal indicators produced by an international organisation. In reaction to the Soviet Union's promotion of state interventionism, Western development agencies preached a view of development in which growth was achieved by 'getting prices right, promoting fiscal discipline, removing distortions created by state intervention, promoting free trade, and encouraging foreign investment'.[12] Trubek and Santos describe this second moment as 'law and the neoliberal market'.[13] As in the 1960s, the interest in law in the 1980s was mainly instrumental and its substantive dimension was much neglected, but the focus was completely different. In this new context, significant efforts in legal reforms went to strengthening the rights of property and ensuring the enforceability of contracts.

The CPIA reflects not only the transition from the first to the second post-war moment of law and development but also an early attempt to assess the rule of law through indicators. On the one hand, the CPIA sought to adapt the World Bank's aid-allocation policy to the changing political conditions, so it could send the right message to borrowing countries and tackle the expansion of communist ideas. On the other hand, the CPIA was the first attempt by the World Bank to measure legal systems in a comparative and sustained manner and to relate them to development policy. They perfectly embodied the idea that law was a formal instrument to foster a market-based economy.

The CPIA contributed immensely to breaking ground for the creation of transnational legal indicators as we know them today. First, it set the conceptual framework according to which law would be evaluated as an instrument of economic development. It focused neither on processes or actors, nor did it focus solely on rules. The CPIA introduced the concept of performance, which measures the actual capacity of legal systems to accomplish certain desirable objectives and functions. Like SLADE, it abandoned the microperspective usually adopted by legal scholars. It was not interested in assessing if criminal offences, contract clauses or administrative acts were correctly defined, interpreted and applied from a doctrinal perspective. It focused on assessing if legal systems effectively protected property rights, enforced contracts and ensured legal certainty, among other things. Good performance was viewed from a global perspective and progress evaluated on the basis of the effects that legal systems produce on the ground.

Second, the CPIA rendered law a measurable and quantifiable concept. It provided the first systematic, comparative and quantified study of law, making possible the identification of macrochanges and patterns of legal systems around the world. From today's perspective, the CPIA indicators look undeveloped, lacking statistical sophistication and methodological rigour. Even with these limitations, the CPIA set the foundation of the third moment of law and development during which the World Bank Institute would develop the World Governance Indicators and the Doing Business indicators.

2   LAW AND PERFORMANCE MEASURES: A NEW ERA IN LAW AND DEVELOPMENT POLICY

In the 1990s, development policy took a radical turn and embraced the governance rhetoric. It radically transformed the way in which regional and international development organisations designed and promoted legal reform, and, more widely, development policy itself. In this section I analyse the shift towards governance in development policy and the inclusion of law as one of its substantive and measurable dimensions.

A New Development Rhetoric: Governance and the Rule of Law

International organisations saw the end of the communist bloc and the intensification of transnational economic flows as an opportunity to sponsor a new rhetoric in which the rule of law embodied the global legal standards favouring transnational economic integration. Ibrahim Shihata, former vice-president of the World Bank, was the first to call this new development rhetoric 'governance'.[14] He acknowledged the importance of the bank's mission to alleviate poverty and foster economic development during the previous decades through lending and development aid. However, he predicted that institutions within states needed to be reinforced because economic growth in the following years would come through the development of the private sector, rather than through the further expansion of state enterprises.[15] Hence Shihata argued that if the bank wanted to accomplish its ultimate mission, it needed to expand its range of action beyond economic policies.[16]

This reasoning constitutes a key moment in contemporary development policy. It built a bridge from 'plain development policy' to what some commentators call 'governance through development'.[17] Shihata argues that getting involved in governance is compatible with the Articles of Agreement of the World Bank because the field is free of political consideration. But, additionally, he claims that the World Bank's involvement is necessary in order to achieve its mandate. Shihata's view depoliticises governance and the rule of law, facilitating the latter's incorporation in the new financing system of the bank, which gradually shifted from project-based to policy-based loans.

For Shihata, the rule of law would function as a magnet to foreign direct investment (FDI) in developing economies, which in turn would fuel economic development and contribute to poverty reduction.[18] Law thus became an institutionalised variable in the decision-making processes of the bank. This shift within the most influential development institution had important repercussions for states and other international organisations, which very quickly endorsed the idea that good governance was the key factor in ensuring economic development.

In 1991, the Council of the European Community issued a resolution setting for the first time the rule of law, market-friendly regulations and development in the wider framework of governance.[19] In 1999 it was the turn of the United Nations (UN). Mark Malloch claimed that globalisation was 'too important to be left unmanaged'[20] and recommended linking market economies to better governance to ensure that the benefits of glo-balisation would reach all sectors of society.[21] In 2004 the UN secretary general endorsed Shihata's proposal and linked governance and the rule of law. Moreover, he argued that the rule of law was a proper suprana-tional concept—a sort of *acquis international*, with autonomous meaning and existence from national rule of law models.[22] The wide acceptance of the governance and rule of law rhetoric inaugurated the beginning of the third moment of law and development, and a prosperous period in the production of legal indicators.

The Third Moment: World Governance Indicators

The main implication of the governance and rule of law rhetoric for law and development policy was that legal and regulatory reforms were seen no longer as a tool for economic reform but as an end in itself. This led development organisations to set a new reform agenda for developing states, which purported to strengthen and improve law as a whole under the idea of the 'rule of law'.[23] As with any other dimension of the World Bank's development policy, the rule of law, and thus state legal systems, were subject to the discipline of measurement, performance and numbers.

In 1996 the bank published *Performance Monitoring Indicators Handbook*, calling on all of its units to measure progress of the bank's projects towards explicit short- and long-term objectives.[24] In 1998 the board of governors adopted the Comprehensive Development Framework to unify the bank's development strategies. It states in principle four that 'development performance should be evaluated on the basis of mea-surable results'.[25] The World Bank acknowledges today that turning to performance measures in the 1990s marked a significant overhaul of its development policy.[26]

These transformations triggered the emergence in 1996 of the World Governance Indicators (WGIs) and the inclusion of the rule of law as one of its six dimensions. The rule of law, set next to proxies accounting for the economic, political and social dimensions of governance, became a proxy indicator of state legal systems. The WGIs sought to fill the lack of follow-up and monitoring instruments in the field of governance as mandated by the Comprehensive Development Framework. They were the first of a new generation of indicators customised to the bank's need to collect information about the effectiveness of its development policies.

Above all the WGIs were a means to ensure governance discipline and accountability from borrowing countries. The World Bank could not directly intervene in the institutional design of borrowers since, pursuant to its Articles of Agreement, it would mean entering into political considerations. This new generation of indicators, which also includes Doing Business and Investing Across Borders, was the missing link of the bank's development policy to enhance its governance capacity over national legal systems and to ensure they were fit, eventually, for the market economy.

In 1999, Daniel Kaufmann, Aart Kraay and Pablo Zoido-Lobatón, the authors of the WGIs, published the first paper of the Governance Matters series in which they correlated governance and rule of law indicators with socioeconomic indicators. They concluded that there 'is a strong causal relationship from good governance to better development outcomes such as higher income per capita, lower infant mortality, and higher literacy'.[27] The study provided strong support for the bank's focus on governance and confirmed that the rule of law was a key dimension of development policy.

Celine Tan has rightly interpreted these changes as a shift towards 'governance through development'.[28] Her insightful study of the World Bank's and the International Monetary Fund's (IMF's) Poverty Reduction Strategic Papers shows that development instruments based on measurable results have become a normative framework for policy reform at national levels.[29] As a consequence, national policy-making is standardised among countries, which facilitates the role of international organisations in streamlining local institutions according to international benchmarks and standards.

3   EVIDENCE-BASED POLICY: THE WAY AHEAD?

The number of legal indicators in the last 15 years has increased dramatically. According to a recent study of the Civil Law Initiative, until the year 2000, only six sets of transnational indicators contained relevant information about state legal systems, in comparison with more than 20 today.[30] Public and private organisations such as the World Bank, the World Economic Forum, the World Trade Organization (WTO), the Civil Law Initiative and the Organisation for Economic Co-operation and Development (OECD), regularly produce and use indicators to assess the performance of state legal systems. Indicators also allow them to design, promote and audit the evolution of legal and regulatory reforms throughout the world. In this section I foreground some key features of Doing Business indicators and the WGIs, and highlight some possible implications of relying on them for conducting legal reform.

Legal Indicators and Legal Reform in Business Law

Legal reform rapidly became a key focus of the new governance and rule of law rhetoric. States needed to ensure good 'fundamentals' at the local level to be competitive in the global economy. Perry Kessaris has rightly noted that legal systems became a component of 'investment climate'—'a "portmanteau phrase" which lumps together law, politics, economy and infrastructure of a given national or sub-national region'.[31] Moreover, if the rule of law was the bottom line of a good legal investment climate, in practice, legal reforms extend well beyond its scope.

In 2005 the World Bank's flagship *World Development Report* stated that investment climate improvements required changes to laws and policies.[32] Most initiatives focused primarily on business law. The World Bank reports in particular to have funded more than 600 legal and judicial reforms in 85 countries, including the drafting of property protection laws in Albania; anti-trust and anti-dumping laws in Egypt; value added tax legislation in India; property, secured transactions and company law in Belarus; commercial, financial and investment laws in Lebanon; and anti-monopoly laws in Argentina.[33]

However, reform alone was not enough. The bank was concerned with effective reform. Its data showed that 90 % of firms in developing countries reported gaps between formal policies and what happens in practice.[34] John Ohnesorge has rightly pointed out that domestic legal reforms in the framework of development policy do not take place in a vacuum.[35] They unfold through mechanisms ranging from UNCITRAL (United Nations Commission on International Trade Law) model laws and WTO treaty-based regimes to externally imposed constraints of loan conditionality and managerial mechanisms identifying good legal reform practices and recommending them to countries. Legal indicators adopt the latter approach. The World Bank, for instance, relies on Investment Climate Surveys and the Doing Business indicators because these benchmark regulatory regimes in more than 130 countries and provide evidence about what governments at all levels can do to create a better investment climate.[36]

The Doing Business project clearly fills a void of quantified legal information which international development organisations require to inform and monitor legal reform in the context of governance.[37] Doing Business indicators claim to provide actionable evidence regarding the specific laws and regulations that enhance or hinder business activity, and the public institutions that supported it.[38] With that purpose, it makes available to reformers a database with good practices and benchmarks in most fields of business law. It also ranks legal and regulatory reforms with proven records of success or failure, and even more impressive, and probably worrying, it makes available a reform simulator. The latter allows governments to test, in advance, the impact of legal reforms on their Doing Business ranking, both at the level of the ease of doing business rank and at the disaggregate level of each of its variables.[39] The combination of the above tools renders national law reformers not only dependent of development agencies' data but also accountable vis-à-vis the reform agenda set at an international level.

Evidence-Based Reform and the Mathematical Turn in Development Policy

By making available legal information that is comparable over time and across countries, transnational legal indicators allow policy-makers to spot systematically legal issues that need reform, design evidence-based legal reform projects and monitor their implementation periodically. In this section I discuss two possible implications that the use of rankings and indicators may convey for the intellectual project of law and development. First, I show that indicators promote an evidence-based conception of legal reform that reinforces en passant the idea that there is only one model of development and only one model of law in development. Second, I show that legal indicators promote a mathematisation of the values and drivers of legal reform to the detriment of public debate and democratic participation.

Evidence-Based Law and Development Policies

Transnational legal indicators have encouraged law and development policy-making to rely increasingly on evidence. Jeffrey J Rachlinski argues that this may be a desirable development. 'Evidence-based law' would be better law because it would be informed by reality.[40] Adam Aft, Craig

Rust and Alex Mitchell, founders of the *Journal of Legal Metrics*, have also claimed that law is far from immune to the subjective biases and beliefs of its observers and practitioners.[41] In their view, more empirical data will chase away anecdotal evidence, popular beliefs or plain factual ignorance, which in their view often underpin the assumptions and judgments of decision-makers.[42]

An evidence-based approach to law and development policy intends to provide more accurate accounts of the relations between law and reality, including the identification of progress made, and to be made, in every society. It would also call on reformers to conduct impact assessments prior to and after legal reforms and, more generally, equip professional decision-makers with the tools to choose a course of action with a proven track record. In other words, it would aim to ensure that legal reforms are carried out on solid factual grounds.

However, this enthusiasm needs to be nuanced. From a practical perspective, the number of legal and regulatory reforms informed by indicators is still relatively insignificant compared with the number pursued every year worldwide. From a theoretical perspective, indicators should not be equated to an unbiased source of empirical evidence. They convey the political and economic views of the issuers as well as their reform priorities. In particular, legal indicators from the World Bank and international development organisations tend to promote the idea that there is only one model of development and only one model of law in development:[43] a private-led model where the rule of law is defined as a proxy of legal systems and its rhetoric is expanded to encompass business law and regulation. Additionally, they tend to be both selective and culturally biased: selective because they emphasise those areas of law related to the functioning of the market economy, and culturally biased because they promote a one-size-fits-all model of law drawn largely from the institutional setting, mode of operation, economic qualities and legal culture of common law systems.

For instance, Doing Business indicators assume that there is a causal link between legal reforms and economic outputs of regulation. The reform simulator reinforces this shortcoming. First, it presents improvement in the ranking as the direct result of legal reforms. Yet, in practice, two-thirds of the variables that Doing Business uses to calculate the rankings relate to economic outputs. These are nonetheless neglected in the simulator as changes in the rank are set to depend only on the legal variables. In other words, the simulator assumes that better economic outputs will follow from the implementation of regulatory reform.

Second, the reform simulator rests on the assumption that less regulation is better for economic growth. Vinod Thomas and Xubei Luo reveal that 7 out of the 10 variables of Doing Business assume that less regulation is better for business, which is a highly controversial and unsettled theory.[44] In turn, this is problematic for two main reasons. First, it disregards the fact that regulation can also bring social and corporate benefits. It depends on the amount of regulation each society starts from and on its social and cultural conditions. On the other hand, it neglects recent evidence showing that regulatory vacuums can also lead to the poor financial performance of economies.[45] Hence, if overall Doing Business may provide reformers with some useful data, its all-inclusive reform packages should be examined carefully.

Indicators and the Mathematical Proceduralisation of Law

As I have explained elsewhere, legal indicators convey a mathematisation of the legal concepts they measure.[46] In the context of policy-making, they also convey a mathematisation of the purposes of the reform. Indicators draw on a process of commensuration of legal phenomena generally made up of three distinct but interrelated stages. First, it disaggregates the concept to be measured into several subvariables. For instance, when Doing Business measures contract enforcement it defines it in terms of the number of procedures needed to obtain a judicial decision, the time it takes to obtain the enforcement and the total cost of the procedure.

Second, indicators quantify each of the different variables. Since legal phenomena are non-observable in the empirical world, indirect measurements are needed. They allow sociolegal scientists to pose measurement problems as problems of statistical estimation or prediction.[47] The reason is straightforward. Contrary to phenomena in the natural world, such as weight or length, most dimensions of the social institution we call law are not readily quantifiable. Indirect measurements build on a collection of directly measurable quantities that are 'believed to reflect the underlying interest to some degree'.[48] They rely on mathematical and statistical techniques to draw abstract variables from the data collected empirically.

The WGI Rule of Law Indicator illustrates clearly the role that mathematics plays in the quantification stage of indicators. Kaufmann et al. produce numerical evidence of the six dimensions of governance, including the rule of law, through a statistical tool known as the unobserved components model.[49] This allows the combination of the values of variables from different data sources into a single score. It builds on the assumption that each variable provides an imperfect signal of the rule of law that is difficult to observe directly. Kauffman et al. assume it is possible to write the observed score of the rule of law in country j based on the relevant variables in source k, y_{jk} as a linear function of the unobserved rule of law in country g_j and a disturbance term ε_{jk}.

$$y_{jk} = \alpha_k + \beta_k \left(g_j + \varepsilon_{jk} \right) \tag{6.1}$$

Here, α_k and β_k are parameters that map the rule of law in country j in the observed data in source k, y_{jk}.

Third, indicators normalise and aggregate individual variables into a single score through mathematical operations. Most indicators rely on the aggregation method of average (or mean) to calculate the estimates. This means that they claim to describe legal systems at a general level, assuming the normal distribution of the values obtained. They identify a model of the legal condition examined—for example, a rule of law standard—and interpret all deviations as imperfections in the realisation of the model. The main implication of quantification and mathematical aggregation is that mathematical operations, such as the method of maximum likelihood or weighted mean, constitute the object measured at the expense of political considerations.

Indeed, the mathematical proceduralisation underlying indicators tends on many occasions to supersede the argumentative and consensual model underpinning international law in the mission of defining the form and content of legal standards with global scope, whether it is the rule of law, contract enforcement, legal certainty and so forth. Transnational economic and social actors commonly perceive international dialogue under democratic conditions as difficult to reach, costly, inefficient and often inconclusive. In other words, the Habermasian model of proceduralisation of law shows practical weaknesses for development policy. In the context of the 'audit society' we live in, mathematical reasoning is gaining predominance in legal reform because it is seen as a technical, often depoliticised, means of setting standards and assessing their compliance.[50]

Finally, mathematisation opens up new horizons for the governance of legal systems and the analysis of law. With legal indicators available, development policy-makers in international organisations can establish relations between law and other quantified variables, such as poverty, economic growth and human development. It allows us to track patterns and trajectories of legal systems over time and to relate them to social and economic change. Yet mathematical rationality strips legal phenomena away from their context and the intrinsic complexity of law as a social institution. Since this simplification is unavoidable in quantitative comparisons of sociolegal phenomena, users of indicators need to make sure they are used only as headlights, and never as 'go' or 'no-go' signals.

4   CONCLUDING REMARKS

Transnational legal indicators exemplify as much as they intensify the transformations of the intellectual project of law and development today. They constitute a clear example of how performance measures and non-binding policy instruments from international organisations become in practice truly transnational normative frameworks guiding legal and regulatory reform projects locally, and eventually shaping states' legal systems. They also confirm the links between development policy and governance, in which the latter tends progressively to instrumentalise and absorb the former. In spite of their evident pitfalls and shortcomings of legal metrics, law and development scholars should not turn a blind eye to them. Empirical evidence is certainly preferable to subjective biases and beliefs in legal reform. The challenge ahead is thus to engage in a sustained critique and improvement of existing metrics. We must ensure that policy-makers have access to more sophisticated data and are equipped with the conceptual and methodological tools to make good use of them.

NOTES

1. New York University has been leading the discussion about indicators and governance in the USA. See Kevin E Davis, Angelina Fisher, Benedict Kingsbury and Sally Engle Merry, Governance by Indicators: Global Power through Quantification and Rankings (Oxford University Press 2012); Sally E Merry, Kevin Engle David and Benedict Kingsbury (eds), The Quiet Power of Indicators: Measuring Governance, Corruption and the Rule of Law (Cambridge University Press 2015).
2. David M Trubek and Alvaro Santos, 'Introduction: The Third Movement in Law and Development Theory and the Emerge of a

New Critical Practice' in David Trubek and Alvaro Santos (eds), *The New Law and Economic Development: A Critical Appraisal* (Cambridge University Press 2006) 1, 5–7.

3. Ibid. 5–7.
4. Ibid. 2.
5. Patrick McAuslan, *Bringing the Law Back in: Essays in Land, Law and Development* (Ashgate 2003) 110–111; David Restrepo Amariles, 'The Mathematical Turn: L'indicateur rule of law dans la politique de développement de la Banque mondiale' in Benoit Frydman, and Arnaud van Waeyenberge (eds), *Gouverner par les Standards et les Indicateurs: de Hume au Rankings* (Bruylant 2014).
6. John H Merryman, 'Law and Development Memoirs II: SLADE' (2000) 48 American Journal of Comparative Law 713.
7. Ibid. 714.
8. William Twining, *General Jurisprudence: Understanding Law from a Global Perspective* (Cambridge University Press 2009) 253.
9. Merryman (n 6) 718–719.
10. Most of it can be found in John H Merryman, David S Clark and Lawrence M. Friedman, *Law and Social Change in Mediterranean Europe and Latin America: A Handbook of Legal and Social Indicators for Comparative Study* (Stanford University Press 1979).
11. Merryman (n 6) 724, 726.
12. Trubek and Santos (n 2) 5.
13. Ibid. 2.
14. Ibrahim F I Shihata, 'The World Bank Facing the 21st Century – Developments in the Eighties and Prospects for the Nineties' in Franziska Tschofen and Antonio R Parra (eds), *The World Bank in a Changing World* (Martinus Nijhoff Publishers 1991) 40.
15. Ibid.
16. Ibid.
17. Celine Tan, *Governance Through Development: Poverty Reduction Strategies, International Law and the Disciplining of the Third World* (Routledge 2011).
18. Shihata (n 14) 35.
19. Resolution of the European Council, 29 November 1991, OJ EEC 11-1991/122 ff.
20. United Nations Development Programme, *Human Development Report* (Oxford University Press 1999).

21. Ibid. 6.
22. Report of the Secretary-General of the United Nations, 23 August of 2004 on The Rule of Law and Transitional Justice in Conflict and Post-conflict Societies, S/2004/616.
23. Shihata (n 14).
24. World Bank, *Performance Monitoring Indicators Handbook* (World Bank 1996).
25. World Bank, *Comprehensive Development Framework* (1998). http://web.worldbank.org/.
26. Ibid.
27. Daniel Kaufmann, Aart Kraay and Pablo Zoido-Lobatón, 'Governance Matters' The World Bank Policy Research Working Paper 2196/1999. http://info.worldbank.org/governance/wgi/pdf/govmatters1.pdf.
28. Tan (n 17).
29. Ibid. 207.
30. David Restrepo Amariles and Julian McLachlan, 'Inventory of Legal Indicators' in Bruno Deffains and Catherine Kessedjian (eds), *Index of Legal Certainty* (Civil Law Initiative 2015). http://www.fondation-droitcontinental.org/en/index-legal-certainty/.
31. Amanda Perry-Kessaris, 'Prepare your Indicators: Economics Imperialism on the Shores of Law and Development' (2011) 7 International Journal of Law in Context 401, 402.
32. World Bank, *World Development Report 2005: A Better Investment Climate for Everyone* (World Bank 2004) 5.
33. World Bank, *Initiatives in Legal and Judicial Reform* (World Bank 2004) 3, 8–9.
34. World Bank (n 32) 6.
35. John Ohnesorge, 'Legal Origins and the tasks of Corporate Law in Economic Development: A Preliminary Exploration' (2009) BYU Law Review 1619, 1620.
36. World Bank (n 32) 1.
37. World Bank, *Doing Business in 2004: Understanding Regulation* (Oxford University Press 2004).
38. Ibid. 1.
39. International Finance Corporation, *Business Reform Simulator.* http://www.doingbusiness.org/reforms/reform-simulator.
40. Jeffrey J Rachlinski, 'Evidence-Based Law' (2011) 96 Cornell Law Review 901.

41. Adam Aft, Mitchel B Alexl and Rust D Craig, 'An Introduction to the Journal of Legal Metrics' (2012) 1 Journal of Legal Metrics 1. http://www.journaloflegalmetrics.org/V1I1/Intro.pdf.

42. Rachlinski (n 40) 910.

43. In this point I follow Trubek and Santos (n 2) 17–18.

44. Vinod Thomas and Xubei Luo, *Multilateral Banks and the Development Process: Vital Links in the Results Chain* (Transaction Publishers 2012) 50–51.

45. Dani Rodrik, *The Globalization Paradox: Why Global Markets, States, and Democracy can't Coexist* (Oxford University Press 2011) 260–266.

46. David Restrepo Amariles, 'Legal Indicators, Global Law and Legal Pluralism: An Introduction' (2015) 47 (1) Journal of Legal Pluralism and Unofficial Law 9.

47. David J. Bartholomew, *Mathematical and Statistical Approaches*, in Kimberly Kempf-Leonard (ed), *Encyclopedia of Social Measurement* vol 2 (Elsevier Academic Press 2005) 633–640.

48. Ibid.

49. Kaufmann et al. (n 27) 5.

50. Michael Power, *The Audit Society: Rituals of Verification* (Oxford University Press 1997).

CHAPTER 7

Institutional Bypasses in Brazil: Overcoming Ex-Ante Resistance to Institutional Reforms

Mariana Mota Prado

Why are some countries rich and others are poor? This question has challenged academics since the end of the Second World War. After decades of controversy, recently, development scholars have been converging towards a possible explanation: *institutions.* In the last decade, independent judiciaries, efficient bureaucracies and non-corrupt agencies have taken centre stage in development discourse.[1] Consequently there has been a massive surge in development assistance for institutional reform projects in developing and transition economies.[2] However, these reforms have had mixed to disappointing results thus far.[3] These failures suggest that scholars in this field may know a lot about functional and dysfunctional institutions but very little about how to transform dysfunctional institutions into functional ones.[4]

The purpose of this chapter is to examine how a particular type of reform, which I call 'institutional bypass', may help policymakers to overcome a prominent obstacle to reforming dysfunctional institutions: resistance to reforms. Instead of trying to fix dysfunctional institutions,

I am grateful for the comments and suggestions I received from my colleagues in the Faculty of Law, University of Toronto, and at the 2014 Yale Law School SELA conference in Lima, Peru. Special thanks go to Emily Satherwaite and Michael Trebilcock for their detailed comments.

M.M. Prado (✉)
University of Toronto, Toronto, Canada

© Palgrave Macmillan, a division of Macmillan Publishers Limited 2017
P. Fortes et al. (eds.), *Law and Policy in Latin America,*
DOI 10.1057/978-1-137-56694-2_7

113

an institutional bypass simply creates a parallel institution that performs exactly the same function as the original institution and competes with it.[5] The chapter focuses on ex-ante resistance—that is, resistance that may prevent a reform from being adopted and that normally takes place at the design stage. More specifically, either interest groups that benefit from the status quo are likely to impose obstacles to change (self-interested resistance), or this is done by people who are risk averse and fear the potential negative consequences of change (cognitive resistance). The chapter is based on two case studies from Brazil: a bureaucratic reform in the state of São Paulo in the 1990s (Poupatempo) and a police reform in Rio de Janeiro in the 2000s (Unidade de Polícia Pacificadora).

The chapter is structured as follows. Section 1 explains what an 'institutional bypass' is and highlights examples of reforms that can be considered bypasses, such as debt recovery tribunals in India and charter schools in the USA. Section 2 describes two institutional bypasses implemented in Brazil: Poupatempo and Unidade de Polícia Pacificadora. Drawing from the Brazilian case studies, Section 3 discusses how bypasses overcome ex-ante resistance to reforms. I conclude by discussing whether these two reforms can be considered successful, and what could then characterise a successful bypass.

1   What Is an Institutional Bypass?

Like coronary bypass surgery, in which transplanted blood vessels are used to create a new circulatory pathway around clogged arteries, an institutional bypass creates new pathways around dysfunctional institutions. An institutional bypass does not try to modify, change or reform existing institutions; instead, it tries to create a new pathway in which efficiency and functionality will be the norm.[6]

There are three characteristics of an institutional bypass:

1. It keeps the original institution in place.
2. It creates an alternative pathway through which to deliver government services or discharge governmental functions (which becomes an option to those using the services).
3. It tries to be more efficient or functional than the original institution.

One example of an institutional bypass is the debt recovery tribunal (DRT) in India. DRTs were established by the Government of India under an act of parliament (Act 51 of 1993)[7] as an executive arm of the government. DRTs fall under the purview of the Ministry of Finance, unlike civil and criminal courts, which are part of the judiciary.[8] Nevertheless, the jurisdiction of DRTs partly overlaps with the jurisdiction of regular courts, offering an alternative pathway to those who want to recover their debts.[9] While all the cases brought to DRTs fall under the jurisdiction of regular courts, the reverse is not true: DRTs do not have jurisdiction over all cases brought to regular courts; they only provide for the recovery of debts owned by banks and financial institutions involving at least Rs1 million (about US$15,000). This means that these tribunals change a specific point in the system. Indeed, 'Debt Recovery Tribunals were established as the Indian government's attempt to improve the legal channels for loan recovery, without overhauling the entire judicial system.'[10] However, some of the expected benefits of faster recovery, such as more and cheaper loans, do not seem to have been achieved.[11]

Another example of institutional bypass is the charter school in the USA. Charter schools are primary or secondary schools established by private parties, such as teachers, parents, non-profit groups, universities or corporations. They are funded with public money and are not allowed to charge tuition. Students can choose to go to a charter school or to remain in a regular public school. Charter schools aim to offer better education than regular public schools, taking advantage of the fact that they are not subject to the same rules, regulations and statutes that apply to other public schools. However, their level of success is much disputed in the academic literature.[12]

2   INSTITUTIONAL BYPASSES IN BRAZIL

Institutional bypasses can be found all over the world, and Brazil is no exception. An example of an institutional bypass in Brazil is a bureaucratic reform called Poupatempo ('saving time').[13] In 1997, the state of São Paulo created a one-stop shop for bureaucratic services. In contrast to the pre-existing system (in which government services were slow, often plagued by corruption and accessed by the public at multiple service points), offices of the federal, state and, in some cases, local administration were placed in one location to provide easy access to a variety of services, such as requesting a driver's licence, obtaining criminal records and filing tax returns. The services were provided more quickly than within the previous bureaucracy, and largely because of that Poupatempo became the main provider of governmental services within the state soon after its creation. Starting with one unit in 1997, it had expanded into 18 units by 2007, providing services to an average of 50,000 people a day or 23 million people a year. By 2012 there were 32 units. Poupatempo provides the same services that were being provided by the previous bureaucracy in a more efficient fashion.

Another example of institutional bypasses is the implementation of the Unidades de Polícia Pacificadora (UPPs, police pacification units)— new police units in the state of Rio de Janeiro.[14] The UPP project takes back territories controlled by drug dealers and criminal organisations, mostly in low-income neighbourhoods with illegal settlements known as favelas.[15] The project is divided into three stages: occupation; pacification; and the creation of a UPP.[16] The occupation and pacification are carried out by an elite police force called Batalhão de Operações Policiais Especiais (BOPE, Police Special Operations Battalion), in some cases with the help of the army.[17] In the third stage, a new unit is created. In 2014 there were 30 UPP units in Rio de Janeiro providing services to an estimated 400,000 citizens.

UPPs can be considered an institutional bypass because, despite not being a new formal police force, they operate largely outside the accountability structures, bureaucracy and authority of the traditional police.[18] This separation may be further reinforced with the creation of a special accountability unit to investigate and prosecute abuse by and misconduct of UPP officers.[19] This gradual separation of UPPs from the traditional police seems to reinforce the idea that UPPs operate as a parallel force. Moreover, the UPPs are trying to perform the same functions of the traditional police force in a more effective manner. In this regard, UPPs have tried to create a respectful dynamic between police officers and members of the community, known as proximity policing. The strategies to create proximity in UPPs are mostly training and a system of financial incentives where police officers receive bonus payments if a certain region has reduced its crime rate and level of police abuse.[20] In sum, UPPs also offer a de facto alternative to those using the services.

3   Overcoming Ex-Ante Resistance to Reforms

One obstacle to implementing institutional reforms in developing countries is ex-ante resistance to their creation, design and implementation. People may resist reforms ex-ante for self-interested or cognitive reasons. In self-interested resistance, those resisting reforms believe (or are able to foresee) that proposed institutional changes will eliminate their privileges, no longer foster their preferences or not offer them any benefits (material or otherwise). Cognitive resistance, on the other hand, is informed by a lack of sufficient information. In this case, the risks (i.e. the lack of any guarantee that one outcome will prevail over another) or uncertainties (i.e. the lack of capacity to predict the possible outcomes) are the main drivers of resistance. These two reasons may not be distinguishable in the real world, but for our purposes we will analyse each of them in turn.

Self-Interested Resistance

People who benefit from the status quo may resist institutional change that is likely to force them to internalise the costs of modifying existing practice or attitudes. This problem is referred to in the academic literature as switching costs[21] and may be addressed with compensation for the costs incurred in the transition.[22] Self-interested resistance can also be related to reforms that will impair rent-seeking activities. For instance, people who receive bribes may actively resist anti-corruption reforms that may deprive them of these rents. One possible strategy to overcome this resistance is to strengthen interest groups that will benefit from the reforms.[23] However, there is no guarantee that those who are willing to promote change will not be overpowered by those who are resisting it.

Resistance to reforms can be hard to overcome owing to the existence of two very distinct interest groups. On one hand, there is a scattered, non-organised mass of citizens who could largely benefit from reforms. This group faces high transaction costs to organise and demand changes. On the other hand, there will be a small group of bureaucrats, concentrated in one place. This group can effectively organise against the reform and strongly voice its preferences at a much lower cost. The reduced coordination costs make it much easier for those resisting reforms to succeed. The prediction is that institutional reforms will only happen if the group demanding reforms has more power and influence, or if there is a critical juncture (i.e. an external event that destabilises the current arrangement, such as a war or a major political crisis). Aside from a critical juncture, empowering the group that wants reforms and weakening the group that does not can be a formidable goal.

An institutional bypass may help to overcome such ex-ante resistance by creating a separate institution that operates in parallel with the dysfunctional one, which creates a very different political dynamic if compared to reforms implemented within existing institutions. While a reform in an existing institution would require reformers to engage in a negotiation process with those operating the dysfunctional institution, the bypass allows them to avoid engaging in such a negotiation process. By contrast, if the reforms were happening in the existing institution, it would have significantly more power to resist.

This may also be the case in the implementation stage: the bypass is a parallel institution and therefore does not require the full cooperation of those operating the dysfunctional institution in order to be implemented. To be sure, some level of cooperation will often be necessary. If nothing else, reformers will at least need information about internal processes and mechanisms that will help them to identify problems and try to design solutions to fix them. In the case of Poupatempo, for instance, reformers benefited from the expertise of public servants who believed that reforms would be beneficial to the system.[24] The same happened with the UPPs: officers in charge of the units are often officials of the military police that excelled in training programmes promoted by the Secretaria Nacional de Segurança Pública (National Secretary for Public Security, SENASP). Such programmes promote new ways of thinking about policing. SENASP also provided training and resources for new UPP recruits and, in many cases, it deployed a federally trained quick response force, the Força Nacional, to occupy favelas, guarding the space as the state hired and trained future 'proximity police' officers.[25]

In sum, the two institutions—the pre-existing one and the bypass—can run relatively independently of each other, making it harder for those resisting reforms to impose the same obstacles to the bypass's creation as they could impose if the changes were happening within the institutions they are affiliated with. For example, previous attempts to change the traditional police force, including community-based policing programmes similar to UPPs, met fierce resistance from police officers.[26] Indeed, one of the earliest and relatively successful community-based policing experiments in the state of Rio de Janeiro remained restricted to a relatively small area of the city (a low-income neighbourhood known as Pavão-Pavãozinho-Cantagalo), never being translated into systemic change.[27] In fact, during the scheme's short existence, colleagues often ostracised the officers working on the project.[28]

This is not to say that there is no self-interested resistance in bypasses, as Poupatempo illustrates. In police stations issuing identity cards, for instance, certain groups were receiving bribes to expedite the process to issue legitimate documents or to falsify documents, and they resisted the proposal for Poupatempo to issue identity cards. The fact that the reform was being implemented at a separate institution, however, is likely to have made their resistance less effective than it would have been otherwise.[29]

Overcoming Cognitive Resistance

Cognitive resistance is informed by a fear of the risks or uncertainties related to the possible outcomes of the reforms. Uncertain as to whether they will be among the winners or losers, or uncertain as to whether society overall will benefit from reforms, some interest groups may adopt a risk-averse position, resisting change. A great deal of this uncertainty comes from the fact that formal institutions—where most reform efforts are focused—are influenced by a set of social, cultural and historical factors. These factors are often referred to as informal institutions[30] and they present a unique set of challenges to reformers because there is a great deal of uncertainty about whether or not we can ever capture and systematise this knowledge in a way that allows us to predict, with some level of certainty, the outcomes of reforms.[31] As a result, they are often perceived to be the black box of institutional change.[32]

Many scholars have supported the idea that academic studies need to acknowledge that there is a complex interaction between formal and informal norms and rules of behaviour, and to develop effective methods to investigate and understand when and how informal institutions and norms can reinforce formal institutions, and vice versa.[33] The question is whether it is possible to ever perform this investigation with a level of certainty that would allow us to overcome political resistance to reforms. In other words, regardless of how scientific these attempts to systematise and generate knowledge about the complex interaction between formal and informal institutions are, they may still be plagued with uncertainties because complex social determinants of institutional arrangements are rarely amenable to a few, simplified formulas.[34]

Many scholars argue that the solution to this conundrum is experimentation—that is, the only way to determine whether or not a reform will work is by testing it empirically. Empirical testing offers the possibility of generating information that will dispel resistance based on a lack of information. More than that, experimentation can actually attract political support from potential beneficiaries, who are assured, based on the results of the experimentation, that the benefits of reforms outweigh their costs (or not). There are many ways in which experimentation can be structured. Banerjee and Duflo propose randomised controlled trials, whereas Charles Sabel subscribes to something more akin to a trial-and-error process.[35]

An institutional bypass may reduce the resistance to reforms that is simply based on a fear of unexpected results for three reasons. First, it has demonstration effects. Those who are afraid of change can observe concrete results before deciding whether or not to support full-scale reforms. This is often touted as one of the advantages of pilot projects, and it can also be a feature of institutional bypasses. In both cases, undoing or abandoning the pilot project or the bypass will not generate significant disruption because the original institution was left untouched.

Second, similar to a pilot project, an institutional bypass allows for direct experimentation because it offers the same services to the same citizens who use the dysfunctional institution. Thus the experiment is based on the actual conditions under which a reformed institution would operate. This is an important difference with an experiment that would be located in a distinct geographic location (another city, institution or country) because such experiments do not offer any guarantee that the same results will be achieved once transplanted somewhere else. Some scholars, including myself, have argued that countries should explore institutional reforms in locations with similar social-cultural-historical circumstances to that where the reform is to be implemented.[36] This may reduce some of the uncertainty, but it is still not as secure (from an informational perspective) as 'testing' the new institution under the actual conditions in which it will operate, as the institutional bypass does. Banerjee and Duflo argue that there is a scientific way of conducting these tests: randomised control trials.[37] While these may be useful and informative in certain circumstances, they present significant financial, logistical, ethical and political obstacles in many others.[38] In such cases, an institutional bypass or pilot project may be a preferable strategy.

Third, a bypass may have an advantage over a pilot project because it can be scaled to size without disrupting the original institution. While experimentation with pilot projects can generate useful information regarding possible outcomes for interested parties, in some cases the positive results obtained are not observed when the institution is scaled to a normal size. At this point, pilot projects are often replacing the original institution, which are being scaled back, while the pilot is being scaled up. This can generate significant costs if the changes resulting from the expansion of the pilot project become hard to reverse. In contrast with this scenario, an institutional bypass may start as a pilot project and evolve into a full-blown institution without promoting any changes in the existing arrangement. Conversely, an institutional bypass could be structured such that it can be quickly abandoned without having much of an impact on the status quo.

In sum, the bypass offers the possibility of effectively dispelling fears about the costs and lingering effects of experimentation even more effectively than a pilot project, as illustrated by both Poupatempo and UPPs. Regarding experimentation, the coordinator of Poupatempo reports that the idea was very experimental, and none of the people involved in its design had done anything similar before.[39] The history of UPPs is very similar. Indeed, two weeks after the second UPP had been created, the Secretary of Public Security stated in an interview to the press, 'Dona Marta [the second community occupied by the police forces] is a laboratory. It is an attempt to put in place something that will certainly succeed. We want to show what we believe about public security and how we want to do it.'[40] Both projects were embedded with a high degree of flexibility and decentralisation to allow those running the operations to modify procedures and plans when necessary, reinforcing the experimental nature of the projects.

Both projects have also relied on feedback mechanisms, constantly collecting information about performance and results achieved, followed by a self-reinforcing system for regular improvements.[41] In this process, both projects have significantly modified the institutional culture of their respective institutions, radically changing how civil servants and police officers conceive their roles and responsibilities. Poupatempo has shifted the focus from processes to outcomes, and inculcated a 'customer service' mentality in all units. Civil servants are trained to provide services in a friendly, efficient and effective fashion.[42]

UPPs, in turn, represent a sweeping change in the way that policing has historically been practised in the city. They follow a model of policing based on the notion of 'proximity'.[43] This approach is based on the idea of having patrolmen and women walking the street, visible and serving as an open conduit of state–society communication. In contrast to the 'old' police, proximity denotes fewer patrols in vehicles, greater decentralisation and special training in community communication techniques. The UPP system seeks to enhance trust directly between citizens and UPP officers, creating an orientation towards the public as opposed to superiors.[44] The strategies to create proximity in UPPs are mostly training and a system of financial incentives where police officers receive bonus payments if a certain region has reduced rates of crime and police abuse.[45] Different training and a small salary increase were also used in Poupatempo.[46]

Regarding demonstration effects, both Poupatempo and UPPs started as small projects, being expanded as they gathered more political support from certain interest groups and from the public in general. Indeed, Poupatempo started with one unit and a budget of R$10 million in 1997, but success created long lines and demand for more units. Such additional units have been created at a significant pace, starting with one in 1997 and reaching 32 in 2012. The budget has also increased significantly: it went from R$150 million in 2008 to R$375 million in 2012.[47] In a similar fashion, the first UPP was created in 2008 and by 2014 the city had 30 UPP units. In the meantime, the total budget for police forces in Rio de Janeiro doubled between 2007 (R$1.9 billion) to 2012 (R$4.1 billion).[48]

It is not clear, however, whether it is desirable or feasible to expand these two projects. As it is often the case with small projects, these are infused with an especially large amount of resources and highly enthusiastic people. In the process of scaling the projects, it may become difficult to sustain similar levels of financing and/or enthusiasm. One of the reasons for this difficulty is economies of scale. For instance, Poupatempo has opened units in smaller cities in the state of São Paulo, where the fixed costs of the unit are similar to those in a larger city, but the demand for services is less. As a consequence, the budget has increased by 709 % from 2002 to 2012 but the number of people using the service has increased by only 85 %. This has increased the price of the service per capita from R$2.77 to R$12.10, raising questions about the need to impose limits on Poupatempo's expansion.[49]

Similar questions may be raised regarding UPPs: between 2007 and 2012 the total budget for the police force in the state of Rio de Janeiro increased by 115 %, while the total number of officers increased by 10 % (they had a salary increase of 101 % in this period).[50] This raises questions about the limits of the UPPs' expansion, as this would require significant resources. The availability of such resources is particularly uncertain if one considers that the external sources of funds (federal government and the private sector) may dry up after the mega-events have taken place in Brazil (the World Cup in 2014 and the Olympics in Rio de Janeiro in 2016).

In sum, public institutional bypasses make room for experimentation, but there is no guarantee that reliable data and impartial evaluation of the results will guide the decisions related to such projects moving forward.

4 Conclusion

Institutional bypasses may be able to overcome obstacles to institutional reforms, becoming a potentially useful tool for reformers, especially in developing countries. This is illustrated in this chapter by the cases of Poupatempo and UPPs in Brazil. One could challenge the general claim presented here by arguing that these two reforms are not particularly successful. In the case of Poupatempo, the decline in the quality of the services, its increasing costs and the construction of new units only in electoral years could be marshalled as evidence of its failure. In the case of UPPs, there have been some critical analyses of the initiative, pointing to a lack of legitimacy, unreported cases of abuse and questionable crime rates.[51] Also, public opinion turned against UPPs after the disappearance of a construction worker at the hands of UPP officers in 2013, which was widely publicised in the media (the Amarildo case).[52] This is often brought as evidence that the initiative is at least questionable, if not a total failure. The underlying question is what can be considered a success in an institutional bypass. How can we draw the line between success and failure in these two cases?

The arguments against Poupatempo seem to rely on the assumption that a successful bypass would need to be eternal. This, however, seems to be an unreasonable expectation. Institutions are always in flux. Some are able to change rapidly enough to adapt to new circumstances and not become obsolete. Others fail to adapt, become redundant or dysfunctional and then disappear. But the failure to adapt to changing circumstances should not be a reason to ignore the fact that these institutions have been effective in performing their functions for a period of time. This was the case for Poupatempo. The units were highly functional in their initial years, and the quality of service provided, albeit declining in recent years, is still superior to that provided to citizens by the offices of the old bureaucracy.

The arguments against UPPs, in turn, assume that a successful bypass needs to be flawless. It needs to be designed and implemented with such precision that no mishaps would occur as a result. However, such an expectation again seems unrealistic. Institutions will fail, no matter how well designed they are. The question is whether they are able to react to such failures promptly, and whether they are able to change fast enough to prevent mishaps from reoccurring. In the case of UPPs, the answer is positive. The officers who tortured and murdered Amarildo were charged and are being investigated. Their hierarchical superior was removed from office.[53] And, perhaps most importantly, the popular uprising that brought the case to the attention of the media suggests that the general population seems to have changed its outlook and expectations regarding the police force. Thus it is possible to argue that the UPPs' success may lie in how the project is changing, however slowly, the way in which citizens in marginalised areas perceive, establish trust in and connect with the police force. This may be reinforced with a series of positive outcomes associated with the UPPs, such as a reduction in crime rates and effective prevention, but the change in perception may occur independently of such indicators.[54]

So what is a successful institutional bypass? It is one that opens up the possibility for institutional change, especially in contexts in which change would have been difficult, if not impossible, otherwise. Institutional bypasses may not succeed in promoting change, being cancelled early on while they are still at the initial stages (e.g. the previous community policing experiences in Rio de Janeiro). In such cases, they may be considered failures. However, institutional bypasses that generate some sort of change inside or outside the existing institutions can be considered successful because they have helped to overcome initial (ex-ante) resistance to reform. In the case of Poupatempo, for instance, identity cards are now only offered at Poupatempo offices, and a major digitalisation project for the identity card system was implemented. In the UPPs, the Amarildo case seems to illustrate that the expectations of the marginalised populations towards the police in Rio de Janeiro have changed significantly, as well as public pressure for accountability for police abuse. Such opportunities may allow us to consider these cases as successful bypasses.

In sum, successful institutional bypasses are those that manage to overcome ex-ante resistance to institutional reforms, even if they do so just for a short period of time. Once the bypass is unable to adapt to changing circumstances and becomes dysfunctional, the solution is to promote another institutional reform. In some cases, the bypass may have sufficient malleability to be reformed from the inside. If not, an institutional bypass of the first bypass may be necessary. Thus the success of a bypass does not lie in its longevity or in its flawless operation, but in its ability to promote change, especially when institutions are not malleable enough and become dysfunctional over time. An institutional bypass is a means to an end, not an end in itself.

NOTES

1. Michael Trebilcock and Mariana Mota Prado, *What Makes Poor Countries Poor? Institutional Dimensions of Development* (Edward Elgar 2011).
2. David Trubek, 'The Rule of Law in Development Assistance: Past, Present and Future' in David Trubek and Alvaro Santos (eds), *The New Law and Economic Development: A Critical Appraisal* (Cambridge University Press 2006) 74.
3. See e.g. Michael Trebilcock and Ronald Daniels, *Rule of Law Reform and Development: Charting the Fragile Path of Progress* (Edward Elgar 2008); Trebilcock and Prado (n 1); Matt Andrews, *The Limits of Institutional Reform in Development Changing Rules for Realistic Solutions* (Cambridge University Press 2013); Michael Trebilcock, *Dealing with Losers: The Political Economy of Policy Transitions* (Oxford University Press 2014).
4. Douglass North, *Understanding the Process of Economic Change* (Princeton University Press 2005) 67. See also Douglass North, *Institutions, Institutional Change and Economic Performance* (Cambridge University Press 1990).
5. Mariana Mota Prado, 'Institutional Bypass: An Alternative for Development Reform' (SSRN 2011). http://ssrn.com/abstract=1815442.
6. Ibid.
7. Recovery of Debts Due to Banks and Financial Institutions Act 1993 (Chennai, India). http://www.drat.tn.nic.in/Docu/RDDBFI-Act.pdf.
8. Sujata Visaria, 'Legal Reform and Loan Repayment: The Microeconomic Impact of Debt Recovery Tribunals in India' (2006). http://www.bu.edu/econ/files/2012/11/dp157-Visaria.pdf.
9. New courts will only be bypasses if they have partial or complete overlapping jurisdiction with pre-existing courts. If they have exclusive jurisdiction they are not bypasses.
10. Visaria (n 8).
11. Sujata Visaria, Ulf von Lilienfeld-Toal and Dilip Mookherjee, 'The Distributive Impact of Reforms in Credit Enforcement: Evidence from Indian Debt Recovery Tribunals' (2012) 80(2) Econometrica 497.
12. See e.g. Caroline M. Hoxby, 'School Choice and School Competition: Evidence from the United States' (2003) 10 Swedish Economic Policy Review 9; Caroline Hoxby and Jonah Rockoff, 'The Impact of

Charter Schools in Student Achievement' (2004). https://www0. gsb.columbia.edu/faculty/jrockoff/hoxbyrockoffcharters.pdf.

13. Mariana Mota Prado and Ana Chasin, 'How Innovative was the Poupatempo experience in Brazil? Institutional Bypass as a New Form of Institutional Change' (2011) 5(1) Brazilian Political Science Review 11.

14. Mariana Mota Prado, Michael Trebilcock and Patrick Hartford, 'Police Reform in Violent Democracies in Latin America' (2012) 4(2) Hague Journal on the Rule of Law 252; Graham Denyer Willis and Mariana Mota Prado, 'Process and Pattern in Institutional Reforms: A Case Study of the Police Pacifying Units (UPPs) in Brazil' (2014) 64 World Development 232.

15. Ricardo Henrique and Silvia Ramos, 'UPPs Sociais: Ações Sociais para Consolidar a Pacificação' in André Urani and Fabio Giambiagi (eds), *Rio a Hora da Virada* (Elsevier 2011) 243; Ignacio Cano et al., 'Os Donos do Morro: Uma Avaliação Exploratória do Impacto das Unidades de Polícia Pacificadora (UPPs) no Rio de Janeiro' (Forum Brasileiro de Segurança Pública and Laboratório de Análise da Violência – UERJ, May 2012) 144–146. See also Clarissa Huguet and Ilona Szabó de Carvalho, 'Violence in the Brazilian Favelas and the Role of the Police' (2008) 119 New Directions for Youth Development 93.

16. Stephanie Gimenez Stahlberg, 'The Pacification of Favelas in Rio de Janeiro: Why the Program is Working and What are the Lessons for Other Countries' (Conference Violence, Drugs and Governance: Mexican Security in Comparative Perspective, Organized by CDDRL, CISAC, FSI Stanford, Stanford, 3–4 October 2011) 8–9.

17. The Economist, 'Conquering Complexo do Alemão' The Economist (London, 2 December 2010). http://www.economist.com/node/ 17627963.

18. This idea was originally articulated by Prado, Trebilcock and Hartford (n 14); and further developed in Willis and Prado (n 14).

19. I. Kopschitz, 'Policia Militar Receberá R$ 1,4 Bilhão em Investimentos' (2 October 2012). http://www.rj.gov.br/web/imprensa/ exibeconteudo?article-id=1252512.

20. Stahlberg (n 16) 13–14, 27.

21. For a summary of the literature, see Mariana Mota Prado and Michael Trebilcock, 'Path Dependence, Development and the Dynamics of Institutional Reforms' (2009) 59(3) *University of Toronto Law Journal* 341.

22. Trebilcock (n 3).
23. Daniels and Trebilcock (n 3).
24. Prado and Chasin (n 13).
25. Willis and Prado (n 14).
26. Sérgio Guimarães Ferreira, 'Segurança Pública no Rio de Janeiro: o Caminho das Pedras e dos Espinhos' in André Urani and Fabio Giambiagi (eds), *Rio a Hora da Virada* (Elsevier 2011) 73.
27. Graziella Moraes D. Da Silva and Ignacio Cano, 'Between Damage Reduction and Community Policing: The Case of Pavão-Pavãozinho-Cantagalo in Rio de Janeiro's Favelas' in Tom Tyler (ed), *Legitimacy and Criminal Justice* (Russell Sage Foundation 2007).
28. Sergio Guimarães Ferreira, 'Segurança Pública nas Grandes Cidades' in Edmar Lismoa Bacha and Simon Schwartzman (eds), *Brasil: a Nova Agenda Social* (Editora LTC 2011) 298–299.
29. Prado and Chasin (n 13) 24–25.
30. North, *Understanding* (n 4).
31. Amartya Sen, 'How Does Culture Matters?' in Vijayendra Rao and Michael Waltron (eds), *Culture and Public Action* (Stanford University Press 2004).
32. Mair Licht, Chanan Goldschmidt and Shalom Schwartz, 'Culture Rules: The Foundations of the Rule of Law and other norms of Governance' (2007) 35 Journal of Comparative Economics 659.
33. Daron Acemoglu and Simon Johnson, 'Unbundling Institutions' (2005) 113(5) Journal of Political Economy 949.
34. Eric Helland and Jonathan Klick, 'Legal Origins and Empirical Credibility', in Michael Faure and Jan. Smits (eds), *Does Law Matter? On Law and Economic Growth* (Intersentia 2011) 99.
35. Charles Sabel, 'Bootstrapping Development: Rethinking the Role of Public Intervention' in V. Lee and R. Swedberg (eds), *Promoting Growth, On Capitalism* (Stanford University Press 2007) 305–341; Abhijit Banerjee and Esther Duflo, *Poor Economics: A Radical Rethinking of the Way to Fight Global Poverty* (Public Affairs 2011).
36. Trebilcock and Prado (n 1).
37. Banerjee and Duflo (n 35).
38. William Easterly and Jessica Cohen, *What Works in Development? Thinking Big and Thinking Small* (Brookings Institution Press 2009); Kevin Davis and Mariana Mota Prado, 'Law, Regulation and Development' in D. Malone et al. (eds.), *Development: Ideas and Experience* (Oxford University Press 2014).

39. Prado and Chasin (n 13) 17.
40. A. Freire, 'Favela da Zona sul é Modelo de Ocupação da Polícia' (2008) *Globo.* http://g1.globo.com/Noticias/Rio/0,MUL913118-5606,00.html.
41. Prado and Chasin (n 13); Willis and Prado (n 14).
42. Prado and Chasin (n 13).
43. Stahlberg (n 16) 9.
44. Willis and Prado (n 14).
45. Stahlberg (n 16) 13–14, 27.
46. Prado and Chasin (n 13).
47. Ibid. 22; Renan Truffi, 'Poupatempo Fica 700% mais Caro em 10 Anos, mas Atendimentos só Crescem 85%', Último Segundo (São Paulo 9 September 2013). http://ultimosegundo.ig.com.br/brasil/sp/2013-09-09/poupatempo-fica-700-mais-caro-em-10-anos-mas-atendimentos-so-crescem-85.html.
48. José Beltrame, 'Apresentação em Audiência Pública da Assembléia Legislativa do Diro de Janeiro' (Governo do Rio de Janeiro Secretaria de Segurança, 7 May 2013). http://www2.camara.leg.br/atividade-legislativa/comissoes/comissoes-permanentes/cspcco/audiencias-publicas/pasta-audiencias-2013/ApresentaoJosMarianoBeltrame 070513.pdf.
49. Truffi (n 47).
50. Beltrame (n 48).
51. Cano et al. (n 15); Julita Lemgruber, Barbara Soares, Leonarda Musumeci and Silvia Ramos, 'Unidades de Polícia Pacificadora: o que Pensam os Policiais' (Universidade Cândido Mendes 2011). http://riorealblog.files.wordpress.com/2011/05/pesquisa-upp-o-que-pensam-os-polciais-com-introduc3a7c3a3o-21.pdf.
52. Samantha Pearson, 'Brazil: Where is Amarildo?', *Financial Times Blog* (3 Aug. 2013). http://blogs.ft.com/beyond-brics/2013/08/03/brazil-where-is-amarildo/.
53. BBC, 'Brazil Police Charged with Rio Murder Over Amarildo Case', *BBC News* (5 October 2013). http://www.bbc.co.uk/news/world-latin-america-24362311.
54. Willis and Prado (n 14).

PART III

Institutional Challenges: Integrating Markets and Regulation

Convergence, Coordination and Collusion in Securities Regulation: The Latin American Integrated Market

Jose Miguel Mendoza

Two bills made their way to the Congress of Colombia, the country with the fastest-growing stock market in Latin America.[1] The first included mainstream corporate governance provisions for listed firms, such as rules on precatory proposals to the board, a mandatory minimum number of independent directors and the obligation to set up internal control systems similar to those regulated under Section 404 of the Sarbanes–Oxley Act. After swift passage through Congress, where few objections were raised, the bill was enacted as Law 964 in July 2005. This law is the cornerstone of Colombia's system of capital market regulation, as well as the main reason this small emerging country is ranked by the Doing Business programme among the top five nations in the world under the category of investor protection.[2]

The second bill, filed for congressional approval in 2011, sought to introduce minor reforms to the country's general company law regime. Among its many provisions, it called for the creation of a registry to record the ownership structure of local firms up to the last real beneficiary.[3]

J.M. Mendoza (✉)
University Los Andes, Bogotá, Colombia

© Palgrave Macmillan, a division of Macmillan Publishers Limited 2017   131
P. Fortes et al. (eds.), *Law and Policy in Latin America,*
DOI 10.1057/978-1-137-56694-2_8

The registry sought to facilitate the process of identifying the controlling shareholders of all companies with operations in the country. This measure targeted the use of special corporate arrangements used for self-dealing and tax evasion practices considered to be widespread in Colombia.[4] A short time after the bill was introduced, local interest groups coalesced against the creation of the registry, harshly criticising the government for what they denounced as an obstacle to foreign investment.[5] Congress promptly dropped the rules concerning the registry.

The story of these bills underlines two issues that are central to understanding how institutional reform can shape development patterns in Latin American capital markets. The issue concerns the nature of institutional reform. Over the last decade, new rules for listed firms have been enacted in countries across the region in accordance with the principles and recommendations of supranational organisations. This top-down reform programme sought to enhance the formal institutions that support capital markets through the introduction of corporate governance rules mostly taken from developed nations, as in the case of Colombian Law 964 of 2005. The mixed results of this programme raise a number of questions concerning institutional reform in Latin America.

The second issue involves a political economy problem.[6] Local institutional arrangements can produce significant benefits for interest groups. These groups can easily coordinate their actions in order to block any changes to the institutions from which they obtain these benefits, regardless of whether reform would also enhance overall welfare.[7] Resistance to institutional reform can manifest itself through the open obstruction of legislative initiatives or by subtler tactics, such as the promotion or acceptance of ineffective rules.[8]

The nature of institutional reform and the opposition of interest groups to institutional changes are intricately related in the analysis of Latin American capital markets. Despite the increased pace of growth that regional stock exchanges have experienced over the last decade, capital markets in Latin America are less developed than expected in light of the region's economic fundamentals.[9]

Addressing this issue is no easy task. Although the development of Latin American capital markets faces numerous hurdles, perhaps the most pressing challenge has to do with the dominance of the *grupos*—family-controlled business groups with considerable political and economic influence—which benefit from institutional configurations that allow them to accumulate wealth and exert social and political influence.[10]

To be sure, the *grupos* are central to economic activity in Latin America. However, the influential insiders in control of them can thwart enforcement actions by regulators and block any efforts to improve the regulatory and enforcement infrastructure of Latin American capital markets. A faulty regulatory framework and incomplete enforcement have made it difficult for firms to rely on the state-backed legal system as a means to supply credible commitments to investors. It follows that many firms have a hard time dealing with adverse selection in Latin America's capital markets.

As a result, access to the region's stock exchanges has been reserved mostly for companies controlled by the *grupos* because they can provide credible commitments to investors without relying on the state-backed system. Without an overhaul of the institutions that support the state-backed system, standalone firms will only have limited access to local stock exchanges and the *grupos* will continue to be the main players in capital markets. Nevertheless, since the *grupos* have both the incentives and the ability to effectively block institutional reform, further capital market development may seem implausible.

This chapter tracks how the creation of the Mercado Integrado Latinoamericano (MILA, Latin American Integrated Market), which currently groups the stock exchanges of Chile, Colombia, Mexico and Peru, can help to overcome some of the barriers to capital market development in Latin America.

1   CONVERGENCE, COORDINATION AND COLLUSION

MILA, launched in 2011 with an opening ceremony that took place simultaneously across three countries, currently groups more than 560 listed companies with a total market capitalisation of $660 billion.[11] The project started in 2008 with negotiations between exchange officials from Colombia and Peru, with the Chilean Bolsa de Comercio de Santiago (Santiago Stock Exchange) joining the discussion in 2009.[12] Soon after, officers from these three countries met to discuss the regulatory changes required to enable the integration of their respective stock exchanges. Initially designed to operate as a joint trading platform, MILA is soon expected to become a consolidated multijurisdiction exchange.

The launching of MILA marked the start of a new chapter in the history of Latin American capital markets. Following Mexico's accession to the integrated market, MILA has more listed firms than Brazil's BM&F BOVESPA (Bolsa de Valores, Mercadorias & Futuros de São Paulo,

Table 8.1 Aggregate data for MILA stock exchanges

	Peru BVL	Colombia BVC	Chile BCS	Mexico BMV	MILA consolidated	Brazil BOVESPA
Market cap (US$ billions)	103	262	313	525	1.203	1.227
Number of issuers	214	76	245	131	646	353
Traded volumes (US$ billions)	6	40	46	126	218	875
Number of intermediaries	25	27	32	34	118	90

Adapted from Bolsa de Valores de Colombia, *Progress Report* (2012)

Brazilian Securities, Commodities and Futures Exchange) and almost equals its market capitalisation (Table 8.1).

Although one of the reasons behind the creation of MILA was to promote deeper capital markets, the integrated market may have a significant impact on the regulation and supervision of listed firms in Latin America. First, the creation of MILA has increased the prospects for regulatory alignment between member states, with convergence on Chile's higher disclosure and governance standards being a likely scenario. Second, MILA has pushed the regulators towards a tight coordination of enforcement policies at the regional level, which has already led to the creation of supranational bodies such as the Supervisory Committee and the Executive Committee of Regulators. Finally, the increasing reallocation of authority from the local to the regional level could dilute the ability of the *grupos* to influence policy-makers and regulators. These ideas are developed below.

Regulatory Convergence

Despite an increasing degree of formal legal convergence over the past decade, there are still important regulatory differences between Chile, Colombia, Mexico and Peru. Of all MILA countries, Chile undoubtedly has the highest disclosure and governance standards.[13] Chile's regulatory reform efforts have been driven by a host of factors, including the pressure exerted by institutional investors and corporate scandals, such as the *Chispas* case. The *Chispas* scandal arose as a result of a 1997 takeover of a local listed firm (Enersis SA) by a Spanish energy company (Endesa

SA), during which several of the former company's directors were found to have been involved in a conflict of interest.[14] In the years following the scandal, Chile introduced Law 19.705 of 2000, with stringent rules on tender offers and transactions that involve conflicts of interest.[15] Chilean policy-makers followed up on these efforts with three major reforms, introduced through laws 19.768 and 19.769 of 2001 (also known as capital market reform I or MKI), Law 20.190 of 2007 (MKII) and Law 20.448 of 2010 (MKIII).

This process of regulatory fine-tuning has resulted in high standards for Chilean listed firms. For instance, although *grupos* are prominent in Chile's stock markets, there is some transparency concerning the ownership structure of business groups and transactions between affiliates.[16] This situation stands in contrast to the other MILA countries, where even the largest *grupos* can still conceal their full ownership structures through cross-holdings and pyramidal structures.

Despite the regulatory differences mentioned above, the onset of MILA has set Chile, Colombia, Mexico and Peru on a path towards convergence. This is due not only to the stated intention of policy-makers to ensure that firms listed on the integrated market are subject to a homogenous set of rules but also to MILA's internal agreements, which compel the harmonisation of capital market regulation. Policy-makers from MILA countries have already started meeting on a regular basis to study proposed changes to their national legislations, with the ultimate goal of '[advancing] towards regional regulation'.[17] In particular, there is some expectation that the new integrated exchange will help to promote convergence between MILA countries with regard to the regulation of related party transactions for listed firms.[18]

Recent developments in Peru and Colombia suggest that both countries might already be moving towards improved capital market standards. For example, Peru has embarked on its first major capital market reform in over a decade.[19] As stated by Peruvian officials, the reform is aimed at improving transparency levels for listed firms and to facilitate overall access to equity finance.[20] The Peruvian reform also seeks to enhance the ability of local institutional investors, particularly private pension funds, to invest in capital markets.[21] Moreover, after a recent meeting of MILA policy-makers, the head of Colombia's financial regulator announced that the country had started working on a major overhaul of capital market rules.[22] The reform's key areas include reviewing governance standards for listed firms, enhancing supervision of *grupos* and allowing institutional investors to participate more actively in capital markets.[23]

The process of regulatory convergence described above has been hastened by the creation of the Pacific Alliance, a trading bloc made up of all four MILA countries.[24] The alliance, currently the largest economic bloc in Latin America, grew out of the Pacific Alliance Treaty of June 2012.[25] Although the countries that form part of the Pacific Alliance have adopted numerous measures to facilitate cross-border exchange, MILA is visibly the centrepiece of the new trading bloc. One of the alliance's stated goals, as noted in the Joint Statement of the Presidents of the Pacific Alliance, is to strengthen the movement 'of services and capital' by procuring the integration of stock exchanges between the member nations.[26] At a recent summit, the treasury secretaries of all four current members of the alliance restated their commitment to ensure regulatory convergence in capital markets.[27] The budding internal structure of the Pacific Alliance, which gathers top officers from each of the four member countries, could facilitate legislative action to reach this goal.[28]

Regional Coordination of Enforcement Policies

Aside from the pressures towards regulatory convergence, the onset of MILA has led to the increasing coordination of enforcement policies at the regional level. Over recent years, regulators from MILA countries have entered into a series of agreements that set out a comprehensive framework for the joint supervision of the integrated market. Although these agreements were initially meant to facilitate cross-border cooperation, there has been a noticeable shift towards the creation of regional institutions charged with the oversight of MILA.

On 15 January 2010, regulators from the MILA states entered into a memorandum of understanding (MOU) with the stated purpose of laying out channels for the exchange of information and facilitating the enforcement of securities regulation through mechanisms labelled 'requests for assistance'.[29] According to the text of the MOU, the agreement between the three regulators was intended to facilitate the integration of capital markets.[30] To this effect, the MOU expressly mentioned areas of interest such as insider trading, initial public offerings and secondary offerings, related party transactions, and the operation of clearing houses, broker-dealers and other intermediaries. More importantly, the agreement set out a commitment for

MILA regulators to engage each other in an ongoing dialogue meant to improve the enforcement of capital market rules.[31]

The initial commitments of the MILA regulators were strengthened in June 2011 through the execution of the First Addendum to the 2010 MOU.[32] Aside from widening the scope of cooperation between the MILA regulators, the 2011 agreement set up the first regional body charged with coordinating joint supervision and enforcement activities within MILA.[33] The creation of the Supervisory Committee, a regional organ that assembles top officers from the regulators of each country, may have laid the foundations for the future delegation of enforcement powers from local to regional authorities. In fact, the Supervisory Committee was granted the power to (1) design rules to facilitate the exchange of information and enforcement within MILA; (2) coordinate joint enforcement actions between the MILA regulators; and (3) set up task forces charged with the design of supervision and enforcement policies for the integrated market.[34]

In 2012 the head regulators of the MILA countries met again to execute the Second Addendum to the 2010 MOU.[35] The language included in this new addendum signalled a clear intention to lodge enforcement authority—as well as the design of regulatory initiatives—at the regional level, as exemplified by the 'harmonization of policies' and 'joint design of objectives' to which the MILA regulators were directed in the agreement. The Second Addendum created yet another regional body for the coordination of supervision and enforcement within MILA, the Executive Committee of Regulators, tasked with facilitating 'top-level coordination … with the ultimate goal of strengthening the process of integration between the three markets'.[36]

Although similar in nature to the defunct Committee of European Securities Regulators, (CESR) the Executive Committee of Regulators is starting to resemble a centralised supervisory agency, along the lines of the European Securities and Markets Authority. To this effect it already has the power to lead joint enforcement actions across borders. The Executive Committee of Regulators has also started to channel the unified positions of MILA policy-makers and regulators.[37]

A quick review of the 2010 MOU and its subsequent addenda reveals how the creation of MILA has moved the regulators towards the increasing coordination of regulatory and enforcement policies at the regional level. The next subsection studies the potential impact of this reallocation of authority with regard to the political economy obstacles identified earlier.

Collusive Delegation and the Political Economy Benefits of MILA

As mentioned earlier, Latin American *grupos* pose a significant challenge to the region's capital markets. A unique combination of traits—strong organisational capabilities, the power to exert influence through their dominance of various industries, close links with the political elite, and the capacity to engage in long-term relations with politicians and policy-makers—grants the *grupos* considerable sway in their home jurisdictions. Through their influence over regulators and politicians, they are often able to thwart enforcement actions and block efforts to introduce effective institutional reforms. The dominance of the *grupos* has led commentators to conclude that any significant improvements to Latin America's institutional infrastructure should be seen as a long-term, incremental prospect.[38]

Despite the problems described above, the integration of the stock exchanges within MILA could potentially speed up the process of institutional reform. The idea here is that the reallocation of authority from the local to the regional level can insulate policy-makers and the regulators from the influence of the *grupos*.[39] Under the theory of *collusive delegation*, the allocation of authority to a supranational body allows officers from the executive branch to form a sort of policy cartel with their counterparts from other countries, 'permitting them to loosen domestic constraints imposed by legislatures, interest groups, and other societal actors'.[40] In other words, the concerted transfer of authority to regional bodies enhances the autonomy of policy-makers by shielding them from domestic pressures.[41]

The idea of collusive delegation has been associated with the allocation of authority for trade negotiations within the European Union (EU).[42] By lodging the power to conduct trade agreements at the EU level, policy-makers can direct negotiations with non-EU countries without being subject to protectionist pressures from local interest groups in each member state.[43] Examples of collusive delegation may also be found in the EU's foreign, security and monetary policies.[44]

In the field of capital markets, collusive delegation might have taken place in the EU through the transfer of legislative power that enabled the implementation of directives and regulations. It has been argued that accession to the EU freed policy-makers in countries such as the Czech Republic from the resistance of entrenched interest groups to capital market reform.[45] The regulators in European member states may also have gained some insulation from local interest groups after the creation of the CESR. Although CESR's powers were limited and it mostly issued non-binding recommendations, this centralised forum for the coordination of EU-wide policies might have provided some cover for the regulators against domestic pressures.[46] The creation of the European Securities and Markets Authority, which further lodged enforcement at the EU level, may have enhanced the insulation of member state regulators from domestic interest groups.[47]

Potential examples of collusive delegation can also be found outside the EU.[48] In the case of Japan, for instance, commentators have noted that the regulators increased their authority over local banks after joining the Capital Adequacy Accords.[49] According to Colombatto and Macey, 'Japanese bureaucrats could not obtain the power unilaterally to impose minimum capital requirements on their own banks because Japanese banks were able to resist this attempt.'[50] After joining the accords, the Japanese regulators gained independence from local banks, a powerful interest group in their jurisdiction.[51] In fact, forming part of the accords 'represented a hands-tying strategy in which the Japanese bureaucrats were able to collude with bureaucrats from other countries in order to obtain more discretionary regulatory authority'.[52]

To sum up, the transfer of authority to a supranational body can erode the influence that interest groups enjoy over the regulators and policy-makers in their home jurisdictions. The available literature points to some of the channels through which the delegation of authority can provide insulation from local interest groups.[53] When the power to set the policy agenda is subject to some degree of coordination with supranational counterparties, local policy-makers can become regulatory gatekeepers who 'strategically manipulate the timing, sequencing and presentation of policies and issues'.[54] At the same time, local interest groups that seek to exert pressure at the regional level will face 'high access barriers' that can reduce their ability to effectively influence policy.[55] The transfer of authority to a regional body also grants policy-makers privileged access to information about policy decisions. This can give rise to an asymmetry of information between policy-makers and local interest groups that makes it more costly for the latter to influence policy.[56] Finally, lodging authority at the regional level increases the number of constituencies that vie for influence, which can set competing interest groups at odds with each other and make it difficult for them to coalesce in order to exert pressure on policy-makers and the regulators.[57]

Turning now to MILA, it must be noted that, at present, the internal authorities of each individual country retain formal powers to enact capital market regulation and lay out enforcement strategies. However, as explained above, the agreements that underpin MILA have embedded the policy-design process within regional bodies such as the Supervisory Committee and the Executive Committee of Regulators. The mandate to coordinate regulatory initiatives, as set out in the 2010 MOU and its addenda, amounts in practice to a partial delegation of authority. In fact, under these agreements, the policy-makers of one MILA nation could hardly propose changes that were opposed by the two other countries. On the contrary, as in the cases of collusive delegation reviewed above, regulatory initiatives will probably flow from MILA's regional bodies to the legislative authorities of each country.

A similar argument could be made with regard to the design of enforcement policies within MILA. Although the regulator of each country retains formal authority over enforcement, the 2010 MOU and its addenda call for the joint design of enforcement policies through the Supervisory Committee and the Executive Committee of Regulators. This amounts again to a reallocation of authority from the national to the regional level. After a specific enforcement strategy has been laid out at the Supervisory Committee or the Executive Committee of Regulators, national regulators would find it difficult to deviate from these commitments made at the regional level.

As in the examples of collusive delegation in the EU and Japan, the allocation of authority described above can shield policy-makers and the regulators from the influence of the *grupos*. First, the mandate to design regulatory initiatives jointly through the Supervisory Committee and the Executive Committee of Regulators may in fact resemble the hands-tying strategy followed by the Japanese regulators that pushed for accession to the Capital Adequacy Accords. By delegating regulatory authority to a regional body, the MILA policy-makers will probably have more control over domestic policy agendas. To this effect, the capital market reforms currently being discussed in Colombia and Peru have been framed as necessary to allow for the proper operation of MILA. In addition, since policy discussions now take place at the regional level, local *grupos* can face information asymmetries that will make it more costly for them to 'distinguish viable alternatives, convince potential supporters of their desirability, bargain internationally over new terms, and draft precise legal language'.[58]

Second, the creation of the Supervisory Committee and the Executive Committee of Regulators can shield enforcement activities from *grupo* interference. Public officials in Latin America can hardly commence enforcement actions against a *grupo* without being promptly forced out of office. However, regulators that are seen to act in accordance with the regional commitments set out within MILA can gain some protection from the *grupos*.[59] Since there may be a high cost for breaching commitments with other MILA countries, local officers have a ready-made avenue to resist interest group pressures. Moreover, the *grupos* would not gain much by forcing uncooperative individuals out of office because new appointees would have an equally hard time breaching MILA policies crafted at the regional level.

Of course, the *grupos* could target regulatory and enforcement policies at the regional level. If the *grupos* in each country had similar interests and independently managed to influence the representatives appointed to MILA's internal bodies, the policies set at the regional level could end up reflecting the joint interests of the *grupos*. Nonetheless, even if the *grupos* had compatible interests, exerting influence over MILA policies would still require sophisticated strategies designed to pressure policy-makers acting simultaneously at the national and regional levels.[60] The complexities of this two-level game could make it hard for the *grupos* to individually manipulate regulatory and enforcement policies within MILA.[61]

It is also possible for the *grupos* to reinforce their regional influence by forming coalitions that facilitate cross-border coordination.[62] In fact, the formation of transnational business coalitions is considered to be a natural response to the delegation of authority to regional or international bodies.[63] Nevertheless, before attempting to exert their influence jointly at the regional level, the *grupos* would have to agree on common areas of interest and design strategies for joint intervention.[64] For this to happen, however, the *grupos* would have to overcome potentially significant collective action problems. Although tight coordination at the national level often allows the *grupos* to overcome collective action problems in order to exert pressure on local policy-makers, these problems may resurface as the *grupos* are forced to form coalitions with an increasing number of cross-border partners.

The formation of coalitions may also be hindered as a result of the process of economic integration between Latin American countries—including the Pacific Alliance—which has set the *grupos* in direct competition against each other in product and capital markets.[65] These competitive pressures can block the formation of cross-border coalitions between rival Latin American *grupos*.[66] Even if *grupos* with competing interests found enough common purpose to coalesce, the expansion of MILA to include countries such as Mexico or Brazil could further complicate efforts to jointly influence regulatory and enforcement policies set at the regional level.

2   CONCLUSION

The dominance of *grupos* poses significant challenges to the development of capital markets in Latin America. The available literature on business groups shows how these structures were successfully dismantled in the USA during the first decades of the twentieth century.[67] In Latin America, however, the *grupos* have proved to be solidly resilient to any attempts to curb their dominance.[68]

If dismantling the *grupos* is not feasible—or even recommendable—in the short term, policy-makers and the regulators should focus on ameliorating the political economy problems posed by *grupo* dominance in local capital markets. This chapter studies how MILA can facilitate this process through regulatory convergence, regional coordination of enforcement policies and insulation for the regulators from interest group pressures through the collusive delegation of authority to supranational bodies.

NOTES

1. See Naomi Mapstone, 'Colombia: Latin America's Equity Issue Superstar', *Financial Times* (London, 16 January 2012).
2. See rankings at www.doingbusiness.org.
3. The information filed with the registry would be strictly confidential except for its use during administrative investigations by governmental agencies.
4. Although this duty to disclose beneficial ownership was to be imposed only on closely held companies, it had the potential to affect firms listed in the local stock exchange that form part of corporate groups with public and private subsidiaries operating in Colombia.
5. 'Por qué están bravos?', *Revista Semana* (Bogotá, 25 February 2012).
6. Ronald J Gilson, Henry Hansmann and Mariana Pargendler, 'Regulatory Dualism as a Development Strategy: Corporate Reform in Brazil, the US and the EU' (2010) Stanford Law and Economics Olin Working Paper n° 390.
7. Brian R Cheffins, 'Law as Bedrock: The Foundations of an Economy Dominated by Widely-held Public Companies' (2003) 23 Oxford Journal of Legal Studies 11, 17.

8. Marco Ventoruzzo, 'Takeover Regulation as a Wolf in Sheep's Clothing: Taking Armour & Skeel's Thesis to Continental Europe' (2008) Penn State Legal Studies Research Paper n° 2008.

9. Augusto de la Torre and others, *Financial Development in Latin America and the Caribbean: The Road Ahead* (World Bank 2012).

10. Tarun Khanna and Yishay Yafeh, 'Business Groups in Emerging Markets: Paragons or Parasites?' (2007) 45 Journal of Economic Literature 331, 372.

11. Andres Oppenheimer, 'South American Stock Exchange: The Way to Go', *Miami Herald* (Miami, 16 February 2011).

12. Marcela Seraylan, 'La integración de mercados y depositarios centrales: Experiencia del MILA' in *Estudio sobre los sistemas de registro, compensación y liquidación de valores en Iberoamérica* (Instituto Iberoamericano de Mercados de Valores 2011).

13. For a historic overview of Chilean capital market regulation, see Rodrigo Cifuentes et al., 'Capital Markets in Chile: From Financial Repression to Financial Deepening' (2002) Central Bank of Chile Economic Policy Paper n° 4.

14. Teodoro Wigodski, 'Caso Chispas: Lealtad Debida en el Directorio de una Sociedad' (2008) Universidad de Chile Working Paper.

15. Superintendencia de Valores y Seguros, 'Desarrollo de las Tomas de Control Corporativo en Chile Despues de la Ley de OPAs' (2004). http://www.svs.cl/sitio/publicaciones/doc/informe_serie_doc_trab4.pdf.

16. David Buchuk and others, 'The Internal Capital Markets of Pyramidal Business Groups: Evidence from Chile' (2012). www.finance.uc.cl/economia_puc/images/stories/FinanceUC/conferences/third/Larrain2012.pdf.

17. 'MILA: Strengthening Financial Integration' (2012) Inter-American Development Bank. http://www.iadb.org/en/topics/trade/mila-strengthening-financial-integration,**6839**.html. See also 'Los Supervisores del MILA Calibran Temas Regulatorios', *Portafolio* (Bogotá, 28 April 2013).

18. OECD, 'Latin American Report on Related Party Transactions' (2012). http://www.oecd.org/daf/ca/LatinAmericanReportonRelatedParty Transactions.pdf.

19. 'Peru Unveils Capital Market Reform', *Emerging Markets* (London, 17 March 2013).

20. 'Peru Espera que Reforma del Mercado de Capitales Potencie su PIB', *La Prensa* (Lima, 4 December 2012).

21. 'Peru Congress to Debate Capital Market Reform Next Month', *Bloomberg* (20 July 2012).
22. 'Los Supervisores del MILA Calibran Temas Regulatorios', *Portafolio* (Bogotá, 28 April 2013).
23. 'Esta es la Ruta que Tomará el Mercado de Valores', *Revista Dinero* (17 May 2013).
24. 'The Growing Pacific Alliance: Join the Club' *Economist* (London, 29 April 2013).
25. 'Pacific Alliance Launched in Chile' *ICTSD* (Geneva, 13 June 2012).
26. 'Joint Presidential Statement of Lima' (28 April 2011). http://embamex.sre.gob.mx/guatemala/images/stories/PDFs/DeclaracionPresidencialAlianzaPacifico.pdf.
27. 'Países de la Alianza del Pacífico Evaluaron Medidas Conjuntas para Fortalecer Integración Económico-Financiera', Peruvian Finance Ministry (25 April 2013).
28. It must be noted, however, that regulatory coordination within economic blocs can also face numerous problems, as exemplified by the long process of corporate law harmonisation within the EU. See Luca Enriques, 'Company Law Harmonization Reconsidered: What Role for the EC?' (2005) ECGI Working Paper n° 53.
29. See MOU executed between *Superintendencia de Valores y Seguros, Superintendencia Financiera* and *Superintendencia del Mercado de Valores del Perú.* http://www.superfinanciera.gov.co/NuestraSuperintendencia/memoperuchile2010.pdf. An earlier MOU, dated 28 October 2009, set out abstract commitments to 'facilitate the project of integrating the capital markets of the three countries'.
30. See Section 2 of the 2010 MOU.
31. See Section 2.1.8 of the 2010 MOU.
32. See First Addendum to the MOU. http://www.superfinanciera.gov.co/NuestraSuperintendencia/memoperuchile2010adenda1.pdf.
33. Brian Ross, 'Successful Integration of Exchanges in Chile, Colombia and Peru', *Fix Global Trading* (15 September 2011).
34. It is also relevant to note that Section 3 of the 2011 addendum refers to the joint intervention of the regulators in response to detected breaches of capital market rules in any of the three MILA countries.
35. See Second Addendum to the MOU. http://www.superfinanciera.gov.co/NuestraSuperintendencia/memoperuchile2010adenda2.pdf.
36. See Second Addendum (Section 3) ibid.

37. 'Los Supervisores del MILA Calibran Temas Regulatorios', *Portafolio* (28 April 2013).
38. Ben Ross Schneider, 'Economic Liberalization and Corporate Governance: The Resilience of Business Groups in Latin America' (2008) 4 Comparative Politics 40, 390.
39. The delegation of powers to supranational authorities often shields local officers from the pressures exerted by domestic interest groups. See Sophie Meunier, 'Trading Voices: The European Union in International Commercial Negotiations' (Princeton University Press 2005).
40. Andrew Moravcsik, 'Why the European Union Strengthens the State: Domestic Politics and International Cooperation' (1994) Harvard Center for European Studies Working Paper n° 521.
41. Mathias Koenig-Archibugi, 'The Democratic Deficit of EU Foreign and Security Policy' (2002) 4 The International Spectator 62, 63.
42. 'The decision of the founding member states of the European Community to delegate trade negotiating authority to the supranational level can similarly be explained by this willingness to insulate international trade agreements from protectionist pressures.' See Sophie Meunier (n 39).
43. See S Meunier (n 39) and A Moravcsik (n 40).
44. See Mathias Koenig-Archibugi (n 41). However, some authors consider that there is scant empirical evidence to support the idea of collusive delegation in the EU. See Andreas Dür (2007).
45. See David Brenneman, 'The Role of Regional Integration in the Development of Securities Markets: A Case Study of the EU Accession Process in Hungary and the Czech Republic' available at http://www.law.harvard.edu/faculty/hjackson/alumnipapers/EU_Expansion.Brennaman.pdf.
46. 'National accountability mechanisms could be threatened by agencies' involvement in CESR—for example, where an agency participates in a CESR decision to develop a controversial new regulatory standard but then clings to the moral high ground of needing to be a "good European partner" to justify imposing that standard in the face of strong, national opposition.' Ellis Ferran, *Building a EU Securities Market* (Cambridge University Press, 2004) 103.
47. On the creation of the European Securities and Markets Authority, see Aneta B Spendzharova, 'Power to the European Supervisory Authorities: Explaining the Incremental Evolution of European

Financial Regulation' (2012) UACES Conference Paper, available at http://uaces.org/documents/papers/1201/spendzharova.pdf.

48. See, for instance, Mathias Koenig-Archibugi (n 41).

49. Ibid.

50. Enrico Colombatto and Jonathan R Macey, 'A Public Choice Model of International Economic Cooperation and the Decline of the Nation State' (1996) 18 Cardozo Law Review 925, 944.

51. Mathias Koenig-Archibugi (n 41).

52. Enrico Colombatto and Jonathan R Macey (n 50) 944.

53. For a more complete explanation of these 'causal mechanisms', see Andrew Moravcsik (n 40) 6.

54. Ibid. The author points out that it is harder for domestic interest groups to oppose an initiative designed at the supranational level than it would be for them to resist initiatives developed locally (9, 11).

55. Julian Schwatrzkopff, 'Splendid Isolation? The Influence of Interest Groups on EU Trade Policy', (2009) Berlin Working Paper on European Integration No. 12, available at http://www.gesis.org/sowiport/search/id/iz-solis-90542108. The author notes that the European Commission is somewhat insulated from member state pressure groups to the extent that it does not rely on them on for financial and political support.

56. Andrew Moravcsik (n 40) 13.

57. Julian Schwatrzkopff (2009). Moravcsik also mentions that 'casting a policy as a foreign policy issue augments the executive's ability to craft persuasive ideological justifications'. See Andrew Moravcsik (n 40) 14.

58. Andrew Moravcsik (n 40) 13.

59. Ibid. 8.

60. David Coen, 'Environmental and Business Lobbying Alliances in Europe: Learning from Washington?' in David Levy and Peter J Newell (eds), *The Business of Global Environmental Governance* (MIT Press 2004) 203.

61. Reallocating authority to regional bodies could in fact give rise to what Putnam has described as a two-level game: 'At the national level, domestic groups pursue their interests by pressuring the government to adopt favourable policies ... At the international level, national governments seek to maximize their own ability to satisfy domestic pressures, while minimizing the adverse consequences of foreign developments ... The unusual complexity of this two-level game is that moves that are rational for a player at one board ... may be

impolitic for that same player at the other board.' Robert D Putnam, 'Diplomacy and Domestic Politics: The Logic of Two-Level Games' (1988) 42 International Organization 3.

62. 'Coalitions are helpful to interest groups when groups find it too costly—relative to the benefits of the policy—to lobby alone': Kasia Hebda, 'Interest Group Coalitions and Information Transmission' (2012) Princeton University Working Paper, available at http://www.princeton.edu/politics/about/file-repository/public/Hebda091411.pdf.

63. Amandine Orsini, 'Thinking Transnationally, Acting Individually: Business Lobby Coalitions in International Environmental Negotiations' (2011) 25 Global Society 3.

64. As authority was transferred from member states to the EU, interest groups representing business 'recognized that to access these restricted entry policy forums, [they] must broaden [their] political and information legitimacy by being more representative of economic and societal interests'. See David Coen (n 61).

65. One example of the growing competition between Latin American *grupos* involves the Chilean Saieh group, a media and financial conglomerate. The Saieh group recently entered the Colombian market with its financial subsidiary Corpbanca, which set that *grupo* in direct competition with the local Sarmiento family group, a Colombian conglomerate that also has substantial interests in the media and financial industries.

66. Amandine Orsini (n 64). The author states that business conflicts can hinder the 'transnationalisation' of business interest groups.

67. For an account of how US utilities groups were dismantled, see Steven A. Bank and Brian R Cheffins, 'The Corporate Pyramid Fable' (2010) 84 Business History Review 435.

68. It is not entirely clear that a policy of dismantling the *grupos* would even be recommended in the short term. Ben Ross Schneider (n 38).

CHAPTER 9

Using Judicial Actions to Address Corporate Human Rights Abuses: Colombia, 2000–2014

Laura Bernal-Bermudez

In October 2014 a lower court in Medellin (Colombia) convicted more than 20 businessmen and women for illicit association with the paramilitaries and forced displacement of the Afro-Colombian communities of Curvaradó and Jiguamiando. Among them were managers and former employees of nine oil palm companies, including Urapalma SA.[1] The judge ordered the restitution of the communal lands and financial compensation for the victims. This is one of the first criminal rulings that we know of where firms have been held accountable for their role in the violence perpetrated during the internal armed conflict, creating an interesting precedent for future cases.

This is an unexpected outcome in Colombia, based on the particular historical, political, social and cultural dynamics, and given what we know from the emerging literature on corporate human rights abuses. It is not difficult to imagine why corporations are involved in human rights abuses in a country like Colombia. On the one hand, the country has an

L. Bernal-Bermudez (✉)
University of Oxford, Oxford, UK

© Palgrave Macmillan, a division of Macmillan Publishers Limited 2017   149
P. Fortes et al. (eds.), *Law and Policy in Latin America*,
DOI 10.1057/978-1-137-56694-2_9

ongoing internal armed conflict, low scores in governance and rule of law indexes, and high levels of corruption. On the other hand, governments have adopted several development plans focused on attracting FDI and aiming to increase the country's participation in global markets. It is, however, difficult to imagine that companies (or business people) could be held accountable through criminal proceedings and much less that reparation for victims would be possible.

This chapter uses Colombia as a case study to explore some of the patterns in the use and outcomes of judicial remedy mechanisms, and to locate the Urapalma case in the broader universe of cases of corporate involvement in human rights violations in the country. It is part of a larger research project that uses a mixed-methods approach to consider expanding the access to justice for victims of corporate human rights abuses in Colombia and elsewhere, while also revealing the persistent barriers to justice for those abuses.

The chapter will be structured as follows. First, it provides background information on the evolution of the current global regulatory framework for corporate human rights abuses because these trials take place within this framework. Second, it explores some of the factors that the literature has identified as relevant to judicial outcomes. Third, it describes Colombia as a case study. Fourth, it presents some preliminary descriptive statistics of the data. Lastly, it offers some conclusions.

For the quantitative analysis I will use a large sample of data extracted from the pilot project on Latin America of Olsen and Payne's Corporations and Human Rights Database (CHRD), which is the first Large-N database on corporate human rights abuses. Although these descriptive statistics do not confirm causal relationships between these factors and the outcome (remedy/accountability), they do show some interesting patterns. The CHRD codes the allegations of abuses recorded by the Business and Human Rights Resource Centre. The unit of analysis is a corporate abuse allegation (CAA)—that is, an instance in which some group and/or individual accuses a company of a human rights abuse (the format of the accusation can be, for example, filing a lawsuit, issuing a report or presenting it to a media outlet). It holds information about the company, the violation, the parties involved, the company response and the remedy mechanisms.[2]

1   Global Regulatory Framework

Although international law is capable of coping with non-state actors[3] and there are international treaties that demand states to take action against corporations,[4] the current global framework has not been able to secure binding human rights obligations for corporations. Nor has it produced treaties demanding home and host states to make human rights law binding for corporations operating in their jurisdiction, or to issue domestic laws to this end.[5] It has, however, produced a series of initiatives that have resulted from the tensions between corporate responsibility (voluntary) and corporate accountability (binding), which I will briefly describe below.

In the 1970s the UN unsuccessfully tried to negotiate a code of conduct of multinational corporations.[6] However, after a series of claims by individuals and communities using the human rights language to challenge companies and seek redress,[7] corporate social responsibility (CSR) initiatives started to appear, not only at the company and industry levels but also at the global level (e.g. within the OECD and the International Labour Organization (ILO)).[8]

In the late 1990s, following a series of corporate scandals (e.g. Union Carbide's Bhopal disaster), continued civil society activism, and pressure from governments and international organisations, companies responded with renewed efforts to establish global CSR frameworks such as the UN Global Compact and the Global Reporting Initiative.[9] Other initiatives that took hold in the early 2000s were a series of public-private schemes (e.g. the Extractive Industry Transparency Initiative).[10]

As a result of escalating advocacy campaigns and lawsuits, in 2005 the UN Commission on Human Rights (today the Human Rights Council) decided to create a special mandate, appointing Prof. John Gerard Ruggie as special representative of the secretary-general on the issue of human rights and transnational corporations and other business enterprises. The mandate resulted in the unanimous endorsement by the Commission of the UN Guiding Principles on Business and Human Rights (UNGPs) in 2011.

The UNGPs rest on three pillars that are then expanded in different principles and markers to measure compliance: (1) the state's duty to protect against human rights abuses by a third party;[11] (2) an independent corporate responsibility to respect human rights; this is a well-established social norm, and non-compliance would affect the company's social licence to operate;[12] and (3) greater access by victims to effective remedy, both judicial and non-judicial, including state-led and non-state-led mechanisms.

The UNGPs did not create any new way of looking at corporate accountability; they simply made sense of the mechanisms that were already in existence, relying on domestic judicial mechanisms for redress, and emphasising the need for home states to prosecute corporations involved in human rights violations abroad. This is because some of the host states are thought to be unwilling or unable to prosecute these corporations.

2   FACTORS INFLUENCING JUDICIAL OUTCOMES

Many have criticised the capacity of the current initiatives to modify corporate behaviour, arguing, for example, that the existing regulatory framework is 'seriously inadequate';[13] that adherence to CSR initiatives, specifically the Global Compact, is best explained by 'organised hypocrisy' and not commitment;[14] or that the UNGPs relied on state- and corporation-led remedy mechanisms, failing to consider instances of collusion of state and company interests, such as in cases against Mercedes-Benz, Ledesma and Ford for their complicity in crimes committed by the dictatorship in Argentina.[15]

A useful way to evaluate the reliance of current regulatory measures on judicial actions to prosecute corporations is by looking at the factors that impact outcomes. In this section I will briefly enumerate some factors that could explain the cases where victims have been able to secure corporate accountability or remedy.

Political Opportunities

The conditions surrounding a judicial claim have a great impact on the political power of the different actors involved in the proceedings and in the outcomes. Political opportunities will arise with social processes that restructure existing power relations. They will open up spaces for certain types of claim that could not have been successful before by either undermining existing political structures (in this case economic and political elites) or giving political leverage to excluded groups (in this case victims of corporate human rights abuses).[16] For Colombia I will take peace processes as political opportunities that shift these power dynamics.

Global Pressure

Some argue for the importance of the use by victims of international mobilisation in a 'boomerang effect' to obtain the support from prominent international NGOs and other international organisations, which will create an additional pressure point on those who are involved in the decision-making process.[17] Modern nation-states are subjected to global pressures and instruction,[18] and are often willing to adjust their behaviour in order to obtain membership of a group of more 'rational' actors in the global sphere.[19]

Profile of the Firm

The increasing economic and political power of corporations[20] has resulted in a reduction in the size and power of the state, now more dependent on the market and less able/willing to monitor and regulate the economic activities of corporations.[21] When a particular business is considered to be essential for the overall economic growth and economic development of a country (in terms of percentage in FDI and gross domestic product (GDP) of the sector where it operates), or is considered to operate in a strategic business sector (e.g. public utilities, security or health), this will increase its political leverage to secure impunity.[22]

On the other hand, a high-visibility brand or name makes a company more vulnerable to negative impacts on its image and reputation, and therefore makes it an easier target for victims and civil society organisations through exposés.[23] Lastly, it has been argued that companies that have codes of conducts and human rights policies, and subscribe to global human rights norms, are easier targets for claimants.[24]

The Role of Civil Society

The likelihood of remedy and accountability increases when there is social mobilisation by the aggrieved party, who can use de facto and legal strategies to achieve their objectives. In turn, mobilisation as a group is more likely when the group has a collective identity that exists before the abuse, and not one that is created by their condition of 'victimhood',[25]—that is, when there are pre-established solidarity and trust networks, as well as a structure around which to organise. The capacity of civil society actors to achieve their objectives is enhanced when they have a set of networks that help to give their claim visibility.[26]

Type of Abuse

Corporations can be involved in abuses of all human rights. However, arguably, the predominant paradigm behind international human rights law, which focuses on the enforcement of civil and political rights to the detriment of economic, social and cultural rights, has an effect on the types of abuse that are prosecuted.[27] Also, within this predominance of civil and political rights, the paradigm also has an unofficial hierarchy of rights, which makes it more likely to successfully prosecute corporations for physical violence crimes and the most egregious violations of international law.[28]

3   COLOMBIA'S CONFLICT AND POLITICAL ECONOMY

Colombia has some of the conditions mentioned in the literature that characterise countries where the most egregious corporate human rights abuses are committed, and where achieving corporate accountability is less likely. It has an ongoing internal armed conflict, low scores in governance and rule of law indexes, and high levels of corruption. It also has legal, social, political and institutional obstacles to justice. At the same time, Colombian governments have adopted development plans focused on attracting FDI and aiming to increase the country's participation in global markets. It is one of the countries where some of the most emblematic cases of corporate human rights abuses studied by the literature have been committed, with allegations of abuses involving companies such as BP, Occidental Petroleum, Nestlé, Chiquita Brands, Drummond and Cerrejón. These abuses range from labour abuses, to environmental degradation, to strategic alliances with illegal and legal armed forces involved in human rights violations during the armed conflict.

This country presents an interesting case for the study of accountability mechanisms for corporate human rights violations because it has some of the most important obstacles to justice identified in the literature, and nonetheless some 'success stories' have been possible where victims have received reparation.

Although some argue that Colombia has one of the most longstanding democratic traditions in Latin America, many have identified the causes of the ongoing armed conflict precisely in the grave deficiencies in the democratic process in the country.[29] Colombia is experiencing the longest armed conflict in the region involving several leftist guerrilla groups,[30] right-wing paramilitary forces, drug traffickers and the armed forces of Colombia. Between 2005 and 2009 the paramilitary group Autodefensas Unidas de Colombia (AUC, United Self-Defence Forces of Colombia) demobilised under the Justice and Peace Law (Law 975 of 2005). This is a transitional justice mechanism according to which, in exchange for demobilising and confessing to past violence, paramilitary leaders receive a dramatically reduced sentence. Since 2012 the Fuerzas Armadas Revolucionarias de Colombia (FARC, Revolutionary Armed Forces of Colombia) and the government are part of a peace process, with ongoing negotiations in Cuba at the time of writing.

The actors in the armed conflict have permeated all spheres of society, including political and economic circles. There is an economic dimension to the armed conflict beyond illegal drugs that is only recently being discovered through the confessions of the leaders of the AUC. For example, the paramilitaries have recounted how forced displacement was used as a war strategy, but it also coincided with the economic interests of both the paramilitaries and the economic elites and companies that were either involved directly in the forced displacements or benefited from the low land prices.[31] The paramilitary leaders have also confessed to being financed by companies in exchange for providing security from the leftist guerrillas.[32] Allegedly, the protection scheme provided by the paramilitaries included the repression of all social protest coming from union members, activists, community leaders, human rights defenders and any other individual who was stigmatised as *guerrillero* (a member of a guerrilla group).[33]

Nonetheless, the internal armed conflict is not the only situation that opens the door to corporate human rights abuses. The CHRD holds cases that have no connection with the conflict, such as the abuses attributed to El Cerrejón regarding the resettlement of indigenous populations in La Guajira, the recent environmental abuses committed by Drummond when the company was caught in 2011 dumping coal into the Santa Marta Bay, and reports of police brutality against protesters opposing the construction of dams across the country. In this way, a broad introduction to the political economy of the country is also necessary.

The government development plans from 2002 to 2014 include FDI as one of the most important components for development. Moreover, in the past decade, the economy has moved towards the extraction of natural resources, particularly the oil, gas and mining sector.[34] According to a 2013 report by the OECD, 'The boom has boosted foreign investment, economic growth and government revenues. However, the rising terms of trade and related capital inflows have contributed to a sharp appreciation of the exchange rate, undermining the competitiveness of other sectors.'[35] Nonetheless, the state is looking to increase the flows of FDI to sectors different from oil, gas and mining, where it is currently concentrated.[36]

Land inequality is also a problem in Colombia. According to the United Nations Development Programme (UNDP), 52 % of lands are catalogued as large properties and these are in the hands of 1.15 % of landowners.[37] Nonetheless, the last two administrations (2002–2014) have followed development plans for the rural areas of Colombia based on promoting national and foreign investment in large-scale agroindustrial projects, which could deepen the concentration of lands in the hands of a few landowners and companies.

The move towards the extraction of natural resources and large-scale agriculture projects is problematic because out of a population of 47 million, 3 % are indigenous peoples who occupy territories with an area of approximately 34 million hectares, which represents 29.8 % of the national territory.[38] There are also a significant number of Afro-Colombian communities that own collective territories that extend across 4 million hectares, which is 4.13 % of the national territory.[39] A significant proportion of the natural resources are located in the territories of indigenous peoples and Afro-Colombian communities, which has led to increasing social conflicts between the communities and companies.

4   Preliminary Findings

The following are some preliminary findings for all sectors of the Colombian economy,[40] using descriptive statistics techniques to show how the data in the CHRD is distributed and what possible patterns can be identified in the use and outcomes of judicial actions to seek remedy and accountability.

There are a total of 193 observations recorded in the CHRD, with the distribution across sectors as shown in Fig. 9.1.

Figure 9.1 shows how those allegations that are recorded by civil society are in the natural resources and agriculture sectors, which are two of the sectors that make up 19 % of the GDP and over 50 % of FDI (with 49.2 % going into the extractives sector). While we cannot state that there are more abuses in these sectors, we can certainly say that more attention is being paid to them there.

Regarding the types of abuse and how these are distributed, 51 % involve physical violence crimes ('abuse'), 21 % are development and poverty abuses,[41] 14 % are abuses impacting the environment, 12 % are labour abuses and 3 % relate to health (Table 9.1). This distribution of abuses, showing a large proportion of them to be related to physical violence, tends to support the hypothesis that civil and political rights violations are more likely to be picked up by the media and by civil society, while economic, social and cultural rights remain slightly behind. There is,

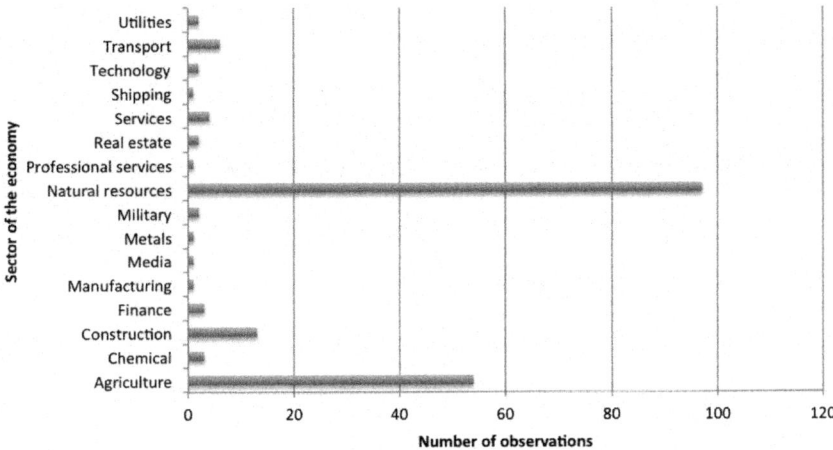

Fig. 9.1 Distribution of observations per sector of the economy (*Source*: Corporations and Human Rights Database, 2014)

Table 9.1 Types of abuse: frequency and percentage

	Frequency	Percentage
Abuse	98	50.78
Development/poverty	40	20.73
Environment	27	13.99
Labour	23	11.92
Health	5	2.59
Total	193	100

Source: Corporate Human Rights Database, 2014

however, increasing concern about development and environment issues, which together make up 35 % of the allegations. Lastly, the large difference between CAAs related to health in comparison with CAAs related to the environment could suggest an under-reporting of health abuses, considering that affecting the environment could have an effect on the health of the local population.

The CHRD records the year when the allegation took place, and this is information that could be used to examine whether, for instance, in the years when there are peaks of particular types of abuse in particular sectors, there were specific turns in the armed conflict, or particular public policies to explain the distribution. This would require further research, but Fig. 9.2 shows interesting patterns.

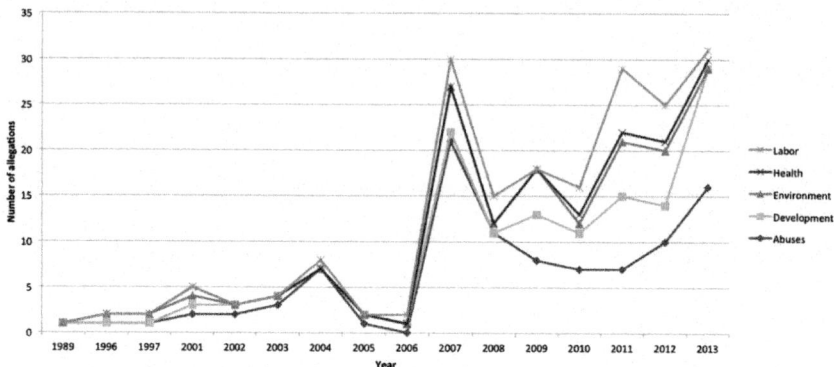

Fig. 9.2 Distribution of types of abuse by year of violation (*Source*: Corporations and Human Rights Database, 2014)

Another piece of information that I find important to examine before moving on to see how aggrieved parties have used domestic judicial mechanisms to seek remedy and accountability, and what patterns we can identify using the CHRD, is who the aggrieved parties are. In 128 cases, local communities were recorded as being those affected by the abuse. This category includes indigenous and Afro-Colombian groups. In 72 cases, workers were named as the victims of the abuse, while in 33 cases the general public appeared to be the affected party (mostly in cases where the environment was concerned).

Lastly, considering that the global regulatory framework has relied on the state and the companies for the realisation of the third pillar of the UNGPs—that is, to guarantee access to remedy for victims—it is interesting to note that in 30 % of the cases the state either was involved in committing the violation (and the company assisted) or assisted the company in perpetrating the abuse. In this way, considering the significant proportion of cases where there was state involvement in the abuse, it is important to question whether the regulatory framework should continue to rely on state- and company-led mechanisms to guarantee remedy and accountability.

Having briefly explored some characteristics of the abuses that have been recorded in the CHRD for Colombia and their distributions across time, sectors and type, I now move to look at judicial remedy mechanisms. In 39 % of the cases a judicial action was initiated. In 35 % of the cases with judicial actions the state was responsible for initiating the judicial action (mostly when there was a criminal investigation), in 53 % of the cases the injured party initiated the action and in only 5 % were the state and the injured party recorded as jointly filing the claim. The CHRD recorded a total of 113 judicial actions, of which 56 % were civil suits (which include constitutional actions for the protection of fundamental rights or *tutelas*), 39 % were criminal proceedings and in 4 % of the cases it was not possible to determine the nature of the action.

The outcomes of these judicial actions, as we expected, mostly tend towards impunity, with 82 % of the cases resulting in no remedy or accountability at the time of writing. However, there are an interesting 18 % of cases where there has been remedy and/or accountability. My broader research project entails a mixed-methods approach to understand the factors that explain these unexpected outcomes. However, for this preliminary exploration of the data I want to see if there are interesting patterns for further research regarding the outcomes of judicial actions and the five factors inferred from the literature and outlined above (i.e. political opportunities, social mobilisation, company profile, international pressure and type of abuse).

The use of judicial actions varies depending on the type of abuse. Of 193 observations, 75 record one or more judicial actions. Of those 75 cases, 60 % are related to physical violence and 24 % to development and poverty. On the other hand, abuses affecting the environment (8 %), health (1 %) and labour rights (7 %) have low levels of judicialisation.

Although the low levels of judicial actions for labour, health and environment abuses could suggest that victims tend to bring judicial claims against corporations when the abuses relate to physical violence crimes, this is hardly confirmed by the data, since this could be explained by less coverage of these types of case by the media. The considerable proportion of cases in which the coders were unable to determine whether a judicial action was taken regarding the labour abuses could suggest that although the media records an intention of filing a claim, they do not follow through in recording what happens after the abuse occurs (Fig. 9.3).

One could consider that victims compensate for the lack of judicial actions for environment, health and labour abuses by turning to non-judicial remedy mechanisms (e.g. administrative sanctions or company grievance mechanisms). However, for health abuses there is no instance recorded where non-judicial remedies were used, and for labour there are only three cases where a non-judicial remedy was sought. For the abuses related to the environment, the situation is different because in 44 % of the

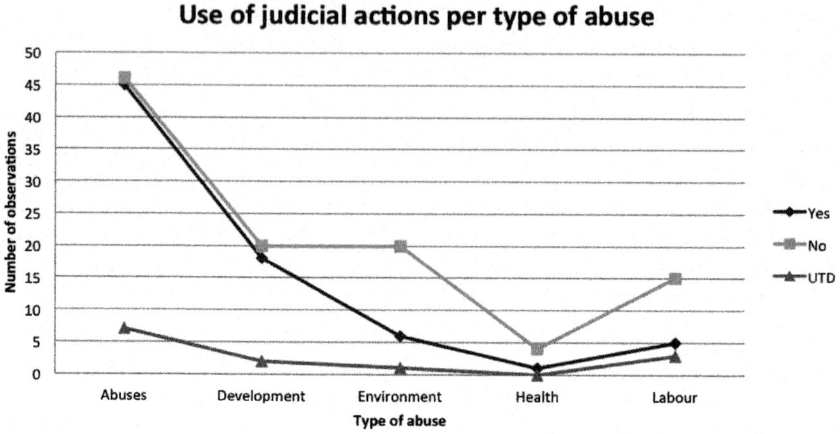

Use of judicial actions per type of abuse

Fig. 9.3 Use of judicial actions by type of abuse (*Source*: Corporate Human Rights Database, 2014)

cases there was a non-judicial action (considerably more than the 22 % of cases where a judicial action was filed). This could suggest a preference in these cases for administrative sanctions imposed by the state.

The outcomes of judicial actions are recorded in the survey for each judicial action as text descriptions. This information is not ready for statistical analysis but it will provide information to create a new variable to describe the outcomes of trials. For now, the CHRD includes variables that indicate whether the judicial action reached court, and if so whether a trial was initiated. Only 12 out of the 26 cases with judicial actions reached trial, of which 11 were civil trials (including constitutional actions) and 1 a criminal trial. This could suggest that although judicial actions for criminal offences, which involve physical violence crimes, are often used, they seldom reach the trial stage. This could be explained either because the prosecutors are unable to identify a perpetrator of the crime or because of the overburden and selective workings of the criminal law-enforcement system in Colombia. Another possible explanation is that victims lack the resources and access to prosecutors to secure the continuity of the investigations.

Using cross-tabulations of the remedy/accountability outcomes of judicial mechanisms and the different variables that refer to the factors outlined above, Table 9.2 summarises the results for the binary variables.

Table 9.2 shows some interesting patterns regarding the role of global pressure, political opportunities, social mobilisation and networks in access

Table 9.2 Remedy and accountability outcomes

	No remedy or accountability (%)	Remedy or accountability (%)	Remedy and accountability (%)
Political opportunities[a]	83.4	1.6	14.9
Global pressure[b]	44.8	3.4	51.7
Brand[c]	96.3	0	3.7
Social mobilisation[d]	84.6	0	15.3
Networks[e]	78.5	0	21.43

Source: Corporations and Human Rights Database, 2014

[a]This is a dichotomous variable coded as '1 = Yes' if the allegation has a '1 = Yes' in the corporate complicity variable, and the date the trial started coincided in time with the following time periods where 'peace processes' have taken or are taking place. 'Peace process' with AUC paramilitary groups: the timeframe of the 'peace process' with the AUC for the purposes of this thesis is 2003–2015. A second 'peace process' is the one with the FARC that started in 2012 and is ongoing. The timeframe for this 'peace process' for the purposes of this thesis is 2012 onwards.

[b]This is a dichotomous variable coded as '1 = Yes' if a foreign state or any of the following international organisations had a role in the case reporting, as other groups involved, as third party or in the judicial or non-judicial remedy: Inter-American Commission of Human Rights, Inter-American Court of Human Rights, UN bodies, ILO, OEC

[c]This is a dichotomous variable coded as '1 = Yes' if the brand of the company or the parent company is listed in Interbrand's 2014 list of the 100 best global brands; 2014 Global CSR Reptrack 100 ranking, which looks at consumers' response to companies' reputation; or in BrandZ Top 50 Most Valuable Latin American Brands 2014. These sources measure the value of the brand, which is derived from the level of visibility of the brand.

[d]This is a dichotomous variable coded as '1 = Yes' if there is a '1 = Yes' coded for the following variables in the CHRD regarding who reported the abuse and other groups involved: repcommunity, repunion or gcommunity, gunion in the CHRD (including cases where there are combinations where repcommunity, repunion or gcommunity, gunion are paired with other reporters)

[e]This is a dichotomous variable coded as '1 = Yes' if '1 = Yes' is in the socmov variable and '1 = Yes' in one or all of the following variables in the CHRD: *repngo, repingo, repun, repmedia, gngo, gingo, gun, gmedia* (including cases where there are combinations of groups involved)

to remedy and corporate accountability. Further inferential statistical tests need to be conducted to determine if there is a relationship between these factors and the outcome, and the strength of this relationship.

Surprisingly, the 'brands' variable, which relates to the company profile, seems to be less relevant when it comes to explaining the outcomes of judicial actions. The two other variables that relate to the company profile and help to determine whether a company is important to the economy of a country are the sector GDP and FDI. In general the data don't seem to reveal any relationship between outcomes of judicial actions and GDP or FDI. This could mean that the importance of the company to the economy, measured by GDP and FDI, is not significant in the comparative analysis across cases. The last company level variable—that is, the subscription to global human rights norms by the company—also does not show any evident patterns in terms of outcomes.

Regarding the type of abuse, there was a remedy and/or accountability in 19.4 % of the cases where there was physical violence; in 22.5 % of the cases related to development; in 18.5 % of the cases where the environment was involved; in 4.3 % of the labour-related cases; and 0 % in those related to health. There does seem to be a pattern where labour and health continue to be sidelined in terms of access to justice.

This preliminary description of the data available in the CHRD for Colombia shows a picture of some of the patterns of abuse and the use of judicial actions. It clearly shows an interesting puzzle and the need for more in-depth research regarding the factors that explain cases where victims receive reparation and the factors that bar other cases from having the same outcomes.

5   CONCLUSIONS

This brief description of the literature on the global regulatory framework and preliminary analysis of the CHRD data shows an important theoretical gap that needs to be filled (i.e. how best to seek remedies for rights violations by corporations), as well as the vast potential of the data recorded in the CHRD. Understanding the patterns of corporate involvement in human rights violations, and the ways in which remedy mechanisms are being used to secure a remedy, should help us to understand the phenomenon, analyse it and make proposals at the policy level. As it is, today academics and practitioners have information restricted to case studies and small-n datasets, which limit the sorts of assertion they can make about where abuses are occurring, which companies are involved and what types of mechanism are more effective in guaranteeing redress for victims.

Understanding other factors that bear on the outcomes of judicial proceedings against corporations involved in human rights violations means recognising the complexity of the phenomenon and the factors beyond legal hurdles and requirements that victims have to face to secure reparations, which extend to the political, social and economic sphere. From the descriptive statistics presented in this chapter, I would like to question the adequacy of continuing to rely on the state and the companies to implement the third pillar of the UNGPs (access to remedy), precisely because of the significant proportion of cases where the state and the company have colluded in the perpetration of the abuse. Regarding the factors that could explain the outcome of judicial actions, it was surprising to see how, in the comparative analysis (i.e. across cases), the variables related to the company profile do not seem to have a significant role in remedy and accountability. There are strong claims in the literature, from activists[42] and academics,[43] arguing that justice for cases of corporate involvement in human rights abuses is an economic story where the state has incentives to protect the company and not its citizens. Although in this preliminary quantitative comparative analysis there is no evidence to support this claim, in the case study of Urapalma SA (included in the broader research project) there is evidence to suggest that the remedy outcomes are explained by a combination of social mobilisation, political opportunities, global pressure and the company having a profile that left it without the protection of the state. This clearly shows the strengths of using a mixed-methods approach.

NOTES

1. Juzgado Quinto Penal del Circuito Especializado de Medellin, 'Sentencia condenatoria y absolutoria.' Radicado 05001 31 07 005 2011 01799, Procesado Gabriel Jaime Sierra Moreno y otros, Delitos Concierto para Delinquir y otros, Víctima La seguridad pública y otros, Sentencia n° 054 of 30 October 2014.
2. For an overview of the CHRD, including its limitations, see Tricia D. Olsen and Leigh A. Payne, 'The Business of Human Rights: Patterns and Remedies in Corporate Abuses in Latin America' (American Political Science Association Conference Annual Meeting, Chicago, IL, USA, August 2013). https://transition-aljusticedata.com/files/Olsen%20and%20Payne%202013.pdf.
3. Phillip Alston, 'The "Not-a-Cat" Syndrome: Can the International Human Rights Regime Accommodate Non-State Actors?' in Phillip Alston (ed), *Non-State Actors and Human Rights* (Oxford University Press 2005).
4. Council of Europe, Convention on the Protection of the Environment through Criminal Law. CETS n°: 172. (1998); Council of Europe, Convention on Corruption. CETS n°: 173 (1999). Also UNGA Res. 58/4 (31 October 2003) UN Doc A/Res/58/4.
5. Andrew Clapham, *Human Rights Obligations of Non-State Actors* (Oxford University Press 2006).

6. John Gerard Ruggie, *Just Business: Multinational Corporations and Human Rights* (WW Norton & Company 2013) xvii.
7. Ibid., xvi.
8. Clapham (n 5).
9. Alwyn Lim and Kiyoteru Tsutsui, 'Globalization and Commitment in Corporate Social Responsibility: Cross-National Analyses of Institutional and Political-Economy Effects' (2012) 77 American Sociological Review 69, 71.
10. Ruggie (n 6) 70.
11. Ibid., 84.
12. Ibid., 91.
13. Surya Deva, *Regulating Corporate Human Rights Violations: Humanizing Business* (Routledge 2012).
14. Lim and Tsutsui (n 9).
15. Juan Pablo Bohoslavsky and Veerle Opgenhaffen, 'The Past and Present of Corporate Complicity: Financing the Argentinean Dictatorship' (2010) 23 Harvard Human Rights Journal 157.
16. Doug McAdam, *Political Process and the Development of Black Insurgency, 1930–1970* (University of Chicago Press 1982).
17. Margaret E Keck and Kathryn Sikkink, *Activists beyond Borders: Advocacy Networks in International Politics* (Cornell University Press 1998).
18. Connie L McNeely, *Constructing the Nation-State: International Organization and Prescriptive Action* (Greenwood Press 1995); David Strang, 'From Dependency to Sovereignty: An Event History Analysis of Decolonization 1870–1987' (1990) 55 American Sociological Review 846.
19. John W Meyer, 'World Society, Institutional Theories, and the Actor' (2010) 36 Annual Review of Sociology 1, 12.
20. Simon Chesterman, 'Laws, Standards or Voluntary Principles?' in Gro Nystuen, Andreas Føllesdal and Ola Mestad (eds), *Human Rights, Corporate Complicity, and Disinvestment* (Cambridge University Press 2011).
21. M Rodwan Abouharb and David L Cingranelli, 'IMF Programs and Human Rights, 1981–2003' (2009) 4 Review of International Organizations 47.
22. Olsen and Payne (n 2).
23. See Clapham (n 5). Also Nicole Deitelhoff and others, 'Business in Zones of Conflict and Global Security Governance: What Has

Been Learned and Where to from Here?' in Nicole Deitelhoff and Klaus Dieter Wolf (eds), *Corporate Security Responsibility? Corporate Governance Contributions to Peace and Security in Conflict Zones* (Palgrave Macmillan 2010).

24. Chesterman (n 20).
25. William A Gamson, 'Social Psychology of Collective Action' in Aldon D Morris and Carol McClurg Mueller (eds), *Frontiers in Social Movement Theory* (Yale University Press 1992).
26. McAdam (n 16).
27. Dustin N Sharp, 'Addressing Economic Violence in Times of Transition: Towards a Positive-Peace Paradigm for Transitional Justice' (2012) 35 Fordham International Law Journal 780, 782.
28. Sharp (n 27).
29. Centro Nacional de Memoria Histórica, 'Basta Ya: Colombia Memorias de Guerra Y Dignidad' (2013). http://www.centrode-memoriahistorica.gov.co/micrositios/informeGeneral/descargas.html; Marco Palacios, *Between Legitimacy and Violence : A History of Colombia, 1875–2002* (Duke University Press 2006).
30. Although several guerrilla groups have been involved in the armed conflict, including the Movimiento 19 de Abril – M-19 and the Ejército Popular de Liberación, there are currently only two guerrilla groups involved in combat: the Fuerzas Armadas Revolucionarias de Colombia and the Ejército de Liberación Nacional.
31. Centro Nacional de Memoria Histórica 71; Juzgado Quinto Penal del Circuito Especializado de Medellin.
32. To some extent, this is also true of the Colombian army, which has legally received funds from corporations in exchange for protection.
33. Centro Nacional de Memoria Histórica, 46.
34. OECD, 'OECD Economic Surveys Colombia Economic Assessment' (2013) 6. http://www.oecd.org/eco/surveys/COL_Overview_Eng.pdf
35. Ibid., 3.
36. Andrés Bermúdez Liévano, 'El Viraje Del Gobierno Por La Inversión Extranjera En El Campo', *La Silla Vacía* (Bogotá, 3 December 2012). http://lasillavacia.com/historia/el-viraje-del-gobierno-por-la-inversion-extranjera-en-el-campo-38017
37. Programa de las Naciones Unidas para el Desarrollo PNUD, *Informe Nacional de Desarrollo Humano: Razones Para La*

Esperanza Colombia Rural (2011). http://planipolis.iiep.unesco. org/upload/Colombia/Colombia_NHDR_2011.pdf

38. Departamento Administrativo Nacional de Estadística, 'Colombia Una Nación Multicultural Su Diversidad Étnica' (2007) 22. http://www.dane.gov.co/files/censo2005/etnia/sys/colombia_ nacion.pdf

39. Ibid., 23–24.

40. There are observations (i.e. CAAs) in the CHRD for the following sectors in Colombia: agriculture/food/beverage/tobacco/ fishing; chemical; construction and building materials; finance; manufacturing/machinery; media/publishing; metals/plastics/ basic materials; military/weapons/security equipment/restraints; natural resources; professional services; real estate/property development; services; shipping and handling; technology; transport; and utilities.

41. This category refers to social, economic and cultural rights, and includes abuses such as denying access to basic needs; destruction of local economies; lack of investment in/exploitation of local economy; encroachment/exploitation of indigenous land/property; no support from local communities/lack of prior consultations; denial of freedom of association; and denial of freedom of expression.

42. Amnesty International, *Injustice Incorporated: Corporate Abuses and the Human Right to Remedy* (2014). https://www.amnesty. org/fr/documents/POL30/001/2014/en/.

43. See Abouharb and Cingranelli (n 21). See also Clapham (n 5).

CHAPTER 10

Multiple Strategies of Financial Regulation Adopted in the Colombian Securities Market: The Case of Over-the-Counter Derivatives

Ligia Catherine Arias Barrera

This chapter aims to open up the discussion, mostly absent in the domestic scholarship, about the different and often inconsistent strategies of regulation adopted in the Colombian securities market. Blanco and Castaño argue that Colombia predominantly implements a risk-based approach to the regulation of its securities market.[1] This was supposedly implemented through the separation of regulation and supervision of the banking and securities systems, and afterwards reaffirmed with the Colombian Securities Law 964 of 2005.[2] However, the case of Colombia responds more to a mixture of regulatory approaches. The evolution of securities market regulation[3] shows a prevailing move towards International Organization of Securities Commissions (IOSCO) Principles of Securities Regulation[4] and OECD Principles of Corporate Governance,[5] some risk-based regulation principles[6] and ultimately a strong emphasis on consumer-investor protection. The inconsistency in the approach to the regulation of the securities

L.C.A. Barrera (✉)
University of Warwick, Coventry, UK

© Palgrave Macmillan, a division of Macmillan Publishers Limited 2017   167
P. Fortes et al. (eds.), *Law and Policy in Latin America,*
DOI 10.1057/978-1-137-56694-2_10

market is palpable in the over-the-counter derivatives market (OTCDM), where it triggers failures in regulation and supervision of this market and affects the use of derivatives in important markets.

This chapter starts with a brief description of the Colombian OTCDM. It then describes the main regulatory approach used in this market, and shows how it interacts rather poorly with a series of institutional issues that are also present in the overall regulation of the market. It then concludes by showing how these interactions affect the development of the OTC derivatives market specifically.

1   BRIEF DESCRIPTION OF THE COLOMBIAN OTCDM

The OTCDM in Colombia was traditionally smaller and less regulated than the Exchange Derivatives Market.[7] Multiple factors converge to explain this situation: the greater confidence in regulated systems as opposed to those less regulated, the degree of development of the Colombian economy, and the lack of information and knowledge about the instrument itself, among others. Moreover, there is a gap in the regulation of the OTCDM in Colombia; most of the rules governing this market are applied by reference to the rules of the exchange-traded derivatives, regardless of the particularities of the market.

The OTCDM includes all those financial instruments traded out of stock exchanges or any other type of securities trading system.[8] The existing regulation regarding the domestic OTCDM is limited to the creation of a Register of Transactions[9] according to the requirements established by the enforcer, the Superintendencia Financiera de Colombia (SFC, Financial Superintendency of Colombia). Moreover, there is an obligation to draft the contract following the standard format approved by the law. However, the terms of such a contract will be enforced only until the time when parties decide to clear and settle the transaction through a central counterparty CCP, when irrevocably the transaction will be governed by the internal regulation of the CCP.[10]

Domestic regulation does not define derivatives transactions. It classifies financial derivatives into two categories according to its complexity: basic derivatives and exotic derivatives.[11] Among the first category are forward, futures, swaps, call-and-put options[12] and others.[13] Moreover, the regulation includes the expression 'any other type of financial derivatives'. This broad category leads to an overcomprehensive characterisation of transactions as financial derivatives. Hence any commercial contract negotiated on the OTC market in which parties have decided to clear and settle through a house of central counterparty risk could be considered a valid derivative transaction. The second category of transactions—exotic derivatives—abstractly covers all those instruments not included within the first category of basic derivatives. The regulation is limited in its nature; it provides a merely declarative list of American, Asian and Bermuda options and the swaps related to credit events. Additionally, it is made clear that mortgage securities (*títulos hipotecarios*)—and any other security resulting from a securitisation process and those defined as security according to the Securities Law 964 of 2005—are not considered to be financial derivatives when incorporated into a simple prepaid option.[14]

2 STRATEGIES OF REGULATION ADOPTED IN THE COLOMBIAN SECURITIES MARKET

In this section I will identify the main regulatory approach used in the OTCDM in Colombia, and explain how it interacts with other institutional elements that are present in the regulation of this market in an unsatisfactory way.

Risk-Based Regulation: The Colombian Approach

Risk-based regulation is a general set of principles that seek to find common and homogenous elements to rationalise the regulatory process.[15] In particular, it prioritises regulatory actions in accordance with an assessment of the risk that the parties will present to the regulatory body's achieving its objectives.[16] This approach to regulation comprehends two stems: prudential regulation and conduct of business.[17] It requires the regulators to clearly define its objectives from the outset. The statutory objectives are closely linked to the risks that firms and individuals pose to its achievement. Therefore regulatory agencies conduct a process of decision-making to decide what risks to address and prioritise. It is highly likely that such a process is biased and affected by some errors in judgement. To explain the subjectivity of the regulators' judgement, the scholarship[18] borrows, from risk perception theory, the classification of two types of error:[19] Type I, erring on the side of caution (judging something as risky when it is not); and Type II, erring on the side of risk (judging something as safe when it is not). Hence any of these types of error, inner perceptions and external factors can influence the judgement of the regulators during the process of selection of risks.

As a result, risk-based regulation requires a strategy of regulation, in which the quality of a firm's internal controls is the focus of attention. The rationale is 'to ensure that a firm's own system of regulation is enhanced to enable the regulator to spend fewer resources monitoring in the future'.[20] This is possible when there is cooperation between the regulators and regulated firms. This cooperation is built on the idea that the primary responsibility of the overall functioning of an area rests on the firms' self-regulation, and that its self-imposed rationale is in line with the regulators' objectives. However, such cooperation is likely to be more effective when the regulators count with enforceable instruments of discretion in implementing their own rules.[21]

Regarding Colombia, Blanco and Castaño argue that the regulatory architecture created in the securities Law 964 of 2007 evidences the inroads of risk-based regulation.[22] They argue that the adoption of a single authority to regulate and supervise the banking and securities market is a manifestation of this approach. We consider that such a view is mistaken because, as international experience shows, adopting a single regulator is not necessarily part of risk-based supervision.[23] In fact the elements of a risk-based approach can be found in the 2011 guidelines issued by the SFC, entitled *Lineamientos Estratégicos*.[24] However, the issues lie in their sluggish implementation.

The guidelines explain how the SFC will carry out its functions[25] as delegated by the president of Colombia. Hence it draws attention to the strategic objectives of financial system supervision. It links the functions of inspection, surveillance and control with specific objectives—namely, institutional strengthening, risk-based supervision, strengthening of prudential rules, consumer protection, finance inclusion and development of capital market. For the purpose of this section the debate is centred on the strategic objective of risk-based supervision.

The SFC created the Marco Integrado de Supervision (MIS, Integrated Supervision Framework). Its purpose is to identify and analyse the 'significant activities of firms, the inherent risks, and the internal mechanisms of control'. The aim is to efficiently allocate the supervision sources according to the levels of risk. It establishes a continuous upgrade of the terms initially proposed and of the methodology for assessing firms' risks.[26] Likewise, the need for a pre-emptive supervision approach is briefly mentioned. However, the guidelines seem more focused on the strengthening of the SFC's capacity and on coordination between internal dependencies than on the implementation of early-stage mechanisms of risk management.

We consider that this flaw deserves special attention. Overall, the SFC's guidelines are still at the design stage and their focus is more on creating a friendly framework for international standards and principles.

Risk-Based Regulation in the Institutional Context

The risk-based approach mentioned above is incomplete and therefore inadequate. Below I will review a series of issues related to its implementation that affect its functioning, and that impair the development of certain financial markets, such as the OTCDM, in Colombia.

Regulation and Supervision

Regulation and supervision are two concepts usually assumed to have similar meaning. However, the distinction between them must be considered in order to understand how authorities perform their mandates. For the purpose of this chapter, regulation and supervision are two complementary stages of the regulators' work. On the one hand, regulation[27] as the setting of standards based on the expectations that the regulators have about regulatees' conduct—that that is, the behaviour regulatees are expected to exhibit in complying with the rules issued by the authorities. On the other hand, supervision[28] alludes to the assessment of compliance by the regulated firms. The carrying out of these functions varies depending on the government's organisation. However, the success of a regulation and supervision system requires the coherent understanding and inevitable link between these two complementary functions.

According to the structure of the Colombian state, the regulatory function is mainly assigned to the bicameral parliament that discusses and approves national laws. However, the initiative to regulate some topics can come from the national government, with the president as head of the executive power. In this case, particularly relevant for the purposes of securities and derivatives regimes, the initiative is conducted by the Ministerio de Hacienda y Crédito Público (MHCP, Ministry of Finance)[29] and is issued through decrees that develop the subject matter announced under the law.

The Colombian Constitution and complementary laws determine how the supervision function takes place. According to the Colombian Constitution, the country's president carries out the inspection, surveillance and control of the financial system. However, those functions are accomplished, by means of delegation, through the SFC, a technical body of the Ministry of Finance. Moreover, Banco de la Republica (BR, the Colombian central bank) has regulatory capability limited to those derivatives related to interest rates, currency exchanges and stock indexes.

To complicate things further, multiple state bodies are organised as *redes de seguridad financiera* (financial safety nets) and share the task of regulation and supervision. This network comprises the MHCP, the BR, the SFC, and two deposit insurance managers (FOGAFIN and FOGACOOP).

The financial regulatory architecture described above denotes an institutional dispersion of tasks, which in turn evidences the need to integrate risk-based regulation and supervision. In particular, supervision cannot be the loose arm of government intervention in the financial system. It is required to integrate the effective risk-led supervision approach with the respective regulation. The surveillance authority alone cannot assume the commitment, while the regulators appear to be estranged from the risk-based approach to supervision. Hence a coherent policy should engage all of the authorities involved in the regulation and supervision process.

Definition of Risk?

When going through the current policy of risk-based supervision in the Colombian securities market, it is not clear to which type of risks the approach is referring. In basic terms it is likely to include credit risk as the main source of systemic risk. Nevertheless, it would be advisable to clarify the term to include, besides credit risk, the other types: liquidity, interest rate, exchange rate risk and so on. This is because any risk can grow to systemic proportions when its negative impact extends beyond an individual institution.[30] The lack of clarity of the term in national regulation may frustrate the implementation of the risk-based approach from the outset.

The Vicious Circle of Risk Assessment

As previously explained, one of the dangers of risk-based regulation systems is the gap between the risk-assessment stage and the enforcement stage. Although this gap is clearly stated in the relevant literature,[31] it is nowhere to be found in the current supervisory approach designed by the SFC. There is no reference to enforcement tools of risk-based supervision because the focus is on reviewing and updating the risk-assessment methodology and strengthening SFC building capacity. Although these two elements are part of the approach, the absence of effective enforcement mechanisms affects the compliance and accountability of the approach itself. Therefore it is advisable to implement enforcement strategies with formal punitive and informal persuasion components.[32]

Regarding the risk-assessment methodology, the Colombian approach in the securities market requires a market-focus study. A general system for the assessment of risk applicable to all regulated firms appears to be insufficient. The degree of complexity and specialisation of certain markets, such as the OTCDM, makes it imperative that the regulators' expertise drives regulatory actions.

Level of Discretion of Supervisors and the Engagement of Regulated Firms
Regulation always involves judgement, but the degree to which judgement is based on observable facts as opposed to what might happen in the future is where differences can occur.[33] Thus when adopting risk-based regulation, it is crucial to establish clearly the degree of discretion that the regulators have. This is translated into powers of intervention and the expectation that the regulators will be more intrusive in order to pre-empt the materialisation of future risks,[34] denoting the forward-looking character of risk- and judgement-led regulation.

The aim is to engage the regulators and regulatees in achieving the general objective of financial stability through the efficient design and execution of a risk-based approach to regulation. As stated by Julia Black, 'risk-based regulation is a modern compromise between the acknowledgment of the realities of the de-centred regulatory space and the limitations of the regulators in providing public goods'.[35] Thus firms are expected to produce internal governance and controls to link financial systems objectives and internal management needs.[36]

In Colombia these internal managerial controls are required to be further developed by the national regulators according to market needs. Here the risk-based approach should be complemented with a notion of prudential and conduct of business regulation. Indeed, the IMF recommends to the SFC and the BR to work on the effective coordination tools for risk assessment and prudential and conduct enforcement. In the IMF's opinion the upgrade of the risk-based supervision will facilitate the monitoring and management of concentration of risk, as well as the control of leverage and collateral quality in the OTCDM.[37]

On the one hand, prudential supervision involves:

not only monitoring the compliance of systematically important institutions with safety and soundness[38] standards, but also evaluating whether these standards are sufficient to protect the rest of the economy adequately from financial distress in a systematically important firm.

This is the macroprudential supervision seeking to limit financial system distress, which is particularly important when regulating highly interconnected and systematically important institutions in the OTCDM. Moreover, it includes microprudential supervision, which is the day-to-day supervision of individual financial institutions.[39] The focus of microprudential supervision is the safety and soundness of individual institutions and also consumer protection. On the other hand, the conduct of business is concerned with consumer protection.[40] However, rather than focusing on the protection of clients from the insolvency of individual financial institutions, it emphasises safeguarding clients from unfair practices.[41]

Although the Colombian regime has an evolving trend of consumer protection[42]—this is one of the strategic objectives of the SFC—there is no link between risk-based supervision and financial consumer protection.[43] Consumer regulation in Colombia is based largely on an extension of the information asymmetry and market failure argument, but conversely it is not based on the overall financial stability objective. Therefore, in order to connect the consumer-investor protection regime with risk-based regulation, I propose to complement that pro-consumer-investor approach by linking market failures[44] in the investor protection feature to the mitigation of systemic risks.[45] Indeed, the consumer protection scheme designed by the SFC could be integrated as one of the pillars of the risk-based approach to regulation and supervision.

Are the IOSCO and OECD Principles Approaches to Regulation?

Although international standards and principles are the trend within financial regulation, they are not regulatory strategies per se. Even so, their national implementation has a positive effect because they pursue the harmonisation of the minimal requirements that will facilitate the integration of safe and sound international markets.

The IOSCO Principles of Securities Regulation and the OECD Principles of Corporate Governance are indubitably useful tools to illustrate strategies of conduct of business and microprudential regulation. However, they are not regulatory strategies in themselves. Therefore their implementation requires the governmental plan within broader, well-directed strategies of regulation. Otherwise the task will not have the expected outcome. It is not about following international trends because it is useful; it is about having a clear strategy to regulate and supervise a market like the securities market.

Only when Colombian regulation is committed to having a coherent framework of regulatory strategies will it be able to enhance confidence in the market, and, more important, improve the resilience of the securities market. The concept of resilience[46] could be the core of a coherent dialogue between the regulators and supervisors of the Colombian securities market, and all of this as part of the comprehensive adoption of a risk-based approach to regulation.

3   WHAT HINDERS THE GROWTH OF OTCDMs IN COLOMBIA?

The traditional rationale for regulating financial markets is the correction of market failures related to asymmetric information and to externalities. The aim is to reduce systemic risks and to ensure that markets are fair, efficient, and transparent.[47] Consistently, there is a persistent movement towards better regulation and a daunting concern to obtain competitive advantage through efficient regulation.[48] One of the difficulties faced by the financial regulators is to deal effectively with the complexity and the rapid pace of the growth of financial markets, especially in complex markets, such as the OTCDM. The design of 'good rules'[49] and coherent regulatory strategies, which support strong, safe and sound markets and avoid malign effects, is not easily achieved.[50] In addition, conducting financial regulation in a manner that procures strong markets, and maintains the balance between securities markets rules and financial sector growth, is challenging.[51]

Accordingly, I argue that the lack of coherence in the design and enforcement of regulatory strategies affects the development of financial markets because it creates a dysfunctional combination of principles and rules. In this sense, the regulators draft relevant rules for each market without a 'plan route' to understand how the risk-based approach, or any other approach, can illustrate the supervision task. This has important implications, such as knowing the market, identifying the risks, prioritising regulatory actions and resources, developing early risk identification and intervention tools, and the implementation of effective enforcement powers. The inconsistency of the Colombian securities approach to regulation has affected the development of OTC derivatives. This section concludes by exploring three issues that affect the development of the OTCDM, which are related to the lack of clarity in the supervision approach adopted in Colombia.

As explained in previous sections, the OTC market is not covered by a proper regulation system. Instead, these transactions are partially governed by the exchanged-traded transactions regime. This shows that the

Colombian regulators have not designed a specialised regime that responds to the particularities of the OTCDM. As a result, the rules governing these transactions come from private contract law and commercial law, as well as the standard contracts issued by intermediaries in the market.

The first issue affecting the growth of the OTCDM in Colombia is the lack of regulatory definition of these transactions. The first task is to set out a comprehensive definition[52] of these instruments of debt financing and raising capital,[53] commonly used by financial and non-financial institutions. It is generally accepted that 'the goal of all derivatives products is to obtain funding at a preferential rate or to take speculative advantage of a movement in a financial market for the investing institution'.[54] This means that, aside from the abovementioned functions, financial derivatives also have a speculative intention.[55]

A clear definition of derivatives in the domestic regulation of OTC derivatives would potentially broaden the scheme to include as many transactions as possible, allowing market participants to create any type of transaction that falls within the derivatives regime. Thus the clarity regarding the regime results in reliability in the rules, and higher levels of transparency and accountability.[56] This lack of certainty regarding the concept of financial derivatives deprecates the clear understanding that both the regulators[57] and market actors are expected to have in a reliable regulatory environment.

The second issue affecting the consolidation of the OTCDM in Colombia is the absence of market infrastructure regulation, in particular the post-trade infrastructure, the CCP.[58] Clearing—the function by which the credit risk is managed—can be carried out centrally by CCPs or bilaterally.[59] Before the Global Financial Crisis (GFC) the vast majority of OTC derivatives were cleared bilaterally with inadequate collateralisation, prompting instability in the market and concretising systemic risk. The post-GFC regulatory reforms promote the use of CCPs, seeking the enhancement and protection of financial market stability. In particular, in the OTCDM, central clearing is focused on the reduction of credit risk.

Immediately after the GFC, the Government of Colombia[60] and the largest market participants[61] set out some key ways to strengthen national capital market infrastructure. Importantly, these proposals were inspired by the international regulatory responses to the failures that contributed to the GFC. First, aiming to provide better credit risk management of OTC derivatives[62] and provision of a clearing and settlement system, the government issued regulation for a CCP in the form of a clearing house.

Unfortunately, after the creation of the Colombian-based clearing house in 2008,[63] the regulation was derogated[64] and has not been replaced. In consequence, the Colombian OTCDM has a clearing house functioning without state regulation.

The rationale is that the CCP imposes itself as the legal counterparty to every trade. This arrangement places the CCP in a unique position in that it has direct interaction and counterparty risk exposure with each trading party.[65] With the creation of the CCP, all those interested in trading derivatives must comply with certain membership requirements.[66] The CCP interposing itself in every trade will support the losses of any cleared transaction. Hence the default will not only affect the large dealer—as it is without a CCP—but will be mutualised among all of the CCP members. The existence of a CCP reduces the risk that the failure of a single counterparty can cascade into a systemic crisis. To this end, a CCP uses several mechanisms to reduce and transform risk—for instance, multilateral netting[67] of trades, margining,[68] loss mutualisation,[69] default management[70] and by imposing more effective controls on all participants. However, the debate lies in the expected benefits that CCPs might bring to the OTCDM—namely improving market resilience by reducing counterparty risk and increasing transparency.[71]

The third issue affecting the consolidation of the OTCDM in Colombia is the limited variety of OTC transactions. This is a consequence of the precarious knowledge of the needs of the domestic market, and the subsequent lack of specialised regulation. After the GFC the national government called for a diversification of financial investment instruments, recognising that the local derivatives market had reduced types of derivatives transactions. The aim was to increase the offering of these financial instruments to both national and international investors, making the Colombian financial system more investor-friendly. However, after seven years the government's initiative has not been achieved and the gaps in OTCDM regulation remain.

4   FINAL REMARKS

The recommendation for the Colombian authorities is to design a regulation and supervision approach to the OTCDM. The strategies of regulation need to avoid the undesirable effects of the widespread reliance on internal risk management models and processes, and the permissiveness of self-regulation. Therefore, the regulators should be empowered with more intrusive intervention tools, with a strong emphasis on the early detection and prevention of risks. Likewise, market infrastructure tools can serve an important role in enhancing the transparency of information available to the relevant authorities and the public, promoting market stability. Finally, the approach needs to assess the particularities of the Colombian market, so the focus should be on increasing the use of regular OTC derivatives for commodities.

NOTES

1. Constanza Blanco and Jorge Castaño Gutierrez, 'La Nueva ley del Mercado de Valores: Manifestación del Derecho Regulativo' (2007) Revista Contexto Universidad Externado de Colombia, 12.
2. Ibid.
3. Constanza Blanco, 'La Regulación como herramienta de protección a los inversionistas' (2010) Revista Contexto Universidad Externado de Colombia, 86.
4. IOSCO Principles of Securities Regulation with three general principles: "protection of investors, ensuring that markets are fair, efficient and transparent, and reducing systemic risk". http://www.iosco.org/library/pubdocs/pdf/IOSCOPD154.pdf. Additionally the incorporation of IOSCO principles is one of the main objectives of Colombian Securities Law 964 of 2005.
5. OECD Principles of Corporate Governance. http://www.oecd.org/corporate/ca/corporategovernanceprinciples/31557724.pdf. These principles are followed on a voluntary basis and in Colombia should be interpreted along with the corporate governance regulation Law 222 of 1995.
6. Following the UK's experience, the source of risk-based regulation principles is the Financial Services Authority risk-assessment framework. In general they are market confidence risk, public understanding risk, consumer protection risk and financial crime risk. http://www.rdec.gov.tw/public/Data/851414194871.pdf.
7. According to the last IMF report 'the derivatives market in Colombia has grown in recent years, mainly to hedge currency and maturity mismatches for real sector currency exchange transactions. The OTC derivatives market is the largest market, dwarfing derivatives traded at the Colombian Stock Exchange or other trading platforms. Equity-based derivatives and local commodities-based derivatives are traded

only in small volumes. At end-2014, gross derivatives exposures in OTC market mounted to US$ 65 billion'. IMF, 'Colombia: 2015 Article IV Consultation-Press Release; Staff Report; and Statement by the Executive Director for Colombia' (2015) 32.

8. Financial Superintendence of Colombia (FSC), Financial and Accounting Circular 100 of 1995 (FAC 100/95), Chapter XVIII: Financial Derivatives and Structured Products ... 2.19 Over-the-counter market. See 'The trading systems of the OTC securities offer registry services to OTC derivatives. These trading platforms are Sistema Electrónico de Negociación, Central Bank of Colombia for public debt instruments; GFI Securities Colombia; ICAP Colombia and Tradition Colombia offer registry and trading services exclusively to their members; *Depósito Central de Valores*, registers all types of authorised securities transactions.' Carlos León and Jhonatan Perez, 'Caracterización y Comparación del Mercado OTC de Valores en Colombia' (2014) 16 (31) Revista Economía Institucional, 226.

9. Decree 2555 of 2010. Section 2.35.1.6.1 (Section 3 Decree 4765 of 2011) Registry of Transactions.

10. FSC, FAC 100/95 Chapter XVIII 3. Minimum Requirements for Derivatives Trading or Offer of Structured Products.

11. FSC, FAC 100/95. Chapter XVIII 5. Types of Financial Derivatives and Structures Products.

12. FSC, FAC 100/95. Chapter XVIII: 5.1.1–5.1.4 Basic Financial Derivatives ('Plain vanilla').

13. FSC, FAC 100/95. Chapter XVIII5.1. Basic Financial Derivatives 5.1.6 Others'.

14. Ibid.

15. Julia Black, 'The Development Of Risk-Based Regulation in Financial Services: Just 'Modelling Through'?' in Julia Black, Martin Lodge Martin and Mark Thatcher (eds), *Regulatory Innovation A Comparative Analysis* (Edward Elgar Publishing 2005).

16. Julia Black, 'The Emergence of Risk-Based Regulation and the New Public Risk Management in the United Kingdom' (2005) Public Law 512.

17. Ibid. 20.

18. See e.g. Black (n 15). Also Julia Black, 'Risk and Regulatory Policy: Improving the Governance of Risk' in OECD (corp. ed), *Risk-based Regulation: Choices, Practices and Lessons Being Learnt* (OECD 2010).

19. Kristin Schrader-Frechette, *Risk and Rationality* (University of California Press, Berkeley 1991).

20. Robert Baldwin, Martin Cave and Martin Lodge, *Understanding Regulation* (Oxford University Press 2012) 105.

21. Julia Black and Robert Baldwin, 'When Risk-Based Regulation Aims Low: Approaches And Challenges' (2012) 6 Regulation and Governance 2.

22. Blanco and Gutierrez (n 1) 12.

23. Julia Black, 'The Development of Risk Based Regulation in Financial Services: Canada, the UK and Australia' A Research Report (ESRC Centre for the Analysis of Risk and Regulation London School of Economics and Political Science, September 2004) https://www.lse.ac.uk/collections/law/staff%20publications%20full%20text/black/risk%20based%20regulation%20in%20financial%20services.pdf.

24. SFC, *Lineamientos Estratégicos 2011–2014* https://www.superfinanciera.gov.co/SFCant/NuestraSuperintendencia/lineamientosestrategicos2011–14.pdf.

25. Decree 2555 of 2010. Section 11.2.1.3.1.

26. The IMF acknowledges that Colombia's derivatives regulatory regime is starting to address the risks of the expansion of the OTCDM. IMF (n 7).

27. See Rosa *M. Lastra*, 'The Governance Structure for Financial Regulation and Supervision in Europe' 10 Columbia Journal of European Law 49, 60.

28. Ibid.

29. Decree 4712 of 2008 Section 20 about the structure of the Ministry of Finance establishes the objective to set up definition, design and implementation of the country's economic policy.

30. Rosa Lastra, 'Defining Forward Looking, Judgement-Based Supervision' (2013) 14 Journal of Banking Regulation 221.

31. Julia Black, 'Risk and Regulatory Policy: Improving the Governance of Risk'. *Risk-based Regulation: Choices, Practices and Lessons Being Learnt (2010) OECD* 215.

32. Baldwin, Cave and Lodge, *Understanding Regulation* (n 20) 422.

33. Andromachi Georgosouli, 'Judgement-Led Regulation: Reflections on Data And Discretion' (2013) 14 Journal of Banking Regulation 209.

34. Ibid.

35. Julia Black, 'The Emergence of Risk-Based Regulation' (n 16) 512.

36. Mads Adenas and Iris H-Y Chiu, *The Foundations and Future of Financial Regulation: Governance for Responsibility* (Routledge 2014) 101.
37. IMF, 'Colombia: 2015 Article IV Consultation-Press Release; Staff Report; and Statement by the Executive Director for Colombia' (n vii) 32.
38. Bert Ely, 'Financial Regulation', The Concise Encyclopaedia of Economics (2008) Library of Economics and Liberty. http://www.econlib.org/library/Enc/FinancialRegulation.html.
39. Lastra, 'Defining Forward Looking' (n 30) 222.
40. The Financial Conduct Authority: Approach to Regulation June 2011 http://www.fsa.gov.uk/pubs/events/fca_approach.pdf
41. Financial Services Authority, The Financial Conduct Authority: Approach to Regulation June 2011. http://www.fsa.gov.uk/pubs/events/fca_approach.pdf.
42. Law 1328 of 2009 Law of Financial Consumer; Decree 2555 of 2010, Articles 2.34.2.1.1 to 2.34.2.1.9 Unit of Financial Consumer Defence, and Article 11.2.1.4.11 (art. 20 Decree 4327 of 2005 Direction of Financial Consumer Protection). Complemented by Law 1480 of 2011 Consumer Protection Statutory Law, Article 57 Judicial Functions to the SFC, and Decree 710 of 2012.
43. Ligia Catherine Arias Barrera, 'Derecho Del Consumidor Y Su Aplicación En El Sector Financiero' (2008) 7 Revista E-mercatoria 1.
44. Regarding Information Asymmetry as market failure, Decision of the Colombian Constitutional Court. Sentencia Corte Constitucional C—973 de 2002.
45. Adenas and Chiu (n 37) 136.
46. Georgosouli (n 34).
47. International Organisation of Securities Regulation (IOSCO), 'Objectives and Principles of Securities Regulation'.
48. Committee on Capital Markets Regulation, Interim Report of the Committee on Capital Markets Regulation (2006).
49. About the discussion of what is 'good regulation', see Baldwin, Cave and Lodge, *Understanding Regulation* (n 20) ch 3.
50. Julia Black, 'The Legal and Institutional Preconditions for Strong Securities Markets' (2001) 48 UCLA Law Review 781.
51. Jose Miguel Mendoza, 'The Fractures in Latin American Finance' http://papers.ssrn.com/sol3/papers.cfm?abstract_id=2394708.

52. Timothy E. Lynch, 'Derivatives: A Twenty-First Century Understanding' (2011) Indiana Legal Studies Research Paper n° 187,14. http://ssrn.com/abstract=1785634.
53. Schyuler Henderson, *Henderson on Derivatives* (Lexis Nexis Butterworths 2003) 1.
54. See Schuyler Henderson speaking on December 8, 1997 at *Legal Accounting and Control Challenges of Credit Derivatives,* IBC. Cited by Alastair Hudson, *The Law on Financial Derivatives* (2nd edn, Sweet & Maxwell 1998) 9.
55. See Lynn A Stout, 'Why The Law Hates Speculators: Regulation And Private Ordering In The Market For OTC Derivatives' (1999) 48 Duke Law Journal 741. Also Hobhouse J, in *Morgan Grenfell & Co Ltd. v Welwyn Hatfield District Council (Islington London Borough Council, Third Party)'* [1995] 1 All ER 1, held that derivatives have 'at least potentially a speculative character deriving from the fact that the obligations of the parties are to be ascertained by reference to a fluctuating market rate which may be higher or lower than the fixed rate at any time'.
56. Lynn A Scout, 'Derivatives and the Legal Origin of the 2008 Credit Crisis' (2011) Harvard Business Law Review 1.
57. Federal Reserve Bank of New York, *Policy Perspectives on OTC Derivatives Markets,* Staff Report n° 424 (March 2010).
58. The post-trade market infrastructure is the term use to include, among others, trade repositories and CCPs. Bank of International Settlements, 'CPSS –IOSCO Principles for Financial Market Infrastructures' (BIS, April 2012). http://www.bis.org/cpmi/publ/d101a.pdf.
59. John Gregory, *Central Counterparties: Mandatory Clearing and Bilateral Margin Requirements for OTC Derivatives* (Wiley Finance Series 2014) 6.
60. The repercussions of the GFC in Colombia affected both the private and the public sectors www.simposiodefinanzas.com/ingles/pdf/analisis_al_comportamiento_del_mercado.pdf.
61. Conference of Colombian Stock Exchange and Colombian Government discussing the required improvements of the derivatives market, both exchange and OTC. www.acolgen.org.co/jornadas-2gen/BVCXMDesarrolloMercadoDerivados.pdf.
62. FSC, FAC 100/95. Chapter XVIII: Financial Derivatives and Structured Products.
63. Decree 2893 of 2007.

64. Decree 2555 of 2010.
65. Douglas D. Evanoff, Daniela Russo and Robert S.Steigerwald, 'Policymakers, researchers, and practitioners discuss the role of central counterparties' (2006) 4Q Economic Perspectives- Federal Reserve Bank of Chicago and European Central Bank. http://econpapers.repec.org/article/fipfedhep/y_3a2006_3ai_3aqiv_3ap_3a2-21_3an_3av.30no.4.htm
66. Craig Pirrong, *The Economics of Central Clearing: Theory and Practice* (ISDA Discussion Papers 2011).
67. 'Netting' is used in derivatives markets (1) to determine the 'net' value of a series of transactions between market participants; and (2) to 'net' the payments to be made by the parties on a given coupon payment date or on a termination or maturity date. See Philip Wood, *Law and Practice of International Finance* (Sweet and Maxwell 2008) 217.
68. CCPs take margin from their members against the risk of the portfolios they clear. See Gregory (n 62) 75.
69. According to the clearing principle of loss mutualisation, the losses above the resources contributed by the defaulter are shared between CCP members.
70. In the event of a clearing member default, CCPs have general rights in relation to managing the risk of that member's portfolio, including suspension of trading, closing out positions, transferring client positions and liquidating margin. See Joanne Braithwaite, 'The Inherent Limits of 'Legal Devices': Lessons for the Public Sector's Central Counterparty Prescription for the OTC Derivatives Market' (2011) 12(1) European Business Organisation Law Review 87, 90.
71. Stephen Cecchetti, Jacob Gyntelberg and Marc Hollanders, 'Central Counterparties for Over-the-Counter Derivatives' (2009) BIS Quarterly Review 45.

CHAPTER 11

A Counterhistory of Anti-Trust in Latin America

Andrés Palacios Lleras

The history of anti-trust law in Latin America is a topic that remains unexplored. While there is a considerable amount of scholarship about its history in other jurisdictions, there is precious little about how anti-trust regimes (ARs) have developed in this part of the world. The few articles devoted to this topic offer a historical narrative that characterises its development as a transition from economic planning towards market liberalisation. In doing so they suggest that the adoption of liberalisation policies amounted to a break from a past characterised by heavy-handed, misguided state interventionism. And although ARs continue to change, they supposedly also reflect a deep commitment to protecting competition.

This chapter engages critically with this narrative, and suggests that a different interpretation of the evolution of this field of law is possible and necessary. Its purpose is to offer a series of arguments that can contribute to a more nuanced understanding of the historical and intellectual development of this field of law. It shows how the development of ARs

This text was originally presented at the Work in Progress Forum at UCL on 27 March 2014.

A. Palacios Lleras (✉)
University College London, London, UK

© Palgrave Macmillan, a division of Macmillan Publishers Limited 2017   185
P. Fortes et al. (eds.), *Law and Policy in Latin America,*
DOI 10.1057/978-1-137-56694-2_11

evidences important continuities amid differences in the economic ideas they incorporate, in contrast to the dominant historical narrative of this field and its emphasis on discontinuities. It also aims to show how particular different ideas shape our understanding of these fields.

The chapter is organised as follows. Section 1 presents the dominant historical narrative of anti-trust in Latin America mentioned before. It describes its core elements and some variants. Section 2 then presents some elements to challenge this narrative. These emphasise the continuity of returning to legal reform to protect competition, even if, in the process, different economic theories are incorporated. These elements do not provide for a new narrative but by advancing them I advocate for a more historically informed and coherent approach to this field of law. Finally, Section 3 offers other ideas that can be helpful in developing a better understanding of the history of anti-trust in this region.

1   THE DEVELOPMENT OF ANTI-TRUST LAW IN LATIN AMERICA: THE DOMINANT NARRATIVE

I begin by analysing the body of literature that addresses the development of anti-trust in Latin America.[1] The core of the dominant historical narrative is composed of two different but related arguments. The first characterises the development of this field of law as a positive occurrence that stands for a sharp break with past and pernicious forms of regulation. In doing so, it presents the introduction and amendment of ARs as events or efforts in the 'right' direction. Changes came in the 1990s, when ARs were adopted de novo or were amended as a complement to liberal economic policies, such as market liberalisation, the privatisation of state-owned enterprises and the like. In turn, the second argument that makes up this narrative sees these events as insufficient. The regimes adopted are inadequate because they fail to meet basic requirements related to the independence of enforcement bodies, the content of legal provisions, and exceptions, among others. The implementation of these regimes also suggests that pernicious beliefs continue to linger in spite of the adoption of these ARs and the ideas for which they supposedly stand. As a result, these regimes should be amended to meet the challenges that prevent their full implementation. The 'big picture' thus suggests that the adoption of ARs is a positive development, but one that should be improved through continuous legal reforms.

A particularly good example of the first argument of this narrative is Julián Peña's article 'The Consolidation of Competition Law in Latin America'.[2] Peña summarises the development of anti-trust in this region in three stages, ranging roughly from the 1930s to the 2010s. In the first stage, only a few countries (Argentina, Brazil, Chile, Colombia and Mexico) had ARs, which were 'basic and vague' and poorly enforced.[3] These were adopted at a time when there was little support for anti-trust enforcement, a situation that followed from the interventionist and protectionist bent of contemporary governments.[4] In the second stage, most countries updated their regimes (Argentina, Brazil, Chile, Colombia and Mexico) or adopted new ones (Costa Rica, Ecuador, El Salvador, Honduras, Nicaragua, Panama, Peru, Uruguay and Venezuela). These processes took place roughly at the same time as the Washington Consensus policies were being implemented. The adoption of ARs and Washington Consensus policies supposedly evidences a break from the interventionist policies that predominated in the past—a 'pendulum shift in the paradigm of state intervention in the markets ...'.[5] Also, this second stage is characterised by the involvement of international organisations such as the United Nations Conference on Trade and Development (UNCTAD), providing assistance for crafting new ARs or amending previously established ones.[6] Finally, the third stage is about the consolidation of the different ARs. This is characterised first by a deeper involvement of other branches of government (notably the legislature), as well as by the support given by the highest levels of governments, civil society and academia (supposedly the case for Argentina, Brazil, Chile, Colombia, Mexico, Panama and Peru). It is also characterised by relying less on legal transplants and more on learning from enforcement experiences. And it is characterised by the involvement of international organisations, both global (e.g. UNCTAD) and regional (e.g. the Latin American Competition Forum).[7]

The second part of this narrative points to limitations that suggest the need for further reforms. In other words, the efforts undergone until now have been necessary but are not sufficient. An example of this part of the narrative can be found in Ignacio de León's book *An Institutional Assessment of Antitrust Policy: The Latin American Experience*.[8] De León argues that the pervasive influence of the colonial mentality continues to influence how Latin American governments understand the relationships between the state and markets. During colonial rule, the Spanish crown controlled economic activities according to its own interests and without regard for establishing well-functioning markets. The independence movements of the first decades of the nineteenth century did not affect the prevailing ideas regarding this issue in the recently independent Latin American states.[9] Quite the contrary: the nascent Latin American states continued to use law to direct economic activities following their own political prerogatives.[10] During the twentieth century, so-called interventionist policies reaffirmed suspicions about free markets at the international level and about competition at the local level.[11] The Washington Consensus, for all its emphasis on market liberalisation, was unable to challenge this legacy of interventionism, and anti-trust enforcement became a tool for it. By relying on images of perfectly competitive markets, competition enforcement authorities are biased against firms that have market power in real markets.[12] The consequences of this mentality can be appreciated in the composition of the ARs and in the predominance of protectionist industrial policies in this region.[13]

Other variants of this part of the narrative emphasise the role that legal formalism has in the development of this field of law. On the one hand, anti-trust enforcement is distinctively rule-bound, leading to economically inaccurate decisions. This results partly from the resistance of judges trained in the civil law tradition who lack the means to rely on economic theories in their reasoning, like their common law peers. The roots of this lay in the adoption of a formalist legal culture that is suspicious of non-literalist interpretations of legal rules.[14] On the other hand, competition authorities have not adapted economic tests to the particularities of their own contexts, characterised by highly concentrated markets and pervasive informality. As a result, they misinterpret the conditions in which competition takes place.[15]

This negative part of the narrative is often intertwined with suggestions for further changes to the different ARs. Some of these analyses suggest further reliance on cooperation programmes, like the Competition and Consumer Protection for Latin America programmes developed by UNCTAD.[16] Others advise taking stock of the limitations identified in order to devise future plans of action.[17] More demanding analyses suggest increasing the independence of local competition authorities, expanding their technical expertise and adopting a less utopian approach to competition.[18] Country-specific reviews of the different ARs in this regime have a similar thrust and offer concrete suggestions.[19]

2   CONTINUITY AND DISCONTINUITY IN LATIN AMERICAN ANTI-TRUST

The dominant narrative places an important emphasis on the legal changes that took place in the 1980s and 1990s as though they represented a significant departure from the past. I challenge this claim by arguing that the changes that took place do not amount to a sharp break from the past but rather as its continuation; legal reform continued to be the privileged mechanism to achieve social (and economic) change, albeit the direction of the changes themselves varied importantly. We can appreciate this by comparing the constitutional context and the ARs adopted in the 1950s with the respective contexts and ARs adopted in the 1990s. Likewise, we can appreciate the change in economic views underlying the adoption of ARs over time. In order to illustrate my arguments I will use examples from Chile, Mexico and Colombia.

The Enduring Allure of Legal Reform

The resort to legal reform as a mechanism for social change is a salient trait of Latin America's legal culture. While this type of reform has a symbolic and practical dimension, the notion that society can be changed via legal reform is quite distinctive.[20] Legal reforms have been part of the programmes of actors of all stripes and colours, ranging from radical socialists to authoritarian and conservative rulers. They have contributed to the adoption of different views about individual rights and communal duties, ranging from the classic liberal civil codes of the nineteenth century to the more communal-oriented social and economic rights of the 1990s. Likewise, the rules resulting from the reforms embed different economic perspectives, which range from developmental theories of the 1950s and onwards to the so-called neoliberal theories of the 1980s and 1990s. The fact that legal rules can be used to establish such a variety of ideas, values and goals points not only to the plasticity of law itself but also to the rich repertoire of perspectives and views that make up this region's legal tradition.

The enactment and amendment of legal rules has been the privileged strategy for protecting competition. The alternative strategy—simply to let markets operate as they do, and let competition take care of itself—has not been considered as a regulatory principle. This is true of the developmental

ARs adopted before the 1990s, as well as of the more neoliberal ARs that were adopted thereafter. Not only is legal reform in the name of competition a pervasive trait in the history of anti-trust in Latin America, it also suggests the pervasive influence of instrumental views about law. This partly explains why authors such as Peña, when writing about the history of this field of law, focus on legal reforms.

The ARs enacted during the large part of the twentieth century grew mainly from changes taking place in constitutional law regarding the capacity of the state to intervene in the economy. These changes signalled the end of the conservative–liberal constitutional balance that characterised the nineteenth century and the dawn of a new form of constitutionalism that addressed what is referred to as the 'social question'.[21] In particular, they refer to the constitutional basis of economic activities and, in particular, to the constitutional protection extended to private property. Nineteenth-century constitutions forbade the amendment of property rights by laws enacted after their promulgation, as well as their expropriation without compensation, but delegated the reach and effect of these rights to the Civil Codes.[22] However, during the first decades of the twentieth century, this protection was relaxed and governments were given the capacity to limit private property rights in the name of the 'common good'. The introduction of doctrines referring to private property as having a 'social function' is particularly important for this transformation.[23] This development is related to the increasing prerogatives accorded to the executive branch for devising and implementing economic policies, which were justified in the name of the expediency required to address economic issues at short notice. Both developments are related because the capacity of the state to intervene in the economy depended on its capacity to alter the rights and duties that stem from private property. ARs were one of several types of regime that, based on the state's capacity to intervene in markets, developed the constitutional ethos of this period.

The history of Colombia's AR evidences how constitutional mandates were developed via laws and administrative decrees. The 1886 Colombian Constitution established in Article 32 that private property rights could not be amended by later laws and that expropriation required compensation.[24] As conservative political forces lost their stronghold over national politics, liberal voices became increasingly more important and their political influence began a process of constitutional transformation. The amendments introduced in 1936 modified this protective constitutional mandate by establishing that property had 'a social function'.[25] Later, in

1945, a new amendment was introduced, and its content was far more sweeping; it established that the state's intervention was required to direct the economy and rationalise to the fullest possible extent the use of the different resources.[26] When discussing what eventually became Colombia's first functional AR in the Congress of Colombia, Senator Campo invoked explicitly this constitutional text to justify why an AR was necessary. This initiative became Law 155 of 1959, which contains some provisions that are applicable today.[27] Just like other ARs enacted at the time in Latin America (e.g. Chile's Law 13.305 of 1959), the enforcement of the law was given to an administrative body—the Superintendence of Economic Regulation—that was attached to a ministry, and thus depended politically on the country's president.

Unfortunately there has been little academic interest in the enforcement record of Law 155 of 1959. The task of enforcing this law was assigned to different administrative bodies over time, and their records are not systematically maintained. As a result, there is little clarity about the number of decisions issued, the sectors addressed or the sanctions imposed. We know, however, that the abovementioned Superintendence issued more than 20 decisions between 1962 and 1968.[28] There are, however, two decisions that offer us a window onto anti-trust legal reasoning in the early 1960s in Colombia. The first is decision 005 of 1961, which concerns an association of raw leather sellers. The association allocated production and selling quotas among its members and negotiated on their behalf with their buyers. The Superintendence noted that there were price increases and argued that they were a consequence of the operation of this association. As a result it ruled against its ongoing commercial practices. It stated that

> the market for raw leather should be organized in a technical, economic, impartial and effective way with the purpose of maintaining a fair balance between all the interested sectors, that are: the production, acquisition and processing [of raw leather].[29]

The second is decision 008 of 1962, where the Superintendence cleared a merger between a national producer of glass and a foreign-owned corporation in a related line of production. The Superintendence argued that the merger would increase the national production of glass products, thus substituting imports (and therefore diminishing foreign currency expenditures), contribute to the exportation of national products (thus positioning Colombia as an international producer), diminish national prices and increase the demand for labour.[30] As these two decisions evidence, anti-trust enforcement was framed in terms of how it contributed to the processes related to industrialisation.

The lack of available information about anti-trust enforcement between the 1950s and the 1990s is common to other Latin American states, with the exception of Chile.[31] Even so, it has become a commonplace to assert that the ARs of the time were hardly enforced, a conclusion that can hardly be sustained without further research. The little research available suggests quite the contrary: these regimes were enforced actively and the relevant authorities made interesting decisions.[32] In any case, the examples from Colombia also show that the considerations for having an AR are quite different from the ones we find today, more in line with modern microeconomic theory.

The economic crisis of the early 1980s exerted considerable pressure on the constitutional and legal framework built around the prevailing views about the role of the state in economic affairs. The crisis prompted the reforms of the 1980s and 1990s associated with the Washington Consensus, which entailed market liberalisation, the privatisation of state-owned enterprises and the protection of private property. The constitutional transformations of this period aimed to set the ground rules for market-based economies based on private property and competition. While the notion that the state can intervene in the economy is maintained, the rationale driving its interventions shifts in focus; the state ought to provide the basic conditions for markets to flourish, not to replace markets or thwart them. This new constitutional rationale was, as before, developed through legal reforms leading to the adoption of contemporary regulation where specialised regulatory agencies aim to maintain market-like conditions in economic transactions.[33]

In spite of the interest in circumscribing the role of the state, the constitutions adopted during the 1980s and 1990s contain provisions resembling the ones adopted in previous decades. It is not without irony that provisions stating that private property has a social function, or that the state should organise economic activities for the benefit of the population, appear during this period when curbing the state's interventions was the paramount goal. An example of this can be found in Article 19(24) of the 1980 Chilean Constitution, ratified under the military regime in place from 1973 to 1990, which states that private property has a social function and that the scope of property rights is a matter subject to laws enacted by the National Congress of Chile.[34]

The ARs adopted during this (second) period reflect this new constitutional rationale but preserve some of its previous features. Regarding their substantive content, the new regimes draw extensively from the USA and the EU, and they tend to frame competition issues in terms of economic efficiency. As for enforcement authorities, during this period we begin to see the development of quite different models. To begin with, in some countries there is a gradual separation of investigative and adjudicative functions, while in others these two functions remain fused. Where this separation takes place, we see either the establishment of proper courts, as in Chile with the creation of the Tribunal de Defensa de la Libre Competencia (Court of Defence of Free Competition), or the transformation of administrative bodies into tribunals, as in Mexico with the 2014 amendments to its Constitution.

The history of anti-trust in Mexico is particularly telling. Anti-trust issues have figured in that country's constitutional tradition since the 1857 Constitution, and Article 28 of the 1917 Constitution was a major development in this field. The substantive contents of this article were developed through laws enacted in 1926, 1931 and 1934, all accompanied by their respective bylaws. It is often claimed that these laws were hardly enforced until the 1990s, but there is little empirical research that corroborates this view. By the early 1980s an amendment to Article 28 contributed to establishing the foundations for a new AR in 1992. The anti-trust law (Ley Federal de Competencia Económica) adopted in that year evidences the influence of US anti-trust analysis in, among other things, forbidding 'hard core' horizontal restraints such as cartels in absolute terms, and forbidding other agreements and unilateral conduct only when they were inefficient.[35] In turn, a new enforcement authority was created, the Comisión Federal de Competencia Económica (Federal Competition Commission), and although it was expected to be more politically independent than its predecessors, it nonetheless retained certain ties with the executive branch.[36] A series of laws enacted in 2006 and 2011 made the Commission more independent and turned it into a quasijudicial institution. The 2014 constitutional amendments to Article 28 furthered this change.[37] As it stands today, Mexico's AR combines both adjudicative and regulatory procedures.

Discontinuity in Economic Doctrines

The ARs adopted before the 1990s reflected essentially a developmental view that was challenged and eventually superseded during the 1980s and 1990s. Some of the texts that contribute to the historical narrative described before consider that these regimes were too interventionist and based on erroneous premises.[38] But could it have been different? These criticisms fail to consider that between the 1930s and the 1970s the prevailing theories about economic development in Latin America were quite different to those that prevailed after that period. One can hardly blame Latin American governments for following the dominant theories and ideas of their time regarding trade and competition, especially when these theories aimed to explain the state of economic affairs in a better way than the available alternatives at the time.

Economic theories about development were based on the premises that the conditions of 'developing' countries were quite different from those present in 'developed' countries. This followed an insight made by John M Keynes, who argued that it was important to distinguish between situations where wages followed the supply and demand of other productive resources smoothly, as envisioned by 'classical economics', and other more common situations where market forces, owing to behaviour not anticipated by 'classical economics', were unable to reach the desired equilibrium. The latter merited the state's intervention to achieve the conditions conducive to higher levels of employment.[39] This separation between the economics of full employment and the economics of underemployment was particularly important for the elaboration of development theories, as can be appreciated in the works of Paul Rosenstein-Rodan[40] and Arthur W Lewis.[41] The thrust of these theories assigned to the state a definitive role in establishing the conditions for development through industrialisation.

The implementation of policies aiming to achieve development through industrialisation also meant strengthening the commercial ties between developing and developed states, to the mutual benefit of both, a view that was in line with classical international trade theories.[42] Latin American economists, and especially Raul Prebisch, were sceptical of this view. Prebisch noted that the terms of trade between developing and developed nation-states fell between 1846 and 1947 in spite of the increases in productivity evidenced at each side of the trade relationship.[43] That is, while the prices of raw materials from developing nations diminished, the export prices of the goods manufactured with these materials in developed nations increased, in spite of the technological improvements involved in their production.[44] Thus he came to a different conclusion than classical trade theories: developed nations at the 'centre' benefit twice from international trade: first, by importing raw materials at increasingly lower prices, and second, by exporting manufactured goods to 'peripheral' nations at prices that did not reflect the technological advances in production.[45] This perspective became the cornerstone of the Economic Council for Latin America and of developmental policies for subsequent decades.[46]

These theories about development complement the 'social' outlook that characterised the constitutional and legal transformations mentioned in Section 2.1. They led to the adoption of policies based on the substitution of imports to boost local industries with unrivalled positions in local markets. But the states did much more than that: they intervened regularly to address the dangers related to external business cycles (e.g. the 1929 crisis), which affected their balance of payments, established different foreign exchange controls, created forced-savings programmes and directed credit to certain sectors. They also organised—sometimes directly—the development of physical infrastructure, and established commercial banks and similar institutions that channelled credit for local industries.[47] Even though local economic processes became the locus of attention, exports were not disregarded and came to be favoured as well. After the late 1950s, when international trade picked up the pace once more, export-oriented policies regained their prominence to some extent and, on the whole, the policy landscape suggested that these states adopted a mixed economic system.[48]

Developmental policies and theories fell under the considerable pressure exercised by both political developments and changes in academia. On the one hand, the success record of development policies was not particularly great and in some instances these policies proved to be counterproductive. Likewise, the political landscape in the USA and England became increasingly less inclined to support developmental policies on account of their purported inefficiency and statism. On the other hand, changes taking place within the field of development economics academia led to acute criticisms. Some of these came from the field itself—that is, they were developed by individuals working within the developmental tradition that aimed to turn it inside out. Other criticisms came from neighbouring academic fields, where views rejecting Keynes' insights were also used to criticise the prevailing theories. In the end the latter criticisms prevailed, leading to a shift in the way development was understood; a single set of premises about how markets work were good for both developing and developed states.[49] This contributed to the ascendancy of the Washington Consensus. Arguments about how markets are better at allocating resources than states, about the importance of sound regulation and about the importance of institutions are the cornerstones of contemporary development theories. The lesson of this shift is that, along with the academic merits of development economics, political confrontations inside and outside academic circles played a determinant role in their demise.

It is hardly surprising that the ARs adopted in the 1990s are based largely on an efficiency approach to competition, just as it is not surprising that the ARs adopted before had a 'developmental' flavour. From a historical perspective, the issue therefore should not be whether the first regimes were misguided but how and why their perspectives changed. To criticise the early regimes for being based on ideas different from the ones held by the anti-trust community today evidences the historicist character of this dominant narrative; it judges the past based on the ideas and values of the present. It should be clear then that continuity (of legal reforms) and discontinuity (of economic theories and policies) complement and run parallel to each other, corroborating the view that continuity and discontinuity can be historically contested. At the end of the day, this narrative evidences the perspectives of the authors that contributed to its development, their own judgments about the past and their belief that their own ideas should inform these regimes.

3   Conclusions

The dominant narrative about the history of anti-trust in Latin America is inadequate for several reasons, as the previous pages suggest. As an alternative, I suggest that we look at this field of law from a perspective that is centred neither on defending nor on attacking the adequacy of free markets. A nuanced approach to the history of anti-trust in Latin America could focus instead on how different views about markets and their adequacy have changed over time.

Equally, a nuanced history of Latin American ARs could also explore the ties created by the process of transplanting these regimes into Latin American contexts. ARs did not develop originally in this region, and it would be quite useful to gain a better understanding of their diffusion. Different jurisdictions treat market power and monopolies differently, and the place anti-trust has vis-à-vis other fields of law, and larger political issues, varies importantly.[50] Latin America is at the receiving end of transnational networks through which different theories circulate between law-producing jurisdictions and their peripheral counterparts. The legal reforms mentioned here were partly about transplanting foreign legal rules and theories. Legal culture mediates the importation of these theories and rules between their original contexts and their new, distinctive ones. Therefore it would be useful to see how these processes have shaped our local understanding of anti-trust law.

Finally, it would also be useful to know more about the actors involved in the development of the ARs. Who were the architects of these ARs at their different stages, and what were their views about competition and the role of the state in economic affairs? Where did these individuals take their theories about anti-trust from, and how did they become acquainted with them? Did they work in the enforcement agencies, provide counsel to the respective governments or engage with them as litigators? Providing a detailed description of the networks of influence and practice regarding this field would bring about highly valuable insights for understanding the particularities of the different ARs.

The texts that have contributed to the history of anti-trust in Latin America have provided us with a narrative that, as faulty as it is, is nonetheless valuable. They stand as historical records of the ways in which people understand what anti-trust is about, and provide some useful insights regarding how to understand its development. As the interest in anti-trust in this region grows, we expect that new generations of lawyers, economists and social scientists will develop more sophisticated accounts of this field of law. We can only expect that they will break the hold of their predecessors and come forward with views of their own.

NOTES

1. Ignacio De León, *An Institutional Assessment of Antitrust Policy: The Latin American Experience* (Kluwer Law International 2009); Ignacio De León, *Latin American Competition Law and Policy: A Policy in Search of Identity* (Kluwer Law International 2001); Julián Peña, 'The Consolidation of Competition Law in Latin America' (2011) Antitrust Chronicle 11; Julián Peña, 'The Limits of Competition Law in Latin America' in D Daniel Sokol & Ioannis Lianos (eds), *The Global Limits of Competition Law* (Stanford University Press 2012); Alfonso Miranda

Londoño, 'Competition Law in Latin America: Main Trends and Features' (2013) 9 Revista Derecho de la Competencia 9; Carlos Pablo Marquez, 'Multilateral Trade Agreements and the Harmonization of Competition Law in Latin America and the Caribbean: A Path to Convergence' Perspectives 05/09-19. http://var./folders/sz/mrsmfs_j2_d8xtp4mg2bdkww0000gn/T/perspectivas19%202.pdf; Ana Maria Alvarez and Pierre Horna, 'Implementing Competition Law and Policy in Latin America: The Role of Technical Assistance' (2008) 83 Chicago-Kent Law Review 91; Julián Peña, 'Competition Policies in Latin America, Post-Washington Consensus' in Philip Marsden (ed), *Handbook Of Research In Trans-Atlantic Antitrust* (Edward Elgar Publishing 2008); Juan David Gutiérrez, 'Competition Laws in Latin America and Caribbean: History, Enforcement and Amendments' (2007) Pontificia Universidad Javeriana, Competition Law & Economics Working Paper 07-05. http://dx.doi.org/10.2139/ssrn.1023811; Bruce M Owen, 'Competition Policy in Latin America' (2003) Stanford Institute for Economic Policy Research Stanford Law and Economics Olin Working Paper nº 268. http://dx.doi.org/10.2139/ssrn.456441; Malcolm B Coate et al., 'Antitrust In Latin America: Regulating Government And Business' (1992) 24 University of Miami Inter-American Law Review 37.

2. Peña, 'Consolidation' (n 1).
3. Ibid. 2.
4. Ibid. 3
5. Ibid. 3.
6. Ibid. 3.
7. Ibid. 3–4.
8. De León, *Institutional Assessment* (n 1).
9. Ibid. 10–12, 14–17.
10. Ibid. 18–22.
11. Ibid. 20–25.
12. Ibid. 47.
13. Ibid. 47.
14. Alvarez and Horna (n 1) 105, 108 fn 41 (Considering that a shortage of economic knowledge can lead to a retreat to formalism). See also Peña, 'The Limits' (n 1) 244, 245, 250. For a quantitative analysis of the primacy of the common law over the Latin American civil law tradition, see Armando E Rodriguez, 'Does Legal Tradition Affect

Competition Policy Performance?' (2007) 21 International Trade Journal 417.

15. Peña, 'The Limits' (n 1) 244–245.

16. Alvarez and Horna (n 1).

17. Peña, 'The Limits' (n 1) 251.

18. De León, 'Institutional Assessment' (n 1) 580–583.

19. See e.g. Jay C Shaffer, *Competition Law and Policy in México—A Peer Review* (OECD 2004) 65–71 (suggesting adoption of a leniency programme and strengthening ties with other branches of power, among other reforms).

20. See Yves Dezalay and Bryant G Garth, *The Internationalization of Palace Wars: Lawyers, Economists, and the Contest to Transform Latin American States* (University of Chicago Press 2002) ch 6. Also Mauricio Garcia Villegas and Cesar A Rodriguez, 'Law and Society in Latin America: Toward the Consolidation of Critical Sociolegal Studies' (2003) 9 Beyond Law 11, 33–36.

21. See, in general, Roberto Gargarella, *Latin American Constitutionalism 1810–2010: The Engine Room of the Constitution* (Oxford University Press 2013).

22. See e.g. Article 27 of the 1857 Mexican Constitution, Article 12(5) of the 1833 Chilean Constitution and Article 32 of the 1886 Colombian Constitution.

23. Regarding the importance of this idea in Chile, see MC Mirow, 'Origins of the Social Function of Property in Chile' (2011) 80 Fordham Law Review 1183. Regarding Colombia, see Daniel Bonilla, 'Liberalism and Property in Colombia: Property as a Right and Property as a Social Function' (2011) 80 Fordham Law Review 1135.

24. Colombia, Constitution of 1886, Art. 32.

25. Colombia, Acto Legislativo 01 de 1936, Art. 10.

26. Colombia, Acto Legislativo 01 de 1945, Art. 28.

27. The first Colombian competition law is Decree 2061 of 1955. However, there is little information about its enforcement. Law 155 of 1959 was enforced, and there is more research about its development.

28. Andrés Palacios Lleras and Juan David Gutierrez 'Una Nueva Visión Sobre Los Orígenes Del Derecho De La Competencia Colombiano' (2015) Revista Derecho Competencia 11, 137.

29. Republica de Colombia. Superintendencia de Regulación Económica. Resolución 005 de 1961 p. 4.

30. Republica de Colombia. Superintendencia de Regulación Económica. Resolución 0008 de 1963 p. 2.
31. See e.g. Dale B Furnish, 'Chilean Antitrust Law' (1971) American Journal of Comparative Law 464. See also Ricardo Paredes, 'Jurisprudencia de las Comisiones Antimonopolio en Chile' (1995) 58 Estudios Públicos 227.
32. Perhaps the best example is Furnish, ibid.
33. David Levi-Faur and Jacint Jordana, 'Toward a Latin American Regulatory State? The Diffusion of Autonomous Regulatory Agencies Across Countries and Sectors' (2006) 29 International Journal of Public Administration 335.
34. Chile, Constitución Política de la Republica de Chile, Art. 19(24).
35. México, Ley Federal de Competencia Económica, Arts. 8–13.
36. Ibid., Arts. 23–29. According to the original text of Article 26 of the law, the members of the Commission were appointed directly by the country's president.
37. For a brief history of the competition law and the pre-2013 amendments, see Eduardo Perez Motta and Heidi Claudia Sada Correa, 'Competition Policy in Mexico' in David Lewis (ed), *Building New Competition Law Regimes: Selected Essays* (Edward Elgar 2013). An overview and critique in English of the recent amendments can be found in Anne Perrot and Assimakis Komninos, 'Mexico's Proposed Reform of Competition Law: A Critique from Europe' (2014). http://dx.doi.org/10.2139/ssrn.2404022.
38. See e.g. De León, 'Institutional Assessment' (n 1) 20–25.
39. John Maynard Keynes, *The General Theory of Employment, Interest and Money—Book 1* (Palgrave Macmillan 1936) ch 2 (IV).
40. Paul Rosenstein-Rodan, 'Problems of Industrialisation of Eastern and South-Eastern Europe' (1943) 53 The Economic Journal 202, 203.
41. Arthur W Lewis, 'Economic Development with Unlimited Supplies of Labour' (1958) 22 Manchester School of Economic and Social Studies 139.
42. Most notably, David Ricardo's theory of international trade.
43. Raúl Prebisch, *The Economic Development of Latin America and Its Principal Problems* (United Nations 1950). http://archivo.cepal.org/pdfs/cdPrebisch/002.pdf.
44. Ibid. 12–14.

45. Ibid.
46. Joseph Love, 'Economic Ideas and Ideologies in Latin America Since the 1930s' in Leslie Bethell (ed), *The Cambridge History of Latin America Volume 6: 1930 to the Present, Part 1: Economy and Society* (Cambridge University Press 1996).
47. Luis Bértola and José Antonio Ocampo, *The Economic Development of Latin America Since Independence* (Oxford University Press 2012) 157.
48. Ibid. 156.
49. See Albert O Hirschman, 'The Rise and Decline of Development Economics' in *Essays in Trespassing: Economics to Politics and Beyond* (Cambridge University Press 1981).
50. On this issue, see Giuliano Amato, *Antitrust And The Bounds Of Power: The Dilemma Of Liberal Democracy In The History Of The Market* (Hart 1997).

Constitutional Engine Room: Between Individual Autonomy and Collective Self-Government

Latin American Constitutionalism, 1810–2010: The Problem of the 'Engine Room' of the Constitution

Roberto Gargarella

In my opinion, Latin American constitutionalism can be organised around two main constitutional ideals—namely, individual autonomy and collective self-government. These ideals refer to two basic claims, which have occupied a fundamental place in US political discussions since the time of independence. Of course, the main military battles that have appeared in the region since those early years were not fought with the idea of 'autonomy' written on the flags of the contenders. However, and just to mention one important example, they did inscribe on their banners expressions such as 'religion or death', which in the end clearly referred to the place of individual autonomy in the new nations. That particular dispute—related to the place of the Church in the organisation of the new societies—was decisive in US public life, for decades (and perhaps until today), and became manifest in multiple debates: How to think about the relationship between the state and the Church? How much influence should the Church have in the writing of education programmes? Should

R. Gargarella (✉)
University Torcuato di Tella, Buenos Aires, Argentina

© Palgrave Macmillan, a division of Macmillan Publishers Limited 2017
P. Fortes et al. (eds.), *Law and Policy in Latin America*,
DOI 10.1057/978-1-137-56694-2_12   205

different religions and cults be tolerated, and for what reasons? However, disputes around individual autonomy went far beyond these (decisive) religious battles: they included conflicts concerning sexual diversity; conflicts about the scope of freedom of expression and association; and conflicts about reproductive rights, among many others.

In addition, it is not difficult to recognise the influence exercised by the ideal of collective self-government in the USA since the early days of independence. It should be enough to state, for example, that the same independence revolutions were crucially based on the republican vindication of the right of the locals to govern themselves. Those revolutions were directly based on a claim of self-government, against the domination of foreign countries—England in the case of the USA; Spain in the case of most Latin American countries; and Portugal in the case of Brazil. From the early claim of 'no taxation without representation', presented by the early American colonist against England, the demand for self-government always occupied a privileged place in the disputes of the new societies. Perhaps more interestingly, that claim continued to occupy a central role in the new nations, after independence, although in a very peculiar way. In most cases, in effect, those who had been called to the war of independence, engaged in it and offered their lives in it began to maintain the ideal of self-government even after the victory. And, as the historian Gordon Wood always emphasised, they began to use the doctrines that were instilled in them against the leaders of the revolution. They demanded a more relevant role for the people at large in the decision-making process; they asked for more spaces for political participation; and they disputed the political organisation that emerged after independence. Let me now explore how these ideals gained expression through different, actual constitutional documents. In order to proceed, I shall now summarily examine the evolution of Latin American constitutionalism, since its independence and until today.

1   1810–1850: CONSTITUTIONALISM IN THE INDEPENDENCE YEARS

The first Latin American constitutions emerged soon after independence (which, in the vast majority of Latin American countries, took place around 1810). Most of them combined foreign ideas, normally of a liberal or radical character. Particularly influential at the time were the constitutions of the USA (both the National Constitution and the early states' constitutions); the French revolutionary constitutions of 1791, 1793 and 1795; and the Spanish Constitution of Cadiz, from 1812. The Venezuelan Constitution of 1811 provides an interesting early illustration of this trend, both in the way it organised power (trying to limit the capacities of the executive branch) and in its Rousseauean phraseology: the Constitution included clear references to the ideas of the social contract, the general will, the sovereignty of the people and so on.

However, this first wave of—quite liberal—constitutionalism was promptly defeated as a consequence of the serious crisis that followed the declaration of independence. In effect, after 1810, Spain made significant military efforts to re-establish its authority in relation to the old colonies, and local leaders began to favour the concentration of authority as the only or main solution to the crisis. Simón Bolívar—one of the most influential public figures of the time, and also a man who was deeply involved in the writing of new constitutions—made this point very clear. In his 'Memorial to the Citizens of New Granada by a Citizen of Caracas', written in 1813, he directly contrasted his own political project (authoritarian and militaristic) with the radical project embodied, in his opinion, in the early Venezuelan Constitution. He stated, 'among the causes that brought about Venezuela's downfall the nature of its Constitution ranks first, which, I repeat, was as contrary to Venezuela's interests as it was favourable to those of her adversaries'. That project was, for him, the 'most grievous error committed by Venezuela'.[1]

We find similar conservative-authoritarian reactions in other Latin American countries, where political leaders also began to advocate military solutions to the independence crisis. In Argentina, many of the most influential revolutionary leaders began to advocate monarchical solutions as the only way out of the crisis. In Mexico, Agustín Iturbide established an empire in 1822. In Chile, General Diego Portales led a military reaction, which came to install the most stable conservative regime in the region, and produced the famed (and strongly conservative) Constitution of 1833. This latter Constitution, in particular, exercised a profound influence on the entire region. Conservative documents—that is to say, texts that combined a preference for a strong and centralised authority, and an official, state-imposed religion—began thus to prevail against liberal constitutions that established a system of checks and balances, and promoted religious tolerance.

2   1850–1917: THE FOUNDING PERIOD OF LATIN AMERICAN CONSTITUTIONALISM

By the mid-nineteenth century, things began to change in the region. In particular, the decades of confrontation (on many occasions, armed confrontation) between liberals and conservatives seemed to be over.[2] Other, more serious concerns, from economic development to the protection of property rights, seemed to prevail within the dominant elites. As a result of this, little by little, liberal and conservative leaders began to come together and try to establish common rules for the (re)organisation of their country. Most of these agreements were signed in the second half of the nineteenth century. In some countries, such as Argentina or Mexico, liberals and conservatives joined forces within the same constitutional assembly. In other cases, such as Chile, what we find is a conservative regime (organised around the 1833 Constitution) that was gradually 'liberalised'. In Colombia we find the opposite, with a long period of liberal constitutionalism becoming gradually more conservative.

The fact is that, by the mid-nineteenth century, we begin to find constitutions that reflected both liberal and conservative ideals. Among many other examples we find the 1853 Constitution in Argentina, the Mexican Constitution of 1857 and also the 1886 Constitution in Colombia, which were written by representatives of both the liberal and conservative groups. Another interesting case of convergence between these two forces appears in the liberal-conservative 'fusion' in Chile (1857–1873); and there are other similar examples in Venezuela and Peru.

The constitutions that liberals and conservatives created during those years appeared as an imperfect synthesis of the legal aspirations of the two groups. More specifically, these new constitutions reflected, on the one hand, the commitment to a system of checks and balances and state neutrality (mainly, religious tolerance), which characterised the aspirations of the liberal group; and the commitment to a system of concentrated authority, regional centralisation and moral perfectionism, which characterised the aspirations of the conservative group. The new constitutions, one could claim, represented a combination between the US Constitution, which was at the time very influential among liberals, and the 1833 Chilean Constitution, which represented the most influential conservative constitution during the nineteenth century. In his influential book *Bases*, Juan Bautista Alberdi—the main intellectual responsible for Argentina's 1853 Constitution—made this point explicit. He first admitted that the

Argentinean Constitution was moulded under the inspiration of the US Constitution. However, he then added that in everything related to the organisation of the presidential powers, 'our Constitution ... needs to distance itself from the example of the U.S. federal Constitution' in order to emulate the Chilean example. This latter Constitution, he asserted, offered 'the only rational solution to republics that shortly before were organized as monarchies'.[3]

Synthetically speaking, these new, liberal-conservative constitutions established religious tolerance, without necessarily affirming state neutrality;[4] defined a system of checks and balances, which was, however, partly unbalanced in favour of the president;[5] and established a centre-federalist model of territorial organisation.[6]

In addition, the liberal-conservative constitutions rejected the incorporation of either social clauses in favour of the disadvantaged, or political initiatives favouring mass participation in the public sphere. That is to say, the liberal-conservative compact was also an exclusionary compact, which implied the displacement of most of the institutional initiatives that radical groups—frequently inspired by Anglo-American radicals and the example of the French Revolution—then proposed. During all those years, in fact, radical groups had advanced numerous constitutional proposals, which included annual elections; the right to recall elected representatives; mandatory rotation; and mandatory instructions, among others. In addition, radical groups had promoted different reforms aimed at addressing the 'social question'. However, the triumph of the liberal-conservative project implied the rebuff of all of those initiatives.

3   1917–1950: THE ADVENT OF SOCIAL CONSTITUTIONALISM

The liberal-conservative constitutional compact was enormously successful in the establishment of regimes of 'order and progress'. This was particularly so from the 1880s onwards, when most countries in the region began to massively export primary goods, and Latin America enjoyed an exceptional period of economic prosperity and political stability.

Things began to change, however, with the arrival of the new century. These changes came as a result of different reasons, which included a growing and increasingly mobilised working class, and also a rising discomfort with the levels of inequality and authoritarianism that distinguished the decades of 'order and progress'.

The first and extremely radical sign of alarm appeared with the 1910 Mexican Revolution. The revolution, as we know, had a quite spectacular constitutional outcome, namely the 1917 Constitution. This was exceptionally long, robust in its declaration of rights and strongly committed to social rights, which was at the time a complete novelty. In fact, the Mexican Constitution became a global pioneer in the development of *social constitutionalism*. It accompanied the enactment of the Constitution of the Republic of Weimar in 1919; the creation of the ILO the same year; and the development of the Welfare State and the Keynesian economic model.

The Mexican Constitution included Article 27, which, among other things, stated:

> The Nation shall at all times have the right to impose on private property such limitations as the public interest may demand, as well as the right to regulate the utilization of natural resources which are susceptible of appropriation, in order to conserve them and to ensure a more equitable distribution of public wealth. With this end in view, necessary measures shall be taken to divide up large landed estates; to develop small landed holdings in operation; to create new agricultural centers, with necessary lands and waters; to encourage agriculture in general and to prevent the destruction of natural resources, and to protect property from damage to the detriment of society.

Another crucial innovation appeared in Article 123, which incorporated wide protections for workers and recognised the role of trade unions; and regulated labour relations reaching very detailed issues, which in a way covered most of the topics that later would come to distinguish modern labour law. This clause made reference, for example, to the maximum duration of work; the use of child labour; the rights of pregnant women; the minimum wage; the right to vacations; the right to equal wages; comfortable and hygienic conditions of labour; work accidents; the right to strike and lockout; arbitration; dismissals without cause; social security; and the right to association, among others.

The 1917 Mexican Constitution decisively changed the history of Latin American constitutionalism. Since its adoption, and little by little, most countries in the region began to change their basic constitutional structure. In fact, and following Mexico's early example, most countries began to include a long list of social rights in their constitutions: Brazil modified its Constitution in 1937; Bolivia in 1938; Cuba in 1940; Uruguay in 1942; Ecuador and Guatemala in 1945; and Argentina and

Costa Rica in 1949. This was the way in which Latin American constitutions expressed, through the use of legal language, the main social change that had taken place in the region during the first half of the twentieth century—namely, the incorporation of the working class as a decisive political and economic actor.

4   1950–2010: CONSTITUTIONALISM AND HUMAN RIGHTS

After this first wave of reforms, the region recognised a second period of constitutional changes, which was fundamentally concentrated between the end of the 1980s and 2000. In this new epoch, Brazil changed its Constitution in 1988; Colombia in 1991; Argentina in 1994; Venezuela in 1999; Ecuador in 2008; Bolivia in 2009; and Mexico in 2011.

Most of these new legal documents were impacted, in one way or another, by two grim events. The first was political and was the emergence of a new wave of dictatorships that affected the region (notably beginning with the military coup against Salvador Allende, in Chile, in 1973). The second event was economic—namely, the adoption of neoliberal reforms and programmes of economic adjustment by the end of the 1980s.

The period of military governments had a profound effect in the region, at different levels. First, it obliged some countries, after the recovery of democracy, to substantively reconstruct their constitutional organisation. This was, for example, the case for Chile, as a consequence of the numerous 'authoritarian enclaves' left by General Pinochet's 1980 Constitution.[7] And this was also the case for Brazil, which had to confront the 1967 Constitution, enacted during the military government of General Humberto Castelo Branco. Among other things, the 1967 Constitution (amended in 1969) imposed severe limitations on the federal organisation of the country, and the political and civil liberties of the population.[8]

In addition, the end of this ruthless era of dictatorships came together with other rights-based constitutional reforms. These changes implied the accordance of special, sometimes constitutional status, to different human rights treaties that the countries had signed during the last four or five decades. These treaties were designed to protect the same basic human rights that had been systematically violated by dictatorial governments.[9] Argentina, Brazil, Bolivia, Colombia, Costa Rica, Chile and El Salvador were among the many countries that tried to ensure more protections for the rights affected by the recent authoritarian governments.

The decision to provide a special legal status to diverse human rights treaties created interesting results. In part, these initiatives expressed the reconciliation of certain parts of the political left with the issue of rights and constitutionalism, which they had frequently resisted. In addition, the new legal status that many of these constitutions granted to human rights had an interesting effect on conservatives. For instance, after these constitutional changes, many conservative judges began to consider more seriously those arguments based on the value of human rights.

The other fundamental constitutional change produced in the region, by the end of the twentieth century, came as a consequence of the application of so-called 'programmes of structural adjustment', by which I mean the harsh economic policies applied in the region during the 1980s, usually by democratic, post-dictatorial governments. These were monetary policies that usually implied a drastic reduction in public expenditures and the elimination of social programmes. These adjustment programmes were originally promoted in the UK under the direction of Margaret Thatcher, and in the USA during the presidency of Ronald Reagan.[10]

The impact of these policies of structural adjustment on constitutionalism was enormous. More directly, the launch of these programmes usually required the introduction of legal and even constitutional changes directed at facilitating the application of economic initiatives.[11] Also—and more significant for our present purposes—the economic changes of the era provoked an economic and social crisis that intensified calls for the introduction of new legal reforms. In effect, the neoliberal programmes provoked social distress and growing levels of unemployment that were not offset by the existence of a solid safety net. As a consequence, millions of people suddenly found themselves in a situation of complete abandonment, without the means to ensure their own subsistence and that of their family. The state, which for the previous 40 years had guaranteed work and social protection for vast sectors of the population, was now shrinking. Most of its most valuable assets were sold in non-transparent and hasty transactions. As a consequence, Latin America began to experience a process of social mobilisation demanding the social protection that many constitutions still promised.

Social protests and counterinstitutional uprisings exploded in the entire region, from south to north, east to west. They included, for example, the insurrection of the Zapatistas (the Zapatista Army of National Liberation) in Mexico, which began in January 1994, a year after the country had signed a free trade agreement with the USA. They also included the 'wars' of water (2000) and gas (2003) in Bolivia, directed against the privatisation of basic sections of the national economy; the occupation of land promoted by the Landless Movement in Brazil; the taking of lands in Santiago de Chile; the 'invasions' of property in Lima, Peru; the emergence of the *piqueteros* movement in Argentina; and also numerous acts of violence against the exploitation of mineral resources in different parts of the region.

Not surprisingly, some of the most relevant sociolegal reforms of the last few decades—including those of Colombia, Bolivia, Ecuador, Venezuela and Mexico—followed the economic crises of the 1990s. The new constitutional changes can be read as a direct response to the social crisis of the previous years. Thus, by the end of the century, most countries in the region had adopted extremely strong constitutions, at least with regard to the social, economic and cultural rights that they included. A first look at the prevalent organisation of these constitutions' bills of rights allows us to recognise the extent of this phenomenon. According to a recent study, current Latin American constitutions guarantee the protection of the environment, culture, health, education, food, housing, work, clothing and so on.[12] In addition, some of the new or reformed constitutions included guarantees for gender equality; incorporated mechanisms of participatory democracy; created the institution of referendum or popular consultation; introduced the right to recall elected representatives; or recognised the right to affirmative action. Still more notably, many of the renewed constitutional documents affirmed the existence of a pluri- or multicultural state or national identity; provided special protection to indigenous groups; and established the duty of mandatory consultation of indigenous communities before the development of economic projects that could affect their communal organisation.

5   The 'Engine Room' of the Constitution

This long but briefly summarised history of the preceding pages reveals both the scope and the limits of constitutional reform in Latin America. Legal reforms could not, or did not want to, go as far as they could have gone in order to ensure that those reforms had the transformative character that their authors—so they declared—wanted them to have. To state this does not deny the value of what has been achieved in the region, in constitutional terms, in recent years. Many of these reform processes managed to advance the interests of the most disadvantaged, at least in the books. Better than that, the practice of these constitutions showed that the changes introduced in the section of rights were far from innocuous. In the last few years (although—and this is a problem—*only* in the last few years), Latin American countries that had adopted more socially robust constitutions have developed an interesting and imaginative practice of judicial enforcement of social rights.[13] However, it also seems clear that these reforms were, in the best case, very limited in their scope and achievements. And one of the main reasons to explain this conclusion is the fact that the reformers seemed to have concentrated their energies on the section of rights, without taking into account the impact that the organisation of power tends to have on those very rights that were then (extra) protected. Notably, legal reformers dedicated most of their energies to the creation of new rights, leaving the organisation of powers essentially untouched. By doing this, legal reforms kept the doors of the 'engine room' of the constitution closed: the core of the democratic machinery was not changed, the engine of the constitution did not become the main object of their attention, as if their mission concluded with their work on the rights section; as if the main controls could only be touched by the closest allies of those in power.

It is interesting to contrast this remarkable omission, typical of recent reformers, with what their old intercessors used to do when engaged in a process of constitutional change. For example, the engineers of the liberal-conservative compact showed no doubt about what they were required to do in order to ensure the life of their most cherished rights—for example, the right to property. For them it seemed totally clear that in order to guarantee protections to such core rights, the first thing to do was to get into the 'engine room' and introduce some necessary modifications. Typically, then, they proposed the restriction of political liberties in order to ensure the enjoyment of broader economic freedoms. This was, for example, Juan B Alberdi's main constitutional lesson for his time: it was necessary to temporarily tie the hands of the majority so as to ensure protection for certain basic economic rights.[14] The 'mistake' of recent reformers also contrasts with what the old radicals used to do when engaged in processes of constitutional change. Radicals concentrated all their energies on producing certain basic political and economic changes (typically, an agrarian reform; a government by assemblies) through the political mobilisation of the masses. In so doing, they never subscribed to the (conservative) model of concentrated authority (as contemporary radicals tend to), and they never spoke the liberal language of rights (as contemporary radicals usually do).

Of course, the problem with the new constitutions is not simply that they did not go far enough, so as to reach the 'engine room' of the constitution. If that was the problem the solution could have simply been to wait until the next reform. The problem is that, by preserving an organisation of powers that is still based on the nineteenth-century model of concentrated authority, the new constitutions put at risk the same initiatives that they advance through their rights section.[15] Thus organised, the new constitutions tend to present a contradictory design: they look democratic and socially committed in their rights section, while at the same time they seem to reject those same social-democratic ideals through their traditionally vertical political organisation. Not surprisingly, and as a consequence, the old hyperpresidentialist political organisation has tended to block all of the initiatives directed at setting in motion the schemes for popular empowerment included in the new constitutions. For example, Argentina's political authorities refused to implement the participatory clauses incorporated in the 1994 Constitution; Ecuador's president systematically vetoed all of the initiatives directed at enforcing the newly created mechanisms for popular participation; and in Peru, Chile, Mexico and Ecuador, indigenous leaders suffered prison or repression every time they wanted to put into practice their newly acquired rights.

For the above reasons, future constitutional reforms should be aimed at rendering the organisation of powers consistent with the new social impulses that have been incorporated through the bill of rights section of the document. In other words, in order to introduce social changes in a constitution, one needs primarily to transform an organisation of power that was designed for old, elitist, nineteenth-century societies.

6   CONCLUSION

Having reached this point, let me conclude this work by going back to the beginning of the chapter and to the reference to the two main ideals behind Latin American constitutionalism: individual autonomy and collective self-government. For those who are still committed to those fundamental ideals, contemporary Latin American constitutionalism has led to disappointing results in at least two ways. On the one hand, the new constitutions tend to maintain a concentrated organisation of power, giving scarce attention to deliberative institutions and limited actual openness—in spite of its own rhetoric—to political participation. On the other hand, the bill of rights section of the new constitutions has become longer and longer, but it still lacks a proper institutional structure capable of guaranteeing the enforcement of the new rights. Partly as a result of that, the new constitutions continue to be lacking not only in terms of self-government but also with regard to the value of individual autonomy. In effect, there are numerous groups that, constitutionally speaking, continue to be within the group of the marginalised among the marginalised (people who did not receive constitutional attention after the social reforms of the mid-twentieth century or the 'multicultural' reform of the end of the century). In the case of women, for example, many Latin American constitutions still remain silent (if they are not directly hostile) with respect to their more basic reproductive rights (a topic that calls our attention to the importance of the link between the constitution and the presence of marginalised voices and viewpoints in constitutional debates).[16]

In addition, we must say that the idea of including long declarations of rights in the new constitutions seems to derive from a simplistic view, according to which social justice's main battle takes place in the 'dogmatic' section of the constitutions. What is still worse, and more important, is that the generous social clauses of the new constitutions seem mostly threatened by a risk that comes 'from within'. In other words, the proponents of those social clauses have not realised or wanted to recognise that one of the main enemies of the enforcement of social rights resided just 'within' the same constitutional text that they proposed. On the one hand, this risk tends to spring from the existing difficulties in distinguishing between reasonable concerns for collective self-government and reasonable concerns for protecting individual autonomy—the result of which is that, on occasion, majorities are allowed to prevail in issues concerning personal morality. On the other hand, this threat emerges from the decision to leave fundamental rights in the hands of the main, centralised, political authority.

NOTES

1. Harold A Bierck (ed), *Selected Writings of Bolívar* vol 1 (Colonial Press 1951) 22.
2. We may recall, in this respect, the brutal way in which Chilean conservatives treated their opponents, from the beginning of the Conservative Republic in 1833; the bloody confrontations between *unitarios* and *federales* in Argentina; the Federal War in Venezuela, which also divided liberals and conservatives; the cruel confrontation between

the two groups in Colombia, which included episodes of civil war; and the battle of the *liberals puros* in Mexico against the forces of the conservative Santanistas. I reviewed some of these events in Roberto Gargarella, *The Legal Foundations of Inequality. Constitutionalism in the Americas (1776–1860)* (Cambridge University Press 2010).

3. Juan Bautista Alberdi, *Bases y Puntos de Partida para la Organización Política de la República Argentina* (Rosso 1960) ch 25.

4. Most of the new constitutions resisted the conservative pressures in favour of establishing a particular religion, and replaced that requirement with some alternative formula. On some occasions, as in Argentina, the liberal-conservative Constitution reserved a special place for the dominant Catholic faith (Article 2 of the Constitution, which ambiguously maintained that the state 'supports' the Catholic religion), while at the same time affirming religious tolerance (Article 14). On other occasions, such as Mexico in 1857 (or, similarly, Ecuador in 1906), the Constitution remained silent on the subject, which was a way of affirming the impossibility of either group consecrating its own viewpoint on the subject. In Chile, the strongly religious profile of the 1833 Constitution was moderated after some decades, when an interpretative law (from 1865) opened up room for (relative) religious tolerance.

5. Most of the liberal-conservative constitutions favoured the traditional system of division of power, accompanied by a system of checks and balances, in line with the US constitutional model. However, and as a consequence of pressure from the conservatives, the new Latin American constitutions introduced some significant changes with regard to the USA's inspiring example. Typically they created an excessively powerful executive, which challenged the structure of equilibriums that characterised the traditional system of checks and balances.

6. The liberal-conservative constitutions emerged after a violent period of disputes between centralist and federalist groups. That is why, in most cases, these constitutions did not want to consecrate either a purely centralist or a federalist territorial organisation of the country. What they tended to do instead was to adopt mixed or more ambiguous solutions in this respect.

7. Those 'enclaves' included the institutions of life-tenured senators (which allowed Pinochet to be part of the Senate during the democratic period) and of 'designated Senators' (which allowed members of the coercive forces to be part of the Senate); a National Security

Congress; an extremely exclusionary electoral system (which made it very difficult for minoritarian forces to participate in electoral politics); and the requirement of qualified majorities in order to change basic aspects of the institutional system (e.g. education, the organisation of Congress or the regulation of the army).

8. Large meetings were subject to prior governmental authorisation; political parties were restricted (only the official party (Aliança Renovardora Nacional, National Renovating Alliance) and an opposition party (Movimento Democrático Brasileiro, Brazilian Democratic Movement) were allowed to function as such); and direct suffrage was suppressed in the main cities for security reasons. In 1969, a provisional military junta introduced a profound amendment to the 1967 Constitution, which strengthened the repressive character of the previous document. For example, it introduced the institution of the death penalty; suppressed *habeas corpus*; created new military courts; and opened the door to new repressive laws, such as the Law of National Security and another that was intended to regulate the press.

9. Kathryn Sikkink, *The Justice Cascade. How Human Rights Prosecutions are Changing World Politics* (Norton & Company 2012); and Carlos H Acuña and Catalina Smulovitz, 'Adjusting the Armed Forces to Democracy. Successes, Failures and Ambiguities in the Southern Cone' in Elizabeth Jelin and Eric Herschberg (eds), *Constructing Democracy. Human Rights, Citizenship and Society in Latin America* (Westview Press 1996).

10. Sebastián Etchemendy, *Models of Economic Liberalization: Business, Workers, and Compensation in Latin America, Spain, and Portugal* (Cambridge University Press 2011); Marcelo Cavarozzi and Juan Manuel Abal Medina (eds), *El Asedio a la Política. Los Partidos Latinoamericanos en laEera Neoliberal* (*Homo Sapiens* 2002); and Maristella Svampa, *La Sociedad Excluyente. La Argentina Bajo El Signo del Neoliberalismo* (Taurus 2005).

11. In this respect we can mention, for example, the 35 amendments to the 1988 Brazilian Constitution that were promoted by the former president, Fernando Henrique Cardoso (amendments that came to facilitate the privatisation process); the reform of Article 58 in the Colombian Constitution of 1991 (which was promoted by the conservative government of Andrés Pastrana in order to provide more guarantees to foreign investment); the modification of Article 27 of the Mexican Constitution (which introduced limits to initiatives for

the distribution of land); the Peruvian constitutional reform in 1993 (which was advanced by President Fujimori after his *auto-golpe*, and directed at eliminating many of the social commitments assumed by the 1979 Constitution); and the guarantees given to the value of the money in Argentina through the constitutional reform elaborated by Carlos Menem. See Gerardo Pisarello, *Un Largo Termidor. Historia y Crítica del Constitucionalismo Antidemocrático* (Corte Constitucional del Ecuador 2011) 186–7. Similarly, one could mention the many different initiatives for judicial reform promoted by the World Bank and other financial multilateral institutions during the 1980s, which were mainly directed at providing a more stable framework for the new types of economic transaction that dominated the period. See Pilar Domingo and Rachel Sieder (eds), *Rule of Law in Latin America* (Institute of Latin American Studies 2011).

12. Roberto Gargarella, Leonardo Filippini and Agustín Cavana, *Recientes Reformas Constitucionales en América Latina*, Report (UNDP 2011).
13. Manuel José Cepeda-Espinosa, 'Judicial Activism in a Violent Context: The Origin, Role, and Impact of the Colombian Constitutional Court' (2004) 3 Washington University Global Studies Law Review 529; Roberto Gargarella, Pilar Domingo and Theunis Roux (eds), *Courts and Social Transformation in New Democracies* (Ashgate 2006); Varun Gauri and Daniel M Brinks (eds), *Courting Social Justice* (Cambridge University Press 2008); and Bruce M Wilson, 'Changing Dynamics: The Political Impact of Costa Rica's Constitutional Court' in Rachel Sieder, Line Schjolden and Alan Angell (eds), *The Judicialization of Politics in Latin America* (Palgrave 2005) 47–66.
14. Juan Bautista Alberdi, *Obras Selectas* (Joaquín V González ed, La Facultad 1920).
15. Carlos S Nino, 'Hyperpresidentialism and Constitutional Reform in Argentina' in Arend Lijphart and Carlos H Waisman (eds), *Institutional Design in New Democracies* (Westview Press 1996); and Carlos S Nino, *The Constitution of Deliberative Democracy* (Yale University Press 1997).
16. In many cases, rights are violated as a consequence of state actions, but also, in many others, by its failure to act in the required way. The importance of the presence of marginalised voices in constitutional debates is discussed at length in Gargarella, *The Legal Foundations of Inequality* (n 2).

CHAPTER 13

Addressing Poverty through a Transformative Approach to Anti-Discrimination Law in Latin America

Alberto Coddou McManus

Anti-discrimination law (ADL) has been developing at an incredible pace throughout the world in recent decades. Although the most sophisticated programmes of regulation in the field have been developed in the Global North, different examples have been emerging recently throughout the developing world. In this context, India, South Africa and Latin America offer prominent examples of attempts to tackle discrimination through diverse legal devices. Moreover, there is an expansion of legal regulation at different levels: on the list of protected grounds; the incorporation of indirect or de facto discrimination clauses; the emergence of intersectionality; and the creation of special equality bodies. However, this development has been uneven: while in Australia, Canada, Europe and the USA there are detailed anti-discrimination legal mechanisms and permanent theoretical scrutiny, this has not been the case in other places. Latin America provides a paradigmatic example of this unevenness: recent years have seen a boom in anti-discrimination regulation. However, this boom has not been coupled with the development of institutional arrangements needed for

A.C. McManus (✉)
Universidad Diego Portales, Santiago, Chile

© Palgrave Macmillan, a division of Macmillan Publishers Limited 2017   221
P. Fortes et al. (eds.), *Law and Policy in Latin America*,
DOI 10.1057/978-1-137-56694-2_13

the effectiveness of such regulation, comprehensive theoretical accounts of conceptual boundaries or reflections of the broader social aims of anti-discrimination regulation.

This work attempts to make a contribution to the debate about ADL in Latin America, a project that has to face the unavoidable fact of poverty and socioeconomic inequality. Indeed, almost one in three Latin American individuals are currently living in poverty or indigence, and, according to the GINI index, this region is the most unequal in the world.[1] This reality inevitably has an effect on legal institutions and their operation on the ground.

Elsewhere I have developed arguments to build a transformative approach to ADL in Latin America.[2] I have offered six constitutive criteria for this approach to be implemented,[3] and argued that ADL could constitute the most accessible step, with the materials we have at hand, to challenge the current institutional and social arrangements in the region. Here I will further develop the criterion of socioeconomic lens and its different articulations, and also provide an analysis of how it has been working on the ground. In particular, I will assess how equality laws have been used to address poverty issues and make a difference for people living in economically deprived areas of Argentina.[4] This country has been leading the wave of anti-discrimination reforms in the region, and it offers a unique example to evaluate legal innovations in this area due to increasing legal mobilisation and judicialisation of public policies; features that are also present in other Latin American countries.

1   A Transformative Approach to Anti-Discrimination Law: Socioeconomic Lens

Purposes and Boundaries

ADL is nowadays crucial for liberal democratic governance and, 'like democracy, the rule of law and human rights, a system of law regulating discrimination has become key to how some states define themselves.'[5] However, like all of these overarching concepts, ADL has also been the site of contestation. ADL in Latin America is considered to be a gateway to further radical reforms: on the one hand seen as a dangerous tool by social conservative constituencies, and on the other as a legal device for empowering disadvantaged groups. Legislative proceedings of the Chilean ADL illustrate this tension: after several trade-offs between negotiating positions, the law ended up including the following clause, which was not contained in the original bill: 'The precepts of this law will not be interpreted as derogations or modifications of other legal precepts currently in force.'[6]

Within this scenario, I will borrow from Gorz, and state from the beginning that a transformative approach to ADL is an example of non-reformist reform that

> set[s] in motion a trajectory of change in which more radical reforms become practicable over time ... nonreformist reforms change more than the specific institutional features they explicitly target [and] alter the terrain upon which later struggles will be waged. By changing incentive structures and political opportunity structures, they expand the set of feasible options for future reform. Over time their cumulative effect could be to transform the underlying structures that generate injustice.[7]

By way of illustration, a transformative approach to ADL would be crucial in the early stages of the development of welfare regimes in the region, built around universal social policies while acknowledging the respect for cultural and social differences. The commitments of a transformative approach allow us to better consider the design of concrete tools for a welfare state that could take into account current economic, social and cultural inequalities. To achieve that, we could start from the already binding anti-discrimination provisions and build a roadmap for future reforms.

As I am also trying to provide a normative account of how we should orient future legal reforms, I should be clear about the broader social aim of this discrete area of law. In that sense, my inquiry lies within the purposive question that every theory of discrimination law must answer in the first place.[8] Although this question is different from the set of distributive questions that a programme of regulation should answer (i.e. about distributing rights and duties to different actors according to particular circumstances), the purposive inquiry remains important for the debate about the institutional articulation of the fundamental values. Indeed, every institutional arrangement could be assessed from the perspective of the values or principles that it is trying to realise.

Most of the debate around the purposive question of discrimination law tends to be very abstract, and at times it relates in uneasy ways to current legal practice.[9] Khaitan has provided an interesting theoretical account of discrimination law as it actually operates in the most important

common law jurisdictions.[10] Here I will follow some of his main theoretical commitments, especially when considering the importance of the
current practice of anti-discrimination legal regimes in Latin America and
the region's particular contexts and challenges. In order to do that, I will
specify how the values and principles that provide the normative foundation of ADL could be realised within a particular social and historical context. The criterion explained at the end of this section is at an intermediate
level of inquiry, which could help us understand the ways in which ADL
in Latin America could transform the lives of the people regulated by it.
Whether the main theoretical grounding of ADL is equality, autonomy
or dignity, a transformative approach should look to the Latin American
context through a socioeconomic lens.

A Transformative Approach to ADL in Latin America

In the context of Latin America, a transformative approach to law and
policy stands against the alternative of placing recent legal reforms under
the development narrative of neostructuralism, which presented itself as
a *via media* between structuralism and neoliberalism. Explicitly, it was
understood as a reaction to the failure of neoliberal policies of structural
adjustment that were rampant during the 1980s and 1990s.[11] Nowadays
it influences policy discourses of the centre-left coalitions that shape the
region's approach to development. Acccording to Leiva,

> its discursive potency derives from being simultaneously an alternative
> vision to neoliberal dogmatism, a comprehensive development strategy, an
> integrated policy framework, and a grand narrative about the path toward
> modernity.[12]

Neostructuralism has been the development narrative of Comisión
Económica para América Latia y el Caribe (CEPAL, or the Economic
Commission for Latin America and the Caribbean (ECLAC)) since the
beginning of the 1990s, and it has fostered anti-discrimination reforms as
a way to trigger the required social integration to enhance international
competitiveness.[13] Indeed, neostructuralism could consider ADL as a crucial policy to balance the change of production patterns with social equity
and, probably, as the main social policy within the path to development.
Alongside economic policies (fiscal reform and a structure of incentives),
ADL is considered to be crucial for the way in which excluded social groups
are incorporated into an economic system of cooperation: vulnerable

groups are now available for the job market, which should be blind to considerations other than job skills. Under this idea, the region would not need radical reforms for the consolidation of democracy: social policies would remain far from universal social rights, and economic and financial arrangements would remain unaltered.

Neostructuralism does not represent a challenge to the free operation of market forces but a reinforcement of its premises: if the market is to function effectively, non-market-based forms of coordination should complement it.[14] For Leiva, '[t]he main characteristic of the neostructuralist policy framework ... is the active promotion of new forms of social coordination beyond those offered by market forces alone.'[15] This discourse considers social cohesion as essential to enhance the adaptability of the labour force required for international competitiveness. Hence neoliberal economic policies remain untouched under this new developmental framework as it 'displaces the center of gravity in policy intervention from economics to the realm of subjectivity, symbolic politics, and the cultural dimension'.[16] The role of the state and the regulatory apparatus should be redirected at the symbolic dimension, empowering historically excluded sectors through ideas with 'a new type of expectations, new citizens, new ways of understanding citizenship'.[17] In other words, neostructuralism is mainly a change in the working environment rather than a radical transformation of the economic institutional arrangement; in a way, it creates a new cultural and social mindset under which market forces should lead us towards development. Far from being an alternative to neoliberalism, 'it completes the historical task initiated by neoliberalism, the consolidation and legitimation of a new, export-oriented regime of accumulation'.[18]

The neostructuralist's groundings of ADL in Latin America could be coupled with its development in Europe. Indeed, the first anti-discrimination provision to be enacted within the European Economic Community, an equal pay gender clause, was born due to the need to prevent unfair competitive advantages in the development of a common market.[19] Even now, some of the most developed anti-discrimination programmes of regulation in Europe have been connected to the struggle for expanding market access,[20] or within a market-based rhetoric of equality of opportunities.[21] For Somek,

> anti-discrimination law ... is not primarily directed at decommodification ...
> it is different from a type of social legislation that aims at backing up the provision of goods with some market-defying or market-bypassing distributive mechanism. Indeed, the very point of anti-discrimination law is to facilitate

market access and not to exempt a certain sphere from the operation of the market.[22]

Although this economic aim has recently been displaced by a broader social aim,[23] it still provides space for criticism, and challenges the allegedly emancipatory character of ADL.

Moreover, equality laws in Europe have not been designed to address inequality or segregation because, 'by tradition, distributive inequalities are dealt with only by political initiatives'.[24] Many of the most relevant domestic programmes of anti-discrimination regulation in Europe originated against the background of the most equal societies in the world. In other words, the development of the European approach was narrowly construed because the distributive task was in the hands of the development of the 'welfare state', and its ancillary concepts of 'social citizenship' and 'decommodification'.

These two ideas have shaped anti-discrimination programmes of regulation in Europe, providing a very restricted scope. Indeed, one could state that the European approach is strong within its narrowness. That is, for example, the case of the EU Equality Directives of the 2000s, which harmonise domestic anti-discrimination regulation within a closed list of protected grounds (race, age, sexual orientation, disability and religion or belief), being considered as one of the most successful regional social policies.[25] Also, the equality jurisprudence of the European Court of Justice and the European Court of Human Rights has been celebrated by many social activists of the region, even though the approach has been rather cautious regarding the possible connections between ADL and social rights, or to the expansion of the list of protected grounds to socioeconomic issues.[26] Despite the innovative work of the European Committee on Social Rights in developing these connections,[27] in European jurisdictions there is still 'a deep reluctance to regard the right to equality as generating social rights in its own right'.[28]

Instead of following the European approach or appeal to a neostructural narrative that could form the basis for recent legal reforms, a transformative approach to ADL acknowledges its role in a region with structural problems such as socioeconomic inequality and poverty. In contrast with the European approach, Latin American ADL has emerged in an era of profound changes. Here I mention just two particular features.

First, the political context. Democratisation and social provisions emerged in the early 1990s, simultaneously with economic liberalisation and privatisation.[29] This tension has influenced the development of constitutional provisions: indeed, many progressive provisions, such as those recognising substantive equality, stand against protections for private property or constraints against state involvement in the economy.[30] Within these contradictions, bottom-up approaches of ADL, in connection with economic and social rights, have worked as tools of resistance against neoliberal programmes of reforms.[31] In the hands of social movements, constitutional and legal equality clauses have been used to reframe the place and meaning of equality in public discourse.[32]

Second, legal operators have to work in societies with structural inequalities and social segregation, with significant portions of the population living in poverty and indigence. Moreover, ethnoracial claims are now part of the official discourse, forcing states to acknowledge the importance of recognition claims in the design of social provisions. If we add the fact that legal operators have to do their work with scarce resources and weak institutional commitments, anti-discrimination programmes assume a very particular shape. This background context has moulded the way in which legal operators understand their role in implementing anti-discrimination provisions. For example, the Inter-American Court understands that the scope of its institutional role is very broad and complex, interpreting that the right to equality refers both to claims of recognition and redistribution,[33] and that its judgments provide guidelines for the development of more detailed protections for rights.[34] Moreover, at the level of reparations, legal operators understand that the role of human rights courts is to effectively apply the guarantee of non-repetition, promoting structural changes in order to tackle causes that lie beneath the surface.[35]

Socioeconomic Lens

This criterion argues that ADL should not be indifferent to socioeconomic concerns, either on substantive provisions or legal infrastructure—for example, on procedural rules in complaints-based models (burden of proof), or special socioeconomic concerns in the exercise of public sector equality duties (like the yet unimplemented Section 1 of the Equality Act in the UK).

For Hepple, 'a truly comprehensive and transformative approach to equality obviously does not mean that all aspects of socio-economic disadvantage have to be dealt with by a single duty or in a single statute'.[36] He remains sceptical about the possibility of addressing redistributive issues through equality laws. However, as I will argue, the context of Latin America forces us to reflect more carefully on this issue.

It is impossible to avoid the socioeconomic lens in the design of anti-discrimination legal devices or in the practice of equality legislation. Traditional protected grounds are over-represented among the poor, especially in Latin America. Moreover, the poor 'experience many of the elements of discrimination experienced by status groups, including lack of recognition, social exclusion and reduced political participation'.[37] There is a consensus in international human rights law that discrimination law should be inextricably linked with 'economic and social situation'.[38] Indeed, many anti-discrimination provisions in Latin America have included, as protected grounds of discrimination, 'economic condition',[39] 'social condition',[40] 'socioeconomic situation'[41] or 'social origin'.[42] These recent reforms are in harmony with Latin American public opinion at large: on average, the majority view discrimination as having structural causes[43] and believe that poverty or lack of money are the main grounds for discrimination, ranking much higher than race, ethnicity or gender.[44] This trend has been confirmed by domestic surveys in Chile, Argentina and Mexico.[45]

As has been clear from the beginning to many social observers, within the emergence of 'new social movements' after the fall of authoritarian governments, the activists' discourse easily accommodated demands for both recognition and redistribution.[46] This reality contrasts the with assumed incompatibility between class and other grounds of protection as tools of emancipation.[47] We may further add that Latin American ADL was not born out of concerns about unfair advantages in the regulation of a common market or about the efficiency or productivity rates in the workforce, but out of a constitutional narrative that gives coherence to both dimensions of equality.

Within this scenario, social movements and legal mobilisation have been developing interesting connections between equality laws and social rights.[48] First, although many jurisdictions recognise the binding character of social rights, they do not include a judicial remedy to redress their violation. Thus litigants have no other alternative but to claim the right to equality in connection with other social clauses, or on its own, under a broad understanding of what equality entails. Second, some jurisdictions have a detailed anti-discrimination regulation that may further economic and social rights, such as provisions on the prohibition of employment discrimination or in the access to public services. Moreover, these provisions may be the only way to make private actors accountable regarding the access to goods or services, where there is no constitutional cause of action against non-state actors. Third, equality laws have been useful to claim a 'ratchet effect' on economic and social rights, especially for groups that cling to modest advances in social protection to extend the scope of beneficiaries. Every time the state makes available the objects of social rights to some of its citizens, equality clauses can be used to argue that the state must extend the same benefits to others. For example, that is the way in which gay couples have obtained access to social security benefits from which they were excluded.[49]

Additionally, the right to equality and non-discrimination has also been used to extend the protection of social rights beyond a 'minimum core'. When social rights are enforceable only to the extent that they protect access to minimum essential levels, equality clauses may be used to 'demand the same treatment as those within the state's jurisdiction who enjoy the highest standards of economic and social rights'.[50] Finally, and specifically on the issue of poverty, ADLs of the region have been relevant to highlight aspects related to social exclusion, marginalisation and vulnerability. In general, ADL may serve to challenge anti-poverty tools that perpetuate and reproduce social conditions associated with poverty. It may do this in four fundamental ways: first, by incorporating 'poverty' (or other related indicators) as a ground of protection; second, by bridging the gap between universal and means-tested policies, incorporating the latter into comprehensive social protection frameworks; third, by drawing links between poverty and other protected grounds through indirect discrimination or intersectionality; and, finally, by crafting positive duties that pay due regard to socioeconomic disadvantages.[51] The interconnection between equality laws and poverty issues allows us not only to make a 'valuable contribution to aspects of poverty based on mis-recognition and social and political exclusion', but also to 'address distributive inequalities in [their] own right'.[52]

2   ADL AND POVERTY IN ARGENTINA

The Argentinian case is well placed to illustrate the link between equality laws and poverty. Argentina was the first country of the region to enact a specific anti-discrimination statute that included an extended list of protected grounds and developed the constitutional equality clause.[53] The constitutional amendment of 1994 impacted the operation of equality laws on the ground, with the incorporation of collective rights and remedies, the establishment of an extended constitutional writ, the explicit constitutional hierarchy of human rights treaties, the creation of an ombudsman (Defensoría del Pueblo) with strong powers, and the constitutional support of positive duties for disadvantaged groups.[54] Although this amendment was also directed at the retrenchment of the state regarding social policies (privatisation, protections of private property and constraining the economic activity of the state), the abovementioned reforms were important for legal empowerment/mobilisation. For example, they provided political support for the creation of a special administrative agency, Instituto Nacional contra la Discriminación, la Xenofobia y el Racismo (INADI, National Institute Against Discrimination, Xenophobia and Racism), in charge of implementing anti-discrimination provisions.[55] The INADI started to explore links between poverty issues and equality, such as the recent campaign for the enactment of a gender identity law, which highlighted both recognition and redistribution claims of transgender people, especially those working in the sex industry.

Furthermore, the Argentinian case is interesting to analyse because of the country's longstanding tradition of social movements and civil rights organisations that have pushed forward the agenda of equality rights. The history of popular resistance to the Argentinian dictatorship highlights the role of social movements in promoting international and domestic pressure to recover democracy. The authoritarian environment also promoted the emergence of 'new social movements': unable to mount full political movements against dictatorship, 'activists began to mobilize around less threatening characteristics, namely ethnic, gender or other identities'.[56] However, with the economic and political crisis of the early 2000s, social movements that included the most deprived socioeconomic groups began to emerge as a resistance to austerity measures.[57] The rapid increase in the number of people living in poverty triggered one of the biggest social mobilisations of recent times in the region. Either called *piqueteros*, because of their distinctive way of social protest, or *villeros*, because of the informal settlements that began to emerge in urban areas, these movements started to construct their identities around socioeconomic conditions, such as the lack of housing or access to a basic income. In a sense, the failures of neoliberal policies 'have contributed to the continuing emphasis on intersecting identities, leading identity-based groups to continue to focus on inequality and economic redistribution'.[58] Beyond that, economically deprived people have found an identity in the shared experience of poverty, and the National Congress of Argentina has recognised this by establishing 7 October as the day of the *Villero* Identity.[59]

Finally, Argentina is interesting to study from the perspective of the judicialisation of politics.[60] It was one of the first countries of the region that granted open access to justice, giving legal standing to public interest associations, and providing judicial review powers to every judge (known as 'diffuse control of constitutionality'). In the context of the crisis of representation and party politics, the courts were gradually considered as an 'institutional voice for the poor'.[61] Legal mobilisation is somehow considered to be an avenue for political participation,[62] and in some cases the only possible way to address complex demands, such as the lack of access to basic services and the structurally deprived conditions suffered by groups of people living in the same area.[63]

In what follows I shall analyse the ways in which equality laws have been used by social movements in order to address poverty issues in Argentina. In the first place, these laws have been used to challenge the lack of access to 'basic' services considering 'social condition' or 'economic situation' as protected grounds. Specifically, they have been used to enforce compliance with state duties to warrant equality of access to these services, and to address structural problems in the functioning of markets in Latin American contexts. However, equality laws have also been used to challenge the stereotyping effects of anti-poverty policies, generating continuities between status inequalities and distributive problems. Moreover, they have been used to extend the scope of social policies that were originally crafted as means-tested policies. Within this second dimension, ADLs have been related to concerns that go beyond the mere expansion of market access, to address challenges against market-based anti-poverty policies. The point of these cases has been 'to influence the original distribution of wealth and income by reorganizing the market economy, not just to try to correct, after the fact, what the market, as now organized, has done'.[64]

A first group of cases concerns situations in which deprived urban areas were lacking access to basic services, a frequent scenario within the struggle for social rights. The reason behind these claims is to enforce compliance with market commitments, especially regarding services that were previously provided by state-owned enterprises, such as water and telecommunications. An interesting case was initiated by the INADI, and later decided by the quasiadjudicatory powers of the ombudsman of the city of Buenos Aires.[65] In this case an old lady living in an economically deprived area of the city of Mar del Plata brought a complaint against a telephone service provider because it refused to install an internet service, claiming that the area was considered a 'risk zone'. The case was started before the INADI, and later a new complaint was initiated before the local ombudsman, who referred the case to the ombudsman of Buenos Aires. In the process, the company replied that there was no technical capacity to provide the service in that area. The resolution issued by the Defensoría de Buenos Aires integrates the reading of the prohibition of discrimination within the administrative regime of public services and the rights of users and consumers. It established that even when dealing with 'improper services' (i.e. not directly provided by the state), the public regime is entrusted to guarantee the permanent, general and egalitarian provision of services that were once the exclusive domain of the state. Moreover, the resolution related the ground of 'social position' included in the Argentinian ADL with the concept of 'social category', and then concluded that the company was arbitrarily distinguishing and imposing a disadvantage on the claimant.

This case has been followed by another group of court cases raised by consumers and users associations using collective actions against telephone providers. These claims are grounded on constitutional equality clauses that allow judges to address these problems from a structural point of view, specifically considering poverty and deprivation within an urban context.[66] Based on Article 75(23) of the Constitution of Argentina, which speaks of 'positive action' and 'real equality of opportunity', and gives examples of 'vulnerable groups', one of the federal courts concluded that 'the role of the judiciary is to make a careful balance in the exercise of rights and protect the weakest'.[67] This line of reasoning was partially based on the harmful effects of the lack of access to phone or internet services, therefore diminishing the market competitiveness of people living in areas considered to be 'risk zones' and reproducing the conditions of poverty.[68]

Anti-discrimination legal provisions have also been used to challenge anti-poverty policies that are considered to be discriminatory, either because of their stereotyping effects or because they do not function as decommodifying devices within the struggle against poverty. In these cases, the main point is to abandon the consideration of poverty as a purely socioeconomic issue and to advance a new perspective of structural discrimination. In other words, these cases consider poverty not as the violation of the content of a specific social right but as an integral problem.[69] Thus the emphasis is placed neither on the unequal treatment of economically deprived people compared with other citizens, nor on the reasons behind pro-poor policies, but on the social context surrounding a certain practice.

An illustrative case was decided by the first instance courts of Buenos Aires, regarding the establishment of emergency measures to deal with the lack of school vacancies for inhabitants of *villas de emergencia*. In 2002, when the effects of the economic crisis were at their peak, the Government of Buenos Aires started to set up 'modular classrooms' to deal with the lack of vacancies for children living in poverty. Although they were originally established as emergency measures to deal with many families that abruptly fell into poverty, in 2005 there was no institutional plan of replacement or reallocation of these children. Those classrooms were popularly known as 'container classrooms', and they were associated with children who lived in *villas de emergencia* or *villas miseria*. The case started with a collective action triggered by an NGO, and was based on anti-discrimination provisions at different levels. The Government of Buenos Aires replied that these emergency measures were considered as positive actions in favour of economically deprived people, so they could not be considered as infringing the people's fundamental rights. The final judgment concluded that the process should not be focused on an analysis of the government's motives for the public policy but rather on the discriminatory effects that it produced. Furthermore, it ordered the government to provide a permanent solution to the lack of school posts, considering the need to respect the other fundamental rights involved, such as the right to education.[70] The decision stressed the importance of budget planning and long-term strategies in the 'war' against poverty in order to pay due regard to the principle of equality and non-discrimination.

3   CONCLUSION

This chapter aims to explore the ways in which ADLs have been used to address poverty issues in Latin America. The case of Argentina illustrates how these laws are unavoidably tied to poverty problems, such as the lack of access to basic services and the stereotyping effects of anti-poverty policies. These examples show the broader tensions between two competing narratives to account for the recent boom in anti-discrimination legal reforms in the region. A neostructural narrative highlights the instrumental character of ADL for economic purposes. However, a transformative approach to ADL provides us with a socioeconomic lens that allows us to properly address poverty as a matter of social justice (redistribution and recognition) and as a structural problem. This chapter is a contribution to evaluating the emancipatory potential of ADL, but further assessments of the functioning of equality laws on the ground are still to come.

NOTES

1. Comisión Económica para América Latina y el Caribe, *Panorama Social* (CEPAL 2014).
2. Alberto Coddou, 'A Transformative Approach to Anti-Discrimination Law' (Working Paper).
3. These are principle of state intervention; ontological lens; socioeconomic lens; challenging stance; political axis; and legal mobilization/empowerment.
4. I will use 'equality laws' and 'anti-discrimination laws' interchangeably.
5. Tarunabh Khaitan, *A Theory of Discrimination Law* (Oxford University Press 2015) 4.
6. Article 18, Law 20.609.
7. Nancy Fraser and Axel Honneth, *Redistribution or Recognition? A Political-Philosophical Exchange* (Verso 2004) 78–79.
8. Khaitan (n 5) 10.
9. George Rutherglen, 'Concrete or Abstract Concepts of Discrimination?' in Deborah Hellman and Sophia Moreau (eds), *Philosophical Foundations of Discrimination Law* (Oxford University Press 2013).
10. Khaitan (n 5).
11. Osvaldo Sunkel and Enrique Zulueta, 'Neo-structuralism versus Neo-liberalism in the 1990s' (1990) 42 CEPAL Review 35.
12. Fernando Leiva, 'Toward a Critique of Latin American Neo-structuralism' (2008) 50 Latin American Politics and Society 1, 3.
13. See the conclusions of the report *Changing Production Patterns with Social Equity* (1992) and the parallel developments in gender or racial equality that made reference to that developmental narrative (ECLAC/CDCC 1995).
14. However, in recent years, ECLAC 'has developed the social and labour market dimensions of its neo-structuralist discourse, moving from a limited concern with "equity" to embrace a rights-based, universalist conception of social protection'. Rianne Mahon, 'Integrating the Social into CEPAL's Neo-structuralist Discourse' (2014) *Global Social Policy* 1, 10. See e.g. one of the latest reports, *Time for Equality* (2010).
15. Leiva (n 12) 6.
16. Ibid. 8.
17. Ibid.

18. Ibid 15.
19. Evelyn Ellis and Philippa Watson, *EU Anti-Discrimination Law* (Oxford University Press 2014).
20. Mark Bell, *Anti-Discrimination Law and the European Union* (Oxford University Press 2002).
21. Michael Connolly, 'Achieving Social Mobility: The Role of Equality Law' (2013) 13 International Journal of Discrimination and the Law 261.
22. Alexander Somek, *Engineering Equality* (Oxford University Press 2011) 83.
23. Christopher McCrudden and Sasha Prechal, *The Concepts of Equality and Non-Discrimination in Europe: A Practical Approach* (European Network of Legal Experts in the Field of Gender Equality 2009) 6.
24. Connolly (n 21) 262.
25. Ellis and Watson (n 19).
26. However, the Strasbourg Court has been using the concept of 'vulnerable groups' in order to 'address different aspects of inequality in a more substantive manner'. Lourdes Peroni and Alexandra Timmer, 'Vulnerable Groups: The Promise of an Emerging Concept in European Human Rights Convention Law' (2013) 11 International Journal of Constitutional Law 1056, 1057.
27. Colm O'Cinneide, 'Bringing Socio-Economic Rights Back into the Mainstream' (2009). http://papers.ssrn.com/sol3/papers.cfm?abstract_id=1543127.
28. Sandra Fredman, 'The Potential and Limits of an Equal Rights Paradigm in Addressing Poverty' (2010) 22 Stellenbosch Law Review 566, 567.
29. Jean Grugel and Pía Riggirozzi, 'Post-neoliberalism in Latin America: Rebuilding and Reclaiming the State after Crisis' (2012) 43 Development and Change 1, 6.
30. César Rodríguez-Garavito, 'Beyond the Courtroom: The Impact of Judicial Activism on Socioeconomic Rights in Latin America' (2011) 89 Texas Law Review 7.
31. Daniel Brinks and William Forbath, 'The Role of Courts and Constitutions in the New Politics of Welfare in Latin America' in Randall Peerenboom and Tom Ginsburgs (eds), *Law and Development of Middle-Income Countries* (Cambridge University Press 2014).

32. Martín Aldao and Laura Clérico, 'La Igualdad "Des-Enmarcada": a Veinte Años de la Reforma Constitucional Argentina de 1994' (2015) 13 Revista Electrónica del Instituto de Investigaciones Ambrosio L. Gioja 8.
33. Rodrigo Uprimny and Luz Sánchez, 'Artículo 24. Igualdad ante la Ley' in Chistian Steiner and Patricia Uribe (eds), *Convención Americana de Derechos Humanos: Comentario* (Fundación Konrad Adenauer 2014).
34. Sergio García, 'The Relationship between Inter-American Jurisdiction and States (National Systems): Some Pertinent Questions' (2014). https://humanrights.nd.edu/assets/134035/garciaramireziaeng.pdf.
35. Alexandra Huneeus, 'Courts Resisting Courts: Lessons from the Inter-American Court's Struggle to Enforce Human Rights' (2011) 44 Cornell International Law Journal 493.
36. Bob Hepple, *Equality: The Legal Framework* (Hart 2014) 227.
37. Fredman (n 28) 567.
38. CESCR, *General Comment no.20* (UN 2009).
39. Law 23.592, Argentina; Article 11, Constitution of Ecuador; Article 37, Constitution of Peru.
40. Law 045, Bolivia; Article 323, Criminal Code, Peru.
41. Law 20.609, Chile; Inter-American Convention against All Forms of Discrimination and Intolerance.
42. ACHR.
43. Edward Telles and Stanley Bailey, 'Understanding Latin American Beliefs about Racial Inequality' (2013) 118 American Journal of Sociology 1559.
44. Latinobarómetro, *Informe Anual* (2001). http://www.latinobarometro.org/latContents.jsp; Alberto Chong and Hugo Ñopo, 'The Mystery of Discrimination in Latin America' (2008) 8 Economía 79.
45. INDH 2013; INADI 2014; CONAPRED 2010.
46. Sarah Warren, 'Latin American Identity Politics: Redefining Citizenship' (2012) 6(10) Sociology Compass 833.
47. Fraser and Honneth (n 7).
48. Equal Rights Trust, *A Litigator's Guide to Using Equality and Non-discrimination Strategies to Advance Economic and Social Rights* (ERT 2014).
49. *Duque v Colombia* [2014] Inter-American Commission on Human Rights, report 5/2014.
50. ERT (n 48) IV.
51. Ibid. 588.

52. Ibid. 567.
53. Law 23.592, of 1988.
54. Aldao and Clérico (n 32).
55. Law 24.515, of 1995.
56. Warren (n 46) 834.
57. Marisella Svampa, 'Movimientos Sociales y Nuevo Escenario Regional. Las Inflexiones del Paradigma Liberal en América Latina' in Maristella Svampa (ed), *Cambio de Época. Movimientos Sociales y Poder Político. Buenos Aires, Argentina* (Siglo Veintiuno-CLACSO 2008).
58. Warren (n 46) 834–835.
59. Law 27.095, of 2014.
60. Gabriela Delamata, 'Movimientos Sociales, Activismo Constitucional y Narrativa Democrática en la Argentina Contemporánea' (2013) 32 Sociologías 148, 156.
61. Roberto Gargarella, Pilar Domingo and Theunis Roux (eds), *Courts and Social Transformation in New Democracies: An Institutional Voice for the Poor?* (Ashgate 2006).
62. Gabriela Delamata, 'Contestación Social y Acción Legal: La (otra) Disputa por los Derechos' 3 Sudamérica 101, 105.
63. Catalina Smulovitz, 'Organizaciones que Invocan Derechos. Sociedad Civil y Representación en la Argentina' (2008) 13 Postdata 1.
64. Roberto Mangabeira Unger, *The Left Alternative* (Verso 2009) xiv.
65. Decision 26/2013.
66. Gustavo Maurino, Ezequiel Nino and Martín Sigal, *Las Acciones Colectivas* (Lexis Nexis 2006). See also the collective action against *Transportes de Buenos Aires* for the unequal conditions of train lanes depending on socio-economic backgrounds: for middle-upper class areas, the Mitre line provided amenities suitable for a trip, such as air-conditioning, television and a reasonable density during peak hours; for the lower classes, the Sarmiento line lacked the minimum safety conditions, had no windows and suffered from persistent overcrowding. The Supreme Court of Argentina forced the company to provide a 'decent service'. *Unión de Usuarios y Consumidores v Sec. Transporte*, 104/01, 24 June 2014.
67. Federal Civil and Commercial Court, n10, 101/2012, 2.b.
68. Ibid. 5.a.3; see another collective action judgment in the dossier 13787/2006 of the same court.
69. Ezequiel Nino, 'La Discriminación Menos Comentada' in Roberto Gargarella (ed), *La Constitución en 2020* (Siglo Veintiuno 2011).
70. Administrative Court of the City of Buenos Aires, n11, 10 July 2006.

CHAPTER 14

Gender Quotas, Legislative Resistance and Non-Legislative Reform

Malu A.C. Gatto

Gender quota policies have gained the attention of international organisations and domestic policy-makers alike for their potential to overcome gender inequality in parliaments throughout the world. Gender quotas are meant to facilitate the entry of women into politics by mandating a defined proportion of candidate nominations or seats in parliament to be reserved for women.[1] In the last two decades, gender quotas have rapidly spread globally and have now been adopted as national-level policies in roughly 50 countries. This type of policy has been particularly prominent in Latin America, where, as of 2015, all democratic countries but one, Guatemala, adopted national gender quota policies.

The literature identifies three general types of quota: party quotas (individual parties voluntarily adopt an internally decided quota); legislated candidate quotas (a law mandates all parties in a given system to nominate the established proportion of female candidates); and reserved seats (a law sets out a proportion of seats in parliament that can only be filled by women).[2] All policies in Latin America fall under the 'legislated candidate quota' typology; nonetheless, variation in quota design still exists. For example, policies adopted throughout the region have established quota

M.A.C. Gatto (✉)
University of Oxford, Oxford, UK

© Palgrave Macmillan, a division of Macmillan Publishers Limited 2017
P. Fortes et al. (eds.), *Law and Policy in Latin America*,
DOI 10.1057/978-1-137-56694-2_14

239

requirements that range from 15 % to 50 %. Furthermore, some policies have included electoral sanctions for non-compliance, while others have been enforced through financial sanctions and many have not established sanctions at all.

As a type of affirmative action policy for women, gender quotas have the potential to intervene in the candidate-recruitment process (otherwise exerted according to party discretion) and limit the space for male candidates—the vast majority of political incumbents and party leaders. Despite this, gender quota adoptions have overwhelmingly taken place inside male-dominated congressional rooms. This pattern seems to defy longstanding assumptions of the rationality of career-driven politicians. According to this view, legislators would act to protect their seats by minimising external competition, and not by adopting a policy that does the opposite: encourage the recruitment of candidates outside the existing pool.

The literature has generally tackled this puzzle in one of two ways. Some scholars have suggested that legislators are indeed self-motivated and, for this reason, adopt quotas as 'empty' gestures of their commitment to gender equality but purposefully design policies that lack the provisions necessary to enact real changes. Others have viewed the role of incumbents more favourably and argued that state actors can be active supporters of women's political representation and activists of change.[3] In this chapter I contribute to this debate by analysing the strength of gender quota designs vis-à-vis their origins. I judge the strength of gender quota policies not by their effective results but by the provisions included in their design. In assessing the origin of policies, I differentiate between processes enacted by *legislative* actors (e.g. electoral changes, encompassing constitutional reforms) and those carried out by *non*-legislative actors (e.g. executive decrees, judicial decisions). I hypothesise that because gender quotas go against the interests of legislative actors, strong gender quota designs are more likely to result from non-legislative processes.

I explore this theoretical proposition by coding and empirically analysing gender quota policies, as originally introduced or subsequently modified by legislative or non-legislative processes. Using data from 40 instances of gender quota policy adoptions and revisions in Latin America, I show that non-legislative actors are responsible for strengthening crucial components of gender quota designs and that their intervention also considerably speeds up the process of design strengthening. By relying on descriptive statistics, the chapter does not seek to exhaustively test the hypothesis posed but, instead, to uncover previously hidden patterns in gender quota-related policy-making, and to highlight important questions about quota policy designs that remain largely unanswered. To the best of my knowledge, this is the first attempt to systematically and comparatively categorise specific provisions of gender quota policies as they pertain to the type of decision-making process that created them. Throughout the chapter the terms 'gender quota', 'quota' and 'quota policies' are used interchangeably.

I divide the chapter as follows. First, I briefly review the literature on gender quota adoption and strengthening. Subsequently, I describe the data used, a dataset that includes all cases of gender quota adoptions (and revisions) in Latin America.[4] In the third section I employ this dataset to analyse the association between the strength of gender quota designs and the type of process through which policies are originated. In conclusion, I summarise my findings and suggest potential areas for further study.

1   Gender Quota Adoption and Strengthening

Scholars generally identify three main forces behind the promotion, adoption and strengthening of gender quotas worldwide: international organisations; transnational diffusion and learning; and the efforts of women's groups, female legislators and party leaders.[5] Most studies agree that the growing popularity of gender quotas is, at least in part, a consequence of international norms and transnational values that emphasise the agenda of gender equality. Studies on gender quotas often claim that international conferences and recommendations, such as the Convention for the Elimination of All Forms of Discrimination Against Women from 1979 and the Beijing Platform for Action from 1995, as well as the creation of UN Women in 2010, have all contributed to the popularity and spread of quotas throughout the world.

Similarly, transnational diffusion and learning have been associated with processes of gender quota adoption and strengthening. This approach suggests that countries learn from each others' policy experiences, prompting policy imitation. In such explanations, policy strengthening results from countries' and policy-makers' engagement in information-sharing on quota provisions/design and observations of what types of policy provision make quotas more or less effective in achieving their stated goals (i.e. increasing women's political representation).

Women's organisations are also often mentioned as the driving force behind the adoption of gender quotas, as well as their subsequent strengthening revisions. Proponents of this view emphasise the importance of women's movements and argue that male-dominated elites do not push for gender quotas unless there is prior women's mobilisation that presses for such a policy. The proportion of women in parliament and party leadership has also been positively associated with the likelihood of a party supporting gender quotas and lobbying for stronger gender quota designs.

Much less has been said about the factors that have the potential to negatively impact the strength of quota designs. For instance, although many authors identify male legislators' resistance to gender quota adoption and/or policy strengthening, few scholars focus on theorising and empirically studying such resistance. The latter group generally suggests that legislators act to minimise the impact of gender quotas on promoting change in elite renovation. To them, the actions of male incumbents represent empty gestures that do not produce strong or effective quotas. Gender quota policies, however, need not be adopted or revised by the very actors that are impacted by them: non-legislative actors may also intervene in the processes of gender quota adoption and strengthening. Baldez has been one of the few authors to place courts at the centre of explanations of quota policy developments. According to her, judicial actors play a crucial role in legitimising quota laws, given that the passing of gender quota legislation often prompts those resisting their adoption to challenge them constitutionally. Courts' willingness to assure compliance with gender quotas and rule against non-compliance has also been described as important in effectively strengthening gender quota provisions. Furthermore, the role of executives in drafting gender quota-related legislation, providing guidance and resources to legislators supporting gender quotas, and enacting executive decrees to address policy design weaknesses, has also been noted.[6]

Although the roles of international organisations, diffusion and female actors within and outside government have been widely documented, much less attention has been dedicated to studying whether the type of decision-making process that led to gender quota adoption/revision matters for policy design. To provide insights into this issue, this chapter disaggregates the design of gender quota policies by provision and type of origin.

2   Measuring Gender Quota Strength

One of the main challenges in carrying out this study is that it requires a measure of gender quota strength. Because I am interested in variation within cases for which gender quotas are in place, I use the index I developed to measure the strength of gender quota designs. The Index of Gender Quota Strength (IGQS) is composed of the different types of provision identified in the literature as responsible for strengthening or weakening a gender quota policy.

However, systematically comparing the strength of gender quota designs is not an easy task. Many authors have contributed to the development of nuanced measures of gender quotas by suggesting frameworks that consider different policy provisions. Schwindt-Bayer, for instance, operationalises quota strength by employing three characteristics of gender quota designs as separate independent variables—namely, 'quota size' (proportion of nominations reserved for women), 'placement mandate' (presence of mandate that establishes that female candidates should be placed in 'electable' positions), and 'enforcement mechanism'.[7] Krook complements this package and argues that, when analysing the effectiveness of gender quota policies, the aspects to investigate should be ambiguity (whether the language of the legislation is clear); requirements (size of the quota demand); presence of sanctions for non-compliance; and, finally, 'perceived legitimacy' (presence of economic or political sanctions for non-compliance).[8] Meanwhile, Jones categorises gender quotas as 'well-designed' or 'poorly-designed' (i.e. 'lax'). According to him, 'lax' refer to policies with loopholes that essentially nullify or substantially diminish the application of gender quotas in practice. Aspects which render a design 'lax' include provisions that allow gender quotas to be avoided in cases in which primaries are conducted.[9] I consider all of these discussions in the development of my indicator.

In sum, from the types of provision identified in the existing literature, I extract five dimensions that contribute to the strength of gender quota designs—namely, (1) size requirements; (2) placement mandates (i.e. ranking systems); (3) compliance mechanisms (i.e. sanctions); (4) office applicability; and (5) obstacles to implementation. For each dimension I create ordinal-level variables that range from 0 to 4, with 0 representing 'no quota/lack of provision' and values 1 through 4 representing different gradations of provision strength from the lowest (1) to the highest (4). For example, on the scale of 'size requirements', a value of 1 refers to a quota between 20 and 29 %, while a value of 4 refers to a quota of 50 %. The IGQS compounds the scores of all five dimensions into a 21-point interval scale (in which 0 signifies the lack of a quota, 1 signifies the weakest and 21 the strongest gender quota designs).[10] It is worth noting that I do not distinguish between parity regimes and quota laws, apart from giving them different values on the parameter measuring 'size requirements'. Although I recognise the debate surrounding the philosophical differences between gender quota laws and parity regimes, I still treat them equally. The reason for this is simple: for the current work, gender quotas represent a type of policy with the potential of breaking the monopoly of political parties in candidate-selection processes and displacing established elites to make room for political outsiders. Parity laws have the potential of prompting similar results.

For the task at hand, I also code the origin of gender quota policies, a process that is not clear-cut. Often, more than one type of actor is involved in the process of policy elaboration. Nonetheless, for the sake of empirical analysis, my coding assigns the origin/authorship of a given policy to the process/actors responsible for finalising it. For instance, a gender quota policy requiring legislative approval to be enacted is counted as originating from the legislature, even if non-legislative actors were involved in earlier stages of the decision-making process. Furthermore, I only consider policies that directly pertain to gender quotas for legislative office. Other gender quota-related policies, including quotas for other government offices, are not included in the current analysis. This variable is coded 0 for policies enacted by legislative actors and 1 for those enacted by non-legislative actors.

To build the dataset used, I first relied on secondary sources to identify relevant policies and complete a list of decision-making processes that affected gender quota policy designs in law and practice. These sources include the Global Database of Quotas for Women,[11] the Observatório de Género of CEPAL/ECLAC[12] and other country-specific secondary sources. I then used primary sources (e.g. congressional decisions, executive decrees and judicial rulings) to individually hand code each policy in accordance with the operationalisation guidelines outlined for the IGQS.

3   RESULTS

A total of 40 procedures of gender quota adoption and revision have taken place in Latin America since 1990. These include policies resulting from legislative processes, executive decrees and judicial decisions. Of the 17 countries from the region that have adopted some type of gender quota, 12 have subsequently revised their respective policies at least once. Although the overwhelming majority of original gender quota policies have been adopted by legislatures, either as specific bills or as part of a larger electoral reform, gender quota policy revisions have sometimes taken place outside congressional rooms. That is, 16 original gender quota policies have been introduced through legislative processes, 1 by executive decree and 1 by judicial ruling;[13] meanwhile, legislators have been responsible for 17 subsequent policy revisions, executives for 2 and courts for 4.[14] This means that non-legislative actors were responsible for 11.1 % of original gender quota adoptions and 26 % of revisions, including one quota retraction.

Figure 14.1 provides an overview of how values of the IGQS are distributed across all 40 policies and breaks down this distribution by each of the IGQS's individual components. As shown, the distribution of the values of the IGQS is skewed left, meaning that policies in the region most frequently score higher rather than lower values on the IGQS scale. The IGQS produces a mean of 11.5 and a median of 12, also reflecting this distributional tendency towards higher values.

Nonetheless, only two of scales of the individual components that make up the IGQS produce means above the scale midpoint (2.5). The scale for size requirements produces a mean of 2.625, while the scale of obstacles for implementation produces a mean of 2.925. This suggests that these

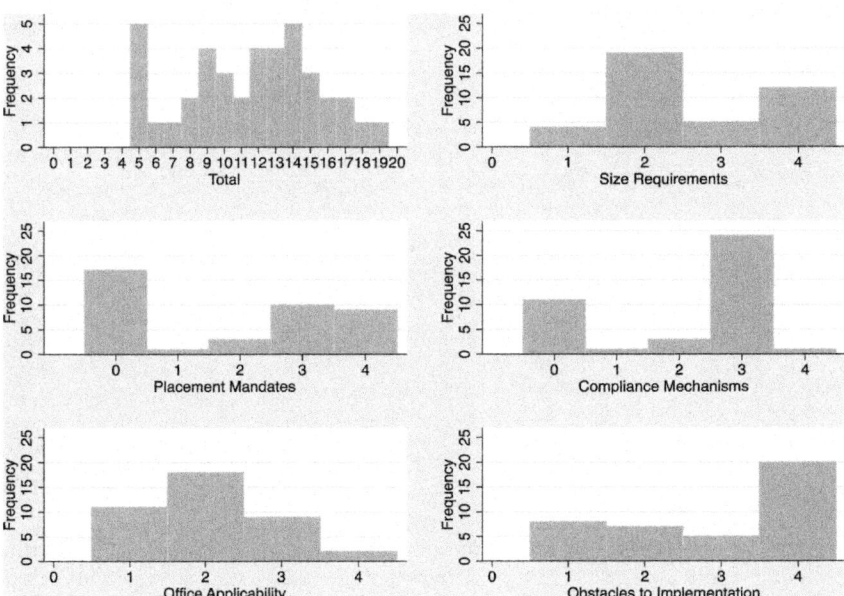

Fig. 14.1   Values of the IGQS and its individual components, as distributed in Latin America (*Source*: Developed by author using own data)

are the scales that, on average, mostly contribute to the strength of gender quota designs in Latin America. This makes sense given that many gender quotas have recently been transformed into parity regimes, thus increasing the size requirements of policy designs, and that many original quotas have been revised (through legislative means or by executive decrees and court resolutions) to close design loopholes.

Despite this seemingly positive snapshot, a number of authors have depicted early gender quota adoptions in Latin America as symbolic gestures to showcase legislators' commitment to gender equality while avoiding increased electoral competition. Others have suggested that although presumably weak, early gender quota policies served as the basis of entrance for women in parliament, who could then challenge weak designs and strengthen quotas from within the system.[15] As Fig. 14.2 shows, weak gender quota designs have indeed been more common among early adopters, with no country other than Nicaragua adopting a quota design scoring less than 10 on the IGQS scale after 1998.

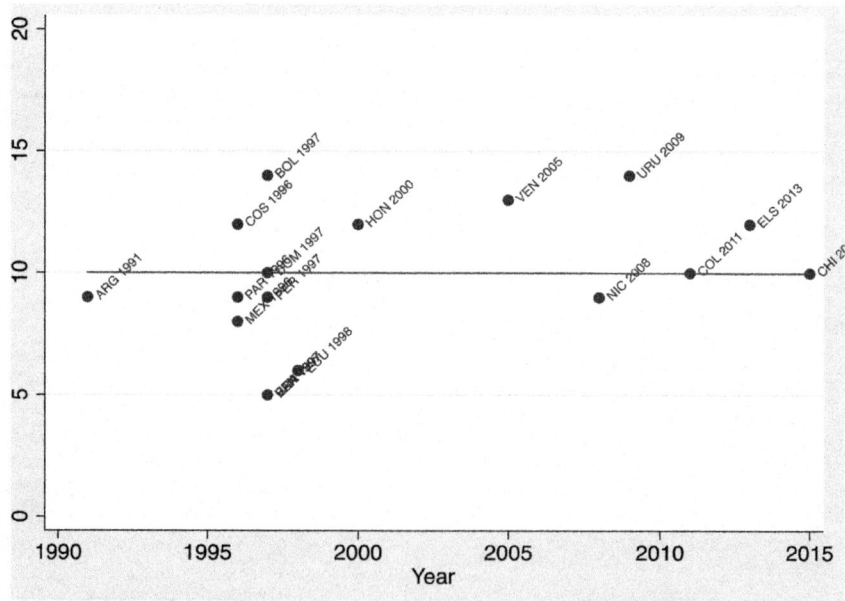

Fig. 14.2 Strength of original gender quota policy designs in Latin America, as measured by the IGQS (*Source*: Developed by author using own data)

Among the early adopters, only one has never revised its quota (Paraguay). All other countries that adopted a quota before 2000 (Argentina, Bolivia, Brazil, Costa Rica, the Dominican Republic, Ecuador, Mexico, Panama, Peru and Venezuela) have since amended their original policy designs. Together, these 11 countries have enacted a total of 20 revisions (and one retraction in Venezuela). Of these, 14 were enacted by the legislature: increasing quotas' size requirements in 8 instances, placement mandates in 6, compliance mechanisms (i.e. sanctions) in 3, extending office applicability in 4 cases, and diminishing or completely closing loopholes in 2.

Albeit less frequently, legislative revisions have also been used to weaken gender quota designs: in the Dominican Republic (2000), a reform repealed the quota from the Senate, leading to a decrease in my measure of office applicability; in two other cases—Mexico (2002) and Ecuador (2000) —revisions created more obstacles to implementation. Two late adopters also reformed their original quotas though legislative means: Honduras and Nicaragua. Honduras' engagement in legislative revision in 2004 also led to the weakening of its quota, which was once again restored and strengthened in 2012.[16] In the same year, the Nicaraguan legislature also strengthened its quota through legislative reform. Although gender quota revisions enacted through legislative means have been frequent, the intervention of non-legislative actors has been less common. Only 6 policy revisions enacted in the region have not been led by legislative actors; of these, 1 retracted the existing quota; 0 addressed size requirements; 2 strengthened placement mandates; 1 enacted sanctions for non-compliance; 2 increased office reach; and 2 addressed loopholes. This brief summary suggests that the role of legislative actors in strengthening gender quota legislation has been extremely prominent and that non-legislative actors may have had only a marginal influence on this process.

However, simple descriptive statistics show that although reforms led by non-legislative actors have been few, they have been significant in magnitude. Table 14.1 summarises the changes in policy strength for the IGQS and all of its individual components, as enacted by legislative and non-legislative actors. The values below refer to the means of policy differences, disaggregated by the type of policy authorship. These values are calculated by first taking the difference in policy strength between a given policy revision and the score of the policy that preceded it (e.g. the Mexican quota policy of 1996 received a score of 8 and its 2002 revision a score of 11; 11 − 8 = 3, thus the difference in policy strength as enacted

Table 14.1   Strength of policy revisions in Latin America as measured by changes in the IGQS and its individual component scales

	IGQS	Size	Placement	Compliance	Office	Obstacles
Mean of Δ	2.68	0.45	1.23	0.41	0.27	0.23
Mean of Δ legislative	2.70	0.58	1.35	0.35	0.18	0.06
Mean of Δ non-legislative	2.60	–	0.80	0.60	0.60	0.80

Note: Based on 22 cases: 17 enacted through legislative means and 5 by non-legislative actors (not considering a case of quota retraction in Venezuela)

by revision is 3), adding-up all of the policy's differences and then dividing the result by the number of policies considered.

When disaggregated by type of policy origin, this measure allows for the analysis of the relationship between the substantiality of quota revisions and their respective authors. Engaging in this exercise, I find that, on average, non-legislative reforms have led to greater strengthening of policy designs in three of the five dimensions of the IGQS: compliance mechanisms, office applicability and obstacles to implementation. Although the mean for the overall IGQS is greater for the distribution of cases enacted through legislative action, this is driven by changes in placement mandates and size requirements. This suggests that although legislative reforms are more frequent, they are also less ambitious in addressing weaknesses in policy designs—especially with regard to compliance mechanisms and loopholes, aspects considered by the literature as crucial for the effective implementation of gender quotas. These findings could be a consequence of the tension between the unwillingness of male legislators to adopt strong gender quotas and increase electoral competition, and the pressure felt by executive and judicial actors to uphold normative values promoted by domestic and international pressure groups.

Non-legislative actors have been particularly important where original adoption has been the weakest. Brazil, Panama, Ecuador, Mexico and Venezuela originally adopted quotas with very weak designs. Brazil, Panama and Venezuela produced original IGQS scores of 5, while Ecuador and Mexico produced designs of scores 6 and 8, respectively. In three cases—Brazil, Mexico and Venezuela—the original policies were reformed (or substituted in the case of Venezuela) by stronger designs enacted by non-legislative actors. Brazil adopted a quota policy of 30 % for the lower house of its National Congress in 1997. Despite the efforts of female legislators and women's groups, the quota was only approved by the Brazilian legislature after the inclusion of loopholes: in passing a 30 % gender quota, the parties managed to simultaneously increase the proportion of candidacies that a party could nominate from 100 % to 150 %, as well as giving the possibility of not complying with the gender quota if not all candidacies were filled. Needless to say, the inclusion of this provision drastically challenged the implementation of the Brazilian gender law. The quota was only reformed again in 2009, when the executive established a tripartite commission to draw up proposals to be submitted as part of a larger electoral reform. Many of the commission's proposals were stripped down and weakened during legislative debates, but their proponents managed to change the language of the legislation from 'reserve' to 'fill', thus implying that it was no longer enough for parties to comply with the quota by 'reserving' extra candidacies for female candidates but not recruiting women to fill them. This change allowed non-legislative actors to intervene more directly in 2010. By ruling that party lists that were not at least 30 % female would not be registered, the electoral tribunal stipulated electoral sanctions for political parties that did not comply with the quota.

In Mexico, the actions of the judiciary were even more emphatic in addressing policy loopholes. The Mexican political parties had been avoiding gender quota compliance in two ways: first, by selecting candidates via party primaries, thus forgoing the need to respect the quota, and, second, by electing women who, upon election, would step down and be replaced by men (*Juanitas*, as they became known). In 2011, Mexico's electoral court ruled that neither tactic could be used to avoid the gender quota, closing the loopholes that for years challenged the implementation of the Mexican quota law. Finally, the original quota repealed by the Venezuelan Constitutional Court in 2000 was replaced by an 11-point stronger one enacted via a judicial ruling of the Venezuelan electoral tribunal in 2005. Through legislative means, Panama and Ecuador were also able to strengthen the policy designs of their original quota policies. Nevertheless, it took Panama two policy revisions through the legislature to strengthen its original policy by only 3e points on the IGQS scale, resulting in what is today one of the weakest gender quota policies in the region. Ecuador, on the other hand, managed to revise its original quota extensively, increasing its policy strength from 7 to 18 in just two years, a process which was implemented as part of the country's efforts to establish general election laws in 2000.[17]

Non-legislative actors have also been quicker to address weaknesses and/or loopholes in gender quota designs than legislative actors. While revisions enacted by legislative actors have taken an average of 5.88 years, revisions by non-legislative actors have happened on average within 3.5 years of an earlier policy. Delays to act can have real consequences for quota policy design. This can be illustrated by a number of cases, Honduras being the most obvious. Honduras first adopted a gender quota in 2000, scoring 12 on the IGQS scale. It then enacted its first reform in 2004, weakening the design of its original policy by decreasing the quota size requirement from 50 % to be reached gradually to 30 %, and by getting rid of its ranking system. Its subsequent reform, concluded by the legislature in 2012, repaired what had been lost in 2004 and produced a quota that was 5 points stronger than the original design established in 2000. In sum, through legislative revisions, it took 12 years for Honduras to strengthen its policy design by 5 points. The Peruvian gender quota, originally adopted in 1997 with a score of 9, has undergone two legislative reforms, one in 2000 and another in 2003. In the course of six years the policy was strengthened by 5 points, but policy developments have stalled ever since, making the Peruvian quota comparatively weak by current standards.

Finally, the contribution of non-legislative actors to the strengthening of gender quota designs goes well beyond their role in enacting change through executive decrees or judicial decisions that directly modify gender quota provisions. In fact, much of the influence of non-legislative actors in strengthening gender quota policies has not been captured in my coding. This results from two factors. First, my coding assigns the authorship of a given policy revision to the actors that finalised/enacted it, meaning that actors' behaviour at other stages of policy-making are not accounted for. Policy-making is much more complex, however, and multiple types of actor are often involved at different stages of the process. For instance, an executive may introduce a policy proposal to be considered in a legislature, which then amends and votes on it. In such a scenario, although the executive had a crucial role in prompting the process of policy-making, the policy would still be coded as originating from the legislature. This, of course, minimises the impact of non-legislative actors in my analysis. This is a particular problem given that the hypothetical scenario described is not uncommon. Most recently, this has taken place in Mexico, when in celebration of the 60th anniversary of women's suffrage, President Enrique Peña Nieto presented a proposal for a parity law. While introducing his proposal on 11 October 2014, Peña Nieto received a standing ovation and he stated that he had 'no doubt [the policy] would be easily adopted' by Mexico's Congress of the Union.[18] Indeed, the Congress incorporated his proposal into a larger electoral reform and approved it only months later. In this example, despite the fact that the reform was largely influenced by the executive, the policy was still coded as originating from the legislature, given that it required the body's approval. Similar policy processes have also taken place in other countries, such as in Chile (2014) and Costa Rica (1990 and 2007).

The second way in which my empirical analysis further minimises the impact of non-legislative actors is by not accounting for the importance of constitutional legitimacy to the implementation of gender quota policies. Challenging the constitutionality of gender quota laws has been a widespread tactic used by political parties and male incumbents to resist the adoption and implementation of gender quotas. In this sense, the willingness of courts to uphold the legitimacy of quota provisions and oversee their compliance has been crucial. Baldez argues that the Supreme Court or Mexico's decision to support the constitutionality of gender quotas was one of the main factors in securing the effectiveness of the policy and in making it difficult for the opposition to prevent the policy from being implemented.[19] In some instances, however, contradicting court resolutions and the reluctance of electoral courts to get involved have also been observed to impact the implementation of quota policies in detrimental ways. On March 2000, the Constitutional Court of Colombia deemed a bill already approved by Congress to be unconstitutional for including a 30 % candidate quota. Although the Court approved other quota provisions in the bill, it decided that a legislated candidate quota would infringe on the autonomy of parties. In May 2000, Law 581 was enacted, instituting gender quotas for non-elected government offices. This decision set back the process of adoption of gender quotas for legislative office by many years: Colombia only managed to adopt a legislated candidate quota in 2011, after making amendments to its Constitution in 2009. These examples show that electoral and higher courts, and their respective interpretations of gender quota policies, are crucial in both legitimising and facilitating the implementation of gender quotas (or accomplishing the very opposite).

4   Conclusion

For more than 20 years, gender quotas have been adopted and revised in Latin America and across the world. The spread of this institutional innovation was accompanied by extensive academic research. The literature has made incredible progress in documenting and analysing the roles of international organisations, transnational diffusion, women's groups and female parliamentarians in processes of gender quota adoption and revision. However, this focus has been at the cost of undertheorising the impact of male resistance, as well as executive and judicial actors.

This chapter hypothesises that the intervention of non-legislative actors in processes of gender quota adoption and revision produce greater positive outcomes regarding the strength of policy designs than when legislators are left to act on their own. This could result from the resistance of male parliamentarians to strengthen gender quota provisions and risk increasing their electoral competition. The reluctance of congressional incumbents to pass strong quota legislation could then give ground for executive and judicial actors to address policy weaknesses and strengthen gender quota policies.

By descriptively comparing and contrasting the overall strength of gender quota policies and its five individual components, I found support for the proposition that executive and judicial actors play a crucial role in strengthening gender quota policies. This conclusion derives from the following observations. First, policy revisions carried out by non-legislative actors are, on average, stronger than those enacted by legislative actors for three of the five components of the IGQS, even though the latter has been the most frequent. Second, non-legislative actors respond more rapidly to policy weaknesses than their legislative counterparts. Furthermore, the impact of non-legislative actors cannot be fully grasped by my empirical analysis: their role also extends to publishing policy recommendations, drafting and presenting bills to the legislature, providing expertise to legislative actors, and granting constitutional legitimacy to the status of quota laws, among other things.

The conclusions drawn at this stage are only exploratory and, more important, can only speak to the observable implications expected as a consequence of the hypothesised behaviour of legislators. In other words, while the results are aligned with my expectations about the behaviour of legislative and non-legislative actors, my findings do not confirm the assumptions I make about the incentives for actors' behaviours (i.e. that legislative actors seek to contain quota strength in order to protect their seats, while non-legislative actors aim to promote gender quotas for exogenous and/or value-oriented reasons).

Given that my conclusions are, thus far, only grounded in theoretical developments and descriptive statistics, they should only be interpreted as providing exploratory ground for future research. This is not to say that the findings presented should not be taken into account: the dynamics between legislative and non-legislative processes have rarely been researched in the context of gender quota adoptions and revisions, and the patterns uncovered certainly deserve further investigation. Combined, my observations suggest that although gender quotas have been studied extensively, many questions remain unanswered. For instance, is the involvement of non-legislative actors in processes of gender quota adoption and revision a consequence of the institutional capacity of each government branch, or a response to the failure of legislatures to properly address and/or comply with the normative commitments of a given government? How do quotas for other branches of government (and the descriptive representation of women in key positions in the executive and court systems) impact the involvement of non-legislative actors in processes of gender quotas for legislative office? These questions illustrate the fruitful ground for research that remains underexplored, and they highlight the need for greater insight into the impact of the roles of specific actors and policy-making processes on the strength of gender quota designs.

NOTES

1. Although quotas can be (and have been) applied to many spheres, this chapter only covers policies for elected legislative office.
2. Mona Lena Krook, *Quotas for Women in Politics: Gender and Candidate Selection Reform Worldwide* (Oxford University Press 2009) 6–9.
3. For a summary of the debate, see Jennifer Piscopo, 'States as Gender Equality Activists: The Evolution of Quota Laws in Latin America' (2015) 57(3) Latin American Politics and Society 27–49.
4. The countries included in the analysis are Argentina, Bolivia, Brazil, Chile, Colombia, Costa Rica, the Dominican Republic, Ecuador, El Salvador, Honduras, Mexico, Nicaragua, Panama, Paraguay, Peru, Uruguay and Venezuela. Guatemala does not have a gender quota and is consequently not included.
5. For a review of the literature, see Krook (n 2) 9–12; Lisa Baldez, 'Elected Bodies: The Gender Quota Law for Legislative Candidates in Mexico' (2004) 44(2) Legislative Studies Quarterly 232–4.
6. See Baldez (n 5); Piscopo (n 3); Krook (n 2) 172.

7. Leslie Schwindt-Bayer, 'Making Quotas Work: The Effect of Gender Quota Laws On the Election of Women' (2009) 34(1) Legislative Studies Quarterly 5–28.

8. Krook (n 2) 11.

9. Mark Jones, 'Gender Quotas, Electoral Laws, and the Election of Women: Evidence from the Latin American Vanguard' (2009) 42(1) Comparative Political Studies 56, 62–3.

10. The codebook explaining the development of indicators and coding of individual quota policies can be accessed at http://www.malugatto.com.

11. The database can be accessed at http://www.quotaproject.org.

12. The database can be accessed at http://www.cepal.org/cgibin/getprod.asp?xml=/oig/noticias/paginas/5/36135/P36135.xml&xsl=/oig/tpl/p18f.xsl&base=/oig/tpl/top-bottom-decisiones.xs.

13. I consider Venezuela to have had two cases of 'original' gender quota adoptions. That is because I consider original adoption as a policy enacted when no other gender quota policy was in place. Given that the first gender quota policy in Venezuela was retracted in 2000, the 2005 policy that reinstated the quota is also coded as an original policy.

14. My analyses exclude the sentence enacted by the Venezuelan Constitutional Court in 2000, which deemed the original 1997 policy unconstitutional. I exclude this case because given that I am only concerned with policy designs, including a case in which a gender quota policy is lacking would only add noise to the analysis.

15. Piscopo (n 3) 36; Baldez (n 5) 235.

16. The latest quota revision in Honduras has been characterised elsewhere as a consequence of executive decree. In fact, all gender-related policies enacted in Honduras (Decreto n° 34-2000; Decreto n° 44-2004 and Decreto No 54-2012) have been initiated and finalised in the National Congress of Honduras. The 2012 law resulted from a bill presented by congresswoman Gillian Guifarro Montes. The confusion might have resulted from the fact that Honduras has two types of *decretos* (decrees): executive and legislative.

17. Note that quota policies originally drafted by non-legislative actors have also been strong. The original parity law enacted by executive order (Decreto n° 29-2010) in Nicaragua in 2010 scored 11 on

the IGQS scale, while the Venezuelan quota enacted by the electoral court in 2005 (CNE Resolución n° 050401-179) scored 17. Given that non-legislative intervention has led to the adoption of original gender quotas only twice, I do not discuss this aspect at length.

18. Parts of his speech can be watched at http://mexico.cnn.com/nacional/2013/10/11/pena-nieto-propone-que-el-50-de-candidaturas-al-congreso-sean-de-mujeres.

19. Baldez (n 5) 234, 244–246.

CHAPTER 15

Human Rights and Remains: A Policy Proposal to Prevent Human Rights Violations in Brazil

Pedro Fortes

Police abuse is often reported as a major source of human rights violation in Brazil.[1] The criminal justice system may function as a filter for police violence because judges are supposed to exclude evidence that results from various forms of police abuse. The link between the confessions extracted under police abuse and the exclusionary rule is part of the law according to law books. However, analysing law in action, Brazil's criminal justice system does not respond effectively to allegations of torture made by criminal defendants. I conducted empirical research in criminal courts in the metropolitan area of Rio de Janeiro in 2007 and 2008, when I interviewed judges, prosecutors and public defenders, and I examined all of the files of ongoing criminal procedures relating to drug trafficking in seven different courtrooms. This research was conducted as part of a thesis written

Previous drafts of this chapter were discussed at the Latin American Studies Association conference and at a research workshop at the Center for Latin American Studies at Stanford University, and the author is grateful for the extremely helpful feedback.

P. Fortes (✉)
FGV Law School, Rio de Janeiro, Brazil

© Palgrave Macmillan, a division of Macmillan Publishers Limited 2017   257
P. Fortes et al. (eds.), *Law and Policy in Latin America*,
DOI 10.1057/978-1-137-56694-2_15

at Stanford Law School, and an article in Portuguese was previously published in the *Brazilian Journal of Empirical Legal Studies* in January 2014.[2]

One year after the publication of my study in Brazil, the chief justice of the Supreme Federal Court of Brazil used his power as head of the National Council of Justice to implement one of the policy recommendations that I defend. Since February 2015, state courts have gradually adopted the custody hearing—a judicial hearing immediately after imprisonment—for an analysis of its legality, necessity and the existence of police abuse. According to Brazil's chief justice, the first year of implementation of custody hearings resulted in the release of approximately half of the detained individuals in the country and resulted in enormous public savings with regard to the potential expenses of penitentiaries.[3] However, had the adoption of a preliminary hearing been accompanied by the introduction of plea bargaining for all crimes and the criminalisation of perjury, Brazil's criminal procedure would have become much more pragmatic, efficient and moral. In many jurisdictions of the North Atlantic, the majority of criminal cases are sentenced immediately after the preliminary hearing because the parties negotiate the terms of a plea bargain and reach an agreement that is favourable to everyone. This scenario could result in effective human rights protection, efficient cost reduction and the application of moral values to criminal law enforcement in Brazil.

This chapter investigates human rights violations and suggests a policy proposal for the prevention of police abuse that goes beyond the adoption of custody hearings. Section 1 demonstrates that criminal defendants often claim that they were victims of physical torture during their judicial testimony, but these allegations almost never trigger an investigation. Section 2 explains that these human rights violations are facilitated by the lack of effective structural devices within Brazil's criminal justice system. Section 3 offers a policy proposal and suggests that different procedural devices should be introduced into the justice system. Section 4 offers some final remarks.

1   ALLEGATIONS OF TORTURE IN CONTEMPORARY BRAZIL

Brazil's criminal justice system fails to investigate allegations of torture made by criminal defendants in courts. Analysing a sample of ongoing trials for drug trafficking in seven different courtrooms of Rio de Janeiro, which included 43 cases, I observed that 20 defendants claimed in their testimonies that they were victims of police brutality—physical torture, psychological torture and manipulation of evidence, among other forms of police abuse—during their imprisonment. There was absolutely no response to these allegations. After hearing these claims, judges, prosecutors and public defenders simply did not take any measures: no investigation was ordered; no request to nullify the imprisonment or the collected evidence was made; and no report was sent to the police internal affairs department. In interviews with 12 of these legal actors, most of them revealed that they never take the initiative to investigate allegations made by defendants. This attitude was observed in judges, prosecutors and public defenders. Paradoxically, they showed a high degree of legal consciousness, stated that torture is a heinous crime and affirmed their commitment to fight for the protection of the physical integrity of criminal suspects.

Exceptionally, some legal professionals admitted the possibility of torture in the so-called 'ticking bomb scenario', and one interviewee even mentioned the concrete circumstances of a kidnapping in which the police captures the intermediary member of a criminal group and must immediately rescue the kidnapped victim so that she is not killed by the other kidnappers. In this case, the police officers are faced with a very difficult judgement call because they have to decide whether they torture the criminal suspect to get information about the victim's location or they simply arrest him and risk the victim's life. In this interviewee's opinion, this exceptional 'ticking bomb scenario' transforms torture into an excusable criminal offence. On the other hand, all other cases of torture are inexcusable and police officers are expected to be investigated, accused and convicted for their criminal conduct if they torture suspects.

Even if these legal professionals showed a high degree of rights consciousness and strongly criticised police violence, they almost never respond to allegations made by criminal defendants in their testimonies. A criminal justice system may function as a filter for episodes of police abuse because criminal defendants will inevitably appear in court. The metaphor of criminal justice as a 'filtering device' implies that, to some extent, judges should extract 'impurities' of illegal police activity from the trial—such as evidence obtained by violent means—through the exclusionary rule. At least in theory, defendants have the opportunity to report any illegal episode to an independent judge.

Nonetheless, Brazil's criminal justice system does not filter episodes of police violence. From a sample of 43 cases, 20 defendants alleged some form of police abuse. Some of them described how the police planted illegal drugs and also inflicted informal punishment by beating the criminal suspect during the detention procedures. Others claimed severe threats, explaining that police officers put a gun to their head and threatened to pull the trigger. Some defendants simply limited their testimony to a general statement of police violence without specifying the abusive conduct of the officers.

The range of accusations varied from a slap in the face to repeated beating for a long period of time. Some 17 defendants alleged that the police faked the possession of drugs in cases of evidence manipulation, and 17 allegations of police violence were made. One of the defendants claimed he was not a drug trafficker but simply a cocaine user. He asserted that he was just trying to buy cocaine for himself when the police suddenly arrived. They covered his head with a plastic bag, depriving him of air for quite a while. Next he was severely beaten by the officials. In his own words, he was 'tortured', even though he did not provide further details about the violent action employed by the police. Nonetheless, his narrative suggested a crescendo of violence, characteristic of physical torture. The criminal suspect reported that the policemen then threatened to kill his co-defendant. He said that they actually put a gun close to the ear of the co-defendant and pulled the trigger. Finally, he was shown a bag with some marijuana attributed to him after he was already inside the police car.

This testimony provides an excellent example of the variety of allegations of police abuse made by criminal defendants. First, even when he confessed, he admitted guilt for a minor offence (drug use instead of trafficking). Second, he alleged that the police subjected him to physical torture by saying that he suffered severe violence and asphyxia through a method called 'submarine'. Third, the criminal suspect also denounced the fact that his co-defendant was a victim of psychological torture, threatened with death and exposed to a gun shot in an extremely traumatic way. Fourth, there is an allegation of evidence manipulation, implying that the police officers fabricated the possession of marijuana to arrest the suspect for trafficking.

Other defendants also reported these many forms of police abuse. Some of the legal actors interviewed also made references to allegations of physical violence, death threats and evidence manipulation as regular complaints of those accused of drug trafficking.[4] Both the observation of practical experience and the analysis of relevant legislation support the following classification of allegations of police abuse:

1. *physical torture and forms of inhuman and degrading treatment*, in which the narrative describes a sequence of violent acts in a crescendo ('escalation'), which possibly cause visible injury and a high or intermediate degree of suffering;

2. *physical abuse*, in which the criminal suspect describes a single act of violence or a sequence that does not imply a high or intermediate degree of suffering;
3. *psychological torture*, in which the defendant describes the infliction of a high or intermediate degree of mental suffering as the consequence of symbolic (non-physical) violence (e.g. death threats, exposure to loud noise and other intellectual processes that may induce paranoia, fear and pain);
4. *non-violent forms of police abuse*, in which the narrative describes a violation of police rules that does not inflict pain or suffering but may nonetheless result in the acquittal of the defendant as a result of exclusion of evidence (e.g. evidence manipulation or a violation of criminal guarantee may result in the exclusion of evidence).[5]

Many defendants reported being victims of police abuse. These allegations were made during judicial hearings. They were made during a criminal trial, in which the defendant was seeking an acquittal. In this context, an allegation of police abuse, at least in theory, also implies a demand for an investigation of police conduct. After all, if evidence was extracted using violence, produced by manipulation or obtained through the violation of a criminal guarantee, the process would be likely to result in an acquittal as a result of the exclusion of illegally obtained evidence. In this sense, a justice system should be ready to respond to these implicit demands of criminal suspects by moving to investigate the veracity of their allegations of police abuse. However, Brazil's criminal justice system did not respond to any of the allegations of police abuse made by the defendants during their judicial hearings.

In none of these 20 cases in which defendants reported both violent and non-violent forms of police abuse did the legal actors move to investigate the veracity of their claims. Prosecutors did not initiate any investigation. Public defenders did not articulate any request to exclude the evidence allegedly obtained illegally. Judges did not consider these allegations to be relevant in their decision-making. In fact, some of these criminal cases had already received a final sentence. A few judges simply ignored the allegations of police abuse in their sentences, making no reference to the content of the defendant's testimony in their decisions. In five criminal sentences, however, the allegations of the defendants were labelled as 'fantasy', a version of the facts completely disconnected from reality. Different judges wrote these sentences, evidencing the fact that there is a tendency to perceive the defendant's words as being untruthful.

2   STRUCTURAL ELEMENTS WITHIN THE CRIMINAL JUSTICE SYSTEM

Human rights groups and academic commentators refer to this lack of response to allegations of torture as a problem caused by the legal culture of Brazil's judges, prosecutors and public defenders. However, empirical evidence collected during this research does not support this conclusion because all legal professionals expressed their stark opposition to police violence. Explanation for this failure to protect the physical and psychological integrity of criminal suspects does not come from the legal culture but from the legal structure. The relevant legal actors do not have adequate instruments to investigate, accuse and punish violent police officers. Time, information and power are decisive factors for effective investigations.

Regarding allegations of torture made by the criminal defendants, these structural elements are also relevant as explanatory factors for the inertia of legal professionals. First, the time gap between the detention of a criminal suspect and their first judicial hearing was so long (on average 60 days, when this empirical research was conducted in 2007–2008) that it significantly detached the legal actors from having the opportunity to meaningfully investigate allegations of physical torture. Second, since Brazil's criminal justice has not established a system of rewards (plea bargaining) and sanctions (crime of perjury), criminal defendants are induced *not* to remain silent. Their version of the facts is strongly disregarded by all legal actors, who usually assume that the criminal defendants are lying. Third, the capacity to investigate these episodes of police violence is extremely limited and does not provide effective control of police abuse. The combination of these three structural factors may explain the inertia of the legal actors, even when their rights consciousness motivates them to punish abusive officers and to try to prevent new cases of police violence.

An important working hypothesis in this research focused on the time gap between the defendant's detention and their first testimony in court. The time gap between the detention and the hearing may be counted in many weeks (as opposed to a few days in most jurisdictions). In the framework established by Brazil's anti-drug legislation, for instance, the police have a 30-day term to collect evidence prior to sending the criminal file to court. Next the criminal prosecutor has a 10-day term to present the written accusation. Only thereafter would the first hearing take place according to Brazil's criminal procedure. This structural variable is extremely important for the investigation of allegations of torture, since the time gap will impact material evidence and prevent any meaningful investigation.[6]

Once a judge is hostage to a structure that provides only the opportunity for the defendant to allege torture after a long period of time, it is also essential to interview the judge and understand their attitude towards and beliefs about the system. What does the time gap tell us? The gap between detention and testimony has proved to be long. The shortest gap was 20 days and the longest was 116 days. On average the time gap observed was approximately 60 days. All of the interviewees considered the terms established by Federal Statute n° 11343/06 to be too long.

When asked if the long time gap between detention and hearing affected their capacity to observe police torture, the common answer was a denial, followed by the explanation that when police agents decide to torture they know how to do it without leaving visible evidence. Nevertheless, all of the interviewees agreed with my insistence that this long time gap would leave agents freer to explore different techniques and be even more brutal, and that evidence would be lost after a couple of weeks. In addition, the passage of time may also have a psychological effect on a defendant. A significant delay may lessen their indignation. It may lessen the significance of the event to a victim of police brutality who still has to pursue an acquittal. It may also increase the difficulty of proof owing to scattered witnesses and failed memories. The passage of time may have both psychological and physical impacts.

The interviews revealed that most legal actors believe that criminal defendants are usually lying. Allegations made in their testimony are generally discredited. One judge suggested that in almost all cases, defendants' versions are untruthful and absolutely disconnected from reality. Some judges were not so radical about the lack of credibility of a defendant's testimony, but they still declared that truth was rare in suspects' versions of the facts. In summary, the judges frequently believe that the version of a criminal suspect is 'fantasy'.

Explanation for this judicial attitude comes from the regime of incentives and sanctions established by the criminal justice system regarding the right to remain silent in the criminal courtroom. For instance, in other jurisdictions the decision to testify or to remain silent is an essential part of the strategy of a criminal defendant. In Brazil, in contrast, criminal defendants almost always give their version of the facts. For example, from the sample of 43 cases analysed, only one criminal defendant did not speak. The data clearly indicate that the right to silence is almost never exercised in Brazil's courts. Why is this right not exercised in Brazil? Is it because a defendant will plead guilty to reduce their punishment?

One might imagine that most defendants confess, seeking a reduction in their punishment. However, the limited options for bargaining in the Brazil's criminal system do not require an admission of guilt. There is currently no comprehensive system of plea bargaining in Brazil, except in the case of minor criminal offences. Confessions are also rare. Since a confession does not ensure a reduction in the prison term, its scope as a defense strategy is extremely limited. In fact, the crime of perjury does not exist in Brazil's criminal justice system either.

All of the interviewed legal actors referred to the so-called 'right to lie' of criminal defendants in Brazil. This 'right to lie' is not granted by any legal statute. It does not exist 'in the books'. In spite of the absence of any formal rule establishing this right, all interviewed legal actors recognised the existence, in practice, of the authorisation to a criminal suspect to lie without consequences. In other words, a defendant may accuse the police officers who arrested him of physical torture, psychological torture and evidence manipulation without fear of being accused of a 'malicious accusation'. The defendant is also free to tell any lie whatsoever since they will not be accused of 'perjury'. Not surprisingly, judges and public prosecutors assigned extremely low credibility to the defendant's account, stating that they often assume that they are lying.

Both the lack of incentives to confess (plea bargaining) and the lack of sanctions for lying (perjury) have induced most defendants to share their version of the facts with the court. However, these legal arrangements provide incentives for a defendant to adopt strategic behaviour (by lying to undermine evidence and police action) and no incentives to adopt cooperative behaviour (by telling the truth to provide more information about other members of their criminal organisation).[7]

Unlike other jurisdictions, there is no necessity to claim innocence or admit fault in Brazil's criminal justice system. In providing testimony, the defendant is only expected to describe their version of the facts and not to declare their innocence or guilt. Even though defendants are not supposed to make a statement of 'guilty' or 'not guilty', some still admitted guilt merely to be able to claim the innocence of their co-defendants. Others admitted the truthfulness of the drug possession but claimed drug dependency (an excuse according to federal legislation).[8] Thus there are still some indirect incentives to admit guilt.[9] In general terms, a defendant's testimony is highly discredited, being frequently considered as 'fantasy'. This lack of credibility may be explained by the structural design of the system and the recognition of the so-called 'right to lie'.

3   A POLICY PROPOSAL TO PREVENT HUMAN RIGHTS VIOLATIONS IN BRAZIL

As Section 2 has demonstrated, structural factors prevent effective investigations of extrajudicial executions and allegations of torture. Therefore policy reform should transform Brazil's criminal justice system and change time gaps, lack of information and power asymmetries.

Particularly in the case of torture, social psychology should not be ignored. In a recent book, Phillip Zimbardo argued that the abuses and torture at Abu Ghraib were fostered by the conditions created by the military prison system there, which established and sustained a 'culture of abuse'.[10] His opinion is directly linked to the Stanford Prison experiment, which led Prof. Zimbardo to conclude that the institutional support, authority and resources that allow these situations to operate as they do are established by the system.[11] Based on this view, he speaks metaphorically about the possibility that bad apples may have become rotten because they had been put in a bad barrel, since 'people and situations are usually in a state of dynamic interaction'.[12]

In an earlier book, Zimbardo had the chance to apply his expertise to the psychoanalysis of Brazilian torturers,[13] reaching many interesting conclusions about the situation and the system that have turned ordinary men into abusive policemen:

1. The policemen engaged in torture were, as a group, isolated from the others. This insularity resulted in an autonomous organisational structure that not only established particular performance expectations about the exercise of power but also supported these practices by protecting the group from outsiders.[14]
2. Belonging to these groups required a violent rite of transition, in which the incoming members were submitted to severe physical suffering and moral humiliation, a process that fostered their blind obedience to authority and lessened their sensitivity to someone else's pain.[15]
3. The search for social approval within the group caused these policemen to internalise a particular moral code with the disengagement of the moral values of society and the incorporation of the group standards that allowed their engagement in torture.[16]
4. Torture was also possible due to the dehumanisation of their victims through communicative processes of social degradation

(stereotyping, labelling, marginalising and blaming them with the support of propaganda).[17]

5. The group of abusive policemen usually neutralised accountability by increasing their sense of anonymity through processes of deindividuation (using masks, painting their faces and sharing the same false name during a mission).[18]

Why is this study relevant for the evaluation of the responses of a criminal justice system to allegations of torture and other forms of police abuse? Primarily, it shows the importance of judicial control to the extent that criminal judges should be capable of deconstructing these traits of systemic police abuse by

1. breaking the isolation through oversight;
2. enforcing obedience to the law, not to the group;
3. fostering moral values through the effective control of police violence;
4. providing the victim with an effective opportunity to report any inhumane and degrading treatment;
5. ensuring accountability.

In summary, professionals responsible for the criminal justice system should be able to impose constitutional checks on the police.[19] These findings lead us to discuss the flaws of Brazil's system of law-enforcement violence control.

Asked about the measures they adopted when they believed that a criminal suspect had been tortured, the interviewed legal actors revealed the non-existence of a consistent mechanism of law-enforcement violence control. In many interviews the legal professionals simply admitted that there is nothing they can do to investigate an allegation of police abuse made by a defendant during his testimony. First, some of the judges and prosecutors referred to the fact that the only mechanism of controlling police abuse is the internal affairs department. Despite a constitutional mandate, governments still did not establish institutional mechanisms of external control of police activity, a function that should be performed by the Attorney General's Office.[20]

In addition, Brazil's criminal lawyers have questioned the constitutional capacity of public prosecutors to conduct direct investigations of criminal offences. They argue that the accusatory role of the public prosecutor must be performed by an impartial public official. In their opinion, collecting evidence bars a criminal prosecutor from accusing. In practice, most criminal prosecutors have been cautious about conducting investigations. Since external control was not established and prosecutors were not reassured about their investigative power, some of the interviewees believe that there is no system for controlling police violence.

Asked about the internal affairs department, many legal professionals seemed to be sceptical about its impartiality or its capacity to meet the demands of the system, given the number of allegations of police abuse. They referred to the extremely small number of allegations that they send to the police internal affairs department or to the Attorney General's office. The reasons for reporting only a few of these allegations were multiple: the lack of infrastructure to investigate a significant number of cases; the high probability that allegations of police abuse are false; the impossibility of collecting evidence of police abuse, since the alleged violence often occurs in slums, and it is difficult to find reliable witnesses there; the impossibility of collecting evidence of the alleged violence, since it was symbolic violence (physical threat), or there is no longer any evidence of physical violence; and the lack of political independence of the branch in charge of investigation.

A few legal professionals had previously documented investigations of police abuse. They reported cases of physical torture to the internal affairs department, supported by a credible allegation of a criminal suspect and physical evidence. The number of cases was very small. In all of these cases they received no feedback from the internal affairs department about their investigation. They explained that police internal affairs officers are not even supposed to notify them of the results of their investigation since it is a completely independent investigation and therefore not connected to the legal process in which torture was alleged. There is no formal institutional channel of communication between the criminal justice system and the police internal affairs department.

4   Final Remarks

This research identifies three systemic flaws in Brazil's criminal justice system. Not surprisingly, I have concluded that these aspects of the system should be reformed. First, the time between detention and hearing should be reduced to one or two days. Shrinking this gap will facilitate investigations. Evidence of physical torture will be preserved; the passage of time will not deter a criminal suspect from reporting police violence; and it will be easier for the internal affairs department to locate witnesses in

Brazil's slums, where most of the episodes of police brutality supposedly occur. Second, Brazil should adopt a plea bargaining system and enact legislation that criminalises perjury. These two mechanisms could significantly impact the behaviour of criminal defendants and improve the credibility of their testimony. Plea bargaining would induce cooperative behaviour, motivating defendants to negotiate with prosecutors. It could also improve communication between prosecution and defence, providing better opportunities for suspects to reveal that they have been victims of police violence. Third, introduction of a shorter time gap, plea bargaining and the crime of perjury will probably lessen the number of false claims of police brutality. These reforms will arguably improve the capacity of legal actors to control the police and will also inhibit malicious accusations. As a result, legal professionals will become much more likely to determine investigations based on allegations made by a defendant in court. The internal affairs department should become more responsive to these allegations, and its investigative structure should be tailored to attend to the demands of the criminal justice system.

Beyond the scenario in Brazil, this research also shows the importance of structural devices that may seem *natural* to legal scholars in the USA and Europe but which are essential for the function of controlling law enforcement violence. Police brutality is likely to increase in the absence of immediate preliminary hearings, clear incentives (plea bargaining) and disincentives (perjury) for cooperative behavior of criminal defendants, and an independent bureau of police control. On the other hand, the existence of these features does not guarantee that torture will never be practised. In his comprehensive history of plea bargaining in the USA, George Fisher highlighted the early adoption of preliminary hearings, defendant-testimony laws, and plea negotiation.[21] Every criminal justice system should be designed to function as a filter of police violence and therefore to protect criminal defendants from torture, evidence manipulation and other forms of police abuse.

Regarding the current situation in Brazil, the recent adoption of a custody hearing did not transform radically the formalism and dogmatism of the country's criminal procedure. Instead of designing a preliminary hearing that could lead to a criminal sentence within a day of the imprisonment, the custody hearing is perceived by many legal actors as a useless act. Because judges, prosecutors, and defence attorneys usually presume that a defendant lies about the circumstances of their imprisonment, many consider the custody hearing to be a massive waste of resources.[22] Others criticise the strong focus on the release of the criminal suspect as being indicative of a leftist perspective of the criminal defendant as a victim of society who should not be imprisoned.[23] Not surprisingly, the National Association of State Magistrates challenged the constitutionality of the custody hearing by filing an Action for Direct Constitutionality Control in the Supreme Federal Court of Brazil.[24]

As my empirical research suggests, Brazil's criminal justice system does not function as a filter of episodes of police brutality. The recent introduction of the custody hearing may have a positive chilling effect on police officers and thus reduce human rights violations. However, without plea bargaining and the crime of perjury, legal actors probably continue to discredit criminal defendants. If so, defendants' allegations do not result in investigations of police abuse. Without a different regime of positive and negative incentives for judges, prosecutors, attorneys and defendants to cooperate and develop more trustworthy interactions, nothing will change. Further empirical research should be conducted. However, the silence of the chief justice on the practical consequences of the custody hearing regarding the investigation of police torture and human rights violations suggests that nothing has really changed.

Finally, the introduction of plea bargaining and the crime of perjury would not violate the fundamental rights of criminal defendants. For instance, the first case of a custody hearing in Rio de Janeiro involved a defendant suspected of attempted robbery. He was released after the custody hearing but with the prospect of experiencing a long criminal procedure that would potentially lead to his conviction. Even if he were released, the existential experience of being accused would follow him for long years of procedural acts and judicial appeals. Likewise, the legal uncertainty relating to a future imprisonment will daunt him and limit his ability to reintegrate into society. On the other hand, a plea bargain could lead to an immediate conviction to a suspended corporal punishment and a monetary fine. Such a sanction would reduce his uncertainty, eliminate procedural and penitentiary costs, and release him fully to reconstruct his social life again. Therefore my policy proposal is optimal not only from the internal perspective of legal actors but also from the vantage point of criminal defendants and their fundamental rights.

NOTES

1. See e.g. James Cavallaro, *Police Brutality in Urban Brazil* (Human Rights Watch 1997). http://www.hrw.org/reports/1997/brazil/.
2. See Pedro Fortes, 'Direitos e Restos Humanos: Uma Hipótese para o Enfrentamento Jurídico-Penal da Tortura no Brasil' (2014) 1(1) Revista de Estudos Empíricos em Direito 28.
3. Ricardo Lewandowski, *Audiência de Custódia e o Direito de Defesa, A Folha de São Paulo* (20 October 2015). http://www1.folha.uol.com. br/opiniao/2015/10/1695906-audiencia-de-custodia-e-o-direito-de-defesa.shtml.
4. One public prosecutor added the total ignorance about the drug found in the possession of a criminal suspect to this list of defence allegations. Observation of cases also suggested that these defendants may argue drug addiction (an excuse that excludes imprisonment and imposes clinical treatment, according to Brazil's legislation) and violation of a criminal guarantee (such as a search without judicial warrant).
5. This typology corresponds to the standards of international human rights norms and Brazil's criminal law: Lei n° 9455/97 (torture) and Lei n° 4898/65 (abuse of authority). It also permitted a clear analysis of the sample of testimonies, since all the narratives easily fit into one of these categories.
6. In the words of Lawrence Friedman, 'legal structure does make some difference; exactly how much, we do not know. If we found two societies, whose social demands on the legal system were identical but whose structures were different, and if we found different outputs and impacts, we could ascribe the variance to structure. Such societies, however, do not exist.' Lawrence Friedman, *The Legal System: A Social Sciences Perspective* (Russel Sage Foundation 1975) 156.

   It is important to explain that the time gap is a structural variable because the legal system defines it as a material circumstance that has a direct impact on the allocation of power between legal actors and the results of the criminal process. In other words, the law limits the power of a criminal judge to investigate, disenfranchising them from the possibility of investigating allegations of physical torture in a meaningful way. When the judge hears the allegation of a defendant, they are no longer able to check if there are injuries to the criminal suspect's body. The passage of time has a direct impact on the criminal judge since it limits their investigative instruments, transforms the material evidence of physical torture and affects the judge's structure of power. Conversely, the long time gap established by the law empowers violent police officers and expands their opportunities for physical violence.

7. In the precise words of George Fisher, 'not only is plea bargaining essential to efficient case management, it also helps win an accused's cooperation in prosecuting his cohorts'. See George Fisher, *Plea Bargaining's Triumph: A History of Plea Bargaining in America* (Stanford University Press 2003) 121.

8. This excuse was extremely popular in one of the courts, in which all three defendants who confessed alleged that the drug found in their possession was for their own consumption and their alleged drug dependency. In all of these cases the procedure had been suspended for their medical evaluation.

9. One judge suggested that all confessions are strategic. According to them, the defendant always has a strategic reason to admit the truthfulness of facts. There is always a strategy behind an admission of drug possession: addiction, drug use or ignorance, for instance.

10. Philip Zimbardo, *The Lucifer Effect: Understanding How Good People Turn Evil* (Random House 2007) ch 15.

11. Ibid. 226. According to Zimbardo, 'the programs, policies, and standard operating procedures that are developed to support an ideology become an essential component of the system. The system's procedures are considered reasonable and appropriate as the ideology comes to be accepted as sacred.'

12. Ibid. 8.

13. In Zimbardo's words, 'the results of the Stanford Prison Experiment, when combined with those of Milgram's, Bandura's, and other related experiments, point to a psychology of evil in which ordinary, even above-average men and women can harm and degrade totally innocent people. These studies suggest that situational power can induce good people to behave in ways that violate their preexisting moral and ethical standards. We have used this research as an analytical backdrop for the transformations of Brazilian policemen into brutal torturers and murderers.' Martha Knisely Huggins, Mika Haritos-Fatouros, and Philip Zimbardo, *Violence Workers: Police Torturers and Murderers Reconstruct Brazilian Atrocities* (University of California Press 2002) 263.

14. Ibid. 248.
15. Ibid. 251–254.
16. Ibid. 250–251.
17. Ibid. 255–257.
18. Ibid. 257–258.
19. Martha Huggins contrasts police violence in Brazil with that in other nations, emphasising the poor constitutional checks on Brazil's police: 'that police violence in modern Western democracies has not reached the level of either military or postmilitary Brazil under routine circumstances may be the result of constitutional checks on the police. However, these checks can be reduced or eroded where specialised squads are given unsupervised (or covertly promoted to carry out) crime control mandates to efficiently regulate dangerous others.' Ibid 190.
20. The exercise of the function of external control of the police force by public prosecutors is a constitutional norm that remains only 'on the books': Federal Constitution of Brazil Article 129, §VII.
21. Fisher (n 7) 106, 166.
22. See http://jota.info/com-regras-atuais-audiencias-de-custodia-representam-uma-politica-equivocada.
23. See http://www.conjur.com.br/2016-jan-11/andre-melo-audiencia-custodia-rito-diretissimo-qual-melhor.
24. See http://jota.uol.com.br/associacao-de-juizes-quer-derrubar-resolucao-do-cnj-sobre-audiencias-de-custodia.

PART V

Mundus Novus: Emerging Technologies and Rights

Mundus Novus: The Construction of a Free Flow of Information from the Navigators of Yesterday to the Internauts of Today

Joaquim Falcão

The 1960s were a time when the world believed to be on the verge of a new period of discoveries. The conquest of space was imminent. The twentieth century was to be the new fifteenth century. The greatest civilisatory adventure ever would be the space race—the exploration not of 'seas where sail was never spread before'[1] but of the endless vastness of outer space. Spaceships would be the new caravels. Instead of the Indies and the Americas, we were heading for the Moon, Venus and Mars. Argonauts or astronauts were the successors of Christopher Columbus, Marco Polo, Pedro Álvares Cabral, Vasco da Gama and Amerigo Vespucci. The twenty-first century did not confirm this belief.

This is a reformed and translated version of Joaquim Falcão, '*Mundus Novus*: Por um Novo Direito Autoral' (2005) 1(2) Revista Direito GV 229 (trans. Kevin Mundy). I am grateful to Diego Werneck, Carlos Affonso, Horácio Falcão, Ronaldo Lemos Antonio Sáenz de Miera and Adriana Lacombe for reading the manuscript and making valuable suggestions.

J. Falcão (✉)
FGV Law School, Rio de Janeiro, Brazil

© Palgrave Macmillan, a division of Macmillan Publishers Limited 2017
P. Fortes et al. (eds.), *Law and Policy in Latin America*,
DOI 10.1057/978-1-137-56694-2_16

275

Just as winds and storms drove Cabral off course, away from the Indies and towards Brazil, so another unforeseen detour has occurred now. Instead of outer space, computerised data processing, a byproduct of the space project pursued by the USA, has turned out to be more significant, bringing in its wake another grand civilisatory adventure—the creation and conquest of cyberspace.

This is the New World.

Cybernetics is decisively shaping the twenty-first century. Software tools are the new charts, maps and itineraries, conduits for information, producers of knowledge and navigational tools. The heroes are not Yuri Gagarin and Neil Armstrong but Bill Gates, Linus Torvalds, Steve Jobs, Mark Zuckerberg and Tim Berners-Lee.[2] Instead of the skies, the twenty-first century navigates the internet.

In this chapter I compare these two grand adventures of contemporary knowledge: the maritime discoveries of the fifteenth century and the creation of virtual space in the twentieth. The focus is on the tension between the free flow of information and intellectual property rights that occurred then and is also occurring now.

How can we shape, at the local and global levels, a free flow of information necessary to foster these discoveries and to advance civilisation? How can we reconcile the public nature of this indispensable flow with the limits of private copyright and the intellectual property rights that would foster innovations? A free flow of information is indispensable to the process of cumulative innovation that is characteristic of periods in which knowledge is expanding.

The fifteenth century shows a correlation between the production of knowledge required for major maritime discoveries to occur and the free, decentralised access to information, as existed between Lisbon, Florence, Genoa, Flanders, Seville and other centres of the age. Is the same free flow that expanded yesterday also fundamental now?

This chapter compares the freedom of the flow of information in the fifteenth century with the limits faced by today's flow owing to rigid intellectual property rights, such as copyright, trademark and patents. None of them existed at that time.

In the fifteenth century there were no individual or government controls to discipline this flow. Freedom prevailed. Today, access to information, even to scientific data, is shaped by national and international laws, as well as by government policies that may stimulate or hinder the adventure of knowledge. How to create and implement a global process of cumulative innovation is the main challenge.

What Can We Learn from the Past?

Today, the key valve regulating this flow is copyright, alongside trade-marks and patents, all of which are privatistic and were forged in the last century. Are they still suited to globalisation, cumulative knowledge and technological development in the twenty-first century?

Analysing what happened in the fifteenth century helps to address a major challenge: What is a fair balance between the free flow of information necessary for the expansion of knowledge in the twenty-first century and the reward needed for private entrepreneurship and protection of the innovation process?

1   THE ROAD OF AUTOGRAPH LETTERS IN THE FIFTEENTH CENTURY

In the fifteenth century the flow of information necessary for the expansion of discoveries travelled in two main ways.

First was through personal contacts, oral history, narratives produced by envoys and travellers who, on returning to Europe, told what they had seen and heard, privately and publicly. The stories told were multiplied. No printed, visual or digital platforms were available. Even so, the news was spread.

Second, knowledge travelled through maps, diaries, itineraries and charts, artistically elaborated manuscripts, and written letters that illuminated knowledge. Back from their trips, the navigators took their daily notes and used them to write travel reports, and letters to their sovereigns and financiers with detailed accounts of their expeditions.

These letters were passed on from one court to another, from banker to banker, from merchant to merchant. Unlike today's books, printed in their thousands, or even millions of times, a handwritten letter would be copied only a few times. A small number of copies gradually found their way into the libraries of clergymen, rich bankers and powerful kings. Some, however, were transformed into pamphlets containing novelesque accounts of adventures, marvels and heroic feats, quasiliterature read out at fairs and sung by troubadours in taverns.[3]

These handwritten letters spread the news. They were fundamental to the maritime discovery process. They performed at least three different functions.

First, they were inspiring letters. They drove hearts and minds—and ambitions. The information contained in them was a veritable engine that fired the reader's lust for a knowledge adventure; in this case, the knowledge available through maritime adventures. They stimulated new projects. They opened bankers' vaults. They channelled seawards the fortunes of merchants, the power of monarchs, the courage of fleet commanders, the strength of midshipmen, the youth of deckhands, and the science of cartographers and astronomers. They fuelled competition between kingdoms, investors, cities and navigators.

Second, they stimulated scientific progress. The information brought back by travellers played a similar role to reports of technical experiments. Each voyage was a 'scientific' mission, a controlled experiment in navigation, as Porto e Albuquerque points out.[4] The sea was a huge lab. Travel writings and letters contained information about the dance of the stars, indispensable to the forging of celestial navigation. They corrected maps and nautical charts. They described the strengths and weaknesses of the caravel in a storm. They were veritable research reports.

Knowledge production had changed radically. The Renaissance no longer sought truth in religion. It was an opening up slowly but permanently to a new secular, decentralised, empirical, experimental and cumulative knowledge-production model. Knowledge depended no longer on faith but on observation and experiments. The free flow of information in letters was fundamental to this empiricisation, decentralisation and diversification of scientific progress.[5]

Alongside diaries, chronicles and maps, letters furnished empirical raw material, which was analysed, compared, studied and systematised to forge the foundations for manuals of navigation and nautical almanacs. The first of these was *Regimento do Astrolábio e do Quadrante*, whose earliest known copy was printed in 1509.[6] These letters were foundational for the knowledge of the new maritime technology, without which the navigators would not have sailed. There would have been no discoveries.

Finally, these letters also had a foundational function for the new world. At the same time as they described the discoveries, they also created them. They invented what had merely been discovered. They gave well-established meanings or significations to mere perceived signifiers.

The engravings with the first images of the New World were based on how their authors would interpret and at the same time describe the new world. They portrayed observed and imagined phenomena at the same time. Europe used the information in the letters to create a new world out of its own imagination and reality—much more the imagination of barbarity than the reality of difference; much more the discoverer's gaze than the object of discovery.

Thus they depicted tropical churches and palaces with steep roofs, ready to receive the snow that never came.[7] They drew native men and women with European features, proportions and muscles. Female Indians looked like Boticelli's Venus. The result was a bizarre graphical ethnocentrism.

The letters did not have the precision of photography. The first picture painted in the Americas was by Franz Post, the *View of Itamaraca*, only in 1637. It was up to the reader to imagine the continent. As such, Vespucci's letters are a good example of this constitutive function.

'We come into the world to name things; so we become either masters of them or servants of whoever names them before us,' as Lya Luft rightly points out.[8]

Factually it would be more correct—but unthinkable today—for us to call the continent Columbia—North, Central and South Columbia. Columbus discovered it, but Vespucci created it. Vespucci's letter—*Mundus Novus* ('New World')—was decisively constitutive. Columbian became American.

The fifteenth century could hardly have been the century of discovery without the free flow of information in these letters. Vespucci's *Mundus Novus* is our case study. What would have happened if the current legal system of intellectual property rights had existed yesterday? And what if Vespucci had decided to enforce it? The analysis of the creation and diffusion of this letter brings history back and surely helps us in the comprehension of today's cybernetic world.

2   *MUNDUS NOVUS* AND THE MISATTRIBUTION OF AUTHORSHIP

Amerigo Vespucci was a lucky man. He was born in the right city—Florence was one of Europe's greatest city-states.[9] He was born in the right century, the late fifteenth, when the human adventure was renascent. He was born into the right wealthy family. He spoke and wrote in Italian as well as in the right language: Latin, the English of his age. He acquired expertise in diplomacy, commerce, banking, maps and astronomy. He had the right interdisciplinary education.

Better yet, he had the right protector: the Florentine Lorenzo de' Medici. No, not Lorenzo the Magnificent but Lorenzo di Pierfrancesco de' Medici, a younger cousin and perhaps richer—the Medici who commissioned Sandro Botticelli to paint two of his greatest masterpieces: *Spring* and *The Birth of Venus*.

He was born at the right time. Still young, Vespucci went to Seville, as a trader and banker, representing Lorenzo. Portugal and Spain were reaping the best and greatest fruits of the strategic Sagres Project—or the Portugal Project, as Luiz Fernando de Souza Pinto rightly prefers to call it.[10] This project was at the origins of the route to the Indies and navigation of the high seas. It made Lisbon the Cape Canaveral and Silicon Valley of the age. It was a victorious Iberian government policy of its time.

While Vespucci was in Iberia, the Sagres Project was under full steam. Portugal's King Manuel the Fortunate and Spain's Catholic monarchs, Queen Isabel I of Castile and King Fernando II of Aragon, were investing their fortune and power. They financed the public policy of the discoveries. They invented the future. They completed the world. They were Schumpeterian entrepreneurs before the title even existed.

In Seville, Vespucci quit the finance business and chose a new profession, a riskier one. He faced the challenge of the maritime exploratory trips. He devoted himself to a new technology that was starting to revolutionise the world: the lateen-rigged caravel and celestial navigation. Then he left the Medicis' bank and became a navigator.

But it was not enough for Vespucci to have been born into the right family, in the right city and in the right century, to leave the right profession at the right time, and to choose the right new profession. More was needed for him to become famous, achieve glory and remain known even today.

Paradoxically, one mistake was indispensable to his glory: the misattribution of the discovery of America by a German cartographer called Martin Waldseemüller. Waldseemüller believed that Vespucci, instead of Columbus,[11] had discovered the new continent. This misattribution gave birth to the naming of America and the immortality of Amerigo Vespucci. Without this error, he would have died misunderstood and practically bankrupt, like Columbus and dozens of other navigators.

With funding from Dom Manuel, Fernando and Isabel, Lorenzo, and friends such as Gianetto Berardi, Vespucci crossed the Atlantic three or four times.[12] He visited what are now Venezuela, Haiti and Cape Verde, as well as Salvador and Cabo Frio in Brazil, via the island of Fernando de Noronha, where he was impressed by the exuberance of its birds, fish, sea and rocks—a quasiparadise.

Whenever he returned to Europe, he had to report back to his sponsors. He wrote letters, memoranda and accounts of his travels. What did these precious repositories of information describe? They described nature and society. Vespucci communicated amazement and awe—breathless admiration of everything that he had never been seen before. He described a new race of men and women with red skin and hard flesh. He wrote of their habits, cuisine, sweet temper, cordiality, treachery and bravery. He was shocked by the cannibalism of these newfound tribes. Some of these natives lived for 150 years, he believed.[13]

The free flow of these letters helped to shape the sixteenth century, influencing investment, power, arts and sciences, and removing from the Catholic Church its authority to dictate the world's geography. It stole from the priests, bishops and the Pope the power to explain the world. The maritime new road played the role of a scientific experiment quickly open to everyone.

These letters reached the thinkers who made the Renaissance: Erasmus of Rotterdam, Michel de Montaigne, Michelangelo Buonarroti, Leonardo da Vinci, Rabelais, Sandro Botticelli, Machiavelli and Thomas More—such an illustrious audience.

Vespucci's letters are said to have been so influential that they served as a basis for More's greatest book, *Utopia* (1509). This seems highly probable.[14] More himself explicitly reveals his source, describing his main character, Raphael Hythloday, as 'so desirous of seeing the world that he ran the same hazard as Americus Vespucius, and bore a share in three of his four voyages that are now published'.[15] The natives portrayed by Vespucci resemble the inhabitants of the island invented by More,[16] who have few laws and live without lawyers. As Vespucci writes,

> Neither do they have goods of their own, but all things are held in common. They live together without king, without government, and each is his own master Beyond the fact that they have no church, no religion and are not *idolaters*, what more can I say?[17]

After they had been read by the sponsors, these letters navigated freely from hand to hand, announcing the awesome news. Little by little, they multiplied, in copies handcrafted by monks, assuming new formats. As pamphlets or booklets measuring 13 by 11 cm, they reached ordinary people in fairs, alleyways and taverns, and then they reposed in libraries as well.

At least five letters are attributed to Vespucci. Three—the *Seville, Cape Verde* and *Lisbon* letters—are considered authentic. Two are apocryphal—that is, their authenticity is unproven: these are *Mundus Novus* and the

Four Voyages. However, the authentic Lisbon letter served as a possible basis for the apocryphal *Mundus Novus.*

Understanding the construction and circulation of *Mundus Novus* enables us to understand the misattribution of authorship and evaluate its legal consequences for our own times, in terms of the challenge of regulating the flow of information. What lessons can be learned from the century of maritime discoveries by legislators in the century of virtual communication?

3   THE FREE FLOW OF COOPERATIVE INFORMATION

Vespucci's authentic Lisbon letter to his protector, Lorenzo de' Medici, in Florence corrected a key geographical error. It interpreted correctly what Columbus had interpreted wrongly. Columbus did indeed find a new continent, but he believed he was in the Indies, in Asia. He was mistaken. In contrast, Vespucci believed he had reached the fourth part of the world. He was right.[18]

This key information was reproduced, argued out and emphasised by the apocryphal *Mundus Novus*:

> I wrote to you at some length concerning my return from those new regions which we found and explored with the fleet ... And these we may rightly call a New World. Because our ancestors had no knowledge of them, and it will be a matter wholly new to all those who hear about them. For this transcends the view held by our ancients, most of whom hold that there is no continent to the south beyond the equator, but only the sea which they named the Atlantic ... But that their opinion is false and utterly opposed to the truth, this my last voyage has made manifest; for in those southern parts I have found a continent more densely peopled and abounding in animals than our Europe or Asia or Africa...[19]

Columbus' journal was wrong about the past; Vespucci's letter confirms the future. *Mundus Novus* is fundamental because it dismantles the structuring dogma of mediaeval religious geography: the earth is flat. It would be no more from then on.

Knowledge based on empirical observation replaced knowledge based on religious dogma. This was the biggest scientific progress ever—as big as Darwin's theory of evolution, centuries later. Both challenged the religious control of the progress of science.

Mundus Novus is a collaborative work because it was not written in a single period of time, in a single city, by a single author. It is a collaborative and cumulative work, written at different times in various cities by several authors. It was modified as it travelled. It is open work, a work in progress. In short, it is a collective letter, almost like Wikipedia.

It is said to have originated from a manuscript in Italian entitled 'Albericus Vespucius offers his best compliments to Lorenzo Pietro di Medici'. It had to be translated into Latin, the language of the elites. The original edition reportedly appeared in Paris circa 1503, already in Latin, freely translated by a certain Jocundus.[20] Its readership and circulation increased.

A free new edition published in Venice in 1504 discards the bureaucratic salutation ('best compliments'), replacing it with *Mundus Novus*, a concise title, easily recalled, attractive, stimulating—a timeless label. Steve Jobs would like it—still modern today, insuperable.

The collaborative process did not stop there. In 1505, in Augsburg, Johann Froschauer freely added an image to the text, with the first woodcut portraying the new continent. The Indians shown there have aristocratic beards, the bodies of hardened mariners with El Greco's noses. From there on, *Mundus Novus* became both image and text and it set everyone's imagination on fire.

More and more editions were published. The news about the discovery of a fourth continent, the dream of Sagres, ignores frontiers. Scholars believe that at least 41 editions were freely published before 1506. A German translation was freely published in Basel, Augsburg, Munich, Leipzig, Nuremberg and Strasbourg. It was a success, as well described by Bueno:

> Mundus Novus is a pamphlet, a chapbook. It was sold on the street, in fairs. It was read by nobles and plebeians. It was as short as a novella and as urgent as an advertisement. It was at once both simple and sophisticated. A mixture of blood, savagery and science, philosophical investigation and picaresque adventure, visions of paradise and Dantean scenes of cannibalism. It was light and profound, analytical without being boring. It had to be a smash hit.[21]

Columbus' wrongness condemned him to bitterness for the rest of his life. Vespucci's rightness perpetuated his name for all time.

The final blow against Columbus was to come from Waldseemüller, a canon of the church of Saint-Dié-des-Vosges, near Strasbourg, in the seventeenth century. *Universalis Cosmographia*, the revolutionary world map produced by this cleric and geographer, was the first to use the name America. His reasoning was simple, as evidenced by Chapter IX of *Cosmographiae Introductio*, the book he wrote to accompany the map:

> Now these parts of the earth [Europe, Asia and Africa] have been more extensively explored and a fourth part has been discovered by Amerigo Vespucci (as will be set forth in what follows). Inasmuch as both Europe and Asia received their names from women, I see no reason why anyone should justly object to calling this part Amerige, i.e., the land of Amerigo, or America, after Amerigo, its discoverer, a man of great ability. Its position and the customs of its inhabitants may be clearly understood from the four voyages of Amerigo, which are subjoined.[22]

Hence the name America appears on the map, labelling the previously unknown lands on the other side of the Atlantic Ocean. Many more maps were produced, multiplying and immortalising the misattribution of authorship. The Europeans took in good faith this act of naming, which was historically mistaken but based on a correct geographical interpretation—an error that gave birth to the identity of the continent's inhabitants as Americans. A false identity, then.

Waldseemüller eventually realised his mistake and wanted to correct it. It was too late.[23] The market, the readers, made the change impossible. The identity of the new world was forged forever. The anonymous monk was the one responsible for the biggest successful mistake ever.

These are the facts. This is the story. Now comes reflection and a proposal. Would this have happened in the twenty-first century? The answer is: probably no.

4   ON THE CURRENT LEGAL OBSTACLES TO THE FREE FLOW OF INFORMATION

There is a clear similarity between the maritime discoveries and the creation of virtual space. On their own, the lateen-rigged caravel, astrolabe, quadrant and balestilha or cross-staff (the hardware) were not sufficient to lead the navigators to new continents. Similarly, computers and other hardware alone will not lead us to the virtual new world. They are necessary but not sufficient conditions.

Charts, itineraries, journals, ships' logs and almanacs were the rudimentary tools, the multiple platforms that created the free flow of information, enabling it to navigate and produce new knowledge. They were the veritable software of today. They established networks of communication, dialogues and debates among navigators, astrologers and cosmographers. They helped to create a new scientific community. They stimulated the innovation process. They made more discoveries possible. They connected the Old World to the New. They built the fifteenth century.

Without software, no one can leave a digital port to navigate through the oceans of the networked society. Without software there is no such a thing as navigation, communications networks, knowledge production and sharing. Without sharing, the virtual world cannot exist. Software makes us more than discoverers; it makes us the creators of ourselves. In the twenty-first century, innovation is not about discovering a distant geographical world; it is about constituting and communicating the non-existent digital world so far.

What would probably have happened to Vespucci's letter if the restrictive copyright laws and patents that govern software today had been enforced in the fifteenth century?

Let us imagine that *Mundus Novus* had been written by Vespucci today. Put yourself, dear reader, in Vespucci's and his lawyers' place. On becoming aware of the successive alterations, translations, illustrations and multiple unauthorised editions, Vespucci's hypothetical lawyers would certainly try to protect their client's rights. How? It varies, of course, from country to country, but Western legislation is much the same. They could take various kinds of action:

1. Denounce criminal copyright infringement and prevent publicity and publishing of the letter, or charge for any permission they might grant.[24]
2. Sue for an injunction to withdraw from circulation all editions published without Vespucci's express permission.
3. Obtain a court order prohibiting the transformation of the letter into stories, chapbooks or ballads by third parties, to be told and sung by troubadours in taverns, fairs and city alleys.
4. Sue Thomas More for plagiarism, comparable to the crime of counterfeiting, in *Utopia*.
5. Claim material and non-material damages[25]—many descriptions of the island of Utopia were taken from Vespucci's letters without due credit and citation.

6. Allege unfair competition by More[26] when Vespucci's letters were sold for his own benefit.
7. Prevent translation and the insertion of unauthorised illustrations[27]—it would not be difficult to obtain a court order obliging the illustrator to pay damages, and preventing circulation of the publication with figures. Without translation and illustration, readership of the letters would decline. It would be impossible to see the dream.

In many countries the lawyers would be successful in all of these actions, but what would be the result of this success? Actually, there would be two different types of consequence: those related to copyright, Vespucci's private rights; and those in respect of advances in maritime discoveries, the public need of scientific progress, the free flow of information.

Vespucci would probably die a wealthier man. Not only would damages be due, but also royalties in accordance with publishing copyright contracts, not to mention that a number of people would be charged criminally and might have gone to prison, including Giocondo (the translator), Froschauer (the illustrator) and Waldseemüller (who cited the letters in his book about the map), as well as many others for criminal breach of copyright.

Vespucci would have paid more taxes but he would have left a richer estate. He would certainly have died rich, but almost anonymous. There would have been fewer editions of the letters. Waldseemüller's misattribution would probably have been corrected. The great geographers would not have read the letter. Vespucci would not have 'discovered' America. America would be known as Columbia, in just homage to Vespucci's greatest rival.

Paradoxically, protection of Vespucci's copyright would not have enabled him to achieve what he most desired in his life. He would have enforced his legal rights and earned a few million dollars or euros, but he would not have achieved fame. Glory would be the price.

From the public standpoint, the consequences for the century of discoveries would have been negative. Probably Montaigne, Botticelli, Leonardo, Erasmus and other navigators and potentates would not have read Vespucci. *Utopia* would have been withdrawn from circulation and we would not know of it. The European imagination would be smaller. Thomas More would not have such a big political and intellectual influence. At best he would be a plagiarist. The world of culture would not have been enriched by intellectual works as distinguished as Bacon's *New Atlantis* or Swift's *Gulliver's Travels,* both directly inspired by More's *Utopia.*

Access to *Mundus Novus* would have been legal only for the happy few financiers: King Manuel the Fortunate, Berardi, Fernando of Aragon, Isabel of Castile and Lorenzo from Florence. Certainly the discoveries would have turned out differently. Fewer financiers, bankers, navigators, mariners, deckhands and scientists would have been willing to participate in one of the greatest adventure of all times. Europe would have accepted Columbus' error a little longer. Geography and science would have remained subordinate to religious faith for longer, instead of empirical observation—more faith and less science.

Briefly, the unrestricted legal freedom allowed *Mundus Novus* and the data it contains to travel throughout Europe. The account 'is everywhere', said Thomas More. There were no legal barriers in terms of national constitutions, the World Intellectual Property Organization, public or private law, national law or international law.

Instead of being an authorial monopoly, as it is today, it was a collective open work—translated freely by some, illustrated freely by others, titled freely by yet others and published freely by many. Over a period of no less than five years, it was collectively produced by several individuals: Vespucci, Giocondo and Froschauer, at least. It was reproduced freely by several publishers in various cities: Paris, Venice and Augsburg. *Mundus Novus* was not private property; rather, it was non-property. It was a 'commons', as Lawrence Lessig would say[28]—a collective work.

The fundamental legal issue posed by *Mundus Novus* is now clear. There is a necessary but not always evident correlation between intellectual property as a private right and the free flow of information required for the progress of knowledge. So how can we reconcile the last century's privatistic copyright law with the gigantic diffusion of cumulative innovation made possible and fostered by technology in the twenty-first century?

Access to knowledge due to legal obstacles is much harder nowadays.

5   THE MULTIPLE NATURE OF AMBITION

Today's copyright law was built on the premise that it is in the public interest to protect and strengthen the innovation process through the capitalisation of the authors and intermediate creators so that they can continue to innovate. But what distinguishes the Digital Age of today from the Industrial Age and the Age of Discoveries is precisely the fact that today's navigators do not depend so heavily on financial capital as Columbus, Cabral, Vespucci or Vasco da Gama did in their day. The latter could navigate only after finding a capitalist, be it King Manuel of Portugal, Isabel of Castile or Lorenzo de' Medici.

Bill Gates in his garage, Linus Torvalds in his bedroom and Mark Zuckerberg in his Harvard dorm embarked on their adventures essentially without capital. They depended much more on access to knowledge than on access to capital. That is the fundamental difference.

A navigator, from yesterday as well as from today, participates in an adventure for many reasons. Neither Columbus nor Vespucci became navigators only to get rich. It is true that they needed financiers—monarchs and bankers. It is also true that Columbus intended to keep 10 % of all the wealth found in the new Indies for himself.

But they were also motivated by other factors. Ambition and lust for power also led Columbus to demand to be made admiral, viceroy and governor-general of any lands he might discover. The fight against the Inquisition's obscurantism was another decisive factor.

The same multiplicity of factors influenced Vespucci, whose greatest desire was to 'leave some fame behind me after I die'. Reducing the drivers of innovation to mere financial gain reduces the complexity of human ambition. It reifies and monetises man's dreams. A government policy for digital innovation must take this multiplicity of factors into account.

Let us stress this point by bringing in the example of another navigator (or aeronaut, as he called himself): Santos-Dumont, the Brazilian who invented the aeroplane. He was the first to build and fly a heavier-than-air plane under its own power, yet he refused to patent the first aircraft offered to the public view worldwide. His plane took off in Paris, covered by world media, without the aid of catapults or other devices, such as those used by the Wright brothers. He considered his invention a 'gift' to mankind. As he said several times, he would rather end his days in poverty than deny others the privilege of performing aviation experiments with his invention.[29]

Santos-Dumont saw inventors as people 'who almost forget about life because they are so absorbed in their dreams'. One of his dreams was to hear in the future that 'an airplane had taken off from the New World and reached the Old [World] in perhaps one day', covering the same distance that Columbus had taken 70 days to travel. Santos-Dumont wanted merely to be 'a contributor to the happiness of mankind'.[30]

This is the greatest challenge posed by humanity's new adventure: construction of the virtual *Mundus Novus*. How do we break with the monopolistic ambition of a copyright law in which only capitalisation of the author via intermediates assures the continuity of creation and innovation and today is captured and embodied in most legal systems? How do we avoid stigmatising as illegal the alternative forms of copyright that already arise in practice?

The new *Mundus Novus* requires a new legal framework governing copyright, trademarks and patents capable of stimulating and driving the advance of the civilisatory adventure. It requires a freer flow of scientific information in favour of innovation processes in order to foster it, instead of controlling it.

NOTES

1. Luís Vaz de Camões, *The Lusiads*, translated into English by William Julius Mickle, 1791 (3rd edn).
2. Inventor of the World Wide Web.
3. Eduardo Bueno, 'Apresentação' in Américo Vespúcio, *Novo Mundo— As Cartas que Batizaram a América* (Planeta do Brasil 2003) 10.
4. Antonio LP Albuquerque, *Os Descobrimentos Portugueses e o Encontro de Civilizações* (Nórdica 1999) 12.
5. Ibid 12 and 30, where we read: 'Nevertheless, we cannot but recognize that once again the old argument from authority was discarded so that knowledge proper could be pursued through observation. This knowledge was built more soundly because it was constructed from the inside out and grounded in the conviction that apparent reality can give anyone who sees and studies it.'
6. Ibid 24–26.
7. The many examples include *A morte do padre Felipe Bourel* ('The Death of Father Filipe Bourel'), by an unknown artist (Museu Nacional de Belas Artes, 'Escola Portuguesa').
8. Lya Luft, 'A Força das Palavras', Veja n° 1862 (14 July 2004), http:// veja.abril.com.br/140704/ponto_de_vista.html.
9. According to João Moreira Salles, 'Florence invented the Renaissance. The Renaissance invented the modern world'. See 'Ao pé do chão', www.nominimo.com.br.
10. Luiz Fernando da Silva Pinto, *Sagres—A Revolução Estratégica* (Editora FGV 2000) 319. Translated as *Sagres: A Strategic Revolution* (Editora FGV 2002).

11. Felipe Fernández-Armesto, *Columbus* (Oxford University Press 1992) 186.
12. According to Eduardo Bueno 'There is only material evidence for Vespucci's participation in three expeditions to the New World.' See Bueno (n 3) 60.
13. Vespúcio (n 3) 45.
14. Bueno (n 3) 61 (referring to the 'Four Voyages' section of the Mundus Novus letter).
15. Thomas More, *Utopia* (Paulo Neves tr, L&PM Pocket 2001) 18.
16. 'There are 54 cities in the island, all large and well-built: the manners, customs, and laws of which are the same, and they are all contrived as near in the same manner as the ground on which they stand will allow. The nearest lie at least 24 miles distance from one another, and the most remote are not so far distant, but that a man can go on foot in one day from it, to that which lies next it. Every city sends three of their wisest senators once a year to Amaurot [the capital] to consult about their common concerns; for that is chief town of the island, being situated near the centre of it, so that it is the most convenient place for their assemblies. The jurisdiction of every city extends at least twenty miles: and where the towns lie wider, they have much more ground: no town desires to enlarge its bounds, for the people consider themselves rather as tenants than landlords. They have built over all the country, farmhouses for husbandmen, which are well contrived, and are furnished with all things necessary for country labour. Inhabitants are sent by turns from the cities to dwell in them; no country family has fewer than forty men and women in it, besides two slaves. There is a master and a mistress set over every family; and over thirty families there is a magistrate.' Available at http://www.bl.uk/ learning/histcitizen/21cc/utopia/more1/island1/island.html.
17. Vespúcio (n 3) 42.
18. Ibid 50–51.
19. Ibid 33–34.
20. Bueno (n 3) 30.
21. Ibid 29.
22. Quoted in Riccardo Fontana, *O Brasil de Américo Vespúcio* (Edílson Alkmim Cunha and João Pedro Mendes tr, UNB 1994/1995) 67. The full title of the map (in Latin) was 'A Map of the Entire World [Universal Cosmography] according to the Tradition of Ptolemy and the Discoveries of Amerigo Vespucci and others'.

23. Fernández-Armesto tells the story in his biography of Columbus: 'Only a year after Columbus's death, Martin Waldseemüller proposed that the new continent be named in honor of Amerigo Vespucci ...; six years later, he retracted the suggestion.' Fernández-Armesto (n 11) 186–187.
24. See Article 29 of the Brazilian copyright law (Law 9610/98).
25. In this sense, see the judgments of the Supreme Federal Court of Brazil in RE-94201, in which the reporting judge was Justice Aldir Passarinho, and of the Rio de Janeiro State Court of Appeal in AC (Civil Appeal) 2000.001.18234.
26. Since the information in the letters would no longer be unpublished. This was the view taken by the Rio de Janeiro State Court of Appeal in AC 1991.001.00612 and AC 1993.001.00092.
27. In accordance with Article 29, III and IV, of the Brazilian copyright law.
28. Lawrence Lessig, *Code and Other Laws of Cyberspace* (Basic Books 1999).
29. Paulo Hoffman, *Asas da Loucura* (Objetiva 2004) 250. A choice that apparently unites the two navigators across the centuries, since 'despite his political positions and Portugal's cultural restrictions at the time (imposed by the policy of secrecy), he [Vespucci] felt a need to discover and derived pleasure from understanding, interpreting and publicizing the fruits of his own intuitions as an elevated example of the universal projection of the Italian Rinascimento'. Fontana (n 22) 71.
30. See Alberto Santos-Dumont, *O que eu vi. O que nós veremos* (Hedra 2000).

CHAPTER 17

Digital Culture, Copyright and the Orphan Works Issue: A View from Brazil

Paula Westenberger

Currently one of the main topics of discussion on the international copyright policy agenda,[1] the digitisation of libraries and archives and the issue of orphan works are deemed illustrative of the extent to which copyright law may impose obstacles to the promotion and preservation of culture. Works are deemed 'orphans' when the copyright owner cannot be identified or located,[2] resulting in the impossibility of obtaining authorisation for preserving and disseminating culturally valuable material.[3]

The fact that authorisation is required for digitising and making works accessible online creates the obligation for cultural institutions to identify and locate every copyright owner in order to ask permission for such uses.[4] The process of clearance of rights is overly expensive and time-consuming, and unauthorised uses entail potential liability for copyright infringement. This situation often prevents cultural institutions from adopting digital technology to preserve and disseminate works, resulting in the 'locking up' of culturally relevant material.[5]

While access to culture should be promoted as a human right and as an essential tool for social development, cultural institutions still need to

P. Westenberger (✉)
Queen Mary University of London, London, UK

© Palgrave Macmillan, a division of Macmillan Publishers Limited 2017   293
P. Fortes et al. (eds.), *Law and Policy in Latin America*,
DOI 10.1057/978-1-137-56694-2_17

respect authors' rights, whose protection also has a human rights basis, and which are subject to complex international and national regulation.

Although the issues of mass digitisation and orphan works have been assessed and addressed in some jurisdictions, Latin American countries still lack a comprehensive solution. El Centro Regional para el Fomento del Libro en América Latina y el Caribe (CERLALC, Regional Centre for Book Development in Latin America and the Caribbean), established by the United Nations Educational, Scientific and Cultural Organization (UNESCO), notes that existing solutions for digitisation focus on preservation rather than promoting wider accessibility to works.[6] CERLALC also points out that orphan works has not yet been directly addressed in Latin American and Caribbean legislations, which has resulted in the need for the promotion of studies on their quantitative, economic and social impact in the region.[7]

Current discussions at the World Intellectual Property Organization (WIPO) are focused on finding an international solution to the copyright-related issues faced by libraries and archives, including those related to digitisation and orphan works, and they have received the input of several Latin American countries.[8] However, finding a balanced solution to the orphan works problem is a complex task in view of the diverse demands of the various stakeholders involved.[9] This chapter will suggest that partial legislative solutions at the national level, justified by the public interest in preservation of and access to culture, can already be formulated[10] to address both the digitisation and the orphan works issues in the context of cultural institutions in Latin America.

Brazil will be examined in view of existing legislative proposals, as contemplated in the copyright law reform project, submitted for public consultation in 2010. The timing is therefore appropriate for discussions that could help to inform the legislator in drafting the relevant provisions.

There is also extra relevance in analysing the Brazilian perspective given that Brazil is currently considered to be a potentially influential world leader in terms of internet rights as a result of the recent implementation of the Internet Bill of Rights,[11] which includes provisions that, inter alia, guarantee freedom of expression online.[12] In this regard, prospective developments in copyright law concerning digitisation and orphan works could become a reference to Latin American countries. Furthermore, the National Library of Brazil, which owns the richest bibliographical collection in Latin America,[13] is currently undertaking an extensive digitisation project[14] and could therefore serve as an important case study on this topic.

This chapter suggests that the main challenges faced by cultural institutions regarding orphan works, including operational impacts and potential liability connected to unauthorised uses of such works, actually result from the lack of legal provisions authorising broader digitisation activities. It is argued, in this regard, that the proposed legislation in Brazil does not sufficiently address the issues associated with digitisation and orphan works in cultural institutions vis-à-vis the human right to take part in cultural life and the constitutional rights to education and culture.

1 DIGITISATION, ORPHAN WORKS AND CULTURAL INSTITUTIONS: FROM HUMAN RIGHTS TO INTERNATIONAL COPYRIGHT LAW

Access to the internet is a key means for individuals to exercise the right to freedom of expression and, hence, is a facilitator in the realisation of other human rights, such as the right to education and to taking part in cultural life.[15] Indeed, the internet serves as a major catalyst for the distribution of culture that is low in cost and high in reach, which, combined with developments in digital technologies, permits the proper preservation of and access to works and expands the possibilities of creative expressions.[16]

In this scenario, the digitisation projects being undertaken by cultural institutions around the world in order to promote access to and preservation of their collections[17] have an important human rights justification, and governments have a mission to provide a legal framework that makes these projects feasible.

According to the Committee on Economic, Social and Cultural Rights (CESCR) of the United Nations, the right to take part in cultural life[18] requires that the states take actions 'ensuring preconditions for participation, facilitation and promotion of cultural life, and access to and preservation of cultural goods', 'culture' being interpreted as encompassing, inter alia, oral and written literature, music and song, non-verbal communication, arts and other forms of human expression.[19] The elements necessary for the full realisation of such a right include, among others, (1) the *availability* of cultural goods and services to everyone, including libraries, museums, theatres, cinemas and the arts in all forms; and (2) the *accessibility* to cultural goods and services, consisting of 'effective and concrete opportunities for individuals and communities to enjoy culture fully, within physical and financial reach for all in both urban and rural areas, without discrimination'.[20]

On the other hand, the protection of copyright also has a human rights basis.[21] However, it is worth pointing out CESCR's interpretation that 'the scope of protection of the moral and material interests of the author provided for by Article 15, paragraph 1 (c), does not necessarily coincide with what is referred to as intellectual property rights under national legislation or international agreements'. In fact, the protection of moral and material interests of authors is 'intrinsically linked' to other Article 15 rights in the Covenant, including the right to take part in cultural life.[22]

However, some aspects of copyright law constitute obstacles to the promotion and dissemination of digital culture, insofar as digitising for the preservation and dissemination of works on the internet requires the authorisation of the copyright owner according to international copyright rules. Such rules concern the exclusive right held by copyright owners of authorising the reproduction[23] and the communication to the public[24] of their works, including making them available online.

It is possible to include some specific uses in copyright legislation that do not require the authorisation of the copyright owner. These are known as limitations and exceptions to copyright. However, they must comply with the 'three-step test', foreseen in the main international copyright treaties,[25] which establishes that exceptions to copyright have to be conceived (1) in certain special cases (2) that do not conflict with a normal exploitation of the work and (3) that do not unreasonably prejudice the legitimate interests of the copyright owner.[26] This means that a provision that allows the digitisation and dissemination of copyright works by cultural institutions should comply with the three-step test.[27]

In view of the above, unless the work is in the public domain or the use is legally permitted by a limitation or exception to copyright, cultural institutions must obtain authorisation of the owner of the copyright prior to the digitisation and dissemination of their work. Such clearance of rights might be unfeasible owing to time and cost issues, or unsuccessful in the case of orphan works, resulting in the 'locking up' of culturally relevant material.

In the UK, orphan works were found to generate a significant operational impact on the functioning of a cultural institution,[28] which showed the urgency of addressing the issue. The United States Copyright Office has developed an extensive study dedicated to orphan works and mass digitisation,[29] concluding that solutions for such issues were 'desperately needed' and proposing legislative responses.[30]

There are no such impact studies on orphan works in relation to Latin American countries, which is a point to be considered in copyright policy, as pointed out by CERLALC.

2   Existing Solutions for the Orphan Works Issue Internationally

There are a variety of solutions being devised worldwide to address digitisation and orphan works issues.[31] One question to be answered is whether any of these solutions allows the creation of a digital cultural environment that addresses specific demands for access to culture in Latin America in a manner that is balanced with the interests of right holders.[32] It is suggested here, however, that, to assist formulating their own solutions, Latin American countries could employ the methodologies of the studies that supported policy discussions in other countries.

Even though the Canadian compulsory licensing system provides legal certainty to the user of orphan works, it has been criticised for its apparent inefficiency, as suggested by the small number of applications filed.[33] The Scandinavian extended collective licensing approach is a possible solution for the issue of mass rights clearance, including for digitisation projects. However, it depends on sufficient representativeness of collective management organisations in those countries, which may not be the same in other jurisdictions,[34] such as Brazil, where collective management is a contentious matter,[35] which may indicate that such a solution may not be widely supported by Brazilian authors.[36] In the USA, although the fair use provision was applied to the Google Books digitisation project,[37] the country still has policy recommendations for implementing legislative solutions specifically for orphan works and mass digitisation. In Europe, Directive 2012/28/EU[38] was issued to regulate certain uses of orphan works by cultural institutions, and the UK passed legislation in 2014 for an orphan works licensing scheme to be carried out by the Intellectual Property Office and for an extended collective licensing scheme - as well as for an exception for certain uses of orphan works by cultural institutions, implementing the EU Directive.[39]

In the absence of legal solutions in some jurisdictions, cultural institutions are either digitising orphan works without authorisation and relying on a risk-management policy, or refraining from using modern preservation technologies for orphan works.[40] The general policy underpinning the 'BN Digital' digitisation project of the National Library of Brazil, for example, is only making available works in the public domain, unless the authorisation of the copyright owners is obtained.[41]

3   BRAZIL'S COPYRIGHT SYSTEM AND CONSTITUTIONAL RIGHTS

The issue of orphan works is not currently addressed in Brazil's Copyright Law,[42] which also does not contain limitations to copyright aimed at cultural institutions. The proposals of copyright reform addressed these issues but still do not provide a comprehensive solution in view of the human and fundamental rights to access to culture.

Cultural institutions hold in their collections various forms of copyright-protected material.[43] Unless the work is in the public domain,[44] digitisation and dissemination online by a cultural institution would require the authorisation of the copyright owners. Authors' exclusive right of use, publication and reproduction of their works are fundamental rights in Brazil's Constitution[45] and are protected under the category of economic rights in the Copyright Law.[46] Authors also own moral rights, which include, inter alia, the rights to be named as author, to keep a work unpublished and to retract a published work when it affects their reputation.[47]

The ownership of rights is another complex element. In order to digitise and make a work available, permission must be obtained from the copyright owner, who can be the author (natural person who creates a work),[48] a legal entity (e.g. collective works, although individual collaborations need to be independently authorised where they can be individualised)[49] or a third party that acquired ownership through contract or inheritance. The lack of formalities regarding the protection of a work—that is, no need for registration[50]—results in difficulties for rights clearance. Uses that may interfere with moral rights are enforceable by authors, their heirs, the director of a film and sometimes even the state, and, even though copyright can be assigned, moral rights are inalienable.[51]

The closest provisions in Brazil's Copyright Law dealing with unknown ownership of rights are those on anonymous works and works of unknown authorship. However, these cannot be considered solutions to the orphan works issue owing to the lack of clarity of these provisions and to their limited scope compared with the orphan works definition.

Anonymous works are defined in legislation as 'any work that does not name the author, either according to his wish or because he is unknown'.[52] The first issue is that the law fails to clearly define *anonymous* works and works of *unknown* authorship, even though it provides different legal treatments for these works: *anonymous* works are owned by the publisher,[53] while works of *unknown* authorship belong to the public domain.[54]

Such drastic differences in ownership with no clear distinction between the definitions of these works result in an unclear rule for their use.

There is disagreement among scholars regarding the application of these provisions. Fragoso understands that anonymous works will belong to the public domain until the author makes themselves known, although he admits that this interpretation has the potential to create issues for the users of these works.[55] Branco disagrees, arguing that anonymous and unknown authorship are different concepts since the law determines a specific deadline of protection for anonymous works, being incompatible with the rule of the public domain, and claiming that, in the case of anonymous works, the author did not want to be known; while in the case of works of unknown authorship, the authorship became unknown over the course of time.[56] However, there is no straightforward way of assessing whether authors are not identified according to their wish or because this information was lost in time, which creates a practical obstacle in applying the relevant rules.

To add further complexity to the discussion, a recent decision by Brazil's Superior Court of Justice has indicated, citing the commentator Elisângela Dias Menezes, that 'anonymous and pseudonymous works can be freely represented, performed, published or in any way utilised without the consent of the author, since the author cannot be identified'.[57]

Furthermore, the provisions for anonymous works and unknown authorship do not sufficiently cover orphan works because they refer only to the unnamed or unknown *author*, not mentioning where the *owner* of copyright is unknown, and they would not apply to the situations where the author or owner is indeed known but not located, which are also within the definition of orphan works.[58]

With regard to the lack of limitations to copyright in Brazil's law concerning the use of works by cultural institutions, it is important to clarify that the limitations clauses[59] have traditionally been interpreted to be exhaustive and narrowly construed.[60] However, another recent decision by the Superior Court of Justice has clarified that the limitations clauses in the Copyright Law should be deemed illustrative, considering the fundamental rights at stake and applying the three-step test.[61]

In the case of the digitisation of works by cultural institutions, the constitutional rights that are relevant to the discussion include the fundamental right to education,[62] which should be provided based on the 'freedom to learn, teach, research and express thought, art and knowledge';[63] the fundamental right of access to information;[64] and cultural rights and access to the sources of national culture, which should be guaranteed by the state, who should support and encourage the dissemination of cultural expressions, as well as promote and protect (including with measures of preservation) Brazil's cultural heritage, which comprises, inter alia, forms of expression and artistic creations.[65]

It can be said that Brazil's Constitution contains provisions that could be interpreted by the courts in order to allow certain cases of digitisation by public institutions without the need for authorisation, applying the understanding of the recent decision in Special Appeal REsp 964.404. However, considering that Brazil is a civil law jurisdiction, relying solely on the case law approach may not provide the legal certainty needed for cultural institutions to carry out their digitisation projects.

In view of the above, Brazil's Copyright Law may not be sufficiently balanced with the human and constitutional rights at stake by not allowing the digitisation of works for preservation and access to culture.

4   PROJECTS OF REFORM OF BRAZIL'S COPYRIGHT LAW

Discussions about the need to update Brazil's Copyright Law culminated with the Ministry of Culture's submission of a project of reform to public consultation in 2010.[66] After the public consultation, some amendments to the original project were proposed.[67] Under a three-step test traditional perspective, it can be said that the amended proposals comply with the interests of rights owners. However, questions remain as to whether they are compatible with social and cultural interests, and, in this regard, the main problems that should be addressed are preservation and accessibility, including online. On this point it is important to stress that the mission of the National Library's digitisation project is to preserve cultural memory and promote wide access to information.[68]

Preservation

The project submitted to public consultation included a provision specifically allowing cultural institutions to reproduce works for the purposes of conservation, preservation and archiving, without commercial purpose.[69] Since no authorisation is required, orphan works would not be an issue for the purposes of preservation.

This solution can be considered three-step test compliant, arguably even under its more conservative approach. It is also, to a certain extent, human and constitutional rights effective because it allows culture to be preserved. However, a question to be asked is whether the concept of preservation of culture should be limited to the reproduction of a work for digital storage or tangible substitution, or if it should be more widely interpreted to include measures for digitally disseminating such works to the public.[70]

Accessibility

The public consultation project also proposed a provision to allow cultural institutions to communicate and make available to the public the works in their collections, for the purposes of research, investigation or study, within their facilities or through their closed computer networks.[71] As a limitation to copyright, this solution would cover works irrespective of their orphan status.

After the public consultation, the proposed amendment imposed further restrictions on such provision, including that it would only apply to works that were rare or unavailable to purchase, and in order to avoid deterioration.

It can be argued that this limitation to copyright should not be restricted to the communication and making available of works within the facilities of cultural institutions; it should also allow, in specific circumstances, the making available on online platforms managed by the cultural institution. Since not everyone is able to visit cultural institutions, narrowing down the access in this manner would be a 'retrograde step in an era of digital culture'[72] and not consistent with the human right of participating in cultural life. This is particularly so in a country of the territorial dimensions and social inequalities of Brazil. Restricting the provision to uses that aim to avoid deterioration and, cumulatively, to works that are rare or unavailable, as reads the proposed amendment, might also be a too narrow formulation.

Relying on the balanced interpretation of the three-step test,[73] it is important to allow the reproduction and communication of certain works by cultural institutions for certain non-commercial cultural uses, both 'cultural institutions' and 'cultural uses' having to be carefully defined.[74] It may be necessary to make a distinction between different categories of work in such limitation, possibly including 'orphan works' in its formulation. Including a low-resolution image of a painting on a museum's website for visitor information purposes, for example, has arguably a smaller impact on the copyright owner than including the full content of an in-copyright, non-orphan book on a library's website. A too widely drafted limitation could violate the three-step test, and a possible solution could be to include a few examples of allowed uses alongside a three-step test wording, akin to Article 46, VIII of Brazil's Copyright Law.

It is therefore crucial that the drafting of this limitation is supported by robust evidence and studies on, inter alia, the functioning of different types of cultural institution and their engagement with copyright law; on the current processes of acquisition, lending and online dissemination of works; and on the contractual architecture involving cultural institutions and rights owners.

Specific Provisions for Orphan Works

A system of non-voluntary non-exclusive licences, including, inter alia, orphan works, was also proposed.[75] The proposed amendment after the public consultation created a provision exclusively for orphan works, which would be licensed by the Ministry of Culture, improving the solution because it separated it from other materials (e.g. out-of-print works), established the allocation of resources, included the need for reasonable and good-faith search for authors (akin to the diligent search requirement in other jurisdictions) and removed some of the restrictions that were imposed in the former proposal.[76] A suggestion that could be made is that Article 52-C, §1, should mention 'owners', while it currently foresees the reasonable search only for 'authors'.

The amended proposal created a balanced licensing solution for orphan works and could be implemented in conjunction with the preservation and accessibility limitations proposed above because it could allow non-cultural or commercial uses of orphan works. Such uses are, however, arguably less urgent than the cultural uses proposed as limitations,[77] and as such should not delay the implementation of the latter.

Problems Not Addressed by the Projects of Reform

No attempt was made to clarify the difference between anonymous works and works of unknown authorship, which are concepts that could create confusion with the definition of orphan works. Suggestions in this case are to redefine anonymous works in order to remove 'works of unknown authorship' from its definition; clarify that where the publisher of anonymous works cannot be identified or located these works could also be considered orphan works; and clarify and rename the works of 'unknown authorship' that belong to the public domain under Article 45, II.

Lastly, the digitisation solutions for cultural institutions should be dissociated from the wider copyright law reform in order to expedite the passing of new legislation, as occurred with the collective management reforms.

5   CONCLUSION

The orphan works issue is real, and it is possible to find a partial solution through legislative amendments that comply with international copyright requirements. A solution that responds to current demands relating to digital culture in Brazil, however, should not be restricted to orphan works but must be thought of in the general context of digitisation by cultural institutions.

It was argued, in this respect, that by creating a general solution for digitisation by cultural institutions, the most urgent issues relating to orphan works (preservation and access) are resolved, which can lead to the conclusion that the magnitude of the orphan works issue is only real in so far as there are no adequate digitisation solutions.

The system being discussed in the reform proposals in Brazil does not appear to fulfil the full potential of the fundamental right of participating in cultural life and the constitutional rights of access to culture, information and education because solutions for an effective dissemination of cultural materials are still required. However, it is vital that the drafting of such a limitation is informed by substantive study and evidence on the current practices of cultural institutions in dealing with copyright works. Empirical methodologies employed in other jurisdictions' studies could also be used in Brazil. Initiatives such as the cooperation between the Brazilian Ministry of Culture and Europeana in the context of the Information Systems and Digital Cultural Collections action within the project Sectorial Dialogues European Union-Brazil, including discussions about copyright, should be strongly welcomed.[78]

NOTES

1. E.g. WIPO's sessions SCCR/26 of 2013 to SCCR/30 of 2015, www.wipo.int/meetings/en/topic.jsp?group_id=62.
2. Anna Vuopala, *Assessment of the Orphan Works Issue and Costs for Rights Clearance* (European Commission DG Information Society and Media Unit E4 Access to Information 2010) 11–12.

3. In UK public sector organisations, works likely to be orphans have arguably little commercial value but great academic and cultural significance. Naomi Korn, *In from the Cold: An Assessment of the Scope of 'Orphan Works' and its Impact on the Delivery of Services to the Public* (JISC 2009) 6.

4. For the purposes of this chapter, 'cultural institutions' are 'libraries, archives, documentation centres, museums, film archives and other museum institutions', following the reform proposal of Article 46, Brazilian Copyright Law, under public consultation in 2010.

5. Korn (n 3).

6. In 2012, 16 CERLALC members had a copyright limitation for libraries, the majority of them only allowing the tangible reproduction of the work required for preservation or substitution of a permanent collection item, whereas only Chilean legislation allowed the electronic reproduction to be consulted in a closed network. CERLALC Circular nº 02, 16 March 2012, 12. For a comparison of legislations, see Annex 2, www.cerlalc.org/Circular_Bibliotecas_Digitales.pdf.

7. Ibid 18.

8. In 2011, Brazil, Ecuador and Uruguay (referring to the earlier African group proposal) made proposals for limitations for libraries and archives (SCCR/23/5), www.wipo.int/meetings/en/details.jsp?meeting_id=22210. In 2013, working document SCCR/26/3 with comments and suggestions, including from Argentina, Brazil, Chile, Ecuador, Mexico and Uruguay, was adopted by the committee, www.wipo.int/edocs/mdocs/copyright/en/sccr_26/sccr_26_3.pdf.

9. For example, heritage institutions and commercial users versus authors and rights holders concerned with the lack of diligent searches and malicious interference in digital files (the 'fake orphans'), and with the lack of proper evidence about the extent of the orphan works issue. Susan Corbett, 'Regulation for Cultural Heritage Orphans: Time does Matter' WIPO Journal: Analysis and Debate of Intellectual Property Issues (2010) 1(2) 180, 182.

10. Similarly, Corbett concludes that 'a partial solution for cultural heritage orphans should not be delayed', in particular in net copyright importing countries such as New Zealand, where the cultural heritage aspect is more immediately significant than the economic one. Ibid 196.

11. Law nº 12.965/2014 (the Internet 'Marco Civil').

12. Melody Patry, *Brazil: A New Global Internet Referee? Policy Paper on Digital Freedom of Expression in Brazil* (Index 2014) 2, www.index-oncensorship.org/wp-content/uploads/2014/06/brazil-internet-freedom_web_en.pdf.

13. Roberto Taddei, *Políticas Públicas para Acervos Digitais: Propostas para o Ministério da Cultura e para o Setor* (São Paulo, 15 June 2010) 34, http://culturadigital.br/simposioacervosdigitais/2010/06/30/politicas-publicas-para-acervos-digitais-propostas-para-o-ministerio-da-cultura-e-para-o-setor/.

14. The digital collection of the National Library of Brazil currently holds more than a million documents, http://bndigital.bn.br.

15. UN, 'Report of the Special Rapporteur on the Promotion and Protection of the Right to Freedom of Opinion and Expression, Frank La Rue' A/HRC/17/27 (16 May 2011) 7, www2.ohchr.org/english/bodies/hrcouncil/docs/17session/A.HRC.17.27_en.pdf.

16. Lea Shaver and Caterina Sganga, 'The Right to Take Part in Cultural Life: On Copyright and Human Rights' (2010) 27 Wisconsin International Law Journal 637, 649–650; and Taddei (n 13) 4.

17. On Brazilian digitisation projects, see Taddei (n 13) 4.

18. Article 27(1) of the Universal Declaration of Human Rights 1948 ('UDHR'); Article 15.1.a of the United Nation's International Covenant on Economic, Social and Cultural Rights 1966 ('ICESCR').

19. UN, General Comment 21 (2009) 2–4.

20. Ibid 4–5.

21. Article 27 (2) of the UDHR and Article 15.1.c of the ICESCR.

22. UN, General Comment 17 (2005) 2–3. Further discussion about the human rights dimension of copyright in UN Human Rights Council, 'Report of the Special Rapporteur in the Field of Cultural Rights, Farida Shaheed' (24 December 2014).

23. Article 9(1) of the Berne Convention for the Protection of Literary and Artistic Works 1886 ('Berne Convention'). Digitisation is a form of reproduction: Agreed Statement concerning Article 1(4) of the WIPO Copyright Treaty 1996, http://www.wipo.int/treaties/en/ip/wct/statements.html.

24. Article 8 of the WIPO Copyright Treaty.

25. Article 9(2), Berne Convention; Article 13, WTO Agreement on Trade-Related Aspects of Intellectual Property Rights 1994 ('TRIPS').

26. The WTO Dispute Settlement Body decided on the interpretation of the three-step test, stating, inter alia, that limitations and exceptions should be clearly defined and narrow in scope and reach (Panel Rep. of 15 June 2000, WT/DS160/R, p. 34). Scholars promoted a declaration about the need for a more balanced application, which rather than a step-by-step approach required a comprehensive overall assessment, considering a balancing of interests of rights holders and

general public, particularly in cases involving fundamental rights. Christophe Geiger, Reto M. Hilty, Jonathan Griffiths and Uma Suthersanen, 'Declaration: A Balanced Interpretation of The "Three-Step Test" In Copyright Law' (2010) 1 Journal of Intelectual Property, Information Technology and E-Commerce Law 119, 119–120, http://www.jipitec.eu/issues/jipitec-1-2-2010/2621/Declaration-Balanced-Interpretation-Of-The-Three-Step-Test.pdf.

27. Corbett discusses the need for compliance with the three-step test by orphan works legislation. Corbett (n 9) 193.

28. Tracing the rights holders for the 13 million works in their online survey would take around 6 million days; there are an estimated 25 million orphans in public sector organisations; due diligences would be complex and costly; the orphan works issue is growing and preventing cultural institutions from serving the public interest as materials of high academic and cultural value are being locked up; and a black hole of twentieth-century content is being created. Korn (n 3) 5–7.

29. The documents related to the study by the US Copyright Office, from 2005 to the final 2015 report, are available at www.copyright.gov/orphan/.

30. US Copyright Office, 'Orphan Works and Mass Digitization: A Report of the Register of Copyrights' (2015) 105, http://copyright.gov/orphan/reports/orphan-works2015.pdf.

31. See Marcella Favale, Fabian Homberg, Martin Kretschmer, Dinusha Mendis and Davide Secchi, 'Copyright, and the Regulation of Orphan Works: A Comparative Review of Seven Jurisdictions and a Rights Clearance Simulation' (2013), https://www.gov.uk/government/publications/copyright-and-the-regulation-of-orphan-works.

32. For a study on libraries exceptions of the world, including Latin American countries, see Kenneth Crews, 'Study on Copyright Limitations and Exceptions for Libraries and Archives: Updated and Revised' SCCR/30/3 (10 June 2015). As regards exceptions for museums, Chile is the only country in Latin America containing a provision expressly for museums, as per Jean-François Canat and Lucie Guibault, 'Study on Copyright Limitations and Exceptions for Museums' SCCR/30/2 (30 April 2015) 19.

33. Stef Van Gompel, 'Unlocking the Potential of Pre-Existing Content – How to Address the Issue of Orphan Works in Europe?' (2007) 38(6) International Review of Intellectual Property and Competition Law 669, 694.

34. Allard Ringnalda, 'Orphan Works, Mass Rights Clearance, and Online Libraries: The Flaws of the Draft Orphan Works Directive and Extended Collective Licensing as a Solution' (2011) 8 Medien und Recht International 3, 10.
35. Escritório Central de Arrecadação e Distribuição (Central Office for Collection and Distribution) faced a Parliamentary Commission of Inquiry discussing the lack of transparency in managing resources. Law 12853/2013 was enacted to regulate the activities of collecting societies and is being challenged by two proceedings before the Supreme Federal Court of Brazil (ADI 5062 and ADI 5065 filed in November 2013).
36. However, this scenario could change in view of new collective management legislation.
37. *The Authors Guild, Inc. v Google, Inc.,* US District Court SDNY, 14 November 2013; USCA 2d Circuit, 16 October 2015.
38. For a detailed analysis of the directive, see Uma Suthersanen and Maria M. Frabboni, 'The Orphan Works Directive' in Irini Stamatoudi and Paul Torremans (ed), *EU Copyright Law: A Commentary* (Edward Elgar 2014) 653; Eleonora Rosati, 'The Orphan Works Directive, or Throwing a Stone and Hiding the Hand' (2013) 8(4) Journal of Intellectual Property Law & Practice 303.
39. http://copyrightuser.org/topics/orphan-works/.
40. Corbett (n 9) 180 and 185.
41. http://bndigital.bn.br.
42. Law n° 9610/1998 ('Brazilian Copyright Law'). English translation on UNESCO's website, http://portal.unesco.org/culture/en/files/30462/11426147383br_copyright_1998_en.pdf/br_copyright_1998_en.pdf.
43. Article 7, Brazilian Copyright Law.
44. Generally 70 years after the death of the author, article 41 of Brazil's Copyright Law.
45. Article 5, XXVII, Brazilian Constitution. English translation available at http://english.tse.jus.br/arquivos/federal-constitution.
46. Articles 28, 29 and 30, Brazilian Copyright Law.
47. Article 24, Brazilian Copyright Law.
48. Article 11, Brazilian Copyright Law.
49. Articles 11, *Sole Paragraph,* 17, §2 and 5, VIII, h, Brazilian Copyright Law.
50. Article 18, Brazilian Copyright Law and article 5(2), Berne Convention.

51. Articles 24, §1 and §2 and 27, Brazilian Copyright Law.
52. Article 5, VIII, b, Brazilian Copyright Law.
53. Article 40, Brazilian Copyright Law.
54. Article 45, II, Brazilian Copyright Law.
55. João Henrique da Rocha Fragoso, *Direito Autoral – Da Antiguidade à Internet* (Quartier Latin 2009) 332.
56. Sérgio Branco, *O Domínio Público no Direito Autoral Brasileiro* (Lumen Juris 2011) 170–171.
57. STJ, Special Appeal REsp 1.322.325 published 14 March 2014.
58. Regarding other Latin American countries, see CERLALC (n 6) 18.
59. Articles 46 to 48, Brazilian Copyright Law.
60. Eg Plínio Cabral, *A Lei de Direitos Autorais: Comentários* (5th edn, Rideel 2009) 111. Souza discusses exhaustive versus non-exhaustive interpretations of the limitations clause, defending the latter. Allan Rocha de Souza, *A Função Social dos Direitos Autorais: uma Interpretação Civil-Constitucional dos Limites da Proteção Jurídica* (Faculdade de Direito de Campos 2006) 271–274.
61. STJ, Special Appeal REsp 964.404 published 23 May 2011.
62. Article 6, Brazilian Constitution.
63. Article 206, II, Brazilian Constitution.
64. Article 5, XIV, Brazilian Constitution.
65. Articles 215, 216 and 216-A, Brazilian Constitution.
66. Unofficially translated by Bráulio de Araújo and Volker Grassmuck of the Research Group 'GPOPAI' of the University of São Paulo, www.vgrass.de/?p=283.
67. Ministério da Cultura, Secretaria de Políticas Culturais, Diretoria de Direitos Intelectuais, 'Relatório de Análise das Contribuições ao Anteprojeto de Modernização da Lei de Direitos Autorais (após a consulta pública realizada de 14/06 a 31/08/2010 e após debate no Grupo Interministerial de Propriedade Intelectual – GIPI)'.
68. http://bndigital.bn.br/sobre-a-bndigital/?sub=missao/.
69. Proposed article 46, XIII. Proposed amendment to 'without profit intent' after the public consultation.
70. CTS/FGV's contribution to the public consultation Article 46, XVI, indicates 'the reproduction for conservation, preservation and archive has undisputable relevance, but only achieves its full potential if it facilitates the access by interested parties' (original in Portuguese), www2.cultura.gov.br/consultadireitoautoral/wp-content/uploads/2010/09/CTS-FGV.pdf.

71. Proposed Article 46, XVI.
72. Corbett (n 9) 194.
73. Christophe Geiger et al. (n 26) 119–122
74. Although not intended as a copyright exception, but as a suggestion for orphan works statutory licensing formulations in the UK, some aspects of Stop 43's definition of 'cultural use' could be used as guidance for the proposed Brazilian limitation. Bearing in mind Brazil's geographical and social particularities, the possibility of adapting such a definition to the Brazilian reality should be considered, http://stop43.org.uk/what_we_stand_for/what_we_stand_for.html#No_commercial_use_of_orphan_wor.
75. Proposed Article 52-B, III.
76. Proposed Article 52-C.
77. See Corbett (n 9) 196, n 10.
78. Geyzon Dantas, 'Mais um Passo para Digitalização de Conteúdos Culturais' (16 October 2015), www.cultura.gov.br/banner-3/-/asset_publisher/axCZZwQo8xW6/content/mais-um-passo-para-digitalizacao-de-conteudos-culturais/10883?redirect=http%3A%2F%2Fwww.cultura.gov.br%2Fbanner-3%3Fp_p_id%3D101_INSTANCE_axCZZwQo8xW6%26p_p_lifecycle%3D0%26p_p_state%3Dnormal%26p_p_mode%3Dview%26p_p_col_id%3Dcolumn-3%26p_p_col_count%3D2. For further information on the Europeana project, see: https://ec.europa.eu/digital-single-market/en/europeana-europeandigital-library-all.

CHAPTER 18

The Incorporation of a Right to Health Perspective into Brazil's Patent Law Reform Process

Emmanuel Kolawole Oke

The tension between patent rights and access to medicines cannot be resolved satisfactorily without incorporating a right to health perspective into the patent law framework. This is because patent rights have an impact on access to medicines, and one of the integral components of the right to health is this access. Incorporating a right to health perspective into the design, implementation and interpretation of a country's patent law entails recognition of the fact that patent rights are instrumental rights that should serve the fundamental needs of a society by facilitating both pharmaceutical innovation and access to medicines. Therefore the incorporation of a right to health perspective into Brazil's patent law reform process, which was launched in October 2013, is a step in the right direction.

This chapter examines the proposed reforms to Brazil's patent law and highlights how these proposals will enhance enjoyment of the right to health. It is structured into three main sections. Section 1 examines the tension between patent rights and the right to health, while Section 2 examines how the relationship between patent rights and the right to

E.K. Oke (✉)
University College Cork, Cork, Ireland

© Palgrave Macmillan, a division of Macmillan Publishers Limited 2017   311
P. Fortes et al. (eds.), *Law and Policy in Latin America*,
DOI 10.1057/978-1-137-56694-2_18

health should be conceptualised. Section 3 deals with the incorporation of a right to health perspective into the recently launched patent law reform process in Brazil. The chapter concludes with the view that other developing countries can follow the Brazilian model by incorporating a right to health perspective into their national patent laws.

1   THE TENSION BETWEEN PATENT RIGHTS AND THE RIGHT TO HEALTH

The Right to Health and Access to Medicines

The right to health is recognised in several international legal instruments (e.g. Article 12(1) of the ICESCR) and in the national constitutions of several countries in the world. In 2000 the UN Committee on Economic, Social and Cultural Rights (CESCR) adopted General Comment No. 14 in an attempt to provide further definition for Article 12 of the ICESCR.[1] Paragraph 12 of General Comment No. 14 is very relevant to the question of access to medicines. It enumerates four essential, interrelated components of the right to health: availability, accessibility, acceptability and quality. In particular, paragraph 12(a) provides that essential drugs (as defined by the World Health Organization Action Programme on Essential Drugs) must be available in a country. In addition, paragraph 12(b) states that healthcare services must be economically accessible to everyone, suggesting that the price of essential drugs should not be so expensive as to be unaffordable for poor patients. This makes access to essential medicines an integral component of the right to health.[2]

In Brazil the right to health is guaranteed in articles 6 and 196 of the 1988 Constitution. The Brazilian Organic Law on Health (Law 8,080/1990) was subsequently enacted in furtherance of the implementation of the constitutional right to health. This law establishes rules for the organisation and functioning of Brazil's unified public health system (Sistema Único de Saúde or SUS). Subsequently, in 1996, Law 9,313 was enacted, setting up a legal framework for the free distribution of anti-retroviral drugs to HIV/AIDS patients.

Many Brazilians have relied on the constitutional right to health to demand expensive drugs by instituting actions in court to enforce this right; and the constitutional right to health has been given an expansive interpretation by Brazil's courts.[3] According to Ferraz, the courts have adopted the stance that the right to health is 'an individual entitlement to any health procedure, equipment, or product that a person can prove she needs, irrespective of its costs'.[4] The favourable disposition towards the right to health and the expansive interpretation given to it by Brazil's judiciary has led to an increase in the number of Brazilians approaching the courts seeking to gain access to medical treatment and medications.[5]

The Tension Between Patent Rights and the Right to Health in Brazil

The successful implementation of Brazil's unified public health programme and free distribution of anti-retroviral drugs, particularly at its early stages, has been attributed to (among other factors) the fact that local pharmaceutical companies (in both the private and the public sectors) were capable of producing anti-retroviral drugs locally at lower rates than the multinational pharmaceutical companies.[6] During this early period, Brazil's intellectual property regime did not provide patent protection for pharmaceutical products and processes.[7] However, this changed in 1996 with the enactment of the Brazilian Industrial Property Law (Law 9,279/1996). Thus, while the Brazilian Government was trying to provide increased access to anti-retroviral drugs (via Law 9,313/1996), it equally had to comply with its international trade obligations by providing patent protection for pharmaceutical products (via the Industrial Property Law 9,279/1996).[8]

Unlike in some developing countries, the Brazilian Government failed to utilise the transition period granted to developing countries under Article 65 of the Agreement on Trade Related Aspects of Intellectual Property Rights (the TRIPS Agreement), permitting it to delay the implementation of patent protection for pharmaceutical products until 2005. It has been argued that if Brazil had utilised this transition period, it 'could have allowed domestic pharmaceutical companies to garner the strength to compete with transnational drug companies specializing in Research and Development'.[9]

In addition, articles 230 and 231 of the Brazilian Industrial Property Law of 1996 permits patents to be granted for certain inventions (including pharmaceutical products) which were previously non-patentable in the country, provided that such inventions were already patented in another country and provided that they have not been marketed in Brazil or elsewhere. This procedure, usually referred to as the 'pipeline patent protection' procedure, is essentially a means of retrospectively granting patent protection for inventions that were already patented in other countries outside Brazil prior to 1996.[10] However, the TRIPS Agreement does not mandate countries to implement pipeline patent protection.[11] Though the duration of the patents granted under this special provision is limited to the remainder of the term of the prior patent granted in the other country, this special procedure significantly impeded the production of generic drugs in Brazil and increased the cost of providing anti-retroviral drugs under the Brazilian unified public health programme.[12]

Thus the introduction of patent protection for pharmaceutical products (particularly pipeline patents) had significant financial implications for the unified public health programme and the free distribution of anti-retroviral drugs. For instance, it has been estimated that 80 % of the Ministry of Health's budget for purchasing anti-retroviral drugs in 2007 was spent on 11 patented medicines, while 20 % was spent on 7 drugs that were manufactured locally by Brazilian pharmaceutical companies.[13]

The situation is further complicated by the fact that a number of Brazilians rely on the constitutional right to health to demand expensive drugs. Ferraz notes that the court orders on the right to health 'force an inevitable reallocation of resources that is potentially harmful to the rational use of funds and to health equity'.[14] Yamin, however, contends that there is simply no 'robust evidence to conclude that the funds for paying for litigated care are systematically coming at the expense of important preventative public health measures or the infrastructure of the health system itself'.[15] A thorough analysis of the problems flowing from this situation, which has been aptly termed the 'judicialisation' of the right to health in Brazil,[16] is beyond the scope of this chapter. The focus here will be on the impact that patent rights have on access to medicines in Brazil. This is because the Brazilian Government, with its constitutional obligation to supply medicines to Brazilians, has an interest in ensuring that the patent system does not hinder the fulfilment of its constitutional obligations. As noted by Shadlen and da Fonseca, '[t]he Brazilian government's concerns with the supply of drugs are rooted in its extensive commitments in the health sector' as 'Brazil's 1988 constitution stipulates health as a constitutional right; [and] the national health system ... offers access to healthcare – including treatments – to all Brazilians.'[17]

Thus for the government it becomes essential to ensure that the patent system plays an instrumental, and not a detrimental, role with regard to the fulfilment of its constitutional obligation to supply medicines to Brazilians. This explains why it has previously utilised the option of issuing a compulsory licence to facilitate access to an essential anti-retroviral drug. In 2007, after unsuccessful negotiations with Merck for price reductions on the drug Efavirenz, the Brazilian Government issued a compulsory licence for the drug and began importation of a generic version from India.[18]

However, the use of flexibilities such as compulsory licensing to facilitate access to medicines is often questioned by developed countries, such as the USA. In 2000, Brazil faced a legal challenge at the WTO brought by the USA concerning the local working requirements contained in Article 68(1)(I) of the Brazilian Industrial Property Law of 1996.[19] However, the dispute was not resolved by the WTO because both countries reached a settlement and the USA withdrew its claim in 2001.[20] However, such challenges against the use of flexibilities to facilitate access to medicines in developing countries demonstrate a failure to understand what should be the true nature of the relationship between patent rights and the right to health. Thus the next section examines how the relationship between patent rights and the right to health should be conceptualised.

2   THE RELATIONSHIP BETWEEN PATENT RIGHTS AND THE RIGHT TO HEALTH

According to Peter Drahos, 'intellectual property rights [including patent rights] are instrumental rights that should serve those needs and interests which human rights discourse identifies as fundamental'.[21] As the CESCR (13) emphasised in General Comment No. 17, 'intellectual property is a social product and has a social function', while 'human rights are timeless expressions of fundamental entitlements of the human person'.[22] Drahos and Braithwaite contend that in any principled national legal system, a fundamental right such as the right to health should take precedence over utilitarian considerations.[23]

Therefore, in the design of a country's patent law system, legislators seeking to improve access to medicines can incorporate a right to health perspective that recognises the essential distinction between the fundamental nature of human rights and the instrumental nature of patent rights. This does not necessarily mean that patent rights should no longer be protected, but it will ensure that patent rights are not exercised in ways that impede access to essential medicines.

It is important to mention that the Brazilian Constitution provides in Article 5(29) that 'the law shall ensure the authors of industrial inventions of a temporary privilege for their use, as well as protection of industrial creations ... viewing the social interest and the technological and economic development of the country'. At first reading, this provision appears to place patent rights on the same level as other fundamental rights. However, a closer reading reveals that the protection of patent rights envisioned by Article 5(29) is with a view to ensuring that patent rights serve the 'social interest' and aid the 'technological and economic development of the country'. In addition, the protection of inventions is equally described as a 'temporary privilege' and not a permanent or eternal right. Thus patent rights are not to be viewed as absolute rights but as instrumental rights that should facilitate the technological and economic advancement of Brazil. Brazilian courts have also delivered rulings that, in effect, recognise that fundamental rights, such as the right to health, should not be trumped by patent rights.[24]

As noted in the Section 1, in its implementation of the TRIPS Agreement, Brazil failed to utilise the transition period that was available to other developing countries. In addition, it also went beyond the minimum requirements of the agreement by providing for a pipeline patent protection procedure. However, there are other key aspects of Brazil's Industrial Property Law that need to be amended in order to facilitate greater access to affordable medicines. In October 2013, the process for reforming the Brazilian patent law was launched in Brazil's Chamber of Deputies.[25] Section 3 highlights how this reform process incorporates a right to health perspective and how the proposed reforms will facilitate access to medicines and improve enjoyment of the right to health in Brazil.

3   BRAZIL'S PATENT LAW REFORM PROCESS AND THE RIGHT TO HEALTH

As pointed out in Section 2, it is in the interest of the Brazilian Government to ensure that its patent law system plays an instrumental role in facilitating access to medicines because of the constitutional obligation imposed on the government to supply medicines to Brazilians. In launching the patent law reform process, the Center for Strategic Studies and Debates of the Chamber of Deputies released a report entitled *Brazil's Patent Reform: Innovation Towards National Competitiveness*.[26] The proposals for the reform of the patent law are contained in Bill No. H.R. 5402/2013, which is annexed to the report.

This chapter will not engage in an extensive analysis of the various sections of the report. It will only highlight how the report incorporates a right to health perspective into the patent law reform process. The report recognises the tension between patent rights and the right to health because it notes that '[t]he negative impact that the system of intellectual property rights has been making on ... access to products or processes protected by patents is notorious. This issue is especially serious in regard to the enjoyment of fundamental rights such as culture, education and health, for instance.'[27] The report further points out that access to medicines is a real challenge for many Brazilians. It states, 'in Brazil, it is estimated that around 50 million people do not have access to medicines and that 51.7 % of Brazilians cease their medical treatment because they are unable to pay for the prescribed medicine'.[28]

The report also recognises the fundamental nature of the right to health and it notes that Article 196 of the Brazilian Constitution established the right to health as a right for all and a duty of the state.[29] Furthermore, the report stresses the instrumental nature of patent rights in its discussion of Article 5(29) of the Brazilian Constitution, which deals with the protection of inventions. According to the report, Article 5(29) states that the grant of patent rights must lead to economic and technological development, therefore the country can adopt measures aimed at the development of sectors that are vital to the population's wellbeing, such as the national pharmaceutical sector.[30] In other words, while the right to health is recognised in the report as a fundamental right, patent rights are considered as instrumental rights, which must play a positive role in the economic and technological development of the country. In addition, measures can be adopted to ensure that patent rights are not detrimental to the population's wellbeing. Patent rights should thus play an instrumental role in facilitating access to medicines for Brazilians because this is vital to their wellbeing.

The report notes that, in implementing the TRIPS Agreement in 1996, Brazil failed to adopt important measures to protect public interest policies that were allowed by the TRIPS Agreement.[31] The report therefore recommends that

> The full adoption of health protection measures and the exclusion of detrimental measures besides the obligations already undertaken in a national scope could minimize the adverse effects of the industrial property system in the implementation of public policies that secure human rights in Brazil.[32]

In other words, this is how a right to health perspective can be incorporated into the design of a country's patent law system. Detrimental measures in the patent law system that hinder the enjoyment of the right to health should be excluded, and measures that protect and secure the enjoyment of the right to health should be introduced into the patent law framework. Incorporating a right to health perspective into the design of a country's patent law does not mean that the patent system will be abolished; rather, it means that the patent system will play an instrumental role in serving the fundamental need to protect the right to health and facilitate access to medicines.

Some of the key proposals contained in Bill No. H.R. 5402/2013 will be briefly examined below.

Eliminating Patents on New Uses or New Forms of Known Drugs

Article 3 of the Brazilian bill introduces a new provision into the Brazilian patent law that will eliminate the grant of patents on new uses or new forms of known drugs. This provision substantially reproduces the provisions of section 3(d) of the Indian Patents Act, which was relied upon by the Indian Supreme Court to deny a patent to Novartis for its anti-cancer drug, Glivec.[33] Some pharmaceutical companies prolong the length of the patent protection on some of their profitable drugs by seeking patent protection for trivial modifications of these profitable drugs (a practice termed 'ever-greening'). This has significant implications for access to medicines because it prevents the quick entry of cheaper generic versions of patented drugs. Provisions such as Section 3(d) are thus useful tools for facilitating the quick entry of cheaper generic drugs into the market.

Article 27(1) of the TRIPS Agreement does not define the standards of patentability to be applied before a country can grant or deny a patent application. While it clearly stipulates that an 'invention' must be 'new', involve an 'inventive step' and be capable of 'industrial application', it fails to provide a definition for these key terms. In other words, countries are free to define in their national patent laws what they deem to constitute an invention, and the standards of patentability they intend to utilise in screening out non-patentable inventions. This flexibility in the TRIPS Agreement provides a basis for prohibiting the grant of patent protection for new forms and new uses of known drugs.

Section 3(d) of the Indian patent law operates by denying patent protection to new forms of known drugs unless a patent applicant can furnish evidence to prove that the new form of the known drug results in the enhancement of the therapeutic efficacy of the previously known drug.

This helps to prevent the grant of patent protection on trivial modifications of previously known drugs. It could be argued that section 3(d) is discriminatory and thus in conflict with Article 27(1) of the TRIPS Agreement because it targets pharmaceutical products. However, it should be noted that Article 27(1) does not forbid the use of bona fide exceptions to deal with problems existing only in certain product areas.[34] In addition, Article 27(1) merely forbids discrimination but it does not prohibit the justified imposition of differential treatment.[35]

Raising the Standard for Determining an Inventive Step

As part of the process of eliminating patents on trivial inventions, Article 3 of the bill also raises the standard for determining what constitutes an inventive step. Under the current Brazilian patent law, Article 13 provides that 'An invention is endowed with [an] inventive step provided that, to a technician versed in the subject, it is not derived in an evident or obvious way from the state of the art.' However, the bill proposes a new Article 13, which provides that an invention must also represent 'a significant technical advance in regards to the state of the art'. Thus it is now proposed that 'The invention carries inventive activity when, for a person skilled in the art, it does not derive in an obvious or evident manner from the state of the art, and provided it represents a significant technical advance in regards to the state of the art.'

The way a country chooses to define its standards of patentability is described by Correa as 'a key aspect of patent policy with implications in other areas, such as industrial and public health policies'.[36] He further argues that 'the best policy from the perspective of public health would seem to be the application of a strict standard of inventiveness so as to promote genuine innovations and prevent unwarranted limitations to competition and access to existing drugs'.[37] According to Correa, the definition of 'inventive step' in a country's patent law is one of the most critical aspects of a patent regime.[38]

Clear Rejection of Data Exclusivity

Data exclusivity is a legal mechanism aimed at ensuring that pharmaceutical companies that spend considerable amounts of money to generate clinical data to establish the efficacy of their drugs, prior to obtaining regulatory approval, are protected against other competitors.[39] Essentially it works by preventing third parties from relying on any such clinical data submitted to the regulatory authorities. Invariably, competing pharmaceutical companies either have to conduct their own clinical trials to generate their own data or wait until the expiration of the period of data exclusivity.

Some developing countries do not provide for data exclusivity because it can be an impediment to the early introduction of cheaper, generic versions of patented drugs. Thus, for example, there is no provision for data exclusivity in India or South Africa. Proponents of data exclusivity argue that it is mandated by Article 39(3) of the TRIPS Agreement. However, opponents of data exclusivity maintain that Article 39(3) does not explicitly provide for data exclusivity and at best it only provides for data protection against unfair competition.[40] In addition, Article 39(3) does not specify any particular time limit for this protection and countries are also permitted to disclose the data where this is necessary to protect the public.[41]

It should be noted that data exclusivity can operate to provide an additional period of protection for a drug beyond the term of its patent, especially where regulatory approval is obtained on a drug a few years prior to the expiration of the patent term or even after the expiration of the patent term. While data exclusivity might be useful in developed countries where several multinational pharmaceutical companies invest heavily in the production of new drugs, it could have a significant impact on public health in developing countries by delaying the production of cheaper, generic drugs.

Article 3 of the bill amends Article 195 (XIV) of the Brazilian patent law by specifically adding a provision that permits the use, by government bodies, of test results or other undisclosed data for the market approval of products. Article 195 (XIV) provides that a crime of unfair competition is committed by anyone who 'divulges, exploits, or utilises, without authorisation, results of tests or other undisclosed data whose preparation involves considerable effort and that were submitted to government agencies as a condition for obtaining approval to commercialize products'. However, the second proviso to Article 195 actually provides that 'the provision in Item XIV does not apply to the disclosure by a government agency empowered to authorize the commercialization of a product, when necessary to protect the public'. Thus it appears that the current patent law permits the drug regulatory agency to use undisclosed data for the market approval of generic drugs because this might be necessary to protect the Brazilian public.

Nevertheless, to make it clear that there is no provision for data exclusivity in Brazil and that the drug regulatory agency is permitted to use undisclosed data for the purposes of approving generic drugs, a third proviso to Article 195 has been proposed under the bill. This states: 'The provision set forth under item XIV does not apply to the use, by government bodies, of test results or other undisclosed data, for market approval of products equivalent to the product for which they were initially presented.'

Clarifying ANVISA's Role in the Examination of Patent Applications for Pharmaceutical Products and Processes

As part of the 2001 Amendment to the Brazilian Industrial Property Law via Law 10,196/2001, a new requirement was introduced with respect to the grant of patents for pharmaceutical products. Article 229C, which was introduced into the Industrial Property Law pursuant to the 2001 amendment, provided that the granting of patents for pharmaceutical products or processes will depend on the prior consent of the Agencia Nacional de Vigilancia Sanitaria (National Health Surveillance Agency, ANVISA). This is a regulatory agency established in 1999 under the Brazilian Ministry of Health pursuant to Law 9,782/1999. As part of its duties, ANVISA is charged with the responsibility of granting regulatory approvals for pharmaceutical products.

The new role granted to ANVISA under the Brazilian patent law led to some friction between the Instituto nacional da propriedade industrial (INPI, National Institute of Industrial Property)—that is, the patent office—and ANVISA.[42] This was due to the fact that Article 229C failed to spell out the precise scope of ANVISA's role in relation to pharmaceutical patents and the law did not clarify the criteria according to which ANVISA should give or withhold consent for applications for pharmaceutical patents.[43]

The real source of the conflict between the two agencies relates to the appropriate standard of patentability for pharmaceutical inventions. While INPI favoured the grant of patents on second and new uses of existing drugs, ANVISA took the opposite view that such applications should not be granted.[44] Basso and Rodrigues have noted that ANVISA currently denies prior consent to, among others, pharmaceutical patent applications filed with insufficient description, patent applications on polymorphs and second medical use patent claims.[45] Shadlen aptly sums up the conflict between the two agencies when he states that it is 'indicative of a broader conflict between two objectives: encouraging and promoting incremental innovation through the patent system, and minimising periods of market exclusivity and preventing the effective extension of patent terms'.[46]

ANVISA plays a crucial role in Brazil by preventing the granting of patents on frivolous inventions. It is thus essential that its role in the examination of applications for pharmaceutical patents be clarified. Article 3 of the bill does this by specifying the grounds on which ANVISA will exercise its power of granting or refusing its prior consent to patent applications. Article 229C currently provides that 'The granting of patents on pharmaceutical products or processes shall depend on the prior consent of the National Sanitary Supervision Agency (ANVISA).'

Article 229C will now be replaced by new text which states that the granting of patents for drugs shall depend on the prior consent of ANVISA, and ANVISA shall examine patent applications in light of public health. It further states that a patent application shall be contrary to public health where the drug in the application presents a health risk, or the application is of interest to an access to medicines policy or to a pharmaceutical care programme under the SUS, and provided that it does not meet the patentability and other criteria established by the patent law. In addition, after the prior consent examination, ANVISA is required to return the application to the patent office, which will examine approved applications and archive unapproved applications.

Furthermore, Article 5 of the bill proposes an amendment to Article 7 of Law No. 9782/1999 (which established ANVISA). The proposed text specifically guarantees the right of ANVISA to participate in the process of examination of applications for patents for pharmaceutical products and processes. According to the proposed text, ANVISA shall 'participate in the process of examination of patent applications for pharmaceutical products and processes, including the analysis of the patentability requirements and the other criterion [sic] set forth under the specific legislation'.

The proposed amendments thus secure the role of ANVISA in the examination of applications for patents for pharmaceutical products and processes. The amendments make it clear that the purpose of ANVISA's participation in the examination process is to scrutinise the patent applications in the light of public health. It is important to stress that the examination of pharmaceutical patents by ANVISA does not infringe Article 27(1) of the TRIPS Agreement, which provides that patents should be available and patent rights enjoyable without discrimination as to the field of technology. This is because ANVISA is not required to apply any new criteria, apart from the criteria contained in Article 27(1) of the TRIPS Agreement—that is, the invention must be new, involve an inventive step and be capable of industrial application. The TRIPS Agreement does not expressly forbid any country from subjecting any invention from any field of technology to stricter standards of examination and scrutiny. In addition, even though Article 27(1) of the TRIPS Agreement forbids discrimination, it does not forbid justified differentiation.[47]

4   CONCLUSION

A common thread that runs through the proposed reforms to Brazil's patent law is the adoption of measures that will make it difficult to obtain frivolous patents for essential drugs, and that will facilitate the early market entry of cheaper generic drugs on the expiration of the patent term of patented drugs. These measures, if eventually enacted into law, will no doubt assist the Brazilian Government in fulfilling its right to health obligations to Brazilians. This approach highlights the importance of incorporating a right to health perspective into the design of a country's patent law. This ensures that measures that are detrimental to the wellbeing of a country's population are not included in the patent law, and it also ensures that patent rights play an instrumental role in facilitating access to medicines.

According to Barratt, it is impossible to resolve the tension between patent rights and public health by relying only on internal principles contained in intellectual property law.[48] Barratt suggests that the best way to resolve this tension is by using external norms contained in the human rights system.[49] Human rights law provides a valuable framework that can be used to define the scope and extent of patent law protection in order to ensure that states can fulfil their obligations to provide access to affordable medicines for their citizens. The TRIPS Agreement does not prevent developing countries from incorporating a human rights perspective into the design, implementation, interpretation and enforcement of patent law at the national level. Thus other developing countries can equally adopt the Brazilian model by incorporating a right to health perspective into the design or amendment of their national patent laws.

NOTES

1. UN Committee on Economic, Social and Cultural Rights (CESCR), 'General Comment n° 14, The Right to the Highest Attainable Standard of Health (Article 12)' E/C.12/2000/4 (2000).
2. Mirela Hristova, 'Are Intellectual Property Rights Human Rights? Patent Protection and the Right to Health' (2011) 93 Journal of the

Patent & Trademark Office Society 339, 356; UN Human Rights Council, 'Access to Medicines in the Context of the Right of Everyone to the Enjoyment of the Highest Attainable Standard of Physical and Mental Health' A/HRC/RES/23/14 (2013).

3. Octavio LM Ferraz, 'Brazil – Health Inequalities, Rights, and Courts: The Social Impact of the Judicialization of Health' in Alicia Ely Yamin and Siri Gloppen (eds), *Litigating Health Rights: Can Courts Bring More Justice to Health?* (Harvard University Press 2011) 76.

4. Ibid.

5. Ibid.

6. Gabriela C Chaves, Marcela F Vieira and Renata Reis, 'Access to Medicines and Intellectual Property in Brazil: Reflections and Strategies of Civil Society' (2008) 8 Sur – International Journal on Human Rights 163, 166.

7. Ibid.

8. Amy Nunn, *The Politics and History of AIDS Treatment in Brazil* (Springer 2009) 91.

9. Chaves, Vieira and Reis (n 6) 167.

10. Ibid 172–173; Duncan Matthews, *Intellectual Property, Human Rights and Development: The Role of NGOs and Social Movements* (Edward Elgar 2011) 130.

11. Chaves, Vieira and Reis (n 6) 172.

12. Matthews (n 10) 130.

13. Chaves, Vieira and Reis (n 6) 164.

14. Ferraz (n 3) 95.

15. Alicia E Yamin, 'Power, Suffering, and Courts: Reflections on Promoting Health Rights through Judicialization' in Yamin and Gloppen (eds), *Litigating Health Rights* (n 3) 352.

16. João Biehl and others, 'Judicialisation of the Right to Health in Brazil' (2009) 373 The Lancet 2182.

17. Kenneth C Shadlen and Elize M da Fonseca, 'Health Policy as Industrial Policy: Brazil in Comparative Perspective' (2013) 41 Politics and Society 561, 566.

18. Chaves, Vieira and Reis (n 6) 171.

19. *Brazil – Measures Affecting Patent Protection – Request for Consultations by the United States* (WT/DS199/1, G/L/385, IP/D/23, 8 June 2000).

20. *Brazil – Measures Affecting Patent Protection – Notification of Mutually Agreed Solution,* (WT/DS199/4, G/L/454, IP/D/23/Add.1, 19 July 2001).

21. Peter Drahos, 'Intellectual Property and Human Rights' (1999) 3 Intellectual Property Quarterly 349.
22. UN Committee on Economic, Social and Cultural Rights (CESCR), 'General Comment n° 17, The Right of Everyone to Benefit from the Protection of the Moral and Material Interests Resulting from any Scientific, Literary or Artistic Production of which He or She is the Author (Article 15, paragraph 1 (c), of the Covenant),' E/C.12/GC/17 (2006) paras 2, 35.
23. Peter Drahos with John Braithwaite, *Information Feudalism: Who Owns the Knowledge Economy?* (Earthscan 2002) 200.
24. Processo n° 2003.51.01.513584-5, 1ª Turma Especializada Tribunal Regional Federal – 2a região. Referred to by Denis B Barbosa and Charlene A Plaza, 'IP in Decisions of Constitutional Courts of Latin American Countries' (PIDCC, Aracaju, Ano II, Edição n° 04/2013, 25 October 2013) 18, http://www.denisbarbosa.addr.com/arquivos/200/internacional/chapter13b.pdf. See also Filipe Fischmann, 'Brazil: Act n° 10.603/2002 on Data Exclusivity for Veterinary Products – "Lexapro" ' (2012) 43 International Review of Intellectual Property & Competition Law 217.
25. PIJIP, 'Brazilian Officials to Launch Report Recommending the Incorporation of TRIPS Flexibilities into Domestic Law' (9 October 2013), http://infojustice.org/archives/30929.
26. Chamber of Deputies – Centre for Strategic Studies and Debates, *Brazil's Patent Reform: Innovation towards National Competitiveness* (2013), http://infojustice.org/wp-content/uploads/2013/09/Brazilian_Patent_Reform.pdf.
27. Ibid 49.
28. Ibid 53–54.
29. Ibid 50–51.
30. Ibid 93.
31. Ibid 60.
32. Ibid.
33. *Novartis AG v Union of India & Ors*, Civil Appeal n° 2706-2716 of 2013 (Supreme Court of India, 1 April 2013).
34. *Canada – Patent Protection of Pharmaceutical Products*, Panel Report, WT/DS114/R, (17 March 2000) para 7.92.
35. *Canada – Patent Protection of Pharmaceutical Products*, ibid para 7.94; SP Barooah, 'India's Pharmaceutical Innovation Policy: Developing Strategies for Developing Country Needs' (2013) 5 Trade, Law and Development 150, 181–182.

36. Carlos Correa, 'Guidelines for the Examination of Pharmaceutical Patents: Developing a Public Health Perspective – A Working Paper' (ICTSD, UNCTAD & WHO 2006) 3, http://www.ictsd.org/sites/default/files/research/2008/06/correa_patentability20guidelines.pdf.
37. Ibid 4.
38. Ibid.
39. See Aaron X Fellmeth, 'Secrecy, Monopoly, and Access to Pharmaceuticals in International Trade Law: Protection of Marketing Approval Data under the TRIPS Agreement' (2004) 45 Harvard International Law Journal 443, 447.
40. Charles Clift, 'Data Protection and Data Exclusivity in Pharmaceuticals and Agrochemicals' in Anatole Krattiger and others (eds), *Intellectual Property Management in Health and Agricultural Innovation: A Handbook of Best Practices* vol 1 (MIHR and PIPRA 2007) 432.
41. Ibid.
42. LMC Povoa, Roberto Mazzoleni and Thiago Caliari, 'Innovation in the Brazilian Pharmaceutical Industry Post-TRIPS' (The 9th Globelics International Conference, Buenos Aires, 15–17 November 2011) 6–7, http://www.ungs.edu.ar/globelics/wp-content/uploads/2011/12/ID-197-Caliari-Mazzoleni-Caliari-Privatization-of-Knowledge-Intellectual-Property-Right.pdf.
43. Ibid.
44. Ibid 6.
45. Maristela Basso and Edson Beas Rodrigues Jr, *Intellectual Property Law in Brazil* (Kluwer Law International 2010) 80.
46. Kenneth C Shadlen, 'The Rise and Fall of "Prior Consent" in Brazil' (2011) 3 W.I.P.O. Journal 103, 105.
47. Barooah (n 35) 181–182.
48. Amanda Barratt, 'The Curious Absence of Human Rights: Can the WIPO Development Agenda Transform Intellectual Property Negotiation?' (2010) 14 Law, Democracy & Development 14, 24.
49. Ibid.

CHAPTER 19

Constitutional Environmental Protection in Brazil: A Rights-Based Approach

Julia Mattei and Larissa Verri Boratti

Debates about the recognition of a right to the environment, in both its substantive and procedural dimensions, have evolved rapidly in many jurisdictions and within international law. The developments have followed the increasing demand for improved legal, policy and regulatory responses to the complexities of environmental problems. The search for these responses has led to the inclusion of environmental protection in various national constitutions and international documents on human rights.[1] However, it has also brought about wide-reaching academic discussion about the advantages of the recognition of a right to the environment itself[2] and on how it would be put into effect by different jurisdictions.

Shelton identifies three main legal frameworks deriving from this link between human rights and environmental protection. First, environmental protection would be advanced through the recognition of other human rights (a precondition to the exercise of existing rights). Second, environmental protection would be promoted through procedural guarantees (access to information and participatory rights). Third, a right to the environment to the 'human rights catalogue' would be included.[3] All of these

J. Mattei (✉)
Nürtingen-Geislingen University, Nürtingen, Germany

L.V. Boratti
University College London, London, UK

© Palgrave Macmillan, a division of Macmillan Publishers Limited 2017   327
P. Fortes et al. (eds.), *Law and Policy in Latin America*,
DOI 10.1057/978-1-137-56694-2_19

approaches can be identified in different legal formulations at the domestic and regional levels. This chapter focuses on the third trend, in particular on the convenience of including such a right into constitutional texts.

It is worth noting that these different legal responses to the relationship between human rights and environmental protection from a constitutional perspective are related to 'context-bound aspects'.[4] In other words, they reflect the particular legal culture, and the institutional, economic and political circumstances, of each jurisdiction. For example, the constitutionalisation of environmental protection within a 'radical-democratic' constitution will assume different forms and shapes than within a 'traditional-institutionalised' constitution. In the former, the constitution is seen as a programme for the state's future, and, therefore, environmental protection is usually framed through a detailed rights-and-duties framework. In the latter, the constitution establishes the fundamental tasks that the state and its agencies have to perform, with environmental protection limited to a statement of public policy (adopting here the distinction of Brandl and Bungert).[5]

This chapter seeks to contribute to the debate by exploring the benefits of a rights-based constitutional approach within a 'radical-democratic' constitution.[6] It does not provide an exhaustive analysis of the intersection of human rights theory, constitutional law and environmental protection; other works have scrutinised such theoretical foundations.[7] Instead, it constitutes an attempt to develop a grounded examination of one specific case of the constitutionalisation of environmental rights by giving an account of the constitutional design adopted by a Latin American country: Brazil. Brazil has played a leadership role within Latin America by developing progressive domestic environmental law and including the right to a healthy environment in the 1988 Constitution as a fundamental right. With Brazil's rise in global influence, both for its economic performance and for the value of its natural resources, its regulatory environmental choices are under scrutiny.

Section 1 explores the structure of a fundamental right to a healthy environment as it is established in the 1988 Brazilian Constitution, in terms of its scope and interpretation ('from inside'). The implementation of this right is also analysed through exemplificative cases selected from recent case law. Next, some contextual and contrasting elements are briefly explored, with the view of enriching the analysis of Brazil. To this end, Section 2 addresses the rise of a Latin American constitutionalism, which gives context to the Brazilian environmental constitutional reforms ('looking backwards'). Section 3 considers alternative models that address the environmental duty of governments without necessarily creating justiciable environmental rights ('looking elsewhere').

1 FROM INSIDE: THE FUNDAMENTAL RIGHTS APPROACH TO ENVIRONMENTAL PROTECTION IN BRAZIL

Brazil is the world's seventh largest economy and has reduced poverty and inequality in recent years (its Gini coefficient is the lowest in decades, at 0.54 in 2013).[8] This notwithstanding, the economy has decelerated and the country is still in the 79th position in the human development index.[9] It is the largest country in terms of territory in Latin America, with a forest area of approximately 59 %,[10] containing biomes that are extremely rich in biodiversity and mineral reserves. However, despite achievements in conservation policy,[11] deforestation and agricultural expansion (major sources of greenhouse gas emissions),[12] and infrastructure development[13] threaten the natural environment and traditional livelihoods. Moreover, 85 % per cent of the Brazilian population live in urban areas,[14] which increases the human impact on ecosystems, as well as raising environmental justice concerns.[15]

A key player in international environmental negotiations,[16] Brazil has also developed advanced domestic environmental legislation, where the sustainable development rhetoric is dominant. At the constitutional level, this appears in the chapters on the economic order (Article 170, VI) and on environmental policy (Article 225). At the statutory level, it is one of the policy goals established in the National Environmental Policy Act (Law 6,938/1981). Nevertheless, the legal framework leaves room for a large degree of discretion, enforcement gaps persist,[17] and a set of controversial proposals for regulatory changes is under debate (e.g. PEC 215 on indigenous lands, PL 5807/2013 on mining and PL 3729/2004 on environmental licensing).[18]

Such a complex reality sets the context for the challenges that Brazil faces in combining economic growth, environmental protection and inclusive development. Here, environmental law, in particular the constitutionalisation of the right to the environment, can make a contribution. This section explores the scope of such an approach within the Brazilian constitutional norms, arguing that it offers an 'overarching legal normative framework'[19] for the promotion of rights and for ensuring environmental goals.

Scope and Structure

The inclusion of a right to the environment in constitutional norms in Brazil was brought about by the 1988 Constitution, even though environmental regulation was already present within the existing set of law.[20] This is a programmatic, broad-ranging constitution, which places considerable emphasis on declaring and strengthening rights. It is an example of a 'radical-democratic' constitution typical of Latin American countries (see Section 2). However, the constitutionalisation of a right to the environment does not merely represent a political statement in such a context.[21] Indeed, it has influenced law- and policy-making in practice. This is because both previous and current regulation has to be interpreted under the new provision and it is a benchmark for the review of executive acts.

The departure point for exploring the scope and structure of the constitutional model adopted is the wording of the heading of Article 225 of the Brazilian Constitution: 'All have the right to an ecologically balanced environment, which is an asset of common use and essential to a healthy quality of life, and both the government and the community shall have the duty to defend and preserve it for present and future generations.' This is a complex provision with multiple functions, calling for some clarification.[22]

First, it recognises the environment as an asset of 'common use'. This means that the environment is not subject to ownership, to disposability or to divisibility: 'It belongs to everybody in general and to nobody in particular.'[23] Therefore environmental policies and environmental decision-making should aim for the preservation of the overall quality of the environment and essential ecological processes, considering the public interest involved. This applies even when environmental regulatory schemes are developed by economic sectors, under both public and private regimes.[24]

Second, the debate surrounding the status that the right to the environment enjoys in the 1988 Constitution is now over. The Supreme Federal Court and the major literature recognise it as a fundamental right.[25] This is based on the understanding of a healthy environment as a condition to the fulfilling of human rights standards, which connects environmental rights to the realisation of human dignity and wellbeing.[26] An outcome of such a rights-based approach is that the right to the environment benefits from the special normative nature of fundamental rights as 'ordre public'. One of those benefits is direct enforceability (self-executing), albeit still requiring further implementing regulation (Article 5 §1). Furthermore, this right is irrevocable, inalienable and not subject to the statute of limitations.[27] The latter aspect has played an important role in claims for compensation for losses and reparation of damage related to long-term contaminated and deforested areas, known as historical hazards.[28]

Moreover, a more rigorous regime for constitutional amendment applies to the right to the environment, which therefore enjoys greater legal certainty: it is covered by the so-called 'eternity clause' in the 1988 Constitution (Article 60 § 4 IV), which precludes the removal or amendment of various fundamental rights and principles. This provision has been further interpreted in environmental matters to perform also the function of 'non-regression' or of a 'no-further degradation test'.[29] This means not only that such a guarantee cannot be abolished but also that the current level of environmental protection cannot be reduced.[30] It represents, in this sense, a barrier to deregulatory efforts.[31] In fact, it has already been used in court decisions as reasoning for constitutional review and application of sanctions (see Section 2).

Third, the right to the environment is presented in the Brazilian Constitution as a 'fundamental right-duty'. At the same time that it grants 'a right for all', it also imposes a duty to protect the environment.[32] This is because environmental rights would be part of the so-called solidarity rights, the ones that 'may be invoked against the state and demanded of it' but 'that can be realized only through concerted efforts of all actors on the social scene'.[33] As a result, they assume enhanced status, and therefore the public interest related to the maintenance of essential ecological processes justifies limiting private property interests.[34] This is translated, for instance, into the doctrine of socioenvironmental function of property that binds environmental and planning permits, as well as landowners' duties towards special protected areas.

Fourth, fundamental rights operate under within two dimensions: objective and subjective.[35] The objective dimension is related to the recognition of certain values that bind public authorities when performing governmental tasks.[36] In this case, environmental protection is recognised as a legitimate fundamental value under the Brazilian constitution, which imposes on the government the obligation of taking such a value into consideration for the constitutional review of statutory provisions, as well as for applying the law and designing policies. There is a general duty to take measures intended to preserve 'essential ecological processes' (Article 225, heading), and also specific duties (Article 225 §1), which encompass matters such as ecological management of species and ecosystems; biodiversity; control of genetic resources; control of technologies, substances and production methods; creation of protected areas; the requirement of environmental impact studies; and establishment of sanction mechanisms. These are to be pursued gradually through law, policy and decision-making.[37] As a result, government discretion is limited to some extent to the fulfilment of those duties,[38] and deviation therefrom may constitute administrative misconduct, and violate criminal and administrative norms.[39] In fact, a comprehensive body of legislation governing those themes has passed since 1988 and institutional aspects have been strengthened.

The subjective dimension of fundamental rights guarantees the enforceability of these rights. Thus recognising the right to the environment as a fundamental right means that there is a justiciable environmental right that can be invoked against interference (by the government or third parties). Most importantly, the Brazilian constitutional provision creates a collective or diffuse right to the environment ('transindividual right'), benefiting the whole society rather than only particular individuals. This is an important feature because it justifies rights-protection instruments on public interest grounds.

In this sense there is a series of constitutional norms recognising collective rights regarding the natural environment (Article 225), the built environment (Article 182), culture (Article 216) and ethnic groups (Article 231). Moreover, procedural guarantees have also been assigned. For example, the publicity of impact assessments is mandatory (Article 225, §1, IV, Constitution), and there is regulation on access to information held by the environmental agencies (Law 10,650/2003). Furthermore, public participation in environmental matters is ensured through several mechanisms, mainly representative councils, consultations, public hearings, and environmental and neighbourhood impact reports.

Finally, there are also administrative and judicial mechanisms for enforcing such guarantees. Relevant here is the Civil Public Action Act (Law 7,347/1985), which allows the judicialisation of collective and diffuse interests, such as the environment. Under this law, prosecutors and civil society organisations, among other actors, can file civil suits against the government or third parties to protect the environment. Moreover, the Constitution also permits every citizen to file class actions against state acts that damage the environment or other assets comparable to it (Article 5 LXXIII).[40] Such procedural guarantees and mechanisms for redress have been used widely by prosecutors, NGOs and community groups to obtain court orders requiring the cessation of harmful activities, and to question the legality of the environmental licensing of large-scale projects, mainly on the grounds of the poor quality of environmental reports, and violation of rights to information, consultation and participation (see, for instance, the judicialisation of the licensing of dam projects before national courts).[41]

Implementation

The rights-based approach adopted has also brought about advances before the courts by allowing the judicialisation of environmental rights. There has been an increasing tendency towards interpretations that give strong effect to environmental constitutional and statutory provisions.[42] This section explores the interpretation given by Brazil's Superior Court of Justice to two key issues in leading cases.[43] Reference is made both to the Forest Code and civil liability, with particular attention to how the language of constitutional and fundamental rights law provides a conceptual framework for singular and plural litigation.

Forest Code and Non-regression

There has been much debate about the Forest Code, which is the key piece of legislation on conservation and forest management. It is at the heart of controversies surrounding Brazilian policies for deforestation and climate change, as well as of conflicts between agribusiness and environmental campaigners in the Congress of Brazil. In 2012 the 1965 Forest Code was replaced by a new law (Law 12,651). Among the most controversial of the provisions reviewed were the reduction of the areas designated as especially protected, and the loosening, or even elimination, of obligations of maintenance and restoration of such areas by rural landowners. The scientific community has argued that the new regulatory framework can lead to the expansion of agricultural land over sensitive ecosystems, a loss of biodiversity and an increase in carbon emissions. Moreover, the changes also impact the urban environment owing to increasing occupation of risk areas.

The legal controversy is related particularly to the violation of the 'environmental eternity clause' or principle of non-regression because of the loosening of environmental protection in comparison with the previous law. In such an argument, constitutional review suits before the Supreme Federal Court have challenged the constitutionality of some provisions of the new Forest Code (outstanding decisions).[44]

While there is much anticipation regarding the position the Supreme Federal Court of Justice will take, the Superior Court of Justice has already ruled in favour of the application of non-regression in environmental matters. This was in response to landowners' attempts to benefit from the new law by demanding the revision of sanctions imposed under the previous Forest Code (e.g. by clearing designated protected areas or failing to recover native vegetation). The Superior Court of Justice framed the dispute over the application of the law under the transindividual dimension of the subjective right to the environment. Accordingly, transindividual rights, such as the right to the environment, also enjoy the legal certainty that is ensured to individual rights. Thus the Superior Court of Justice concluded that the sanctions already imposed could not be reversed.[45]

Compensation for Moral Damage

Civil liability for environmental damage is also an example of how the interpretation of environmental provisions has advanced. Under Brazil's legal regime,[46] environmental liability claims seek to guarantee (1) the reparation of the damage when possible; (2) compensation for permanent harms; and (3) compensation for both pecuniary and non-pecuniary losses. Compensation for non-pecuniary losses, the so-called moral damage, is particularly relevant because the understanding put forward by the Superior Court of Justice on the subject relates to the rights-based constitutional provision.

The Superior Court of Justice's interpretation has advanced towards the recognition of moral damage as a harm that can be redressed in an environmental liability claim in all its dimensions: individual, collective and diffuse.[47] Compensation for individual and collective moral damage that derives from environmental degradation events is less controversial. Examples cover environmental nuisance that results in harm to the health, property or wellbeing of individuals or specific groups.[48] However, the courts are more reluctant to recognise the diffuse dimension of moral damage relating to environmental harm.

Only recently has the Superior Court of Justice's understanding shifted towards an innovative interpretation on the matter, including such an element within compensatory measures. The leading case was a civil public action decided in 2013, addressing the manufacture and disposal of asbestos products. Upholding the State Court of Appeal decision, the Superior Court of Justice ordered the defendants to provide compensation not only for pecuniary losses suffered by the neighbourhood of an asbestos disposal site but also for diffuse moral damage. The ruling was based on the constitutional provision recognising the diffuse nature of the environment, both as an asset of common use and as a transindividual right. It concluded that environmental degradation affects the wellbeing of the entire society, which is prevented from enjoying the ecological services provided by environmental goods or, as in this case, is exposed to health risks, uncertainty and disturbance.[49]

2   Looking Backwards: Environmental Protection in the Context of Latin American Constitutionalism

Following the analysis of the scope of the environmental constitutional provision in Brazil, it is also relevant to explore what underlies the adoption of such a rights-based framework. Therefore this section looks backwards to contextualise the Brazilian experience within the constitutional developments in Latin America. It is argued that the constitutionalisation of rights in the region has shaped environmental policies towards a rights-based approach and, more recently, even further.

In enacting the 1988 Constitution, Brazil was at the forefront of a wave of major constitutional reforms carried out by Latin American countries from the late 1980s (redemocratisation) up to recent times,[50] the so-called New Latin American constitutionalism.[51] The two features that mainly characterise this movement are the widening of democratic participation and the recognition of new constitutional rights (see Gargarella's contribution to this volume, Chapter 12).[52] Besides the classical democratic-liberal political and civil rights, most of the new Latin-American constitutions have notably detailed economic, social and cultural rights, as well as collective rights.[53] They regulate a range of rights and duties, which classical European constitutionalism does not usually consider as constitutional subjects.

This mostly political option for a comprehensive constitution derives from contextual elements common to Latin American countries, which is well explored in the literature.[54] In particular, it is a reaction to the authoritarian regimes of the 1970s, and to the socioeconomic crisis associated with the implementation of neoliberal programmes in the 1980s.[55] In this scenario, constitutional texts gave prominence to values such as pluralism and diversity (in societies highly plural in ethnic groups and with persistent forms of discrimination), combined with democratic participation.

Furthermore, owing to structural social inequality, distributive justice was articulated within constitutional principles mainly through the prescription of social rights.[56] In addition, the constitutionalisation of socioeconomic rights and the establishment of mechanisms for their implementation allowed litigation and judicial activism to emerge. This contributed to the development of a constitutional and human rights theoretical framework on rights justiciability, while enhancing courts' legitimacy when intervening in institutional issues.[57]

The variety of changes introduced by the new Latin American constitutionalism has also influenced the environmental policies adopted. The recognition of environmental rights at the constitutional level comes along with this rights-oriented approach in a context where grassroots movements emerged, campaigning for environmental protection balanced with social justice.[58] In most cases the environment has only constitutional value when linked to the human, meaning that the anthropocentric view remains unchallenged. Nevertheless, being proclaimed as a collective or diffuse good, the constitutional recognition of environmental rights surpasses a pure economic value ('enlarged anthropocentrism'). It encompasses the protection of both ecological processes and public interest litigation, as demonstrated in the Brazilian case. Moreover, the increased litigation has enhanced environmental law enforcement.[59]

More far-reaching approaches do exist. Some constitutional provisions come closer to an ecocentrism, having the potential to enable a transition to a deeper ecological paradigm.[60] The constitutions of Ecuador (2008) and Bolivia (2009) are the most celebrated examples,[61] being announced as representatives of a 'new Andean Constitutionalism',[62] a 'pluralist'[63] or a 'transformative' constitutionalism.[64] These examples represent a step forward in relation to the Latin American constitutions that have already addressed the 'social question' because they also incorporate the 'indigenous question'.[65] Based on the constitutional recognition of political pluralism and multiculturalism, these constitutions promote the institutionalisation of indigenous ancestral values and organisational systems within the legal order, such as the ones encapsulated in the concept of *buen vivir* (Article 12ss e 340ss, Ecuadorian Constitution; Article 8, Bolivian Constitution).[66]

For example, adopting the holistic approach proclaimed by indigenous traditions, the Ecuadorian constitutional text goes further than recognising a fundamental right to a healthy environment. It actually entitles nature ('Mother Earth') to subjective rights,[67] therefore protecting nature's right to exist and to maintain its regenerating capacity (see e.g. Article 71). It also adopts a consistent constitutional environmental policy, including provisions for sectorial policies and implementation mechanisms (see, mainly, Article 395ss). A domestic court recognised substantive rights of nature for the first time in 2011 based on the new constitutional provision.[68] However, the outcomes of this novel political and regulatory understanding—and to what extent it actually promotes further environmental protection—remain largely disputed.

Finally, major problems deriving from a 'hyper-regulation' of themes at constitutional levels in Latin America are not ignored. For instance, this may lead to a significant number of constitutional reforms, weakening effectiveness, a loosening of the normative strength of constitutional law[69] and, in some cases, increasing the power of the executive branch.[70] Environmental policies are not immune to such concerns, as reflected in the persistent gap between the strong constitutional framework and limited regulatory enforcement and trade-offs on the ground,[71] yet to be empirically studied.

3   Looking Elsewhere: Other Approaches to Environmental Protection

The Brazilian example suggests that the recognition of a right to the environment is legitimate and convenient—in particular, owing to the Latin American context, where claims for enhancing democracy and the protection of rights forged constitutional reforms. However, this is one among many models, and we are left with the question of whether a provision for a right to the environment is necessary. To reflect on that question, we have to look elsewhere.[72] The EU and some of its members, for instance, adopted a very different path, which is worthwhile briefly outlining here.

Environmental protection spreads through various EU documents as an objective of public policy, ranging from policy documents to treaty law.[73] Moreover, it is linked to procedural rights, particularly with the adherence to the UN Economic Commission for Europe's Aarhus Convention[74] and the implementation of strong procedural secondary EU legislation, such as the Environmental Impact Assessment Directive,[75] and the directives on access to environmental information[76] and on industrial emissions.[77] However, the EU makes no legislative reference to a substantive right to the environment.[78] Therefore no justiciable, autonomous environmental right can be clearly invoked.[79] At the domestic level, environmental constitutional provisions have been adopted in a variety of ways. While there are countries with a rights-based framework,[80] others have chosen to frame environmental protection as a state duty (under 'traditional-institutionalised' constitutions).[81] It is therefore a constitutional value that binds governmental action, but it neither prescribes duties nor gives rights to individuals.[82]

Despite the absence of environmental rights, both European and domestic courts of countries which have adopted a 'state's objective' approach[83] do offer effective mechanisms for environmental law enforcement. This is done mostly through existing human rights law. For example, the European Court of Human Rights and the European Court of Justice case law has derived individual rights from interpreting the European Convention on Human Rights[84] and environmental obligations established in EU secondary law[85] by linking environmental quality to the guarantee of individual rights (largely health, physical integrity, privacy and property). Moreover, the European Court of Justice has interpreted procedural rights broadly, extending standing to enforce environmental law to individuals and interested parties.[86] Therefore the courts have recognised a positive duty of states to take measures when those rights might be at risk owing to environmental nuisance, or to enforce environmental law.

Based on individual rights, this approach seems to contrast with the Brazilian rights-based grounds because it does not benefit the community at large. Although dynamic interpretations of rights and procedural guarantees, the standing requirements in the European model are more stringent and do not allow broad public interest litigation.[87] It is clear that these differences are also 'context-bound', deserving a more thorough examination,[88] which is beyond the scope of the current contribution.

4   Conclusion

This chapter aims to present an overview of the framework of constitutional environmental protection adopted in Brazil, which is an example of a rights-based constitutional framework that enhances environmental policies, despite remaining largely anthropocentric. The Brazilian Constitution grants an enforceable fundamental right to an ecologically balanced environment (subjective dimension) on both an individual and a collective basis, and it establishes environmental protection as a state binding duty (objective dimension). Moreover, it links rights with duties, and envisages the prohibition of regress in environmental matters. This model offers not only a conceptual framework to public policies but also important avenues for judicial protection, through litigation on public interest grounds. This is evidence that the legal benefits of constitutionalisation mentioned in the literature—namely, a positive influence on legislation and courts decisions, enhanced participatory rights and access to justice, and barriers to 'rollbacks'[89]—have been delivered. To assess the impact of constitutionalisation on the country's environmental performance and shortcomings requires a more sophisticated empirical study.[90]

The chapter also seeks to put the Brazilian case into perspective by referring to further existing frameworks. At a regional level, it presents some of the recent constitutional developments in Latin America. This provides a glimpse of how changes in environmental policy are intertwined with political processes in the region, leading to the recognition of the fundamental status of the right to environment. Expanding the analysis, the chapter shows that the European 'state guideline' approach provides an alternative to the direct protection framework. The former has the advantage of allowing the environment to be judicially protected without necessarily linking environmental harm to the violation of other existing rights. The latter, although limited in scope, is anchored in human rights law and has not prevented the development of strong environmental law. This suggests that there is no best model, and the alternatives are to be interpreted, taking into account contextual aspects, judicial nuances and the aspirations of each community.

NOTES

1. Edith Brown Weiss, *In Fairness to Future Generations* (Transnational Publishers 1989); Ernst Brandl and Hartwin Bungert, 'Constitutional Entrenchment of Environmental Protection: A Comparative Analysis of Experiences Abroad' (1992) 16(1) Harvard Environmental Law Rev 1.
2. Tim Hayward, 'Constitutional Environmental Rights: a Case for Political Analysis' (2000) 48 Political Studies 558.
3. Dinah Shelton, 'Human Rights, Environmental Rights, and the Right to Environment' (1991) 28 Stanford Journal of International Law 103.
4. Gunter Frankenberg, 'Comparative Constitutional Law' in Mauro Bussani and Ugo Mattei (eds), *The Cambridge Companion to Comparative Law* (Cambridge University Press 2012) 171.

5. Brandl and Bungert (n 1) 83.
6. On the criticism of a rights-based approach in advancing environmental protection, see Christopher Miller, *Environmental Rights: Critical Perspectives* (Routledge 1998); Catherine Redgwell, 'Life, the Universe and Everything: A Critique of Anthropocentric Rights' in Alan E Boyle and Michael R Anderson (eds), *Human Rights Approaches to Environmental Protection* (Clarendon Press 1996).
7. See Jeremy Waldron, 'A Rights-based Critique of Constitutional Rights' (1993) 13 Oxford Journal of Legal Studies 18; Boyle and Anderson (n 6).
8. Available at http://www.worldbank.org/en/country/brazil/overview.
9. Available at http://hdr.undp.org/en/content/table-1-human-development-index-and-its-components.
10. Available at http://data.worldbank.org/indicator/AG.LND.FRST.ZS/countries.
11. Jeff Tollefson, 'Stopping Deforestation: Battle for the Amazon' (2015) 520 Nature 20.
12. Accounting for 34.6 % of total emissions by sector. Available at http://www.seeg.eco.br/.
13. The government launched the Growth Acceleration Plan in 2007 in order to increase investment in infrastructure. See http://www.pac.gov.br/.
14. See https://data.un.org/CountryProfile.aspx?crName=BRAZIL.
15. See http://www.atlasbrasil.org.br.
16. The position that Brazil has assumed in climate change negotiations is an example, putting forward a strong argument in favour of the historical responsibility of countries and voluntarily committing to emissions reductions.
17. Lesley K McAllister, *Making Law Matter: Environmental Protection and Legal Institutions in Brazil* (Stanford University Press 2008) 20.
18. Available at www.camara.gov.br.
19. Hayward (n 2) 6.
20. José Drummond and Ana Flávia Barros-Platiau, 'Brazilian Environmental Laws and Policies, 1934–2002: A Critical Overview' (2006) 28 Law and Policy 84.
21. Joseph L. Sax, 'The Search for Environmental Rights' (1991) 6 L. Land Use & Environmental Law 93, 94.
22. The analysis is based on Brazilian legal doctrine.

23. Drummond and Barros-Platiau (n 20) 95.
24. José RM Leite and Patryck A Ayala, *Dano Ambiental: Do Individual ao Coletivo Extrapatrimonial* (6th edn, Revista dos Tribunais 2014).
25. See Supreme Federal Court, ADI-MC 3540/DF, DJ 03.02.2006, http://www.stf.jus.br.
26. Sax (n 21) 100; Joshua Bruckerhoff, 'Giving Nature Constitutional Protection: A Less Anthropocentric Interpretation of Environmental Rights' (2008) 86 Texas Law Review 622.
27. Luís R Barroso, *Interpretação e Aplicação da Constituição: Fundamentos de uma Dogmática Constitucional Transformadora* (Saraiva 1996).
28. See Superior Court of Justice, REsp 1.120.117/AC, DJe 19.11.2009, http://www.stj.jus.br
29. Bruckerhoff (n 26) 638.
30. Ingo W Sarlet and Tiago Fensterseifer, *Direito Constitucional Ambiental: Estudos sobre a Constitutição, os Direitos Fundamentais e a Proteção do Ambiente* (Revista dos Tribunais 2011) 222.
31. This would have to be justified by a compelling public interest or by the necessity of realisation of other constitutional rights: Bruckerhoff (n 26); Antonio H Benjamin, 'A Constitucionalização do Ambiente e a Ecologização da Constituição Brasileira' in José JG Canotilho and José RM Leite (eds), *Direito Constitucional Ambiental Brasileiro* (Saraiva 2007) 122.
32. Sarlet and Fensterseifer (n 30) 68.
33. Shelton (n 3) 123.
34. Nicholas Bryner, 'Brazil's Green Court: Environmental Law in the Superior Tribunal de Justiça (High Court of Brazil)' (2012) 29(2) Pace Environmental Law Review 470, 481.
35. Ingo W Sarlet, Luiz G Marinoni and Daniel F Mitidiero, *Curso de Direito Constitucional* (Revista dos Tribunais 2012).
36. Filippe AS Nascimento, 'A Dimensão Objetiva dos Direitos Fundamentais: É possível Reconhecer os Direitos Fundamentais como uma Ordem Objetiva de Valores?' (2011) 13(1) Revista Direito e Liberdade da Escola da Magistratura do RN 215.
37. This duty might manifest either through positive obligations (non-omission and non-insufficient protection) or through negative obligations (non-interference). Sarlet et al. (n 35) 574. Brazil's Supreme Federal Court has recognised that the judiciary can even determine that the executive branch takes measures to ensure the realisation of

social and ecological rights under special circumstances, and that budgetary deficiency cannot be claimed for not fulfilling this duty. However, the issue remains controversial. See Supreme Federal Court, REsp 658171/DF, DJe 21.02.2014, http://www.stj.jus.br.

38. José JG Canotilho, 'Estado Constitucional Ecológico e Democracia Sustentada' in Heline S Ferreira, José RM Leite and Larissa V Boratti (eds), *Estado de Direito Ambiental: Tendências* (2nd edn, Forense Universitária 2010) 159.
39. Benjamin (n 31) 74.
40. McAllister (n 17).
41. See http://www.prpa.mpf.mp.br/news/2013/processos-judiciais-do-caso-belo-monte-sao-publicados-na-integra-pelo-mpf.
42. Bryner (n 34) 532.
43. The Superior Court of Justice is internationally acknowledged for its consistent body of decisions on the matter. See its index of environmental case law, available at http://www.stj.jus.br/internet_docs/jurisprudencia/jurisprudenciaemteses/Jurisprud%EAncia%20em%20teses%2030%20-%20direito%20ambiental.pdf.
44. These are ADIn 4901; ADIn 4902; ADIn 4903.
45. Superior Court of Justice, PET no REsp 1.240.122/PR, DJe 19.12.2012, http://www.stj.jus.br.
46. The National Environmental Policy Act (Article 14) and the Civil Code (Article 927) establish strict liability for environmental damage.
47. Leite and Ayala (n 24).
48. See Superior Court of Justice, REsp 1.374.284/MG, DJe 05.09.2014 (riverside communities); REsp 1.318.917/BA, DJe 23.04.2013 (fishermen community), http://www.stj.jus.br.
49. Superior Court of Justice, REsp 1.367.923/RJ, DJe 25.09.2014, http://www.stj.jus.br. The compensation awarded was approximately US$125,000.
50. Rodrigo Uprimny, 'The Recent Transformation of Constitutional Law in Latin America: Trends and Challenges' (2011) 89(7) Texas Law Review 1587.
51. For a further analysis, see Roberto Gargarella, *Latin American Constitutionalism, 1810-2010: The Engine Room of the Constitution* (Oxford University Press 2013).
52. Uprimny (n 50) 1601.
53. ibid 1591.

54. For further analysis of contextual aspects, see Miguel Schor, 'Constitutionalism Through the Looking Glass of Latin America' (2006) 41 Texas International Law Journal 1; Diego López-Medina, 'The Latin American and Caribbean Legal Traditions: Repositioning Latin America and the Caribbean on the Contemporary Maps of Comparative Law' in Bussani and Mattei (n 4).
55. Schor (n 54) 34.
56. ibid.
57. César Rodríguez-Garavito, 'Beyond the Courtroom: The Impact of Judicial Activism on Socioeconomic Rights in Latin America' (2011) Texas Law Review 1669, 1671.
58. Henri Acselrad, 'Grassroots Reframing of the Environmental Struggles in Brazil' in D Carruthers (ed), *Environmental Justice in Latin America: Problems, Promise, and Practice* (MIT 2008) 77.
59. For other examples, see David Boyd, *The Environmental Rights Revolution: A Global Study of Constitutions, Human Rights and the Environment* (University of California Press 2012) 125ss.
60. Germana Moraes and William P Marques Júnior WP, 'A Construção do Paradigma Ecocêntrico no Novo Constitucionalismo Democrático dos Países da Unasul' (2013) 5(3) Revista de Direito Brasileira 42, 44.
61. For an account of the constitutional changes in Bolivia and Ecuador, see Ruben M Dalmau, *El proceso Constituyente Bolivariano (2006–2008) en el Marco del Nuevo Constitutionalism Latinoamericano* (Enlace 2008); Eduardo Gudynas, 'La Ecologia Política del Giro Biocéntrico en la Nueva Constitución de Ecuador' (2009) 32 Revista de Estudios Sociales 34.
62. Boaventura de Sousa Santos, *Refundación del Estado en América Latina: Perspectivas desde una Epistemología del Sur* (Antropofagia 2010).
63. Antonio C Wolkmer and Milena P Melo, *Constitucionalismo Latino-Americano* (Juruá 2013).
64. Ramiro A Santamaría, Alberto Acosta and Esperanza Martínez, *El Neoconstitucionalismo Transformador: el Estado y el Derecho en la Constitución de 2008* (Abya-Yala 2011).
65. Gargarella (n 51).
66. Thomas Fatheuer, *Buen Vivir: A Brief Introduction to Latin America's New Concepts for the Good Life and the Rights of Nature* (Heinrich Boll Foundation 2011).

67. Ibid 64.
68. A domestic court considered that the construction of a road without environmental licensing, and involving the deposit of debris in a river, violated nature's rights, established in the new constitutional order. In addition, the precautionary principle, the rights of future generations, the presumption regarding the burden of proof and diffuse standing rules were the subjects of debate, and they supported the imposition of reparation measures. Provincial Court of Loja, Protection Action nº 11121-2011-0010, http://www.funcionjudicial-loja.gob.ec/index.php?option=com_wrapper&view=wrapper&Itemid=205.
69. Gargarella (n 51) 152.
70. Almut Schilling-Vacaflor, 'Bolivia's New Constitution: Towards Participatory Democracy and Political Pluralism?' (2011) 90 European Review of Latin American and Caribbean Studies 3, 259.
71. McAllister (17).
72. For a constitutional comparative analysis, see Jonathan B Wiener, 'Something Borrowed for Something Blue: Legal Transplants and the Evolution of Global Environmental Law' (2001) 27 Ecology Law Quarterly 1295; and Boyd (n 59).
73. See Article 3(3) TEU; Article 11, 114(3) and 191 TFEU.
74. Declaration 2005/370/EC OJ L124/1.
75. Directive 2011/92/EU, amended by Directive 2014/52/EU.
76. Directive 2003/4/EC.
77. Directive 2010/75/EU.
78. Even though the European Union Charter of Human Rights refers to environmental duties (articles 35, 37, 38), as do resolutions on fundamental rights (European Parliament Resolutions of 12 April 1989 [1989] OJ C120/51 and of 8 April 1997 [1997] OJ C223/74), they are not drafted as legal rights.
79. Ludwig Krämer, 'The Environmental Complaint in EU Law' (2009) 6 Journal for European Environmental & Planning Law 13; Nicolas de Sadeleer, 'Enforcing EUCHR Principles and Fundamental Rights in Environmental Cases' (2012) 81 Nordic Journal of International Law 39.
80. For example, Portugal, Spain, Belgium, France and Sweden.
81. For example, Germany, Austria, Netherlands, Bulgaria and Italy.
82. For a comparative study, see Brandl and Bungert (n 1).

83. The example of Germany is analysed in Michael Kloepfer, *Umweltrecht* (3rd edn, Beck 2004) 121.
84. See *Lopez Ostra v Spain* (1995) 20 EHRR 277; and *Guerra v Italy* (1998) 26 EHRR 357.
85. See C-361/88 *Commission v Germany* EU:C:1991:224; and C-297/08 *Commission v Italy* EU:C:2010:115.
86. See C-75/08 *Christopher Mellor v United Kingdom* EU:C:2009:279; and C-115/09 *Trianel Kohlekraftwerk v Germany* EU:C:2011:289.
87. The Additional Protocol to the ACHR includes a right to a clean environment (Article 11). However, the Inter-American System of Human Rights is limited to the protection of individual rights, not allowing public interest litigation. Like the European Court of Human Rights, the Inter-American Court and Commission have made use of human rights law to afford environmental protection. Christian Schall, 'Public Interest Litigation Concerning Environmental Matters before Human Rights Courts: A Promising Future Concept?' (2008) 20 Journal of Environmental Law 417.
88. Boyd (n 59).
89. Ibid 26–28.
90. OECD, Environmental Performance Reviews: Brazil (OECD 2015).

INDEX

A

access to information, 139, 276, 299, 300, 303n2, 327, 332
access to medicine, xxxvii, 311–18, 322, 323, 324n2324n6
accountability, xxxiv, xxxiii, 28, 36n34, 102, 116, 124, 145n46, 150–4, 156, 158–63, 172, 176, 266
ACHR. *See* American Convention on Human Rights (ACHR)
ADL. *See* anti-discrimination law (ADL)
Africa, 15, 16n3, 17n8, 71n1, 83, 96, 221, 282, 284, 320
American Convention on Human Rights (ACHR), 7–14, 18n25, 25, 27, 28, 39, 41, 48–50, 53n14, 55n30–2, 60, 61, 71n13, 72n15, 345n87
amnesty, 9, 11, 13–15, 19n48, 20n67, 26–30, 33, 36n32, 36n34, 55n31
anonymous work, 298, 299, 302
anti-discrimination law (ADL), xxxv, 221–37

antitrust, 187, 197–8n1
armed conflict, 149, 150, 154, 155, 157, 165n30
attorney general's office, xxxvi, 266, 267
autonomy, xxxv, 6, 17n21, 138, 205, 206, 215, 216, 224, 251

B

Bolivia, 29, 37n53, 72n29, 210, 211, 213, 236n40, 247, 253n3, 336, 343n61, 344n70
Brazil, xxxi, xxix, xxxvi, xxxvii, xxxiii, 4, 7–9, 11, 13, 17n8, 17n24, 18n28, 20n67, 25–9, 31, 35n18, 37n47, 72n29, 83, 113–28, 142, 142n6, 187, 206, 210, 211, 213, 247, 248, 253n4, 257–72, 276, 280, 291n25, 293–309, 312–23, 324n3, 324n6, 325n24, 327–45
business groups, 132, 135, 142, 143n10, 143n16, 145n38

Note: Page numbers with "n" denote notes.

C

case-law, xxxi, 4, 6, 11–14, 40, 42, 59, 63, 69, 70, 79, 300, 328, 338, 342n43

charter schools, 114, 115, 126n12

Chile, xxxi, xxxix, 12–14, 19n46, 26–8, 36n33, 62, 64, 66, 67, 72n29, 83, 133–5, 143n13–16, 187, 189, 192, 193, 199n23, 199n31, 207, 208, 211, 213, 215, 217n4, 228, 236n41, 251, 253n4, 304n8, 306n32

collusion, 131–47, 152

Colombia, xxix, xxxiv, 6, 10, 11, 13, 19n46, 29, 72n29, 80, 81, 83, 86, 87, 90n3, 91n16, 91n22, 93n38, 131–5, 140, 142n4, 149–71, 173–7, 178n1, 178n3, 178n5, 179n8, 181n37, 182n60, 187, 189, 191, 192, 199n23, 208, 211, 213, 217n2, 251, 253n4

Commission, 7–10, 18n24, 18n27, 18n28, 24–6, 28, 30–2, 35n7, 35n18, 40, 50, 53n14, 55n31, 57–60, 63, 64, 66–9, 71, 73n45, 73n46, 73n51, 103, 146n55, 151, 161, 193, 200n36, 224, 249, 303n2, 307n35, 337, 345n87

compensation, 8, 9, 40–7, 51, 53n10, 58, 117, 149, 190, 218n10, 331, 334–5

compliance, xxxi, 9, 11, 12, 24, 28, 29, 32, 33, 38n62, 39–51, 52n3, 52n6, 53n10, 53n12, 53n13, 54n17, 54n18, 55n33, 56n34, 56n35, 58, 60, 107, 151, 171–3, 231, 240, 242, 243, 247–9, 251, 306n27

constitutionalism, xxx, xxxv, xxxviii, 16n3, 17n8, 20n68, 190, 205–19, 328, 335, 336, 343n54, 343n61

constitutional law, xxxi, 3, 4, 10, 21, 22, 24, 29, 32, 33, 79, 190, 235n26, 328, 329n4, 337, 342n50

convergence, 23, 24, 27, 29, 30, 131–47, 197n1, 208

coordination, 117, 131–47, 170, 173, 225

copyright, xxix, xxxvi, xxxvii, 276, 277, 285–7, 289, 293–309

corporate governance, 131, 132, 145n38, 165n23, 167, 174, 178n5

corporations, xxxiv, xxxiii, 23, 81, 95, 115, 149–53, 157–9, 161, 162, 165n32, 191

Costa Rica, 60, 72n29, 187, 211, 219n13, 247, 251, 253n4

Country Policy and Institutional Assessment (CPIA), 98–9

Court, xxx, xxxi, xxxii, xxxvi, xxxix, xxxviii, 3–20, 22–34, 36n29, 38n62, 39–71, 71n1, 71n10, 71n13, 72n29, 73n45, 73n51, 81, 92n25, 93n38–40, 115, 125n9, 149, 160, 161, 181n44, 193, 218n8, 219n13, 226, 227, 231–3, 235n26, 235n31, 236n35, 237n66, 242, 245, 246, 249, 251, 253, 254n14, 255n17, 257–9, 262–4, 268, 269, 271n8, 277, 285, 286, 291n25, 291n26, 299, 300, 307n35, 312–14, 316, 318, 324n3, 324n15, 325n24, 330, 331, 333, 334, 336–9, 341n34, 341n37, 342n42, 344n68, 345n87

coverage, xxxi, 59, 61–7, 69, 70, 73n51, 89, 93n38, 159

CPIA. *See* Country Policy and Institutional Assessment (CPIA)

criminal justice, xxxvi, 127n27, 257–9, 261–9

criminal procedure, 26, 257, 258, 262, 268, 269

cyberspace, 276

D

debt recovery tribunal (DRT), 114, 115, 125n8, 125n11

democracy, 3, 7, 59, 211, 213, 218n9, 219n15, 222, 225, 230, 337, 344n70

derivatives, xxxiv, 167–83

development, xxx, xxxv, xxxiv, xxxii, xxxiii, 9, 22, 33, 56n36, 77–93, 95–111, 113, 125n2, 126n14, 126n15, 126n21, 127n35, 127n38, 132, 133, 135, 142, 142n6, 146n62, 150, 153–7, 159, 162, 166n40, 168, 170, 171, 175, 185–90, 193–7, 199n27, 208, 210, 213, 221–7, 234n13, 242, 243, 250, 252, 254n10, 277, 293–5, 313, 316, 317, 327, 329, 335, 336, 339

dictatorship, 5–7, 25, 59, 60, 152, 164n15, 211, 230

digital culture, 293–309

discretion, xxxv, 170, 173–4, 180n33, 240, 329, 332

Doing Business, 95, 99, 102–6, 131

domestic violence, 8, 25, 26

Dominican Republic, 72n29, 247, 253n4

DRT. *See* debt recovery tribunal (DRT)

drug trafficking, 257, 258, 260

E

ECLA / ECLAC / CEPAL, 224, 234n14, 244

Economic doctrine, 193–6

economic planning, 81, 185

economic rights, 88, 89, 189, 214, 298

economy, xxxiii, 80–2, 90n13, 91n19, 97, 99, 102, 103, 105, 127n33, 132, 137–42, 142n7, 154–7,

161, 164n9, 166n41, 168, 173, 190–2, 213, 227, 231, 329

Ecuador, 29, 37n56, 72n29, 187, 210, 211, 213, 215, 217n4, 219n11, 236n39, 247–9, 253n4, 304n8, 336, 343n61

environmental protection, xxix, xxxviii, 327–45

equality, xxxv, xxxii, 84, 87, 213, 221, 222, 224–33, 234n4, 234n13, 234n14, 235n21, 235n23, 240, 241, 246, 253n3

Europe, 3, 4, 15, 16n2, 98, 109n10, 143n8, 146n61, 163n4, 200n37, 200n40, 221, 225, 226, 235n23, 268, 277, 278, 280, 282, 284, 287, 297, 306n33

European Court of Human Rights, 4, 13, 15, 16n3, 40, 58, 59, 64, 69, 70, 226, 338, 345n87

European Court of Justice, 69, 226, 338

Evidence-based reform, 104

F

FDI. *See* foreign direct investment (FDI)

finance, xxix, 115, 135, 144n27, 166n40, 170–2, 180n29, 183n67, 280

foreign direct investment (FDI), 100, 150, 153–6, 161

freedom, xxxiv, xxxvii, 13, 71–2n13, 166n41, 206, 214, 276, 287, 294, 295, 299, 304n12, 305n15

free flow of information, xxxvii, 275–91

fundamental rights, xxix, xxxviii, 4, 6, 7, 9, 13, 21–38, 55n31, 93n38, 159, 216, 233, 269, 298, 299, 303, 306n26, 315–17, 328–36, 338, 344n78, 344n79

G

gender quota, xxxv, xxxvi, 239–55
Germany, 13, 345n83
governance, xxxii, 22–4, 32–4, 96,
  99–104, 106–8, 108n1, 110n27,
  126n16, 127n32, 131, 132, 134,
  135, 145n38, 146n61, 150, 154,
  164n23, 167, 173, 174, 178n5,
  179n18, 222
government, xxxi, xxxv, xxix, xxxvi,
  xxxviii, 4, 6, 8, 10, 20n67, 32,
  49, 50, 57, 67, 79–81, 83–5, 88,
  93n38, 95, 103, 104, 114, 115,
  122, 132, 142n3, 146n62, 150,
  151, 154, 155, 171, 172, 176,
  177, 182n61, 187, 190, 194,
  197, 198n1, 205, 206, 211, 212,
  214–16, 218n8, 218n11, 228,
  233, 242, 244, 251, 253, 266,
  276, 280, 281, 288, 295,
  306n31, 313–16, 320, 321, 323,
  329–32, 340n13
Guatemala, 72n29, 144n26, 210, 239,
  253n4

H

Honduras, 27, 72n29, 187, 247, 250,
  253n4, 254n16
human rights, xxx, xxxi, xxxiv, xxxvi,
  xxxiii, xxxvii, 3–73, 149–66,
  211–13, 218n9, 222, 226–8,
  230, 234n26, 236n35, 257–72,
  293–7, 301, 305n16, 305n18,
  305n22, 315, 317, 323–4n2,
  324n6, 325n21, 326n48, 327,
  328, 330, 336, 338, 339, 339n2,
  340n6, 344n78, 345n87
human rights abuse, xxxiv, xxxiii, 7, 9,
  149–66
Human rights database, xxxiv, 150,
  157, 158, 160, 161

human rights violation, xxxvi, 8, 10,
  14, 27–9, 47, 48, 58, 60, 150,
  151, 154, 162, 257–72

I

indicators, xxxv, xxxii, 12, 64, 95–111,
  124, 229, 243, 254n10
indigenous, 18n27, 155, 156, 158,
  166n41, 213, 215, 329, 336
industrialization, 82, 84
innovation, xxx, xxxvii, 210, 222, 251,
  276, 277, 285, 287–9, 311, 316,
  319, 321, 325n35, 326n42
institutional bypass, xxxiii, 113–28
institutional reform, 113–28, 132,
  133, 138
institutions, xxx, xxix, xxxii, xxxiv,
  xxxvii, xxxiii, xxxviii, 6, 17n11,
  22, 23, 26, 29, 33, 57–65, 68,
  70, 78, 80, 82, 85–8, 92n25, 97,
  100, 102, 104, 106, 108,
  113–15, 117–21, 123, 124,
  125n7, 127n33, 127n38, 132,
  133, 136, 172–4, 176, 193, 195,
  213, 215, 217n7, 218n8,
  219n11, 222, 293–303, 304n4,
  304n9, 306n28
instrumentalist approach, 79
integration, xxx, xxxi, xxxiii, 100, 133,
  136–8, 141, 143n17, 144n33,
  145n45, 146n55, 174, 224
intellectual property, 276, 279, 287,
  294, 296, 297, 304n9, 305n25,
  307n33, 307n38, 313, 315, 317,
  323, 323n2, 324n6, 325n21,
  325n24, 326n40, 326n42
Inter-American Commission, 7, 8,
  10, 18n27, 18n28, 24–6, 28,
  30–2, 35n18, 40, 50, 53n14,
  55n31, 57, 63, 64, 71, 73n46,
  73n51, 161

Inter-American Court of Human
Rights, xxx, xxxi, 3–20, 38n62,
39–56, 161
Inter-American System, 5, 7–10, 12,
21, 22, 26, 31, 33, 34, 40–2,
49–51, 53n9, 57–73, 345n87
Inter-American System of Human
Rights, 53n9, 57–73, 345n87
international organisations, 22, 23, 95,
97, 98, 100, 102, 107, 108, 151,
152, 161, 181n47, 187, 239,
241, 242, 252
internet, xxxvii, 232, 276, 294–6
Internet bill of rights, xxxvii, 294

J
Judicial dialogue, 17n10
judicialisation of politics, 3, 4, 231
jurisprudence, 4–6, 11–15, 16n5,
19n57, 58, 66, 69, 226

L
labour, xxxi, 17n13, 69, 151, 154,
156, 159, 162, 191, 200n41,
210, 225, 234n14, 290n16
Latin America, xxx, xxxi, xxxv, xxix,
xxxiv, xxxvi, xxxii, xxxiii, 5, 13,
15, 16n3, 16n6, 17n11, 17n19,
21–38, 52n7, 58, 63, 67, 69–71,
83, 89, 96, 98, 126n14, 131–4,
136, 141, 142, 143n9, 145n38,
150, 154, 163n2, 185–201, 209,
212, 213, 218n9, 218n10,
219n11, 219n13, 221–37,
239–41, 244–6, 248, 251, 253n3,
294, 297, 306n32, 328, 329,
335, 337, 339, 342n50, 343n54,
343n57, 343n58, 343n66
law and development, xxxii, 77–93,
95–111, 235n31, 325n35

legal education, 83, 84, 91n21
legal metrics, xxxiii, 105, 108, 111n41
legal reform, xxx, xxix, xxxii, xxxvii,
26, 58, 85–7, 95–9, 103–5, 107,
108, 125n8, 186, 187, 189–93,
196, 212–14, 223, 224,
226, 233
liberal-conservative constitutions, 209,
217n5, 217n6

M
market, xxxiv, xxxii, xxxvii, xxxiii, 78,
82, 83, 86–9, 91n19, 98–100,
102, 105, 131–47, 150, 153,
154, 167–83, 185–92, 194–6,
225, 226, 228, 231, 232,
234n14, 284, 318, 320, 321, 323
Mathematical turn, 104, 109n5
media, xxxi, 8, 55n31, 57–73, 123,
124, 147n66, 150, 156, 159,
166n40, 224, 288, 303n2
Mexico, xxxi, xxix, 29–31, 38n72, 62,
64, 66, 68, 69, 72n29, 133–5,
142, 187, 189, 193, 198n19,
200n37, 207, 208, 211–13, 215,
217n2, 217n4, 228, 247–50,
253n4, 253n5, 304n8
moral damage, 334–5

N
Neo-liberalism, 234n11
Nicaragua, 72n29, 187, 246, 247,
253n4, 254n17
non-regression, 331, 333–4

O
OAS. *See* Organization of American
States (OAS)
ombudsman, 230–2

Organization of American States (OAS), 7, 10, 50, 57, 59–61
orphan works, xxxvii, 293–309

P

Pact of San Jose, 60
Panama, 72n29, 187, 247–9, 253n4
patent law, xxxvii, xxxviii, 311–26
patent rights, xxxvii, 311–17, 322, 323
perjury, xxxvi, 258, 262, 264, 268, 269
Peru, 11, 13, 29, 37n58, 72n29, 95, 113, 133–5, 140, 144n33, 187, 208, 213, 215, 236n39, 247, 253n4
plea bargain, 258, 269
police, xxxvi, xxxiii, 9, 26, 114, 116, 118, 121, 122, 124, 126n14, 126n15, 155, 257–64, 266–9, 271n6, 271n13, 272n19, 272n20
police abuse, xxxvi, 116, 122, 124, 257–62, 266–9
police violence, xxxvi, 257, 259, 260, 262, 266–8, 272n19
policy, xxx, xxxv, xxix, xxxvi, xxxii, xxxiii, xxxviii, 3, 5, 7–10, 16n6, 22–4, 26, 33, 34, 34n5, 78, 79, 82–4, 87–9, 91n22, 92n23, 96–108, 110n27, 125n3, 125n12, 134, 135, 137–42, 143n13, 145n41, 145n55, 146n57, 147n63, 147n65, 147n69, 162, 172, 179n18, 180n29, 180n31, 187, 195, 197n1, 198n14, 198n19, 200n37, 224, 225, 233, 234n14, 239–53, 254n13, 254n14, 257–72, 280, 288, 291n29, 293, 297, 304n12, 319, 322, 324n17, 325n35, 327–30, 332, 337, 339, 340n20, 342n46
policy-making, 33, 34, 84, 102, 104, 106, 241, 250, 253, 330

political participation, 206, 215, 228, 231
politics, 3, 4, 6, 16n5, 17n19, 22, 24, 33, 103, 145n38, 145n40, 147n62, 190, 218n7, 218n9, 219n13, 225, 231, 235n31, 239, 253n3, 324n17
Poupatempo, xxxiii, 114–16, 118, 119, 121–4, 126n13, 128n47
poverty, 82, 83, 91n22, 91n23, 100, 102, 107, 127n35, 156, 159, 221–37, 288, 329
principles, xxxv, xxxiv, xxxvii, 27, 79, 91n19, 92n25, 93n40, 101, 132, 151, 164n20, 167, 169, 171, 174–5, 178n4–6, 181n47, 182n58, 183n69, 189, 223, 224, 233, 234n3, 323, 331, 333, 336, 344n68, 344n79
proceduralisation, xxxii, 106–8
property, 86, 88, 89, 98, 99, 103, 166n40, 166n41, 190, 192, 199n23, 208, 210, 213, 214, 227, 230, 276, 279, 287, 294, 296, 297, 304n9, 305n25, 306n26, 307n33, 307n38, 313, 315–17, 321, 323, 323n2, 324n6, 325n21, 325n24, 326n40, 326n42, 326n48, 331, 334, 338
prudential supervision, 173
public interest litigation, 336, 338, 345n87

R

rankings, 104, 105, 108n1, 109n5, 161, 228, 243, 250
recognition, xxxviii, 26, 227–30, 233, 264, 311, 327, 331, 334–7, 339
redistribution, 80, 84, 87, 227, 228, 230, 233
regional transnational community, 15

regulation, xxxiv, xxxii, xxxvii, xxxiii, 23, 68, 80, 82, 83, 89, 100, 104–6, 115, 127n38, 131–47, 167–83, 186, 191, 192, 195, 218n7, 221–3, 225, 226, 228, 294, 304n9, 306n31, 330, 332, 337

religion, 205–7, 217n4, 226, 278, 281

remedies, xxxiii, 58, 159, 162, 163n2, 230

reparation, xxxi, 28, 37n47, 39–42, 46–8, 53n9, 54n17, 56n36, 150, 154, 162, 227, 320, 331, 334, 344n68

resistance, xxxv, xxxiii, 4, 5, 15, 17n10, 17n23, 23, 24, 29, 30, 36n34, 113–28, 132, 138, 188, 227, 230, 239–55

revolution, 206, 209, 210, 289n10, 343n59

right to a healthy environment, xxxviii, 328, 336

right to health, xxxvii, xxxviii, 93n38, 311–26

right to lie, 264

risk, xxxiv, 88, 93n38, 114, 117, 119, 167, 169–78, 178n4, 178n6, 179n15, 179n16, 179n18, 180n23, 180n26, 183n70, 215, 216, 232, 252, 259, 280, 297, 322, 333, 335, 338

rule of Law, xxxii, 32, 78, 83, 85, 89n1, 90n14, 98, 100–3, 105–7, 108n1, 109n5, 110n22, 125n2, 125n3, 126n14, 127n32, 150, 154, 219n11, 222

S

self-government, xxxv, 205, 206, 215, 216

SLADE. See Studies in Law and Development (SLADE)

social and economic rights, 88, 89, 189

social transformation, 77, 87, 91n21, 219n13, 237n61

stock-market, 131, 135

strategy, xxxiii, 26, 29, 82, 91n19, 95, 117, 120, 139, 140, 142n6, 155, 170, 174, 189, 224, 263, 264, 271n9

Studies in Law and Development (SLADE), 97–9, 109n6

Supreme court, xxx, 3, 4, 11, 13, 15, 16n1, 16n8, 19n47, 25–8, 30–2, 36n29, 38n62, 58, 61, 69, 73n42, 81, 237n66, 251, 318

T

TLP. See Transnational legal process (TLP)

torture, xxxvi, 18n25, 29, 123, 257–69, 270n5, 270n6, 271n13

Transnational legal process (TLP), 16n6, 21–38

transversal human rights, 22, 32–4

Trinidad and Tobago, 42, 55n30

TRIPS agreement, 313, 314, 316–20, 322, 323, 326n39

U

Unidades de Polícia Pacificadora (UPPs), 116, 118, 121–4, 126n13, 126n15, 128n51

United Kingdom, 15, 20n68, 179n16

United States, 13, 61, 86, 92n25, 125n12, 296, 324n19

United States Agency for International Development (USAID), 83, 86, 92n33, 96–8

UPPs. See Unidades de Polícia Pacificadora (UPPs)

USAID. See United States Agency for International Development (USAID)

V

Venezuela, 4, 29, 37n59, 49–51,
55n30–2, 62, 64, 71n13, 72n29,
187, 207, 208, 211, 213, 216n2,
247–9, 253n4, 254n13, 254n14,
255n17, 280
victims, xxxi, xxxiii, 8, 25, 26, 28, 46,
47, 60, 149–54, 158–60, 162,
163n1, 258–61, 263, 265, 266,
268, 269

W

Washington consensus, 187, 188, 192,
195, 198n1
women, xxxv, xxxvi, 8, 26, 121, 149,
210, 216, 239–44, 246, 248–50,
252, 253, 254n7, 254n9,
271n13, 279, 281, 284, 290n16
World Bank, 78, 85, 89n1, 95, 97–103,
105, 109n14, 110n27, 219n11

Printed by Printforce, the Netherlands